THE RULE OF LAW IN BRAZIL

The rule of law is not a simple concept when it comes to defining the political, economic, and legal developments of a country like Brazil, which is a young democracy struggling with its longstanding extractive institutions and entrenched interests. In this book, Juliano Zaiden Benvindo offers a broad perspective of the functioning, evolution, and dynamics of the rule of law in Brazil from different perspectives. The book explores how Brazilian democracy has dealt with the high levels of social inequality and the authoritarian mindset that still play a big role in its fate, and asks whether the country's democratic achievements and institutional framework are sufficiently strong to enforce the rule of law as an imperative for Brazil's development, especially in times when the country is most in need of them.

Volume 2 in the series Rule of Law In Context

Rule of Law In Context

By exploring the rule of law in different jurisdictions around the world, the series makes an original and insightful contribution to the rule of law scholarship by moving past intractable debates over what the rule of law should mean to find out what it actually means and how it works 'on the ground', with an implicitly comparative objective as it explores these issues in the context of different legal systems.

Series Editors

Lorne Neudorf
Gabrielle Appleby

Associate Editors

Rosalind Dixon
David Landau
Lawrence McNamara
Arun Thiruvengadam

Recent titles in this series:

The Rule of Law in the United States: An Unfinished Project of Black Liberation
Paul Gowder

The Rule of Law in Brazil: The Legal Construction of Inequality
Juliano Zaiden Benvindo

The Rule of Law in Brazil

The Legal Construction of Inequality

Juliano Zaiden Benvindo

•HART•
OXFORD • LONDON • NEW YORK • NEW DELHI • SYDNEY

HART PUBLISHING

Bloomsbury Publishing Plc

Kemp House, Chawley Park, Cumnor Hill, Oxford, OX2 9PH, UK

1385 Broadway, New York, NY 10018, USA

29 Earlsfort Terrace, Dublin 2, Ireland

HART PUBLISHING, the Hart/Stag logo, BLOOMSBURY and the Diana logo are trademarks of Bloomsbury Publishing Plc

First published in Great Britain 2022

A catalogue record for this book is available from the British Library.

A catalogue record for this book is available from the Library of Congress.

Library of Congress Control Number: 2022934803

ISBN: HB: 978-1-50993-495-9
ePDF: 978-1-50993-497-3
ePub: 978-1-50993-496-6

Typeset by Compuscript Ltd, Shannon

For Pedro and Nina

Acknowledgements

I SIGNED THE publishing agreement for this book at the ICON-S conference in Chile in July 2019. There would be no better place for it. Every year, this is the place where constitutionalism expresses itself in many different ways, and where I can meet several of my best friends in the field. But Chile was special: Brazil had just elected Bolsonaro as President, and we were all very concerned about country's prospects. Brazil's future looked grim, but not even the most pessimistic could foresee what it would hold only a few months later.

I left Chile already focusing on this book, which I would begin writing, a month later, during my CAPES/Alexander von Humboldt fellowship at the Max-Planck Institute for Comparative Public Law and International Law in Heidelberg, Germany. Wonderful months were spent having fruitful conversations with scholars from all over the world, and particularly those participating in the research project *Ius Constitutionale Commune en América Latina*, where we discussed several subjects on Latin American constitutionalism. My book would not exist without those days in Heidelberg, and special thanks are due to Armin von Bogdandy, Mariela Morales Antoniazzi, Pedro Villareal, Juan Herrera, Roberto Miccú, David Geng, Johannes Mikuteit, Franz Ebert and Sabrina Ragone. Rafaela Giordano, a Brazilian librarian at MPIL (what luck!) and all the MPIL staff helped me immensely with research material and were always available, making that research period a great experience.

My return to Brazil would bring me back to the reality I was investigating in my book, and the radicality of what was happening made everything look so surreal that my writing was just not quick enough to keep pace with the downturn that the country was enduring, then aggravated by the COVID-19 pandemic. Writing about the rule of law in Brazil in this context was extremely frenetic: every day there was a new development that meant rewriting large parts of this book, all the while running the risk of this text being overtaken by history. It was such a challenge that it reminded me of Llewellyn Woodward's advice that 'some sort of after-knowledge is necessary if history is to be written at all'. Ideally, I would like to know 'what happened next', but the challenge of not '[knowing] what happened next' makes such an endeavour somehow very attractive: it triggers a psychological drive of analytical brainstorming of imponderable variables whose conclusions may prove wrong afterwards, but which are nevertheless worth it.

Taking into account such a degree of uncertainties and imponderable variables, the years I have been writing posts and columns for the *International Journal of Constitutional Law Blog (I-CONnect)* on several developments in Brazil and Latin America helped me understand how to cope with the radicality of time in constitutional law. Those posts and columns have been received with such generosity by David Landau and Richard Albert, two leading scholars who became such great friends, that I can frankly say that I would not be able to write such a challenging book without learning from their expertise and friendship. Rosalind Dixon, Tom G Daly, Yaniv Roznai, Tom Ginsburg, Oran Doyle, Sebastian Eickenjäger, Marianne Ulriksen, Christian Prener, Ane Karoline Bak Foged, Mohamed Arafa, Carlos Bernal, Vicente Benítez, Gonzalo Ramirez Cleve, and Chiara Graziani have, in one way or another, helped me brainstorm some fundamental subjects of this book, from comments on the first drafts to debates over impeachment, constitutional moments, constitutional courts, threats to liberal democracy and a number of other interesting topics that enrich many discussions in this book.

I have been able to rely on several Brazilian friends and brilliant scholars, who provided me with insights that relieved some of the burden of dealing with the insecure future of our country. Special thanks go to Daniel Bogéa, Cristiano Paixão, Argemiro Martins, Marcelo Neves, Pablo Holmes, Roberto Bueno, Debora Diniz, Gabriela Rondon, Estefânia Barbosa, Marcelo Cattoni, Emilio Peluso Meyer, Conrado Hübner Mendes, Thomas Bustamante, Jane Reis, Alexandre Araújo Costa, Fernando Acunha, Virgílio Afonso da Silva, Miguel Godoy, Rafael Mafei, Diego Werneck Arguelhes, Gisele Cittadino, Thomaz Pereira, Alexandre Veronese, Vera Karam de Chueiri, Cláudio Ladeira, Aline Osório, Luis Roberto Barroso and Miroslav Milovic (in memoriam). The members of the Centre for Comparative Constitutional Law at the University of Brasília also helped me greatly with their comments on the book, particularly Ramiro Barroso, João Paulo Santos Araújo, Julio Gonçalves Melo, Gustavo Torres, Henrique Neubauer, André Demétrio, Manuellita Hermes Rosa Oliveira Filha, Taiz Costa, Ingrid Dantas, João Paulo Araújo, Tayná Frota, Matheus Depieri, Maria Letícia Sousa Borges, Maria Antonia Melo Beraldo, and Geovana Soares.

'The Rule of Law in Context' Hart series editors, Gabrielle Appleby and Lorne Neudorf, were fantastic in helping me plan and organise the main topics of this book. Their enthusiasm and insights regarding the best strategy to provide the reader with a rich but accessible discussion of such a complex subject guided me throughout my writing.

Rosemarie Mearns and Kate Whetter were the perfect team at Hart during the development of this book. Their careful and gentle support and communication are all an author could wish for. They certainly know how this can make a difference! I would also like to thank Claire Banyard and Linda Staniford for their great help during the editing process.

During the writing of this book, I was a fellow of CAPES/Alexander von Humboldt Stiftung, the National Council for Scientific and Technological Development (CNPq), and the Research Support Foundation of the Federal District (FAP-DF). I am also very indebted to the entire staff of the University of Brasília, my *alma mater* and where I have the pleasure to work with such wonderful friends and colleagues in this fascinating world of teaching, learning and researching.

Most of this book was written during the COVID-19 pandemic. Brazil was dealing with its worst crisis ever, and in particular I lost a dear friend and colleague, the great philosopher Miroslav Milovic, to the disease. Yet, during the pandemic, there was also life. My daughter Nina was born while I was writing this book. The joy of having Nina and Pedro (my four-year old son) growing up together is just magical. Daniela, my wife, gave me the love and strength I needed to keep working on this project during such surreal times. My parents, Ângela and Benvindo, and my brother Aldo and sister Érica, provided me with wonderful insights on the reality of life in Brazil when we were able to meet during the pandemic. My parents-in-law Denise and Alberto provided me with such a wonderful support during my stays in their beautiful house in Vila de São Jorge, Chapada dos Veadeiros. During the pandemic, being close to nature, waterfalls and pure air was all I needed to write this book. Thank you!

The painting on the cover of this book is part of my memories. It is on the wall of my parents' house, just in front of the dinner table. I grew up looking at it and it has always brought me such a close connection with the simple life of Brazilians. It is titled 'Vila', painted by my mom Ângela Zaiden, who has always given me such an inspiration for the beautiful things of life.

This book is dedicated to my kids. I'll have a bit more time to enjoy life and play with them now that it is published!

Contents

Acknowledgements .... *vii*

Introduction 1
- I. What Happened to the Brazil that was 'Taking Off'? 1
- II. The Structure of this Book 7

1. The Conceptual Evolution of the Rule of Law in Brazil 14
- I. Introduction: A Prosaic Approach to the Rule of Law 14
- II. Democracy and Social Justice in the Core of the Rule of Law: A Normative Dispute? 19
- III. Estado de Direito in Brazil: Between Preservation and Democratisation 22
- IV. Estado de Direito in Brazil: Social Inequality as a Hindrance to Coordination 26
- V. The Rule of Law and Coordination in Unequal Societies 28

2. The Local Lived Experiences of the Rule of Law in Brazil: The Impacts of Social Inequality 31
- I. Introduction: A Persistent Inequality 31
- II. Brazil and its Longstanding Struggle with Social Inequality 33
- III. Inclusiveness and Historical Inequalities in Brazil 39
  - A. Racial Inequality 39
  - B. Gender Inequality 45
  - C. Indigenous People 50
  - D. Regional Inequalities 54
- IV. Inequality and Brazil's Declining Rule of Law 59

3. The Authoritarian Mindset and the Rule of Law in Brazil 63
- I. Introduction: Hobsbawm's Omen and the Authoritarian Mindset in Brazil 63
- II. The Theoretical Justification of the Authoritarian Mindset: The Three Main Pillars 66
- III. The Reinvention of the Authoritarian Mindset in History 67
  - A. The Authoritarian Mindset in Authoritarian Regimes 67
  - B. The Authoritarian Mindset in the Awakening of Democracy: A Clash of Narratives 71
  - C. The Authoritarian Mindset and the Revival of the Military under Jair Bolsonaro 78

IV. The Reinvention of the Authoritarian Mindset after Years of Democratic Life 84

4. The Rule of Law and Brazilian Political Institutions: A Reshaped 'Coalition Presidentialism' 87
I. Introduction: Some Cautionary Remarks About the Brazilian Political System 87
II. The Brazilian Political System: Efficiency or Deep Dysfunctionality? 92
A. A Strong Presidentialism? 92
B. A Highly Fragmented and Oligarchical Congress 98
C. Clientelism and 'Coalition Presidentialism': A Necessary Correlation? 103
III. A Reshaped 'Coalition Presidentialism' 110

5. The Rule of Law and Brazil's Politicised Judicial System 113
I. Introduction: The Judiciary in a Country in Crisis 113
II. The Judiciary's Constitutional Design 116
A. The Federal, State and Specialised Courts 116
B. The Federal Supreme Court 120
C. The 'Ancillary' Institutions of Justice: The Public Ministry, the Advocacy-General of the Union and the Public Defender's Office 129
III. A More Accessible, Though Still Unaccountable, Judiciary and the Increasing Culture of Rights 132
IV. Privileges and the Judicial System: The Judiciary as a Blatant Illustration of Brazil's Inequality 135
V. Criminal Justice and Police Forces 138

6. The Extra-Legal Influences on the Rule of Law and Mechanisms of Accountability in Brazil 146
I. Introduction: The Paradoxical Relationship Between the Private and Public Sectors in Brazil 146
II. The Data of Corruption in Brazil According to International Indicators 148
III. The Combat of Corruption in Brazil: The Effects of Path Dependence, Inequality, and Institutional Design Flaws 153
IV. Accountability Institutions, Incremental Improvements in Combatting Corruption and Political Backlash: Two Steps Forward, One Step Back? 157
A. Accountability Institutions 157
B. The Expected Political Backlash 160
V. The Organised Civil Society and the Quest for Fairness Amidst Self-Preservation Movements: A Permanent Struggle 163

VI. A Free and Independent Media? ... 168
A. The Media as a Key Player in Brazilian Democracy and in its Backsliding ... 168
B. The Power of the New Media: Fake News as the New Normal ... 174

7. The Rule of Law in Brazil and the Challenges of International Law ... 179
I. Introduction: Brazil as a Soft Power? ... 179
II. The Rule of Law in Brazil and International Law: Impacts on the Domestic Level ... 181
III. Brazil and Regional Integration: The MERCOSUR ... 186
IV. Brazil and International Tribunals: The Inter-American Court of Human Rights ... 191
V. The International Perception of Brazil's Compliance with the Rule of Law ... 195

8. The Future of the Rule of Law in Brazil ... 198
I. The Destabilising Factors of the Rule of Law in Brazil ... 198
A. The Growing Polarisation in Society and Politics ... 200
B. The Disarrangement of the Political and Judicial Systems ... 202
C. A New 'Equilibrium'? ... 203
II. The Future of Brazil's Rule of Law ... 207

Bibliography ... *216*
Index ... *235*

Introduction

I. WHAT HAPPENED TO THE BRAZIL THAT WAS 'TAKING OFF'?

IN NOVEMBER 2009, a cover of *The Economist* portraying the Christ the Redeemer in Rio de Janeiro taking off announced that Brazil was rapidly heading towards becoming the fifth biggest economy in the world and that the country 'suddenly [seemed] to have made an entrance onto the world stage'.[1] A special report was dedicated to this rise of Brazil as a world power and a country that, instead of '[being] all promise', was finally 'beginning to deliver'.[2] Brazil already had some political stability, with a regular turnover of power between two major political parties – the Brazilian Social Democracy Party (PSDB) and the Worker's Party (PT) – and elections were well-organised and peaceful. The improvements in institutional capacities, governance, and the rule of law pointed to a path that seemed to lead to more democracy and not the other way around, while several social indexes were improving.[3] Brazil ranked comparatively well both in Latin America and among middle-income countries in terms of governance, judicial independence, legislative strength, diversified and independent media, a professionalised civil service and accountability institutions.[4] However, although in 2009 those positive developments were visible and progress in several areas was still being made, a series of both gradual and accelerated radical events was about to lead Brazil in the opposite direction.

In 2013, a new cover of the same magazine again portrayed the Christ the Redeemer, but now, instead of taking off, it appeared to be falling onto the wonderful mountains that surround the stunning landscape of Guanabara Bay. The cover also had a very provocative title – 'Has Brazil Blown It?'[5] – and argued that the optimism of the 2009 cover was already showing signs of wear. Subsequent cover pages on Brazil exposed how, step by step, the country was seriously losing sight of that optimistic future. In January 2016, a cover with a crestfallen Dilma Rousseff, the then President, forecast a grim picture: 'Brazil's

[1] 'Brazil Takes Off' (*The Economist*, 14 November 2009) www.economist.com/leaders/2009/11/12/brazil-takes-off.

[2] 'Getting It Together at Last (*The Economist*, 14 November 2009) www.economist.com/special-report/2009/11/14/getting-it-together-at-last.

[3] See ch 2.

[4] See MA Melo and C Pereira, *Making Brazil Work: Checking the President in a Multiparty System* (Palgrave Macmillan, 2013) 1–23.

[5] 'Has Brazil Blown It?' (*The Economist*, 28 September 2013) www.economist.com/leaders/2013/09/27/has-brazil-blown-it.

Fall: Dilma Rousseff and the disastrous year ahead'.[6] *The Economist* would support her removal on two other covers. The first one came with the heading 'Time to Go' and suggested her resignation as a less traumatic solution than her impeachment.[7] One month later, when the impeachment bid had already been approved in the Chamber of Deputies, the cover 'The Betrayal of Brazil' extended criticism to the whole political class, which, it was suggested, had also betrayed the country.[8] Now the cover had the Christ the Redeemer holding a SOS sign.

That SOS sign, now looking back, is indicative of how that year – 2016 – was a portent of a future that would remind Brazilians of their past. It is when Pandora's box was opened and released some of the country's past evils that until then had seemed to be under control. It is also when the country, as never before since the transition to democracy in 1985, could see the pillars of its democracy beginning to tremble. A sequence of developments at that time laid the groundwork for the rise of Jair Bolsonaro as President two years later, a shocking and unexpected outcome for many. The country that around a decade ago was 'beginning to deliver' would now feature the 'Latin America latest menace',[9] a statement that has since proven true as the country has rapidly backslid in various markers of democracy and the rule of law. *The Economist* could not better depict such a rapid transformation: the Christ the Redeemer would now breathe through an oxygen mask[10] – and not only because Brazil had one of the world's worst responses against the COVID-19 pandemic.[11]

It is a strange feeling to follow the chronology of those covers: it seemed that Brazil was finally crossing the threshold where the ladder to development could no longer be kicked away,[12] where democracy was 'the only game in town',[13] and where the commitment to the rule of law had found an 'institutional equilibrium'[14] that could stabilise the political forces and society at large. Naturally, there was still a long way to go: the high levels of social inequality,

[6] 'Brazil's Fall' (*The Economist*, 2 January 2016) www.economist.com/leaders/2016/01/02/brazils-fall.

[7] 'Time to Go' (*Tne Economist*, 16 March 2016) www.economist.com/leaders/2016/03/26/time-to-go.

[8] 'The Great Betrayal' (*The Economist*, 26 April 2016) www.economist.com/leaders/2016/04/23/the-great-betrayal.

[9] 'Jair Bolsonaro, Latin America Latest Menace' (*The Economist*, 22 September 2018) www.economist.com/leaders/2016/04/23/the-great-betrayal.

[10] 'Jair Bolsonaro Is Not the Only Reason His Country Is in a Ditch' (*The Economist*, 5 June 2021) www.economist.com/leaders/2021/06/03/jair-bolsonaro-is-not-the-only-reason-his-country-is-in-a-ditch.

[11] 'Covid Performance Index' (*Lowy Institute*, 13 March 2021) https://interactives.lowyinstitute.org/features/covid-performance/.

[12] See H-J Chang, *Kicking Away the Ladder: Development Strategy in Historical Perspective* (Anthem Press, 2002).

[13] A Przeworski, 'Democracy as an Equilibrium' (2005) 123 *Public Choice* 269.

[14] See A Przeworski and JM Maravall, 'Introduction' in A Przeworski and JM Maravall (eds), *Democracy and the Rule of Law* (Cambridge University Press, 2003) 3. See also ch 1.

the stubborn authoritarian mindset and the institutional dysfunctionalities on multiple levels were barriers to structural changes. In a young democracy with such 'self-reinforcing processes'[15] blocking or hindering structural measures aimed at attacking the country's longstanding evils, changes are limited, incremental, and simply not enough, but they do occur and bring some progress. It seems, though, that there is also a threshold beyond which the risk of backlashes significantly increases. Brazil crossed this last threshold without having crossed the previous one. In such a clash of thresholds, Brazil's downfall has been so rapid and intense that it has increasingly appeared to be a 'state that flouts the law and scoffs at the constitutional state or state of law' (*état de droit*).[16]

However, the question is whether such a downfall is just a deviation, even if a radical one, from that path towards the 'entrance onto the world stage'[17] or, on the contrary, an eternal return journey to where Brazil has long belonged. Short-term history, especially such an intense one, has a powerful capacity of blurring our analytical eyes in relation to events that have lingered, to processes that have reinforced themselves throughout history, even if they have also changed based on current events. For a multifaceted concept such as the rule of law, short-term history naturally matters, but it is how the country incrementally and consistently evolves in its institutional capacities and in its markers of democracy over long stretches of time that it can more accurately reflect what the country has achieved, what it is currently enduring and what may happen next.

That said, the rise of a figure like President Bolsonaro, more than the phenomenon itself, reveals the deep wounds of Brazilian democracy that have not been properly treated over the years of democratic life and which are now bleeding fast. They will take longer to heal once Bolsonaro leaves office, so the damages, in such a short period of time, have already been projected as part of the country's long-term history: they transcend their own temporality as wrongs that will demand even stronger tools to protect democracy thereafter. *Bolsonarismo*, as this phenomenon has been called, describes the country's incapacity to deal with its past and also its propensity to reconcile with the irreconcilable. It is by far the country's most severe test of democratic resilience since Brazil transitioned from the civilian-military dictatorship (1964–85). But it is also the country's most revealing experience of the need to confront its longstanding evils, 'to make the world more transparent for us, to make us think about what we have forgotten'.[18] These words, written by my dear friend,

[15] P Pierson, *Politics in Time: History, Institutions, and Social Analysis* (Princeton University Press, 2004) 52.

[16] J Derrida, *Rogues: Two Essays on Reason* (Stanford University Press, 2005) xiii. Jacques Derrida's *état de droit*, in his book *Voyoux*, was translated into 'state of law' in its English version, which sounds unconventional but also shows the difficulty in directly translating *état de droit* into *rule of law*. Such a loss of translation will be examined in ch 1 of this book.

[17] See n 1.

[18] M Milovic, 'Vírus do Capitalismo' (*Prerrô*, 14 April 2020) www.prerro.com.br/o-virus-do-capitalismo/.

professor, and colleague Miroslav Milovic, who left this world as a victim of the COVID-19 tragedy in Brazil, say much of the country's need to finally learn from its past, and not make its present – and its future – a reinvention of the worst of it.

Brazil's present has, however, embraced that past, with its long-term history now radicalised in all its disruptive force within a short period of time. This explains why Brazil, which could until recently enhance its institutional capacities and the rule of law, fell into a slump. This is also the reason why understanding Bolsonaro as a culmination of both the country's structural flaws and the misfortunes of the time may better explain where Brazil currently stands and where it may go from now on. The country was already struggling with its longstanding democratic shortcomings, but contingencies also matter: unfortunately it featured an opportunistic politician who had been strategically planning for a long time to become president through a far-right agenda that could easily gather the support of a resentful people and satisfy the interests of wealthy segments of society. His mystifying and salvationist rhetoric won the hearts of the people with a power of affection that challenges reason.

Brazil is naturally not alone. In various countries, to a greater or lesser extent, recent developments have raised serious concerns about the quality of their democracies as the symptoms of their decay have become more pronounced.[19] Adam Przeworski points out some typical signs in this direction: the erosion of traditional party systems, the rise of right-wing populism and the decline of support for democracy. Moreover, potential causes for such a phenomenon may be found in a stagnant economy, rising inequality, lower social mobility and growing polarisation in society.[20] Zachary Elkins stresses this last point by arguing that 'divided publics [is] the single most important factor that threatens and undermines democracy, at least in modern presidential systems',[21] and, when extended to politics, this polarisation is indeed dangerous: 'party polarization threatens the most basic objectives of governance',[22] so 'understanding polarization comparatively should be at the top of the agenda for comparative political scientists'.[23]

These symptoms are strongly felt in Brazilian democracy. However, two key developments may help explain why Brazil resorted to such a strong example of an extreme-right movement as a way out of a political crisis that had been brewing since the popular protests of 2013, or earlier.[24] The first is the typical

[19] See MA Graber, S Levinson, and M Tushnet, 'Constitutional Democracy in Crisis? Introduction' in MA Graber, S Levinson and M Tushnet (eds), *Constitutional Democracy in Crisis?* (Oxford University Press, 2018) 3.

[20] A Przeworski, *Crises of Democracy* (Cambridge University Press, 2019) 81–122.

[21] Z Elkins, 'Is the Sky Falling? Constitutional Crises in Historical Perspective' in Graber, Levinson and Tushnet (n 19) 53.

[22] ibid.

[23] ibid 59.

[24] See JZ Benvindo, 'Brazilian Elections and Demonstration of June 2013: The Rise of Conservatism?' (*International Journal of Constitutional Law Blog*, 1 November 2014) www.iconnectblog.com/2014/11/brazilian-elections-and-demonstrations-of-june-2013-the-rise-of-conservatism/.

argument that has historically proven strong enough to destabilise governments: the anti-corruption rhetoric, but now boosted by a judiciary heading at a rapid pace toward politicisation and even partisanship.[25] The second is the erosion of the political system through increased party fragmentation and decreased institutionalisation,[26] which creates incentives for corruption.[27] Bolsonaro surfed on the wave of the anti-corruption crusade prompted by 'Operation Car Wash', a massive anti-corruption probe,[28] which positioned the judiciary as an instigator of the crisis by disregarding basic constitutional principles in favour of an alleged public outcry. He also benefited from an eroding party system,[29] exactly when the Worker's Party (PT) was suffering its most severe backlash in history after years in power. On the other hand, the Brazilian Social Democracy Party (PSDB) was unable to grasp the support of a growing mass of resentful people, who saw in Bolsonaro, from the marginal Social Liberal Party (PSL), a way out of the crisis.[30]

However, Bolsonaro has proven to be too heavy a burden for a country that, despite its flaws, has learned to live with democracy and whose institutional framework, even if weakened, still has some capacity to react to such a crisis. Particularly in view of the disastrous handing of the COVID-19 pandemic, but also the mismanagement of all sectors of governance and economy, Bolsonaro increasingly looks like a transitory phenomenon, though *bolsonarismo* will not be. The radicality of such a short-term event will impact future developments in the country in a way that obviously remains to be seen. Despite their serious dysfunctionalities and disruption under Bolsonaro, the country's democratic

[25] See ch 5.

[26] See ch 4. See also S Mainwaring, F Bizzarro and TJ Power, 'The Uneven Institutionalization of a Party System: Brazil' in S Mainwaring (ed), *Party Systems in Latin America: Institutionalization, Decay, and Collapse* (Cambridge University Press, 2018) 164–200.

[27] See P Schleiter and A Voznaya, 'Party System Institutionalization, Accountability and Governmental Corruption' (2018) 48 *British Journal of Political Science* 315.

[28] See E Valarini and M Pohlmann, 'Organizational Crime and Corruption in Brazil: A Case Study of the "Operation Carwash" Court Records' (2019) 59 *International Journal of Law, Crime and Justice* 100340, 100340; PF Lagunes and J Svejnar, *Corruption and the Lava Jato Scandal in Latin America* (Routledge, 2020).

[29] See Przeworski (n 20) 83; TG Daly and BC Jones, 'Parties versus Democracy: Addressing Today's Political Party Threats to Democratic Rule' (2020) 18 *International Journal of Constitutional Law* 510.

[30] PT lost various seats in parliament in the 2018 elections, but, as it is the party with the strongest attachment to its social base and is very ramified, it ended up being the party with most seats in the Chamber of Deputies (it fell from 69 in the 2014 elections to 56 in the 2018 elections) and still disputed with Bolsonaro in the second round, obtaining roughly 45% of the votes with Fernando Haddad. Bolsonaro was, however, much more disruptive for the centre-right parties, particularly the Brazilian Social Democracy Party (PSDB), which had long figured as the traditional opponent to PT in the presidential elections. The number of deputies fell from 54 in 2014 to 29 in 2018, and his presidential candidate, Geraldo Alckmin, received merely 4.8% of the votes. The centre-right Brazilian Democratic Movement (MDB), the biggest party then, had 66 seats in the Chamber of Deputies in 2014, but merely 34 in 2018. Bolsonaro's Social Liberty Party (PSL), on the other hand, saw a rise from 4 seats in 2014 to 52 seats in 2018. Bolsonaro would later leave PSL and govern without any party affiliation for most of his government.

institutions as well as organised civil society have shown a reasonable degree of resilience and capacity for reaction. Therefore, for a concept such as the rule of law, it is what has led to such a phenomenon and what will possibly linger for a long time thereafter that deserve further attention and reflection. This may better explain the quality and functioning of the rule of the law in the country, which is marked by several layers of self-reinforcing processes[31] that transcend this very specific moment and that have impacted various other critical moments in Brazilian history.

All such historical clashes, in recent and past history, imply methodological dilemmas that should be announced in advance. Discussions of the rule of law in such a radical and intense political moment are certainly under continuous threat of falling into analytical pitfalls. The history of our own time is always a risky endeavour, but even more so when short-term history tends to transcend its time and greatly affect our interpretation of the 'actors and factors [that are] relevant to the (declining) health of the democratic system'.[32] It has a powerful capacity of distorting the interpretation not only of this very moment, but also of what happened previously, and what may happen next. *Bolsonarismo* is a phenomenon that certainly reveals much of Brazil's wounds, but it is also one that overshadows what is beyond the radicality of its very presence.

We thus need to go far beyond the spectre of *bolsonarismo*. This book focuses on some key 'actors and factors'[33] that have moulded the rule of law in Brazil over time. Its main thesis is that the rule of law in Brazil has greatly improved over the years of democratic life but still pays the high price for simply 'normalising' longstanding tensions and not challenging them. By 'normalising' such tensions, the rule of law has been strategically identified with legal mechanisms to maintain, justify and even construct inequality. This also reveals how a certain authoritarian mindset clashing with democracy is still pervasive in the country. The alarming levels of social inequality and the still widespread authoritarian mindset, when combined as deeply as they currently are, cause the country's mechanisms of democratic protection to be placed under severe stress, thus exacerbating their structural dysfunctionalities. Social inequality and an authoritarian mindset are therefore not only the central guidelines for understanding the functioning and quality of the rule of law in Brazil, but also the long-term features that create incentives for short-term junctures to resound for a long period of time. Despite that, this book has hope that Brazil's democracy will survive the radicality of present times and prove itself stronger, even if the path toward its consolidation now looks bumpier and more distant.

[31] See Pierson (n 15) 12.

[32] TG Daly, 'Understanding Multi-Directional Democratic Decay: Lessons from the Rise of Bolsonaro in Brazil' (2020) 14 *Law & Ethics of Human Rights* 199.

[33] ibid.

II. THE STRUCTURE OF THIS BOOK

The rule of law is not a simple concept when it comes to defining the political, economic and legal developments of a country like Brazil. Similar to many other Latin American countries, Brazil is a young democracy struggling with its long-standing extractive institutions[34] and entrenched interests. The very concept of rule of law in such a scenario is thereby both unstable, because of its recurring connections with a past that does whatever it takes to keep itself virtually untouched, and promising, because of the legitimising forces of a democracy that has become part of Brazilian life, even if it is a flawed one. Brazil features one of the most interesting democratic transitions that also turned out to be a constitutional transition marked by the great involvement of organised civil society[35] and the promise of a new era.[36] If this new constitutional moment laid the groundwork for positively transforming Brazilian institutions and strengthening the rule of law, it has nonetheless suffered from the memory of much of that authoritarian era. As Anthony Pereira points out, 'the legacy of authoritarian legality has cast its shadow over democracy'.[37] This clash between instability and promise, on the one hand, and authoritarianism and democracy, on the other, is what makes the investigation of the rule of law in Brazil such a fascinating subject.

This book aims to discuss the functioning, evolution and dynamics of the rule of law in Brazil from different perspectives. It stresses not only how the rule of law has developed in the legal system, but also how the political institutions and extra-legal organisations have transformed the foundations of the rule of law in Brazil. Moreover, in a context of a crisis of liberal principles and 'democratic decay'[38] in global constitutionalism, the book explores the visible threats to the rule of law in a young democracy like Brazil. Past history provides a rich background to show how the transition to democracy has fostered a greater commitment to the rule of law while, at the same time, raising new dilemmas that democracies, and especially young ones, often face. The central question

[34] D Acemoglu and JA Robinson, *Why Nations Fail: The Origins of Power, Prosperity and Poverty* (Crown Business, 2012) 168.

[35] See L Barbosa, *História Constitucional Brasileira: Mudança Constitucional, Autoritarismo e Democracia no Brasil Pós-1964* (Biblioteca Digital da Câmara dos Deputados, 2012) 145–248; C Paixão, 'Autonomia, Democracia e Poder Constituinte: Disputas Conceituais na Experiência Constitucional Brasileira (1964–2014)' (2014) 43 *Quaderni Fiorentini* 450; C Michiles, *Cidadão Constituinte: A Saga das Emendas Populares* (Paz e Terra, 1989).

[36] See JZ Benvindo, 'The Forgotten People in Brazilian Constitutionalism: Revisiting Behavior Strategic Analyses of Regime Transitions' (2017) 15 *International Journal of Constitutional Law* 332.

[37] AW Pereira, *Political (in)Justice: Authoritarianism and the Rule of Law in Brazil, Chile, and Argentina* (University of Pittsburgh Press, 2005) 172.

[38] TG Daly, 'Public Law and the Puzzle of Democratic Decay in Brazil' (2017) *Law and Society Association (Working Paper)*, www.democratic-decay.org/s/Daly_Pub-Law-Democratic-Decay-Brazil_finaldraftRev.pdf.

of the book is how Brazilian democracy has dealt with the high levels of social inequality and the authoritarian mindset that still play a big role in its fate, and whether the country's democratic achievements and institutional framework are sufficiently strong to enforce the rule of law as an imperative for Brazil's development, especially in times when the country is most in need of them.

The first chapter – 'The Conceptual Evolution of the Rule of Law in Brazil' – will examine the doctrinal debate over the rule of law in Brazil, the evolution of its meaning in important moments of Brazilian history and the way legal institutions have dealt with it over time. The investigation is, therefore, both doctrinal and historical and focuses on a diachronic analysis of the concept of rule of law. More importantly, it explores the various subtle ways in which the rule of law can be lost in translation. A necessary discussion is found in the confusions and misconceptions that occur when the rule of law is simply translated into *Estado de Direito*,[39] as normally employed in Portuguese. The legal doctrine, statutes and precedents refer to the concept of *Estado de Direito* when they aim to express a similar understanding to what is internationally called the rule of law. The evolution of such a concept is also an interesting topic, because the Brazilian legal doctrine and institutions, even under authoritarian rule, used a deviating concept of *Estado de Direito* to justify some of the major atrocities of those regimes, in a clear case of abuse of such a concept. Brazil, more than many of its Latin American neighbours, is rich in experiences of abuses of legal concepts, with a number of legal documents mentioning them as a way to promote the goals of dictatorial regimes, as took place during Getúlio Vargas's *Estado Novo* (1937–45) and the civilian-military dictatorship (1964–85). On the other hand, the concept of *Estado de Direito* has itself evolved with the transition to democracy in 1985, and, particularly, with the 1988 Constitution, whose democratic quality is very visible by calling it *Estado Democrático de Direito*.

In this regard, *Estado de Direito* is a compelling concept to observe the clash between preservation and democratisation in Brazil, and also how it has been subverted by the country's high social inequality and deep-rooted authoritarian mindset. This chapter acknowledges and briefly examines some normative assumptions that are usually connected to the concept of rule of law as well as its traditional conceptual distinctions with, in particular, the German *Rechtsstaat* and the French *état de droit*. It assumes, in any case, that, for an adequate assessment of the rule of law, it needs to address the constraints that inequality and authoritarian legacies constitute for such a concept. For this purpose, this chapter will adopt a game theoretic modelling for the rule of law by focusing on concepts such as equilibrium, coordination, behaviours and incentives, but tempered with those normative debates as well as historiographic

[39] See M Rosenfeld, 'The Rule of Law and the Legitimacy of Constitutional Democracy' (2001) 74 *Southern California Law Review* 1307.

concerns of temporal processes over long stretches of time in political and legal institutions.[40]

The second chapter – 'The Local Lived Experiences of the Rule of Law in Brazil: The Impacts of Social Inequality' – introduces the first fundamental element for understanding the rule of law in Brazil: the country's structural social inequality. The main argument is that Brazil is marked by a history of strategically keeping inequality virtually unchanged despite the various political and social transformations in the country. Brazil has certainly become more democratic and has improved as regards social welfare, but inequality is a serious hindrance to the political, economic and legal development as well as to the consolidation of the rule of law. It also helps explain why the country still suffers from moments of serious democratic crises, such as under the Bolsonaro government, by arguing that inequality negatively impacts the capacity of the democratic institutional and legal framework to function as a self-enforcing coordination device,[41] while creating incentives for formal and informal institutions to preserve a strategy of exclusion of those most in need. This chapter will also discuss whether and how the rule of law, in the years since democratisation, has fostered greater inclusion of minorities in Brazil (such as women, the Black community and Indigenous people) and lessened regional differences. It ends by examining some comparable empirical markers of the quality of Brazil's democracy and rule of law according to international surveys and indexes. By contextualising those empirical data and connecting them with the previous discussions, the chapter ends by arguing that those surveys and indexes do matter but should be taken with a pinch of salt, especially in a country with such high social contrasts.

The third chapter – 'The Authoritarian Mindset and the Rule of Law in Brazil' – introduces the second fundamental element that has largely impacted the rule of law in the country: the persistence of an authoritarian mindset, which has been manifested not only in simple behaviours that are usually entangled with inequality, but also in the most critical moments of Brazilian history. This chapter aims to show how such an authoritarian mindset has reinvented itself as democratic in both explicit authoritarian periods and moments where democracy seemed to be heading to a point of no return. Brazil features one of the most compelling constitutional transitions in Latin America, when distinct sectors of organised civil society could effectively influence the drafting of the 1988 Constitution. Yet, as usually happens in democratic transitions,[42] this same Constitution also preserves various legacies of the previous authoritarian years.

[40] See Pierson (n 15).

[41] See B Weingast, 'The Political Foundations of Democracy and the Rule of Law' (1997) 91 *American Political Science Review* 251.

[42] See T Ginsburg, '¿Fruto de la Parra Envenenada? Algunas Observaciones Comparadas sobre la Constitución Chilena' (2014) 133 *Estudios Públicos* 1.

This is the paradox that is beneath many of Brazil's recent developments: on the one hand, there is a visible institutional improvement, so the commitment to the rule of law has indeed become more effective; on the other hand, that authoritarian mindset, which expresses itself through distinct practices (clientelism, corruption, attacks on minorities and a rather unstable civilian control over the military) keeps causing serious damage to the country. A clash of narratives between authoritarianism and democratisation has played a relevant role in Brazilian history and is a fundamental subject for grasping the main nuances of the rule of law in Brazil.

The fourth chapter – 'The Rule of Law and Brazilian Political Institutions: A Reshaped "Coalition Presidentialism"' – delves into the functioning and dysfunctionalities of Brazil's political system. This chapter will show how parliament and the executive have managed to comply with the rule of law and how they have also overlooked it in order to keep entrenched mutual benefits virtually untouched. The goal is to discuss some of the core institutional political improvements the country has visibly achieved over the democratic years as well as some forms of abuse of constitutional tools to jeopardise the rule of law.[43] This chapter will examine the main features of Brazil's Congress and Executive, notably by focusing on the functioning of its so-called 'coalition presidentialism'.[44] The analysis will revolve around the fascinating debates over whether 'coalition presidentialism' is suitable for governance or, on the contrary, is so dysfunctional that political deadlocks[45] have raised the stakes of power and destabilised the constitutional system.[46] It also explores the significant party fragmentation and the still-oligarchical National Congress, two key defects that tend to foster clientelism and corruption. The chapter also raises the question of whether clientelism and 'coalition presidentialism' are a necessary correlation.

The fifth chapter – 'The Rule of Law and Brazil's Politicised Judicial System' – examines the judiciary in Brazil, a major player in Brazilian democracy. The judiciary has become significantly stronger over the democratic years, but notably the Supreme Court has transformed itself into a central political player, in a way that is not easily translatable into the language normally adopted by constitutional courts elsewhere. The main constitutional and political matters are now decided by that Court, sparking a fierce debate over whether it has, or has not, overstepped the principle of

[43] See R Dixon and D Landau, *Abusive Constitutional Borrowing: Legal Globalization and the Subversion of Liberal Democracy* (Oxford University Press, 2021); D Landau, 'Abusive Constitutionalism' (2013) 47 *University of California, Davis* 189.

[44] S Abranches, *Presidencialismo de Coalizão* (Companhia das Letras, 2018); S Abranches, 'Presidencialismo de Coalizão: O Dilema Institucional Brasileiro' (1988) 31 *Dados – Revista de Ciências Sociais* 5.

[45] See B Ames, *The Deadlock of Democracy in Brazil* (University of Michigan Press, 2001).

[46] See B Weingast, 'Designing Constitutional Stability' in R Congleton and B Swedenborg (eds), *Democratic Constitutional Design and Public Policy Analysis and Evidence* (MIT Press, 2006) 343–66.

separation of powers, no matter how this principle has been normatively interpreted. It has behaved as an important player in protecting democracy and enforcing the rule of law, but it does not follow that, by acting as such, it has left behind the authoritarian mindset that has long pervaded Brazilian institutions. It has defended the rule of law and constitutionalism, but it has also transgressed them by other means, through either a preservationist behaviour or sheer politics – not to say partisanship in some cases. It has become more accessible, but it still lacks accountability. The judiciary is one of the most independent in Latin America[47] but is also a very successful corporation that institutionally embodies and constructs inequality. This chapter also delves into Brazil's judicial criminal system and police forces, which have proven highly inefficient and caused the levels of violence to increase (eg, the shocking numbers of police killings), thereby fostering inequality even further.

The sixth chapter – 'The Extra-Legal Influences on the Rule of Law and Mechanisms of Accountability in Brazil' – investigates other actors, organisations and institutions that have played an important role in fostering the rule of law in Brazil, such as accountability institutions, movements of organised civil society and other public interest groups. Corporations and economic sectors have cooperated with the state on several fronts, though some such relationships have been plagued by clientelism and corruption. For this purpose, it reviews some empirical data on corruption according to international indicators and delves into some mechanisms Brazil has adopted to combat corruption, particularly by focusing on the effects of path dependence, inequality and institutional design flaws. It also shows the challenges of changing such a reality even by means of incremental improvements, since political and social backlashes have become commonplace. On the other hand, there is a growing movement of organised civil society in favour of new policies aimed at democratising the institutional framework and designing strategies to tackle the longstanding inequalities in the country. This chapter looks into how civil society has coordinated conflicting interests in its quest for fairness through a series of actions and mobilisations that have resulted in important public policies. It ends by discussing the role, structure and dynamics of the media, which, though seemingly free and independent, is very concentrated and influential in Brazil. The power of social media (Facebook, Twitter, WhatsApp, etc) is also an important factor in understanding their impact on the enforcement of the rule of law and the challenges they bring to Brazilian democracy.

The seventh chapter – 'The Rule of Law in Brazil and the Challenges of International Law' – is aimed at discussing how international law and institutions have impacted the development of the rule of law in Brazil. Previously

[47] See J Ríos-Figueroa, 'Institutions for Constitutional Justice in Latin America' in G Helmke and J Ríos-Figueroa (eds), *Courts in Latin America* (Cambridge University Press, 2011) 33, 36.

seen as a 'global development power',[48] Brazil has more recently been in the spotlight as a growing antagonist of international relations and regional integration. This is a radical deviation from its previous path, when Brazil aimed at strengthening the rule of law by projecting its rising power through regional associations such as MERCOSUR and UNASUR as well as other partnerships with poor and middle-income countries. The participation of Brazil in other international associations, such as the Organisation of the American States (OAS), and its commitment to international law and rulings by international courts, in particular the Inter-American Court of Human Rights, is also addressed in this chapter. It ends by discussing how the international community has interpreted Brazil's compliance with the rule of law, especially in view of the recent critical developments that have undermined its appeal as a world's soft power in the promotion of democracy and the rule of law.

The eighth and final chapter – 'The Future of the Rule of Law in Brazil' – provides a deeper analytical approach by summarising the main conclusions of the previous chapters and connecting them to some debates over the current context in Brazil. This chapter links long-term history to short-term events, thus assessing their impact on possible future developments for the rule of law in Brazil. The goal is to foresee potential scenarios for the rule of law amid the challenges of the political crisis that the country has been enduring. The main question is whether Brazil has achieved a mature institutional framework and a cohesive civil society that are strong enough to cope with the recurring risks of democratic backsliding. This chapter delves into the factors that have destabilised the rule of law in the country, such as the growing polarisation in society and politics and the dysfunctionalities of the political and judicial systems. It begs the question of whether Brazil will find a new 'equilibrium' to stabilise its democratic and constitutional system and how the country will overcome Bolsonaro's disruptive years.

This book ends by arguing that Brazil has had ups and down throughout its democratisation process, but, overall, it has achieved significant institutional progress, fostered mechanisms of social inclusion, and enhanced its culture of democracy. It is still a country marked by significant social inequality, where extractive institutions have managed to keep their influence and power untouched, and where the authoritarian mindset, through distinct forms, has found a way to disrupt democracy whenever the opportunity arises. Brazil needs to learn from its past and address the wrongs that have long plagued its capacity to face the challenges of a young democracy. This book reveals its profound concern about Brazil's democracy, especially given recent critical events, but it is confident that Brazilian democracy is here to stay, even if its path to consolidation now demands more energy and vigilance. The rule of law in Brazil has

[48] P Dauvergne and D BL Farias, 'The Rise of Brazil as a Global Development Power' (2012) 33 *Third World Quarterly* 903.

been built upon the legal construction of inequality and this has handicapped the country's capacity to overcome its longstanding evils, frequently reappearing in different forms. This book aims to show that Brazil, despite its setbacks, has made some progress in its commitment to the rule of law, but unless it challenges its deep-rooted inequality, it will always be the country where the Christ the Redeemer will keep falling onto the wonderful landscape of Guanabara Bay.

1

The Conceptual Evolution of the Rule of Law in Brazil

I. INTRODUCTION: A PROSAIC APPROACH TO THE RULE OF LAW

ONE OF THE most difficult challenges for someone exploring the concept of rule of law is to feel lost in translation. Countries not sharing the Anglo-American legal tradition may find, in such a concept, only a very imperfect equivalent. Most commonly, we see rule of law being translated, for example, into *État de Droit* (French), *Estado de Derecho* (Spanish), *Stato di Diritto* (Italian), *Estado de Direito* (Portuguese), and *Rechtsstaat* (German) – and vice-versa. If the concept of rule of law is what we could call a 'multi-faceted ideal'[1] that has become 'an international hurrah term, on the lips of every development agency, offered as a support for economic growth, democracy, human rights, and much else',[2] it would be nonetheless wrong to simply assume that such an ideal is unique across the globe. *Rechtsstaat*, for instance, has evolved in such a way that it can mean the constitutionalisation of politics and the promotion of substantive values of constitutional justice and welfare.[3] *État de Droit*, in turn, is intrinsically connected to the debate over the limits of parliamentary sovereignty.[4] Depending on how we translate rule of law – for example, based on a substantive/axiological approach (*Rechtsstaat*) or on the institutional limits of popular representation (*État de Droit*) – it looks like we are sailing on troubled waters. Not only is rule of law a highly contentious concept,[5] but the way the literature has assimilated it into distinct political contexts varies significantly.

[1] J Waldron, 'The Concept and the Rule of Law' (2008) 43 *Georgia Law Review* 6.

[2] M Krygier, 'Four Puzzles about the Rule of Law: Why, What, Where? and Who Cares?' in JE Fleming (ed), *Getting to the Rule of Law* (New York University Press, 2011) 64.

[3] M Rosenfeld, 'The Rule of Law and the Legitimacy of Constitutional Democracy' (2001) 74 *Southern California Law Review* 46, 1328–29.

[4] ibid 1330–33.

[5] See J Meierhenrich and M Loughlin, *The Cambridge Companion to the Rule of Law* (Cambridge University Press, 2021); TP Costa and D Zolo (eds), *The Rule of Law: History, Theory and Criticism* (Springer, 2007); JE Fleming, *Getting to the Rule of Law* (NYU Press, 2011); T Ginsburg and M Versteeg, 'Constitutional Correlates of the Rule of Law' in M Adams, A Meuwese, and EH Ballin (eds), *Constitutionalism and the Rule of Law* (Cambridge University Press, 2017) 506–25; N MacCormick, *Rhetoric and the Rule of Law: A Theory of Legal Reasoning* (Oxford University

Yet there are points of contact, which have become stronger still as legal traditions have become more intertwined than ever. The concept of rule of law itself, though highly contestable, is based on the 'deployment and enforcement of procedural safeguards',[6] a formal understanding that recalls the Lockean perspective of individuals owning fundamental rights that transcend social contract and civil society.[7] It is not easily translatable – such a Lockean perspective would sound rather inconsistent with various legal traditions, after all – but it is common sense that predictability, fairness and determinacy are part of the core of what we usually expect from a legal system and its institutions.[8] Normally, the immediate associations of such premises are found in the separation of powers, the general commitment to the law by all individuals and the state, and – particularly important for the Anglo-American tradition – the fairness of all trials and procedures. It could also embrace substantive contents (human dignity,[9] or the recognition of multicultural identities,[10] for example), though such an appeal to substance rather than procedure (and the several disputes over the scope of each one) transforms the rule of law into a more contestable and dependable concept.

If we ask a Brazilian lawyer what the concept of rule of law means, he or she will most likely assume that we are referring to the Portuguese concept of *Estado de Direito*. A more literal translation of rule of law into *regra do direito* or *regra da lei* (or even *império do direito*) sounds odd and, in fact, detached from the country's legal tradition, even if some scholars have used such literal translations to express their distinctive features.[11] *Estado de Direito*, like the rule of law, can encompass distinct shades of meanings, but, to put it simply, it embraces the premise that state acts must be determined and limited by law.[12] As such,

Press, 2005); GJ Postema, 'Law's Rule: Reflexivity, Mutual Accountability and the Rule of Law' in X Zhai and M Quinn (eds), *Bentham's Theory of Law and Public Opinion* (Cambridge University Press, 2013) 7–39; J Waldron, 'The Rule of Law as a Theatre of Debate' in J Burley (ed), *Dworkin and His Critics: With Replies by Ronald Dworkin* (Blackwell, 2004) 319–36; T Bustamante and TL Decat, *Philosophy of Law as an Integral Part of Philosophy: Essays on the Jurisprudence of Gerald J. Postema* (Hart Publishing, 2020); S Holmes, 'Lineages of the Rule of Law' in A Przeworski and JM Maravall (eds), *Democracy and the Rule of Law* (Cambridge University Press, 2003) 19–61; M Adams, A Meuwese and EH Ballin, *Constitutionalism and the Rule of Law* (Cambridge University Press, 2017); M Krygier, 'The Rule of Law: Pasts, Presents, and Two Possible Futures' (2016) 12 *Annual Review of Law and Social Science* 199–229; J Møller and S Skaaning, *The Rule of Law: Definitions, Measures, Patterns and Causes*, (Springer. 2014); J Waldron, 'The Concept and the Rule of Law' (2008) 43 *Georgia Law Review* 1; A Przeworski and JM Maravall *Democracy and the Rule of Law* (Cambridge University Press, 2003). On the future of the rule of law, see Y Roznai, 'The Rule of Law in 2030' in C Bezemek (ed), *Constitutionalism 2030* (Hart Publishing, 2022).

[6] Rosenfeld (n 3) 1335.

[7] ibid 1334.

[8] See LL Fuller, *The Morality of Law* (Yale University Press, 1969).

[9] J Waldron, 'The Rule of Law and the Importance of Procedure' in Fleming (n 2) 16. See also C Brettschneider, 'A Substantive Conception of the Rule of Law: Nonarbitrary Treatment and the Limits of Procedure' in Fleming (n 2).

[10] Rosenfeld (n 3) 1351.

[11] See JJG Canotilho, *Estado de Direito* (Gradiva Publicações, 1999).

[12] ibid 4.

however, it says little, and it is no wonder that it has evolved to also embrace a myriad of new contents that brought to it a more coloured and nuanced dimension. Despite its contextual differences, the concept of *Estado de Direito* would also be significantly affected by the global trend of embracing democratic values as part of its core. Constitutional scholars and the Brazilian Constitution have added the adjective *democrático* to this concept, thereby distinguishing *Estado Democrático de Direito* from the emptier *Estado de Direito* as a means to spotlight that, nowadays, a state determined and limited by law should fundamentally be a democratic state determined and limited by law.

History helps explain this need to stress the democratic value of *Estado de Direito*: both Brazil and Portugal – just to focus on two Portuguese-speaking countries – have endured years of dictatorships in the twentieth century. Their Constitutions, drafted in the aftermath of the transition to democracy, highlight at the beginning that they are *Estado Democrático de Direito* (Brazil) or *Estado de Direito Democrático* (Portugal).[13] Such a concept is, therefore, deeply ingrained in a historical narrative of overcoming authoritarianism. It would be misleading to investigate the rule of law in Brazil – and also in Portugal – without acknowledging that *Estado de Direito* has evolved to embrace a set of social-democratic values that are embedded in their constitutionalisms. Although the concept of *Estado de Direito* could simply be narrowed to express that state acts should be determined and constrained by law – and therefore be flexible enough to be employed even by authoritarian governments – it would be contextually wrong to see it detached from the movements toward democratisation that have formed the core of those countries' current constitutional identities.[14]

However, like the debates over the scope and limits of contents and procedures of the rule of law, establishing this intrinsic liaison between *Estado de Direito* and democratic values is a recipe for endless, though fascinating, discussions. The normative assumptions that underlie such a concept serve as ideals that should be deeply valued and largely sought. Moreover, they help connect those several analogous concepts (rule of law, *état de droit*, *Rechtsstaat*, etc) to more consensual and internationalised standards. Despite the contextual differences among such concepts, there are also common values that foster a more translatable dialogue. In some respects, some translators, in order to distinguish the civil law tradition from the common law one, use *legal state* instead of rule of law in English.[15] However, it is undeniable that rule of law has become the internationally adopted concept, though it could also mean different things for different realities. It could concentrate in itself such diverse core ideals, but it

[13] See Article 2 of the 1976 Portuguese Constitution; Article 1 of the 1988 Brazilian Constitution.

[14] See M Rosenfeld, *The Identity of the Constitutional Subject: Selfhood, Citizenship, Culture, and Community* (Routledge, 2009).

[15] See JR Silkenat, JE Hickey and P Barenboim (ed), *The Legal Doctrines of the Rule of Law and the Legal State (Rechtsstaat)* (Springer, 2014).

could distinctly operate in each reality. Martin Krygier is right when he says that we should be 'universalist about the value of it, [but] deeply contextual about how to get there'.[16] *Estado de Direito* is not rule of law, but it does not follow that *Estado de Direito* could not be translated into rule of law, as if both were completely different concepts. The rule of law has achieved such a degree of abstraction from its original Anglo-American tradition that it came to embrace general values that are also intrinsically found in current interpretations of those other analogous concepts. Context obviously matters, but so do the shared values among them.

For this reason, this book adopts an unconventional understanding of the rule of law, at least among legal scholars. It acknowledges the value of those normative assumptions – after all, they help connect those analogous concepts with each other – but it is not concerned with exploring much further the various nuances that have led to distinguishable and controversial comprehensions of the rule of law, nor does it aim to pinpoint the potentially untranslatable elements found in *Estado de Direito* or anywhere else. It obviously recognises the structural differences among those analogous concepts and it will briefly discuss some of its core features and historical connections. Moreover, it will bring some introductory arguments on how *Estado de Direito* has shaped Brazilian constitutionalism, particularly its longstanding difficult relationship with a certain authoritarian mindset and the pervasive degree of social inequality in the country. The following chapters will explore further such a relationship, which will inevitably lead to the conclusion that *Estado de Direito*, like those other similar concepts, is indeed contextually dependent. However, for now, the main goal is just to show that, regardless of its distinguishable historical and normative attributes, there is something that transcends its localised narrative and can be explained in much more prosaic terms.

The main argument is that, if *Estado de Direito* (like the rule of law) has come to embrace some fundamental values, it is nevertheless intrinsically reliant on an 'institutional equilibrium'[17] that will lead political forces to understand that following the law is strategically beneficial to them, and, mostly, that their powers are constrained by the powers of other political forces and dispersed among various organised interests. Such an understanding clearly acknowledges that the *raison d'être* of the rule of law relates to the ability of legal norms to constrain the sovereign power for the benefit of individuals.[18] However, this equilibrium-focused argument hinges less on axiological assumptions and more on behavioural incentives. It finds that the legal framework and institutions are, first and foremost, coordination devices, and that the rule of law is basically a

[16] Krygier (n 2) 99.

[17] A Przeworski and JM Maravall, 'Introduction' in Przeworski and Maravall (n 5) 3.

[18] P Costa, 'The Rule of Law: A Historical Introduction' in P Costa and D Zolo (ed), *The Rule of Law: History, Theory and Criticism* (Springer, 2007) 74.

consequence of overcoming difficulties in coordinating people's behaviour.[19] To be sure, it acknowledges the relevance of the values embedded particularly in the last developments of the rule of law and those other analogous concepts. It also recognises their deep contextual differences. Yet, it is exactly by exploring this more prosaic nature of human behaviour that they seem more translatable. Most importantly, by assuming that, in the end, the rule of law and its analogous concepts are part of the coordination dilemmas of societies,[20] it is history and the way the political forces have managed to deal with an increasingly complex society[21] that gain analytical relevance. If we are using the concept of *Estado de Direito* instead of rule of law – or vice-versa – it is not because they are intrinsically distinct in the very nature of such a coordination dilemma, but rather in how history, traditions and language have shaped them.

This chapter will, therefore, begin by briefly discussing how democratic values and social justice have shaped the normative assumptions usually associated with the rule of law and its continental counterparts. Despite their differences, they have all been marked by theoretical disputes and evolutionary narratives that show the growing presence of substantive conceptions in their core throughout history. The more substantive they have become, the more contentious their normative assumptions have been, which have intensified with several democratisation processes worldwide.

The following section will discuss some elements of how *Estado de Direito* was shaped by the Brazilian civilian-military dictatorship (1964–85), and how such a concept has been manipulated and abused in favour of preservation instead of democratisation. It will stress, nevertheless, that *Estado de Direito* should currently be understood as *Estado Democrático de Direito*, though inequality combined with an authoritarian mindset still greatly impacts Brazilian democracy. This chapter will focus on the premise that *Estado de Direito*, now interpreted as *Estado Democrático de Direito*, is seriously concerned with social justice, not because social justice has to be part of the core of *Estado de Direito* nor because such a concept hinges on normative assumptions to become reality. The claim for social justice is rather prosaic and follows Maravall's and Przeworski's argument that people – citizens and public officials alike – obey the law not necessarily due to a moral obligation, but by reason of effective incentives for compliance.[22] In this regard, a society that continuously fosters inequality fails to deliver incentives that will enhance coordination among individuals against encroachments on their rights and among public officials to abide by the rules, thereby impairing the *Estado de Direito*. The main

[19] See BR Weingast, 'A Postscript to "Political Foundations of Democracy and the Rule of Law"' in Przeworski and Maravall (n 5) 111.

[20] ibid.

[21] See N Luhmann, *Law as a Social System* (Oxford University Press, 2004) 230–73.

[22] Przeworski and Maravall (n 5) 2.

argument is that the rule of law (and *Estado de Direito*) should, according to such a perspective, be an egalitarian rule of law to effectively take root.

This chapter concludes by arguing that *Estado de Direito* will be henceforth translated into rule of law not only because it has become the internationally standardised concept, but mostly because, when prosaically interpreted, all those analogous concepts will lead to discussions of 'institutional equilibrium',[23] coordination, behaviours and incentives. If such a viewpoint is also disputed, at least it facilitates the analysis of distinct features normally associated with the concepts of rule of law and *Estado de Direito*. This is the main aim of this book.

II. DEMOCRACY AND SOCIAL JUSTICE IN THE CORE OF THE RULE OF LAW: A NORMATIVE DISPUTE?

As part of the civil law tradition, *Estado de Direito* is naturally closer to concepts such as *Rechtstaat* and *État de Droit* than the Anglo-American rule of law. The continental counterparts of the rule of law were highly influenced by the German doctrine of the *Rechtsstaat*, though their distinct constitutional histories and cultures raise particular challenges and imply some structural differences.[24] In all those cases, the intricate balance between formal and substantive conceptions of the rule of law as well as the normative disputes over the meaning and extent of the core values they should embody have marked their histories. However, there is a fundamental feature that underlies all such continental conceptions and makes them particularly distinct from the Anglo-American rule of law: the emphasis on the state.[25] As Krygier points out, it is not an accident that the continental versions of the rule of law have the state in their concepts, unlike the Anglo-American version.[26]

This reflects on a different relationship between the state and individuals, and it also lays the groundwork for the 'principle of legality', one of the hallmarks of those concepts. The continental versions of the rule of law have been greatly impacted by the historical developments of constitutional law, and, particularly after World War II, some core values began to be directly associated with them. The German *Rechtsstaat*, whose nineteenth century interpretation pointed to a 'symbiosis between the law and the state'[27] and the primacy of the state over legislation,[28] evolved to embrace substantive principles and values, particularly

[23] ibid.
[24] See Costa (n 18) 102.
[25] See DN MacCormick, 'Der Rechtsstaat und die Rule of Law' (1984) *JuristenZeitung* 65.
[26] Krygier (n 2) 47.
[27] Rosenfeld (n 3) 1319.
[28] See G Gozzi, 'Rechtsstaat and Individual Rights in German Constitutional History' in Costa and Zolo (n 5) 238.

human dignity.[29] It became a constitutional *Rechtsstaat*[30] and a democratic *Rechtsstaat*[31] which could, in a more restricted version, set the administrative goal of realising social rights or, in a broader version, determine the constitutional duty of doing so.[32] It is no wonder that the *Bundesverfassungsgericht*, the German Federal Constitutional Court, has become a prominent player in the promotion of social welfare in Germany.[33] By the same token, the French *État de Droit*, unlike the more formalist *État Légal* that was mostly based upon the 'principle of legality',[34] was coined to embody substantive principles in its core, and it has as such been adopted by the French *Conseil Constitutionnel*.[35] Despite their original differences, both concepts have thus become more analogous.[36]

The Portuguese *Estado de Direito* would adopt a similar narrative: a gradual, though impactful, transition from a formalist to a substantive conception. The 'principle of legality', which is one of its bedrocks, would also follow this route. Both the Brazilian and Portuguese debates over the *Estado de Direito* usually stress the developments from a 'liberal *Estado de Direito*' to a 'social *Estado de Direito*', and then to a 'democratic *Estado de Direito*'.[37] *Estado de Direito*, like the French *État Légal*, is also inspired by the German *Rechtsstaat*.[38] Therefore, the emphasis on the state and individual autonomy (encompassing both freedom and property) is dominant, but, as with *Rechtsstaat*, history would lead to significant changes in its originally formal meaning. Gradually, like the turbulent relationship between constitutionalism (interpreted mainly as negative freedoms) and democracy, *Estado de Direito* would demand a *legitimate power*, and thus a *democratic power*.[39] In order for this power to be democratically legitimate, social justice would inevitably become a central concern.

The normative debates on the subject predominate in both the Portuguese and the Brazilian constitutional literatures. Depending on how *Estado de Direito* is interpreted and whether it embodies substantive values in its core, the impacts on political agents' and constitutional courts' behaviours are not

[29] Rosenfeld (n 3), 1328; D Zolo, 'The Rule of Law: A Critical Reappraisal' in Costa and Zolo (n 5) 12–13.

[30] Costa (n 18) 132.

[31] ibid 120.

[32] ibid 132.

[33] See D Grimm, 'The Role of Fundamental Rights after Sixty-Five Years of Constitutional Jurisprudence in Germany' (2015) 13 *International Journal of Constitutional Law* 19; Gozzi (n 28) 251.

[34] See A Laquièze, 'État de Droit and National Sovereignty in France' in Costa and Zolo (n 5) 278.

[35] See D Rousseau, 'The Conseil Constitutionnel Confronted with Comparative Law and the Theory of Constitutional Justice (or Louis Favoreu's Untenable Paradoxes)' (2007) 5 *International Journal of Constitutional Law* 28.

[36] See Laquièze (n 34) 286.

[37] See Canotilho (n 11); JA da Silva, 'O Estado Democrático de Direito' (1988) 173 *Revista de Direito Administrativo* 15.

[38] See Canotilho (n 11) 9.

[39] ibid 10.

negligeable. JJ Gomes Canotilho, one of the leading Portuguese constitutional scholars, wrote that 'the proclaimed tension between "constitutionalists" and "democrats", between *Estado de Direito* and democracy, is a myth of the modern political thought'.[40] His argument is similar to José Afonso da Silva's, a prominent Brazilian constitutional scholar, who points out the gradual transition from a *liberal Estado de Direito* to a *democratic Estado de Direito*.[41] For Silva, Brazil's 1988 Constitution adopts an even stronger democratic core than Portugal's 1976 Constitution: *Estado Democrático de Direito* instead of *Estado de Direito Democrático*. This difference – he argues – means that the Brazilian Constitution first highlights the democratic quality of the state, which 'radiates the values of democracy all over its constituent elements, and thus over the legal order',[42] though such a difference is, in practice, of little relevance.[43] Canotilho and Silva acknowledge the risks of a *social Estado de Direito*, because it could, firstly, be associated with totalitarian states and dictatorships,[44] and, secondly, engender a clientelistic relationship between the state and citizens.[45] However, a *democratic Estado de Direito* 'incorporates a revolutionary component of transformation of the *status quo*',[46] and is thereby a '*state of social justice*' that aims to foster 'solidarity' and the 'inclusion of the other'.[47]

The upshot is that, though the origins of those concepts are marked by particularities that are not easy to translate into other contexts, the continental counterparts of the rule of law have evolved to embrace the genuine concern with enhancing democratic inclusion as well as incrementally providing instruments for social justice. There is an insurmountable debate over whether and how *Estado de Direito* or any such analogous concepts should embrace substantive values. In many respects, setting the boundaries and extent of the rule of law and its analogous concepts overlaps the conflictive relationship between constitutionalism and democracy.[48] This normative debate is well portrayed in the constitutional literature,[49] as is the discussion of the importance, impacts and risks of such substantive assumptions for political institutions[50] and

[40] ibid 11.
[41] See Silva (n 37).
[42] ibid 21.
[43] See ibid 21; Canotilho (n 11) 11.
[44] Silva (n 37) 17; Canotilho (n 11) 13.
[45] See J Habermas, *Between Facts and Norms* (MIT Press, 1996) 427.
[46] Silva (n 37) 21.
[47] Canotilho (n 11) 14–15; Silva (n 37) 22–24.
[48] See L Thomassen, 'A Bizarre, Even Opaque Practice: Habermas on Constitutionalism and Democracy' in L Thomassen (ed), *The Habermas-Derrida Reader* (The University of Chicago Press, 2006) 179.
[49] See Habermas (n 45) 388; M Adams, EH Ballin and A Meuwese, 'The Ideal and the Real in the Realm of Constitutionalism and the Rule of Law: An Introduction' in Adams, Meuwese and Ballin (n 5) 3–33; Meierhenrich and Loughlin (n 5).
[50] See Habermas (n 45) 388; L Ferrajoli, 'The Past and the Future of the Rule of Law' in Costa and Zolo (n 5) 323–52.

constitutional courts.[51] These normative debates are important and have defined much of the functioning of legal institutions over history. Yet, as with many concepts with such a degree of normative disputes, *Estado de Direito* has also been largely conceptually manipulated and abused.[52] In Brazilian history, such normative ideals have clashed with its preservationist adoption as justification for maintaining and constructing inequality.

III. ESTADO DE DIREITO IN BRAZIL: BETWEEN PRESERVATION AND DEMOCRATISATION

'The new Constitution would present itself as the consolidation of the commitment of the military regime to the *Estado de Direito*, even if it had originated from a practice that denies each of its premises.'[53] Leonardo Barbosa's words, which correctly portray a key feature of the Brazilian civilian-military dictatorship (1964–85), are a good description of what *Estado de Direito* has come to mean in Brazil. The dictatorship could draft a new Constitution – in this case, the 1967 Constitution – and, despite its authoritarian content,[54] still argue that it was acting according to the *Estado de Direito*. Years later, during the debates on the need for a new constitution, conservative forces allied with the military employed the concept of *Estado de Direito* to fend off more radical moves toward democratisation. They argued that it would be by enforcing the 1967 Constitution that the *Estado de Direito* would be preserved, not by drafting a new constitutional document.[55]

This narrative exposes how legal concepts can be strategically manipulated and abused. *Estado de Direito*, in both cases, could not embrace the formal version of a state limited and determined by law, whose acts preserve at least the negative individual freedoms, let alone those versions stressing substantive values in their core.[56] Instead, *Estado de Direito* could mean a generic exonerating concept for an increasingly authoritarian government and a barrier to changes that would affect those who supported it. In the first case, the Constitution – and an authoritarian one such as the 1967 Constitution – would be the central

[51] See Habermas (n 45) 194–286; K Günther, *The Sense of Appropriateness: Application Discourses in Morality and Law* (SUNY Press, 1993); JZ Benvindo, *On the Limits of Constitutional Adjudication: Deconstructing Balancing and Judicial Activism* (Springer, 2010).

[52] See D Landau, 'Abusive Constitutionalism' (2013) 47 *University of California, Davis* 189; R Dixon and D Landau, *Abusive Constitutional Borrowing: Legal Globalization and the Subversion of Liberal Democracy* (Oxford University Press, 2021).

[53] L Barbosa, *História Constitucional Brasileira: Mudança Constitucional, Autoritarismo e Democracia no Brasil Pós-1964* (Biblioteca Digital da Câmara dos Deputados, 2012) 107.

[54] ibid 77–119; C Paixão, 'Past and Future of Authoritarian Regimes: Constitution, Transition to Democracy and Amnesty in Brazil and Chile' (2015) 30 *Journal of Constitutional History* 89–105.

[55] JN Cerqueira Neto, 'O Supremo Contra a Constituição' (PhD. Thesis, University of Brasília, 2020).

[56] JJG Canotilho, *Direito Constitucional e Teoria da Constituição* (Almedina, 2003) 98.

document expressing the regime's commitment to the *Estado de Direito*. As a typical dictatorship, the authoritarian Constitution was used as a democratic symbol of that regime.

However, the Constitution was not the hierarchically superior document of the legal framework. There was always a '*reason of state*'. In Brazil, this was embodied in what was then called '*Revolution*', which prevailed over any interpretation and enforcement of the law.[57] Such a '*Revolution*' was stamped on the so-called '*Institutional Acts*', which were authoritarian executive orders not subject to judicial review[58] regardless of their blatant unconstitutionalities – even in the face of the 1967 Constitution.[59] Part of the legal doctrine at that time not only justified them as being in accordance with the *Estado de Direito*, but also as having the nature of a 'transitory and exceptional constitutional amendment'.[60] What mattered in the end was not whether the state would be constrained by law, but how that law would be constrained by the '*Revolution*', which would '[reflect] not only the interests and will of one group, but the interests and the will of the nation'.[61] There would be no *Estado de Direito* were it not 'revolutionary'.

During the transition to democracy, such a 'revolutionary' *Estado de Direito* would be profoundly preservationist: no change should be made to the point of destroying the bedrock of the '*Revolution*'. Democracy was knocking on the door and the political forces were devising the best strategy to cope with the inevitable transition to a new political regime. People were thronging the streets and Brazil would experience the powerful impact of the popular masses, which gained strength in the last dictatorial years and would greatly impact the 1987/1988 Constituent Assembly.[62] On the one hand, there were those aiming to keep the past virtually untouched – and this is where *Estado de Direito* was employed as a preservationist concept. On the other hand, there was an increasingly powerful and influential organised civil society. As Barbosa points out, 'for the first time in Brazilian history, the protagonists of the constitutional change were not confined to the institutional circles'.[63] That pluralist document made

[57] See Paixão (n 54).

[58] See Ato Institucional n. 1, de 9 de Abril de 1964, Article 1, § 4; Ato Institucional n. 2, de 27 de Outubro de 1965, Article 19, I. For an English translation, see CW Guerchon, 'Institutional Acts of the Brazilian Government' (1971) 1 *International Journal of Politics* 258.

[59] See M Feinrider, 'Judicial Review and the Protection of Human Rights under Military Governments in Brazil and Argentina' (1980) 5 *Suffolk Transnational Law Journal* 171–99.

[60] See HL Meirelles, 'Natureza, Conteúdo e Implicações do Ato Institucional N.º 5: Notas e Comentários' (1969) 20 *Revista de Direito da Procuradoria Geral* 1.

[61] Ato Institucional n. 1, de 9 de Abril de 1964. See Guerchon (n 58) 9.

[62] See JZ Benvindo, 'The Forgotten People in Brazilian Constitutionalism: Revisiting Behavior Strategic Analyses of Regime Transitions' (2017) 15 *International Journal of Constitutional Law* 332–57; Barbosa (n 53) 149–85; C Michiles, *Cidadão Constituinte: A Saga das Emendas Populares* (Paz e Terra, 1989).

[63] Barbosa (n 53) 242.

Brazil an important example of academic disputes regarding the impacts of both preservationist and popular movements on constitution-making.[64]

The conceptual transition of *Estado de Direito* is visible in those contexts. It needed to be paradoxically 'revolutionary' to embrace preservation through authoritarianism, and later on be preservationist to counter progressive agendas in constitution-making. The political forces adopted it as a rhetorical concept to fend off any threat to the authoritarian regime, and later on as a constraint on a more democratic constitutional design. As the transition to democracy revealed itself to be more pluralist and participatory than first expected, and the top-down elitism in constitution-making did not occur as planned,[65] *Estado de Direito* could not be that previous top-down concept, either. In the new democratic order, *Estado de Direito* became *Estado Democrático de Direito*. There was no point in adopting either the formal version of this concept nor, worse, the axiological concession of that authoritarian '*Revolution*'. The 1988 Constitution would spotlight the democratic quality of *Estado de Direito* in its first Article: 'The Federative Republic of Brazil, formed by the indissoluble union of states and municipalities and of the Federal District, is a *Estado Democrático de Direito* …'.[66]

The democratic value added to the concept of *Estado de Direito* is a common outcome of democratic transitions. It sets a new standard that should guide the relationship between the state and individuals. In addition to this normative standpoint, there is the reconfiguration of institutional incentives that foster coordinated forms of inclusion of new players in the political arena, distributing thereby larger shares of power. As Maraval and Przeworski point out, the relationship between democracy and the rule of law is 'no more than that: a world of populated institutions in which actors may have conflicting interests and different powers behind them'.[67] The Brazilian constitutional project sought to be more inclusive and pluralist. As a consequence, the institutional framework was designed to strengthen checks and balances, improve transparency and accountability and include new actors in the political arena. Democracy became the normative standpoint, but it was how political actors accepted and embraced such a standpoint that effectively changed the landscape of the country's new regime.

Disputes over this new constitutional project have since changed. Like most democratic transitions, what was then preservation would turn itself into

[64] See TA Eisenstadt, AC LeVan, and T Maboudi, *Constituents Before Assembly: Participation, Deliberation, and Representation in the Crafting of New Constitutions* (Cambridge University Press, 2017) 47; Benvindo (n 621); F Hagopian, '"Democracy by Undemocratic Means"?: Elites, Political Pacts, and Regime Transition in Brazil' (1990) 23 *Comparative Political Studies* 147.

[65] During the transition, the so-called Comissão Afonso Arinos drafted a model of constitution, but it was not even seriously discussed during the Constituent Assembly. See Barbosa (n 53) 207–10.

[66] Article 1 of the 1988 Constitution.

[67] Przeworski and Maraval (n 17) 13.

strategies to hinder or even block policies aimed at distributing shares of political and economic benefits to new actors. These strategies would also manage to roll back some gains already made via the new constitutional document.[68] In such an unequal country, with a legacy of authoritarianism that has favoured specific sectors of society,[69] it is no wonder that the backlash against such a constitutional project would be particularly consistent. The concept *Estado de Direito*, now *Estado Democrático de Direito*, would be again reshaped to embrace the argument that there is only *Estado de Direito* where governability is feasible and sustainable. This argument was already raised by preservationist movements during the Constituent Assembly, but now, instead of identifying themselves with authoritarianism, the word 'modernisation' would become the new slogan. A modern *Estado de Direito* (and a modern *Estado Democrático de Direito*) is one that, while seemingly including new social groups, is, in reality, much more interested in devising policies to preserve the privileges of those already benefitting during the dictatorship. Other sectors and social groups that could largely benefit from the new Constitution would also find new ways to preserve their privileges.

This is to be expected: preservation, in its old and new forms, is a natural phenomenon of disputes among conflicting interests. In a democratic regime, however, what matters is how such conflicting interests are internalised in institutional practices, and how new behavioural incentives provided by the new constitutional order can lead to greater levels of inclusion, even if imperfectly and insufficiently. The strength of preservationist movements, in democratic regimes, should be offset by mechanisms that bring other social actors into the political arena, and, more specifically, by instruments that enable new arguments to be publicised, discussed, and well-received by institutions.[70] *Estado de Direito* is therefore intimately related to the capacity of such a system to open itself up to various arguments and transparently react to them. The 1988 Constitution, with its all imperfections, is by far the Brazilian constitutional document that has most consistently and extensively provided a set of institutions, tools, and principles that favour transparency, accountability and constraints in the relationship between the state and citizens. It has also proven an effective coordination device in the political realm, although some controversies, which will be later examined,[71] persist among political scientists and constitutional lawyers.

[68] See Barbosa (n 53) 249–323; JZ Benvindo, 'Brazil in the Context of the Debate over Unamendability in Latin America' in R Albert and B Oder (eds), *An Unamendable Constitution?* (Springer, 2018) 345–64.

[69] See PHGF Souza, *Uma História da Desigualdade: A Concentração de Renda entre os Ricos no Brasil (1926–2013)* (Hucitec, 2018).

[70] See Habermas (n 45).

[71] See ch 4.

IV. ESTADO DE DIREITO IN BRAZIL: SOCIAL INEQUALITY AS A HINDRANCE TO COORDINATION

Brazil has indeed democratised, but it has been a democratisation defined by high levels of social inequality. This is why there is a feeling of being lost in translation when *Estado de Direito* is associated with rule of law. Marcelo Neves goes straight to the point when he states that the rule of law without a 'sensible reassessment of our peculiarities' is not 'transposable to the Brazilian legal-political reality'.[72] Oscar Vilhena Vieira, by the same token, argues that 'extreme and persistent social and economic inequality erodes reciprocity, both in the moral and the mutual advantage sense, thus impairing the integrity of the Rule of Law'.[73] The country's staggering social inequality and also the authoritarian mindset are features that cannot be overlooked when the rule of law is at stake.

The reason for this is quite straightforward. If we adopt the premise that 'we cannot explain why the rule of law does or does not emerge in a specific historical context by invoking nothing but the strategic calculations of powerful political actors',[74] an unequal society, with a legacy of authoritarianism, will inevitably lead to more conflicting and less consensual behaviours among those actors. The rule of law, in this context, will be based on a less stable equilibrium since those with larger shares of power will not find sufficient incentives for consensus, whereas the typical coordination devices, such as the legal framework, will prove less effective than needed.

As seen, the 1988 Constitution was the result of a democratic transition that brought a more inclusive design with incentives for consensus. Preservationist movements were successful in keeping many of their privileges untouched, but the transition to democracy was one such moment when the increasing participation of organised civil society changed the landscape for greater pluralism, a more robust system of checks and balances, and therefore a stronger compliance to the rule of law. The years that followed also brought an increasing social participation at the institutional level.[75]

The difficulty in translating the rule of law into *Estado de Direito* is that Brazil, despite such progress, has not overcome its most structural shortcoming: the relationships between the state and individuals and also among individuals themselves are largely dependent on the levels of wealth and poverty, race and gender. This is obviously not a Brazilian singularity – even in advanced

[72] M Neves, 'Luhmann, Habermas e o Estado de Direito' (1996) 37 *Lua Nova* 94.

[73] OV Vieira, 'Inequality and the Subversion of the Rule of Law' (2007) 4 *Sur – International Journal on Human Rights* 27.

[74] S Holmes, 'Lineages of the Rule of Law' in A Przeworski and JM Maravall (n 5) 19.

[75] See L Avritzer, 'Um Balanço da Participação Social no Brasíl Pós-Constituição de 1988' in L Avritzer (ed), *Experiência Democrática, Sistema Político e Participação Popular* (Fundação Perseu Abramo, 2013) 11–20.

economies social inequality also leads to shocking outcomes[76] – but the rule of law cannot be correctly translated into *Estado de Direito* and vice-versa unless inequality is examined as a structural element. In such a context, the rule of law must be interpreted as an egalitarian rule of law. It needs to both provide welfare and regulate behaviours by '[protecting] people with law'.[77]

Brazil has built a rather solid institutional framework, which, in some respects, is comparable to those of some advanced economies,[78] but it visibly lags behind in promoting social mobility and inclusion of underprivileged groups of society.

Normally, the difficulty in translating rule of law into *Estado de Direito* and vice-versa falls into the conceptual disputes over historical origins, legal traditions and normative ideals.[79] These differences are relevant, but, if we assume beforehand that the rule of law (or *Estado de Direito*) is mostly related to the capacity of individuals to '[police] the state' and 'react in concert to potential transgressions by the state',[80] inequality is not a secondary element but a crucial one for overcoming potential coordination problems, thereby playing a major – though sometimes neglected – role for such a translation. Inequality also impacts the capacity of individuals to react against other private agents encroaching on their rights, thereby affecting the duty of protection the state should provide in order to preserve the rule of law more broadly.[81] The lack of incentives for inclusion and coordination will certainly impair the rule of law by denying the equal protection and enforcement of democratic rights, disrupting the growing need to connect this concept with democratic ideals.[82]

The argument in favour of social justice as part of the core of *Estado de Direito* is, however, very controversial. It leads to the disputed field of an evolutionary narrative in history, and, more importantly, it stresses the difficulties in migrating concepts from diverse legal traditions. Furthermore, the impacts on institutional behaviour given the extent and scope of this concept are not

[76] See EM Uslaner, *Corruption, Inequality, and the Rule of Law* (Cambridge University Press, 2008); DL Bennett and B Nikolaev, 'Factor Endowments, the Rule of Law and Structural Inequality' (2016) 12 *Journal of Institutional Economics* 773–95; DM Brinks, 'Inequality, Institutions, and the Rule of Law: The Social and Institutional Bases of Rights' (2008) 351 Kellogg Institute Working Paper.

[77] J King, 'I-CONnect Symposium on "Constitutional Boundaries" – The Social Dimension of the Rule of Law' (*International Journal of Constitutional Law Blog*, 27 April 2018) www.iconnectblog.com/2018/04/i-connect-symposium-on-constitutional-boundaries-the-social-dimension-of-the-rule-of-law.

[78] See MA Melo and C Pereira, *Making Brazil Work: Checking the President in a Multiparty System* (Palgrave Macmillan, 2013).

[79] See Canotilho (n 11); Silva (n 37) 15–24.

[80] Weingast (n 19) 110.

[81] See B Magaloni, 'Authoritarianism, Democracy and the Supreme Court: Horizontal Exchange and the Rule of Law in Mexico' in S Mainwaring and C Welna (eds), *Democratic Accountability in Latin America* (Oxford University Press, 2003) 269; Postema (n 5) 25.

[82] See Brinks (n 76) 5.

negligible: political institutions and, notably, the judiciary tend to take a more proactive approach to social welfare in this context. Whether a more formal or substantive conception of the rule of law should be adopted is therefore a topic with practical implications, even though this discussion will surely lead to insurmountable normative disputes. Maravall and Przeworski were possibly excessively harsh when they argued that 'the normative conception of the rule of law is a figment of the imagination of jurists', but they might have a point: perhaps it would be more productive to focus, as they say, on the 'political forces, their goals, their organization, and their conflicts'.[83]

V. THE RULE OF LAW AND COORDINATION IN UNEQUAL SOCIETIES

The rule of law seems stuck between the very limits of formalist conceptions and the vast margin of appreciation of substantive ones, which are impacted by their own historical origins and institutional developments. How such conceptions affect constitutional democracy is one of the fascinating subjects that have provided countless dialogues in the field, as this chapter has briefly introduced. However, this book will not explore them much further. Its focus is rather more prosaic: it is not whether the quest for social justice should or should not be in the *core* of the rule of law, because what such a *core* means is up for grabs. Rather, social justice will be a central concern for as long as it matters for the rule of law to effectively take hold. Social justice strongly influences mutual commitments that are expected from this concept: an unequal society fails to create sufficient incentives for individuals and public officials to abide by the law. In other words, an unequal society fails to solve the coordination problem that is typical of complex societies.[84]

Estado de Direito will thus be translated into rule of law in this book but not without acknowledging its structural differences from its Anglo-American and analogous continental counterparts. Every Brazilian scholar knows, for example, the centrality that the state plays in Brazilian constitutionalism, and, similarly to the German model, it has historically been given precedence over the constitution. However, also like that model, after the transition to democracy, the constitution has increasingly shaped the Brazilian reality. Increasingly, it is not the constitution whose legitimacy derives from the state, but it is the state whose legitimacy derives from the constitution.[85] The transition to democracy in 1985 and the drafting of the 1988 Constitution built a set of institutions and coordination devices that have since provided a more resilient, though

[83] Przeworski and Maravall (n 176) 2.

[84] See Weingast (n 19).

[85] See B Schlink and AJ Jacobson, 'Introduction – Constitutional Crisis: The German and the American Experience' in B Schlink and AJ Jacobson (eds), *Weimar: A Jurisprudence of Crisis* (University of California Press, 2000) 1–2.

imperfect, 'self-enforcing equilibrium' for its democracy.[86] Political forces and private agents have incrementally observed limits on their behaviours,[87] but the challenges are still significant to convincingly support the claim that Brazil has adopted the rule of law as a standard practice.

On the one hand, Brazil has a set of institutions and practices that follow the guidelines of the rule of law: separation of powers, generality, non-retroactivity and publicity of legal acts and formal equality of all citizens before the law, among others. Brazil's Constitution also features an extensive bill of individual, social and economic rights. In spite of that, it still lags behind in commitment to the law, very much because inequality is pervasive and the country's authoritarian past has ingeniously reinvented itself in the new democratic environment, thereby reinforcing inequality. As Oscar Vilhena Vieira correctly states, 'social and economic exclusion, deriving from extreme and persistent levels of inequality, obliterates legal impartiality, causing the *invisibility* of the extreme poor, the *demonization* of those who challenge the system, and the *immunity* of the privileged, in the eyes of individuals and institutions'.[88] The rule of law in Brazil should place social justice as a central concern, and for pragmatic reasons: inequality affects the capacity of institutions and the constitution to effectively work as coordination devices.

The following chapters will delve into various dimensions of this debate. While *Estado de Direito* will be translated into rule of law by pointing out this more prosaic viewpoint, it will nonetheless place social inequality and the deep-rooted authoritarian mindset as powerful hindrances to the rule of law. Although context matters – and this is why inequality and the authoritarian legacy are so central in the case of Brazil – it will also assume that, despite the diverse experiences, there is some conceptual identity among the several translations of the rule of law.[89] It might come from general principles such as legality, generality, publicity and non-retroactivity of legal precepts. It might also come from the premise that, despite the distinct realities, the central goal is basically to protect individual freedom by limiting state power. More generally, it could also come from the perception that, over the years, the analogous concepts to the rule of law have become more universally connected, following the trend of embedding it with some substantive content (or setting the procedures to make it more democratically legitimate).[90]

Pragmatically speaking, though, this book will adopt the premise that individuals and public officials will behave according to the rule of law primarily because they have effectively '[constructed] a focal solution that resolves their

[86] B Weingast, 'The Political Foundations of Democracy and the Rule of Law' (1997) 91 *American Political Science Review* 245.

[87] ibid.

[88] Vieira (n 73) 27.

[89] See Zolo (n 29) 19; MacCormick (n 25) 67.

[90] See Habermas (n 45).

coordination dilemmas about limits on the state'.[91] The constitution, the legal framework and a set of institutions will function as coordination devices as long as they prove themselves 'self-enforcing', that is, individuals and public officials have an interest in abiding by them and will react in concert whenever there is a violation of the limits imposed on them.[92] Social inequality and an authoritarian legacy hamper such a coordination, fostering thereby the expansion of extraconstitutional means and the noncompliance with the law, while transforming potential consensus between social masses and elites into a much more challenging endeavour.[93] The following chapters will reveal how far Brazil has gone in preserving and enforcing such coordination devices and how strong its institutions and civic culture are in order to effectively place limits on those who must abide by – but also eventually have the power to transgress – the rule of law.

[91] Weingast (n 86) 246.
[92] ibid 251; Weingast (n 19) 110.
[93] Weingast (n 86) 252.

2

The Local Lived Experiences of the Rule of Law in Brazil: The Impacts of Social Inequality

I. INTRODUCTION: A PERSISTENT INEQUALITY

BRAZIL IS HIGHLY unequal, and the country's history keeps this state of inequality virtually untouched. Economic crises, political instabilities and regime changes have left this landscape practically unaffected. The few events that slightly flattened inequality had a brief lifespan, without changing the inertia that has long plagued the country.[1] Wealth and poverty live side by side: the view from penthouse windows in Ipanema and Leblon in Rio de Janeiro shows, alongside one of the world's most astonishing natural landscapes, favelas with thousands of families struggling to survive.

There seems to be a correlation between regime change, political crises and the level of inequality in Brazil: whenever there is some movement towards decreasing – or merely potentially decreasing – inequality, the backlash tends to be quite severe. Though the empirical data lead to more nuanced interpretations – it is not simply that dictatorial periods were more unequal and democratic ones were more equal –[2] they show that Brazil's dictatorships in the twentieth century, notably Getúlio Vargas's *Estado Novo* (1937–45)[3] and the civilian-military regime (1964–85)[4], were inequality boosters by benefitting historical oligarchical and business sectors, despite the previous period of lower inequality.[5] This pattern remains valid in more recent developments. The political backlash

[1] PHG Ferreira de Souza (2016), 'A Desigualdade Vista do Topo: A Concentração de Renda entre os Ricos no Brasil, 1926–2013' (PhD. Thesis, University of Brasília, 2016).

[2] See PHG Ferreira de Souza, *Uma História da Desigualdade: A Concentração de Renda entre os Ricos no Brasil* (1926–2013) (Hucitec, 2018) 232 ('the influence of the political context cannot be reduced to a simple opposition between more inequality in dictatorships and less inequality in democratic periods').

[3] See PHG Ferreira de Souza, 'A History of Inequality: Top Incomes in Brazil, 1926–2015' (2017) 167 Working Paper – International Policy Centre for Inclusive Growth (IPC-IG) 1–43.

[4] ibid 19.

[5] ibid.

that led to the rise of President Bolsonaro could, for example, be interpreted according to such a rationale, as an illiberal backlash against the years the Worker's Party (PT) remained in power,[6] even though President Dilma Rousseff's (PT) last years in power were also marked by 'the overlapping of the political and economic crisis'.[7] Corruption scandals and the economic downturn certainly played a role,[8] but we cannot overlook that redistributive policies and a more progressive agenda would be met with fierce resistance and would help shape the melting pot of conservatism and authoritarianism that led to Bolsonaro's victory.

Inequality and authoritarianism are thus closely intertwined in Brazilian history: the moments when Brazil endured the greatest levels of equality were also those that paradoxically paved the way for a democratic backsliding. Just to focus on those two dictatorial periods of the twentieth century, both *Estado Novo* (1937–45) and the civilian-military dictatorship (1964–85) followed moments of greater equality in the country, also as an outcome of the 'mild levelling' Brazil experienced after the Great Depression in the early 1930s and World War II.[9] Both authoritarian periods reversed this trajectory and provided the country with its most authoritarian Constitutions (1937 and 1967). On the other hand, the 1988 Constitution is, by far, the most democratic ever in Brazilian history and it has proved rather resilient at its core despite various attempts to reverse some of its social rights and mechanisms of social inclusion.[10] It is no accident that regressive movements against that constitutional social core[11] and the strategy of deconstitutionalisation of core constitutional commitments[12] have

[6] See W Hunter and TJ Power, 'Bolsonaro and Brazil's Illiberal Backlash' (2019) 30 *Journal of Democracy* 68–82; TG Daly, 'Populism, Public Law, and Democratic Decay in Brazil: Understanding the Rise of Jair Bolsonaro' (2019) *International Human Rights Researchers' Workshop: 'Democratic Backsliding and Human Rights'* 22, https://ssrn.com/abstract=3350098; S Abranches et al., *Democracia em Risco? 22 Ensaios sobre o Brasil Hoje* (Companhia das Letras, 2019); JZ Benvindo, 'Brazil's "False Consciousness of Time": The Rise of Jair Bolsonaro' (*International Journal of Constitutional Law Blog*, 10 November 2018) www.iconnectblog.com/2018/11/brazils-false-consciousness-of-time-the-rise-of-jair-bolsonaro/.

[7] L Avritzer, 'The Impeachment of Dilma Rousseff: Introduction' (2017) 11 *Critical Policy Studies* 349.

[8] See ch 6.

[9] Ferreira de Souza (n 3) 19.

[10] See JZ Benvindo, 'The Brazilian Constitutional Amendment Rate: A Culture of Change?' (*International Journal of Constitutional Law Blog*, 10 August 2016) www.iconnectblog.com/2016/08/the-brazilian-constitutional-amendment-rate-a-culture-of-change/.

[11] See R Albert, *Constitutional Amendments: Making, Breaking, and Changing Constitutions* (Oxford University Press, 2019) 63–66; JZ Benvindo, 'Preservationist Constitutional Amendments and the Rise of Antipolitics in Brazil, (*International Journal of Constitutional Law Blog*, 26 October 2016) http://www.iconnectblog.com/2016/10/preservationist-constitutional-amendments-and-the-rise-of-antipolitics-in-brazil/.

[12] See C Paixão and JZ Benvindo, 'Constitutional Dismemberment' and the Strategic Deconstitutionalization in Times of Crisis Beyond Emergency Powers' (*International Journal of Constitutional Law Blog*, 24 April 2020) www.iconnectblog.com/2020/04/constitutional-dismemberment-and-strategic-deconstitutionalization-in-times-of-crisis-beyond-emergency-powers/; EPN Meyer, *Constitutional Erosion in Brazil: Progresses and Failures of a Constitutional Project* (Hart Publishing, 2021).

intensified in the last few years. The pattern, even if less intense now, remains, but it is at least a positive sign that the 1988 Constitution is still firmly in force and that Brazilian democracy has provided some tools to protect itself and its Constitution from breakdown.

This chapter examines the rule of law as it has been experienced in a country with such high inequality. Its impact on the institutional framework is significant and, as will be further examined in the following chapter, is intimately connected to an authoritarian mindset that is still pervasive. This chapter also explores specific kinds of inequality, such as gender, race and that affecting Indigenous people. Brazil scores comparatively low in gender and racial equality, even for regional standards, which is certainly an issue for the rule of law. Also relevant is how the country deals with its longstanding regional inequalities and how the commitment to the rule of law depends on your location. This chapter ends by critically assessing some empirical data on the quality and functioning of Brazilian democracy and rule of law, and contextualising them with the conclusions of the previous sections.

II. BRAZIL AND ITS LONGSTANDING STRUGGLE WITH SOCIAL INEQUALITY

Inequality impacts on the resilience of a democratic regime. Przeworski, Alvarez, Cheibub and Limongi, in their *Democracy and Development: Political Institutions and Well-Being in the World, 1950–1990*, concluded that 'it appears that democracies are less stable in societies that are more unequal to begin with, in societies in which household income inequality increases, and in societies in which labour receives a lower share of value added in manufacturing'.[13] Brazil has been a democracy since 1985 and it is undeniable that the Brazilians' welfare has improved over those years. Yet, unlike income inequality,[14] for example, welfare is a very controversial concept to be objectively measured[15] and usually encompasses a set of abstract variables (political liberties, health, and education, for example[16]) that add even more difficulty to such a task. Brazilians enjoy greater political liberties and are healthier and better educated. They are also wealthier, as indeed the country has become wealthier. However, income inequality has little changed. The most recent data on income inequality point out that, in Brazil, 'democracy is not a sufficient condition for redistribution' since the 'concentration of income at the top remained very high, following a

[13] A Przeworski, et al., *Democracy and Development: Political Institutions and Well-Being in the World: 1950–1990* (Cambridge University Press, 2000) 122.

[14] See M Arretche, 'Conclusion: A Half-Century of Change' in M Arretche (ed), *Paths of Inequality in Brazil: A Half-Century of Changes* (Springer, 2019) 331.

[15] ibid 4.

[16] ibid.

sine wave trend: top shares ebbed and flowed over time, frequently in tandem with political and institutional disruptions'.[17] Brazilians are better-off, but their lives are marked by the challenges of an unequal society: its political system tends to be more turbulent, the levels of violence are high,[18] and the rule of law features various structural fragilities.

Though still marked by inefficiency and underfunding, Brazil has advanced policies to help overcome poverty, such as universal health care, public education, a rather protective labour law, an ample social security system, and social programmes such as *Bolsa Família*, a successful conditional cash transfer programme.[19] The 1988 Constitution, which resulted from a 'set of fragmented political and ideological projects from various sectors of society',[20] is an important example of a constitutional project seeking to enhance democracy, strengthen the rule of law and combat poverty. It features an extensive bill of civil, political, social and economic rights, many of them protected by unamendability.[21] The typical democratic credentials are all there, such as a fairly robust institutional framework of accountability institutions, a presidential system in which both the legislative and judicial branches share their powers and check each other, a legal system that complies with the premises of generality, predictability, and transparency[22] and a rather vibrant civil society.[23] Moreover, Brazil is a signatory of various international treaties on human rights, having participated in international efforts to combat poverty and improve welfare worldwide.[24]

However, democratic legislation, institutions, and policies, though representing important elements for the rule of law, struggle in a society used to coping with the typical hurdles of social inequality. An unequal society is disruptive for coordinating conflicting interests and '[exacerbates] the distributive trade-offs among individuals'.[25] The consequences for the rule of law are many. Without proper coordination, individuals do not feel assured that they will be better-off by following the rules nor do they truly believe that the legal and institutional

[17] Ferreira de Souza (n 3) 3.

[18] See P Fajnzylber, D Lederman and N Loayza, 'Inequality and Violent Crime' (2002) 45 *The Journal of Law and Economics* 1–39.

[19] See T Campello and MC Neri, *Bolsa Família Program: A Decade of Social Inclusion in Brazil* (IPEA, 2013).

[20] JZ Benvindo, 'The Forgotten People in Brazilian Constitutionalism: Revisiting Behavior Strategic Analyses of Regime Transitions' (2017) 15 *International Journal of Constitutional Law* 356.

[21] Article 60, §4, of the 1988 Constitution. See also Y Roznai, *Unconstitutional Constitutional Amendments: The Limits of Amendment Power* (Oxford Univeristy Press, 2017) 36 ("Brazil has a long history of unamendability").

[22] See MC Cunha Filho, 'A Construção da Transparência Pública no Brasil: Análise da Elaboração e Implementação da Lei de Acesso à Informação no Executivo Federal (2003–2019)' (PhD. Thesis, University of Brasília, 2019).

[23] See L Avritzer, 'Um Balanço da Participação Social no Brasil Pós-Constituição de 1988' in L Avritzer (ed), *Experiência Democrática, Sistema Político e Participação Popular* (Fundação Perseu Abramo, 2013) 11–20.

[24] See ch 7.

[25] P Beramendi and D Rueda, 'Inequality and Institutions: The Case of Economic Coordination' (2014) 17 *Annual Review of Political Science* 266.

frameworks are aimed at benefitting them instead of some privileged social groups. They also feel less empowered because many are deemed second-class individuals, who are not able to claim their rights nor present any significant leverage in negotiations that could lower the distributive injustice of their labour force.[26] Less coordination also implies less reciprocity. An unequal society tends to see the law not as 'an instrument of social organization and pacification',[27] but rather as a barrier to their own interests. 'The result is that the state is negligent with the invisible, violent and arbitrary toward the moral outcasts, and docile and friendly towards the privileged that place themselves above the law.'[28]

Most current and influential studies on Brazil's social inequality have shown two seemingly contradictory routes. On the one hand, despite the most recent downturn, the country has become wealthier, poverty has declined, and individuals have benefitted from higher living standards and welfare. On the other hand, income inequality has remained virtually stable over the years, even when compared with the beginning of the twentieth century and the several regime changes and crises the country has since endured.

The data on income inequality are staggering. Marcelo Medeiros, Pedro Ferreira de Souza and Fábio Ávila de Castro have provided outstanding empirical studies on its dynamics. By concentrating their analyses on the top richest through income tax tabulations, their conclusions are less optimistic than other studies that have focused on household surveys. Such a methodology has the benefit of more accurately assessing the capital flow that household surveys can barely collect and has proven highly convergent with other empirical tabulations.[29] Their impactful paper *The Upper Top of Income Distribution in Brazil: First Estimates with Income Data and a Comparison with Household Surveys (2006–2012)*[30] has raised some of the most interesting debates on inequality in the country as they concluded that 'income data reveals the concentration at the top that is substantially greater than other sources and, in general terms, remained stable in the period examined'.[31] The underlying argument, which Medeiros had previously pointed out,[32] is that that only by focusing on the richest is the real inequality in Brazil effectively disclosed.

Pedro Ferreira de Souza wrote the prizewinning book *Uma História da Desigualdade: A Concentração de Renda entre os Ricos no Brasil 1926–2013*

[26] ibid.

[27] See OV Vieira, 'Inequality and the Subversion of the Rule of Law' (2007) 4 *Sur – International Journal on Human Rights* 43.

[28] ibid.

[29] See M Medeiros and PHGF Souza, 'A Estabilidade da Desigualdade no Brasil entre 2006 e 2012: Resultados Adicionais' (2016) 46 *Pesquisa e Planejamento Econômico* 7–31.

[30] M Medeiros, PHGF Souza and FAD Castro, 'O Topo da Distribuição de Renda no Brasil: Primeiras Estimativas com Dados Tributários e Comparação com Pesquisas Domiciliares, 2006–2012' (2015) 58 *Dados – Revista de Ciências Sociais* 7–36.

[31] ibid 35.

[32] M Medeiros, *O Que Faz os Ricos Ricos: O Outro Lado da Desigualdade Brasileira* (Hucitec, 2005).

(*A History of Inequality: The Income Concentration among the Richest in Brazil 1926–2013*) and his conclusions are breathtaking. Based on income tax tabulations, Brazil has endured few periods of lower inequality, but they were rapidly reversed, normally coinciding with the collapse of democracy or more liberal regimes.[33] More interestingly, though the 1988 Constitution has enhanced Brazil's democratic credentials and provided a more robust safety net for the poorest, it has not represented the equality booster that the literature normally claims.[34] In fact, it has kept virtually unchanged a set of privileges and benefits for the richest as a bargaining chip during constitution-making and afterwards. Despite the improvements for the poorest, accommodation and not redistribution from the top is a more accurate description of the new democratic period.[35] Inertia, corporatism,[36] tax breaks and indirect taxation favouring the richest[37] have greatly impacted the new democratic order, proving that regime change alone cannot alter such a reality.[38]

The numbers on income inequality are indeed appalling. Ferreira de Souza's findings reveal that, from 1926 to 2015, 'on average, the share of total income received by the top 1 per cent was about 24 per cent'.[39] This number remained quite unchanged despite some steep and structural changes in the country.[40] Whenever there was a critical juncture – normally coinciding with the country's political cycles[41] – the level of inequality oscillated, and, if it decreased slightly, it regained its former level shortly afterwards.[42] Such numbers show that, for example, in 2013, the 0.1 per cent, 1 per cent, 5 per cent, and 10 per cent richest received 11 per cent, 24 per cent, 42 per cent and 53 per cent of the national income, respectively.[43] Briefly, the 'bottom 90 per cent' share less than 50 per cent of the national income. Brazil did not endure the 'Great Egalitarian Levelling' observed in other currently more equal countries after the traumatic events of the twentieth century, like the Great Depression and the World Wars.[44]

[33] See Ferreira de Souza (n 2) 230; Ferreira de Souza (n 3).

[34] Ferreira de Souza (n 2) 234. ('… the 1988 Constitution revealed itself far less redistributive than it is normally claimed, and, in practice, the democracy took place more as a negotiated transition than as an inflection point.'). See also Ferreira de Souza (n 3) 12.

[35] See Ferreira de Souza (n 3) 12.

[36] See PHG Ferreira de Souza and M Medeiros, 'Diferencial Salarial Público-Privado e Desigualdade de Renda per Capita no Brasil' (2013) 43 *Estudos Econômicos* 5–28.

[37] See Ferreira de Souza (n 2) 229; Ferreira de Souza (n 3) 12; Medeiros, Ferreira de Souza and Castro (n 30).

[38] See Ferreira de Souza (n 2) 235.

[39] Ferreira de Souza (n 3) 9.

[40] ibid.

[41] Ferreira de Souza (n 2) 231 (the 'ups and downs of inequality are more related to the country's political cycles of the last century than to structural transformations …').

[42] ibid 232.

[43] Medeiros, Ferreira de Souza and Castro (n 30) 25.

[44] See JG Williamson, 'Latin American Inequality: Colonial Origins, Commodity Booms or a Missed Twentieth-Century Leveling' (2015) 16 *Journal of Human Development and Capabilities* 324–41.

Instead, Brazil, which was already slightly more unequal before those events, merely experienced a 'mild levelling', which was later reversed.[45] This phenomenon helps explain why Brazil lags behind in equality,[46] only competing, among those with available data, with Argentina, Colombia, South Africa, and, more recently, the United States.[47]

In truth, there has never been a long-term trend towards income equality in Brazil,[48] even though some redistribution reaching the 'bottom 90 per cent' has taken place – and this is why the Gini coefficient shows a decline over the years.[49] In this respect, there is some space for optimism. Ferreira de Souza's findings focus on the top richest, whose income concentration has oscillated from 20 to 25 per cent over those years,[50] but there are data showing that the 'bottom 90 per cent' have also become wealthier and better-off, and that absolute poverty has significantly decreased (even though a reversal of this trend has taken place from 2014 onwards).[51] This improvement, however, does not exclude the fact that a large part of the country's wealth has been distributed for the benefit of longstanding interests through public policies that keep the same logic of wealth concentration.[52]

The 1988 Constitution has not really affected the top richest, who could take advantage of inertial effects and entrench their interests in the new constitutional framework. However, it provided a net protection that has benefitted many Brazilians. Marta Arretche, a leading Brazilian scholar on the subject, argues that this difficulty in assessing inequality lies in the perception that 'inequality reduction is the result of a combination of factors, which means that any monocausal theory of the phenomena cannot capture its encompassing dynamics'.[53] Her thesis is quite straightforward: democratisation and the new constitutional order in Brazil have reduced inequality, interpreted according to such a 'combination of factors' that go beyond income and 'its sheer monetary dimension'.[54] Despite her claim that Brazil has also experienced a systematic decline in income inequality since 1989[55] – which may not hold up when confronted with Ferreira de Souza's thesis[56] – her emphasis on inequality embracing a 'combination of factors' is crucial for understanding the impact of inequality on the rule of law through a set of other key variables. Income inequality certainly matters for the

[45] See Ferreira de Souza (n 3) 20.
[46] ibid.
[47] ibid 16.
[48] Ferreira de Souza (n 2) 232.
[49] Ferreira de Souza (n 3) 11.
[50] ibid 9.
[51] See M Ciaschi et al, 'A Reversal in Shared Prosperity in Brazil' (2020) 344111 *The World Bank*.
[52] See M Medeiros and PHGF Souza, 'Estado e Desigualdade de Renda no Brasil: Fluxos de Rendimentos e Estratificação Social' (2013) 28 *Revista Brasileira de Ciências Sociais* 141.
[53] Arretche (n 14) 331.
[54] M Arretche, 'Preface' in Arretche (n 14) viii.
[55] ibid v; Arretche (n 14) 332.
[56] Ferreira de Souza (n 3).

rule of law, but so do the levels of poverty, welfare and public access to social benefits and services, which have undeniably improved over the country's years of democratic life.

Arretche's argument is that the 'inclusion of outsiders' gained momentum in the early 1990s through a growing access to a vast array of social benefits 'de-linked from income and social background'.[57] Based particularly on the demographic censuses by the Brazilian Institute of Geography and Statistics (IBGE) between 1960 and 2010, she and other prominent scholars[58] examined distinct variables (level of education, female fertility rate, market labour, social policies such as health care and social security, infant mortality, life expectancy, female and racial inclusion, religious pluralism, electoral transparency and participation, etc) and concluded that Brazilians' living standards have indeed improved despite the still 'many unacceptable inequalities'.[59] Democracy has played a role for the 'shift in the history of inequality in Brazil', but what has since visibly changed is that the country has gradually implemented long-term policies aimed at including the 'outsiders' and some major shifts in individuals' behaviours (higher women's entry in labour market and education, for example).[60]

For the rule of law, it certainly matters that the 'bottom 90 per cent' receive greater public protection, and, though such a change has not really altered the mean level of income inequality, better life conditions tend to engender stronger social compliance to the institutional framework and lead to more effective coordination of conflicting interests. The 'inclusion of outsiders'[61] by enforcing social rights also implies that these individuals will exert and claim their individual rights, many of which do not demand monetary redistribution, with more positive outcomes. Therefore, inequality, in such multiple dimensions, has declined, but there are still various gaps that place Brazil in a humiliating position in comparison to other democracies. There have been improvements in access to education,[62] political participation[63] and civil society engagement,[64] but the levels of racial and gender inequality,[65] regional disparities and the quality and reach of public services are still very disturbing,[66] let alone the aforementioned

[57] Arretche (n 14) 332.
[58] ibid.
[59] Arretche (n 14) viii.
[60] ibid ix.
[61] Arretche (n 14) 341.
[62] See N Menezes Filho and C Kirschbaum, 'Education and Inequality in Brazil' in Arretche (n 14) 69–88; M Lima and I Prates, 'Racial Inequalities in Brazil: A Persistent Challenge' in Arretche (n 14) 113–36.
[63] See F Limongi, JA Cheibub and A Figueiredo, 'Political Participation in Brazil' in Arretche (n 14) 3–24.
[64] See AG Lavalle and LS Barone, 'Councils, Associations, and Inequality' in Arretche (n 14) 25–46.
[65] See CAC Ribeiro and R Schlegel, 'Horizontal Stratification in Brazil's Higher Education (1960–2010)' in Arretche (n 14) 89–112.
[66] M Arretche, 'The Geography of Access to Basic Services in Brazil' in Arretche (n 14) 137–62.

high income inequality. The changes, in some areas, have been 'dramatic', but inequality has also proven very resilient.[67]

The quality of the rule of law in Brazil is not properly understood without exploring further the particular effects of inequality in such distinct dimensions. The support for democracy, the trust in democratic institutions, and the level of civil education on the rule of law are all intimately associated with how social inclusion has taken place. Brazil is a young democracy whose previous political crises have not largely disturbed the data of income inequality, especially for the richest citizens, but democracy and incremental public policies targeting the worst-off have positively impacted the quality of the rule of law in Brazil.

III. INCLUSIVENESS AND HISTORICAL INEQUALITIES IN BRAZIL

When delving into Brazil's inequality, there are contrasts: on the one hand, income inequality is extremely high and has not really changed since the beginning of the twentieth century.[68] On the other hand, Brazilians' welfare and overall wealth have improved during the democratic years.[69] Therefore, if 'democracy is not a sufficient condition for redistribution',[70] it, at least, matters a great deal for the 'inclusion of outsiders',[71] who share other benefits this system supplies.

Some specific types of inequalities provide a comprehensive overview of the historically entrenched exclusions and incremental, though still insufficient, inclusions. Despite some relevant improvements in the last decades, the country was and still is largely structured in racial and gender discrimination, and the economic and development gap between the country's poorer north and wealthier south is still shocking, not to mention the discrimination towards those who migrated to the south in pursuit of better living conditions.

Although inequality can be explored on different fronts – it has, after all, multiple causes and encompassing dynamics[72] – the next section will briefly discuss and present some empirical data that expose how distinct types of inequality have affected Brazilian society and impaired the rule of law.

A. Racial Inequality

Inequalities are difficult to overcome not only because of longstanding practices and entrenched benefits that are largely supported and protected by the

[67] Arretche (n 14) 331.
[68] See Ferreira de Souza (n 2); Ferreira de Souza (n 3).
[69] See Arretche (n 14).
[70] Ferreiera de Souza (n 3) 20.
[71] Arretche (n 14) 332.
[72] ibid 331.

institutional framework, but also because they develop strategies to justify themselves or hide themselves from scrutiny. An important example of the first type is the claim that individuals who work hard and persevere will be better-off. This has long been, for example, a central argument to justify the so-called 'American dream' despite the undeniable forms of discrimination and the sheer luck of being born into a privileged family.[73] Let us call such a strategy the paradigm of success. A more perverse strategy is to transform a certain type of discrimination into an economic one, hiding it from scrutiny and connecting it to that paradigm of success. This has been Brazil's myth of 'racial democracy', which is based on the premise that inequality in Brazil is not racial, but economic. In the extreme, it means that people suffer discrimination because they are poor, not because they are Black, and they are poor not because they are Black, but because they do not work hard and persevere.[74]

The myth of 'racial democracy' gained theoretical strength particularly after the publication of Gilberto Freyre's *The Masters and the Slaves*, first published in 1933. According to Freyre, Brazil is a 'society whose national direction is inspired not by blood-stream of families, much less that of a race, as the expression of a biological reality', but, rather, 'one of diverse ethnic origins …'.[75] Brazil is 'a society that is democratic in its ethnic, social, and cultural composition',[76] where 'individuals of the most widely varied social origins and personalities, differing likewise in race or religion … have risen to the highest positions'.[77] This book strongly influenced anthropological studies on Brazil's social formation, and the argument of 'racial democracy' has since been replicated as a mantra and, strikingly, not only by those who benefit from it. As Layton and Smith put it, 'powerful societal narratives of racial democracy will lead observers, including targets and perpetrators themselves, to misattribute discrimination triggered by the target's skin color instead to class or gender'.[78]

The myth of 'racial democracy' is largely embraced by white Brazilians from middle and upper classes and, though functioning as a mechanism of organisation of public discourses and sentiments, it is strategically announced as a symbol

[73] See R Dworkin, *Sovereign Virtue: The Theory and Practice of Equality* (Harvard University Press, 2002).

[74] See GM da Silva and EP Reis, 'Perceptions of Racial Discrimination among Black Professionals in Rio De Janeiro' (2011) 46 *Latin American Research Review* 55; GM Silva and E Saldivar, 'Comparing Ideologies of Racial Mixing in Latin America: Brazil and Mexico' (2018) 8 *Sociologia & Antropologia* 417.

[75] G Freyre, *The Masters and the Slaves: A Study in the Development of Brazilian Civilization* (University of California Press, 1986) xiv.

[76] ibid xv.

[77] ibid.

[78] ML Layton and AE Smith, 'Is It Race, Class, or Gender? The Sources of Perceived Discrimination in Brazil' (2017) 59 *Latin American Politics and Society* 55.

of Brazilian culture and nationalism.[79] Such a myth has become so entrenched among Brazilians that even for disadvantaged groups – the 'outsiders' – discrimination is still associated with class, not race, even though having dark skin is the key determinant of discrimination.[80] More interestingly, contrary to common wisdom, Blacks and Browns who occupy more prestigious positions and are part of the middle and upper classes tend not to report discrimination based on their skin colour, unlike those in low prestige positions.[81] There is a vast amount of empirical evidence of what scholars call 'whitening' as individuals move up the education and income ladders.[82]

It is no wonder that Brazil has become a paradigmatic case for debates on racial inequality. Racial discrimination is widespread, no serious empirical evidence corroborates the myth of 'racial democracy', but its negative impacts on individuals' behaviours and the institutional reaction to such types of discrimination are nothing short of deleterious to the rule of law. Discrimination, after all, largely amplifies distrust in institutions of all sorts.[83] Yet, the myth of 'racial democracy' serves as a powerful strategy to keep benefits and privileges virtually untouched for the mostly white upper and upper-middle classes by disguising sheer racial prejudice and, more importantly, by naturalising 'racially inflected class differences' through a set of behaviours and practices.[84] The violence springing from such a reality is not simply a matter of culture or class. It is racial discrimination to a large extent,[85] but the myth of 'racial democracy' builds the narrative that public policies should be colour blind, not therefore targeting structural and longstanding racial discrimination nor the various forms of 'state-orchestrated anti-black violence'.[86]

[79] See RE Sheriff, *Dreaming Equality: Color, Race, and Racism in Brazil* (Rutgers University Press, 2001) 7; C McCallum, 'Racionalized Bodies, Naturalized Classes: Moving Through the City of Salvador da Bahia' (2005) 32 *American Ethnologist* 100.

[80] See Layton and Smith (n 77) 52–54; EP Monk, 'The Consequences of 'Race and Color' in Brazil' (2016) 63 *Social Problems* 413.

[81] See N Kopkin and G Mitchell-Walthour, 'Color Discrimination, Occupational Prestige, and Skin Color in Brazil' (2020) 15 *Latin American and Caribbean Ethnic Studies* 45.

[82] See LF Schwartzman, 'Does Money Whiten? Intergenerational Changes in Racial Classification in Brazil' (2007) 72 *American Sociological Review* 940–63; SR Bailey, M Loveman, and JO Muniz, 'Measures of "Race" and the Analysis of Racial Inequality in Brazil' (2013) 42 *Social Science Research* 106–19; JA de Carvalho, CH Wood and FC Andrade, 'Estimating the Stability of Census-Based Racial/Ethnic Classifications: The Case of Brazil' (2004) 58 *Population Studies* 331–43.

[83] See BS Levitt, 'Discrimination and Distrust of Democratic Institutions in Latin America' (2015) 3 *Politics, Groups, and Identities* 417–37.

[84] McCallum (n 79) 113.

[85] See TB Fenwhick, 'Avoiding Governors: The Success of Bolsa Família' (2009) 44 *Latin American Research Review* 102–31 (showing that race matters a great deal for discrimination by controlling factors related to class).

[86] JA Alves, *The Anti-Black City: Police Terror and Black Urban Life in Brazil* (University of Minnesota Press, 2018) 19.

There is a vast literature pointing out how skin colour has a significant impact on:

(a) education years;[87]
(b) access to better paying jobs;[88]
(c) successful electoral outcomes;[89]
(d) state violence in general (such as police killing);[90]
(e) prison demographics;[91]
(f) residential segregation;[92]
(g) health outcomes;[93]
(h) access to basic services;[94] etc.

Also very interesting are the discussions and challenges derived from the national census classification of 'pretos' (Blacks) and 'pardos' (Browns). Some scholars have pointed out, for instance, the distinct perception of discrimination between those groups – the self-declared 'pardos' feel less discriminated against – despite the socio-economic data showing that both groups face equivalent challenges in social mobility and victimisation through discrimination.[95] Other studies, on the contrary, have stressed that the binary classification – 'whites' and 'non-whites' – may fail to grasp existing differences between Blacks and Browns.[96] This debate is endless, but, regardless of the methodological challenges involved, the numbers are dramatic: racial inequality is not only historically entrenched but also strategically fostered by a set of private and public practices and policies.

Some numbers help us to understand the structural inequality related to skin colour in Brazil. According to the 2018 data from the Brazilian Institute of

[87] See LAO Gonçalves, NND Silva and N Brooke, 'Brazil' in PAJ Stevens and AG Dworkin (eds), *The Palgrave Handbook of Race and Ethnic Inequalities in Education* (Palgrave Macmillan, 2019) 143; LJ Marteleto and M Dondero, 'Racial Inequality in Education in Brazil: A Twins Fixed-Effects Approach' (2016) 53 *Demography* 1185–205.

[88] See O Arias, G Yamada and L Tejerina, 'Education, Family Background and Racial Earnings Inequality in Brazil' (2004) 25 *International Journal of Manpower* 355; Bailey, Loveman and Muniz (n 82) 106.

[89] See A Janusz, 'Candidate Race and Electoral Outcomes: Evidence from Brazil' (2018) 6 *Politics, Groups, and Identities* 702–24; K Kay, G Mitchell-Walthour and IK White, 'Framing Race and Class in Brazil: Afro-Brazilian Support for Racial versus Class Policy' (2015) 3 *Politics, Groups, and Identities* 222–38.

[90] See Alves (n 86) 324.

[91] See JA Alves, 'On Mules and Bodies: Black Captivities in the Brazilian Racial Democracy' (2016) 42 *Critical Sociology* 229–48.

[92] See EE Telles, 'Residential Segregation by Skin Color in Brazil' (1992) 57 *American Sociological Review* 186–97; ECL Marques, 'Housing and Urban Conditions in Brazil' in Arretche (n 14) 163–82.

[93] See JAF Santos, 'Desigualdade Racial de Saúde e Contexto de Classe no Brasil' (2011) 54 *Dados – Revista de Ciências Sociais* 5–40; VSP Coelho and M Dias, 'Health and Inequalities' in Arretche (n 14) 183–205.

[94] See Arretche (n 66).

[95] See VT Daflon, *Tão Longe, Tão Perto: Identidades, Discriminação e Estereótipos de Pretos e Pardos no Brasil* (Mauad, 2018) 17.

[96] See Bailey, Loveman and Muniz (n 82) 116.

Geography and Statistics (IBGE), Blacks and Browns amount to 55.8 per cent (9.3 per cent Blacks and 46.5 per cent Browns) of Brazilians, while whites comprise 43.1 per cent, yet they lag behind in various indicators. For example:

(a) among those studying between the ages of 18 and 24 years old, 55.6 per cent of Blacks and Browns are in higher education ('78.8 per cent of whites), and 28.8 per cent of Blacks and Browns (and 17.4 per cent of whites) have less than 11 years of study and were not at school at the time of the survey;
(b) 9.1 per cent of Blacks and Browns are illiterate (3.9 per cent among whites), and only 10.1 per cent of Blacks and Browns earned a university degree (24.0 per cent among whites);
(c) Blacks and Browns amount to 64.2 per cent of the unemployed, and 47.3 per cent of them have informal jobs (34.6 per cent of whites);
(d) whites earn, on average, 73.9 per cent more than Blacks and Browns, and, among those with a university degree, whites earn 45 per cent more per hours worked;
(e) only 29.9 per cent of managerial positions are occupied by Blacks and Browns;
(f) Blacks and Browns represent 75.2 per cent of the 10 per cent of the population with the lowest wages, and only 27.7 per cent of the 10 per cent with the highest wages;
(g) 32.9 per cent of Blacks and Browns earn less than U$ 5.50/day (15.4 per cent among whites), and 8.8 per cent of Blacks and Browns earn less than U$ 1.90/day (3.6 per cent among whites);
(h) 44.5 per cent of Blacks' and Browns' households lack one or more services of basic sanitation (27.9 per cent among whites' households);
(i) the murder rate among Blacks and Browns reaches the staggering number of 98.5/100,000 youths between 15 and 29 years old (among whites, this number is 34/100,000);
(j) Blacks and Browns are politically sub-represented: they amount to only 24.4 per cent of federal deputies, 28.9 per cent of state deputies and 42.1 per cent of city councillors, and even though they account for almost half of the contenders (41.8 per cent; 49.6 per cent; 48.7 per cent, respectively), only 16.2 per cent of them obtained electoral funding of over R$ 1 million (approximately U$ 200.000,00) in the last elections.[97]

Other data specifically on violence against Black people illustrate even further the gap between whites and Blacks (also including Browns). According to the *Atlas da Violência 2021*, 77 per cent of the victims murdered in Brazil were Black, and the likelihood of a Black person being murdered is 2.6 times higher than that of a non-Black person. Moreover, Black women amount to

[97] IBGE, 'Desigualdades Sociais por Cor ou Raça no Brasil' (*IBGE*, 2019) https://biblioteca.ibge.gov.br/index.php/biblioteca-catalogo?view=detalhes&id=2101681.

66.6 per cent of all murdered women and are 2.5 times more likely to become a victim than non-Black women. From 2009 to 2019, the homicide rate has decreased by 20.3 per cent, but that number was 15.5 per cent for Blacks and 30.5 per cent for non-Blacks, so the reduction was 50 per cent higher for the latter group.[98]

The scenario is shocking from all angles, but there have been some important developments aiming at more fairly including Blacks and Browns in Brazilian society. Some of the positive developments stem from the beneficial effects of democratisation, economic stability and growth as well as changes in demographics (such as declining fertility) and better living standards.[99] However, Brazil has also amplified the adoption of policies aimed at including Blacks and Browns, such as affirmative action in higher education[100] and public careers,[101] and income transfer programmes, such as '*Bolsa-Família*' (a monthly conditional cash transfer programme aiming at combatting extreme poverty), which reaches mostly Blacks and Browns.[102]

Although the numbers are upsetting, a comparable trend with the studies on income inequality can also be seen on those of racial inequality: there has been some progress in including Blacks and Browns in society, but the gap between them and the whites has little changed. Overall, Blacks' and Browns' living standards and welfare have improved, but so do the whites', keeping the gap between these two groups high. Moreover, despite a minor reduction in labour market inequality due to the country's larger trade openness to international competition, racial prejudice is prevalent.[103] Nonetheless, there are some positive movements. For instance, in higher education, even though the landscape is still very grim for the 20 per cent poorest (only 8.1 per cent of Blacks and 8.4 per cent of Browns are in higher education, compared to 25.5 per cent of whites), among the 20 per cent richest, the numbers are much closer: 86 per cent among whites, 73.5 per cent among Blacks, and 76.5 per cent among Browns.[104] Moreover, since 1980, the growth of Black and Brown university graduates has

[98] See D Cerqueira, H Ferreira and S Bueno (ed), *Atlas da Violência 2021* (Instituto de Pesquisa Econômica Aplicada, Fórum de Segurança Pública, 2021) 49, www.ipea.gov.br/atlasviolencia/arquivos/artigos/1375-atlasdaviolencia2021completo.pdf.

[99] See Lima and Prates (n 62) 116.

[100] See J Bernardino-Costa and AE De Carli Blackman, 'Affirmative Action in Brazil and Building an Anti-Racist University' (2017) 20 *Race Ethnicity and Education* 372; A Dias Lopes, 'Affirmative action in Brazil: How Students' Field of Study Choice Reproduces Social Inequalities' (2017) 42 *Studies in Higher Education* 2343; Bailey, Loveman and Muniz (n 82); GHGD Silva and O Skovsmose, 'Affirmative Actions in Terms of Special Rights: Confronting Structural Violence in Brazilian Higher Education' (2019) 11 *Power and Education* 204.

[101] See TD Silva and JMD Silva, 'Reserva de Vagas para Negros em Concursos Públicos: Uma Análise a partir do Projeto de Lei 6.738/2013' (2014) 17 *IPEA (Nota Técnica)*.

[102] See AW Pereira, 'Bolsa Família and Democracy in Brazil' (2015) 36 *Third World Quarterly* 1682; Fenwhick (n 85).

[103] See G Hirata and RR Soares, 'Competition and the Racial Wage Gap: Evidence from Brazil' (2020) *Journal of Development Economics* 102519.

[104] See Lima and Prates (n 62) (data from IBGE Census 2010).

been higher than whites, even though they are more concentrated in less prestigious degree programmes and face much greater challenges to access better paid jobs after graduating.[105] Intergenerational improvements have also occurred: the gap between children of Black and Brown university graduates and children of white university graduates who entered university has also shrunk over the years.[106]

Racial inequality is largely entrenched in Brazilian society and, though it mingles with various elements of income inequality more broadly, it deserves a special place in our analysis of the rule of law in Brazil. Racial inequality goes way beyond class divisions or income distribution. It has a perversity of its own that certainly affects how institutions behave in providing equal treatment for Blacks and Browns, and, more importantly, in pursuing inclusion in a context of a historically segregated society. True, there have been some improvements, but they are slow and first target inequalities at the base of the system, not significantly affecting those inequalities that are seen at the intermediate and higher levels of society.[107] The rule of law in Brazil will never be fully effective unless racial inequality is targeted as such, and not merely as an effect of class divisions and economic disparities that reproduce the myth of 'racial democracy'. Despite some progress, Brazil still has a long way to go to catch up with the minimum standards of an inclusive democracy, and to make its institutions trustworthy enough for every single Brazilian, regardless of his or her skin colour.

B. Gender Inequality

Gender inequality in Brazil follows the pattern of most Latin American countries whose patriarchal and religious (especially Catholic and, now, also evangelical) legacies have placed women and the LGBTQIA+ community in disadvantageous positions across diverse segments of society.[108] However, there has been some important progress over the years. The 1988 Constitution strongly affirms the principle of equality between men and women[109] and the promotion of well-being regardless of 'origin, race, sex, colour, age, and any other forms of discrimination'.[110] Though the 1934 Constitution already featured a clause prescribing 'equal rights' to all,[111] the 1988 Constitution qualified such

[105] ibid 123; Dias Lopes (n 100) 2343.
[106] See Lima and Prates (n 62) 131.
[107] ibid 132.
[108] See MM Camou and S Maubrigades, 'The Lingering Face of Gender Inequality in Latin America' in L Bértola and J Williamson (eds), *Has Latin American Inequality Changed Direction?: Looking Over the Long Run* (Springer, 2017).
[109] Article 5, I.
[110] Article 3, IV.
[111] Article 133, I.

a principle as an unamendable clause and extended it more explicitly to the family,[112] labour[113] and prisoner's rights.[114] Legislation has also provided for better protection of women.[115]

Empirically, there has been what Marta Arretche calls a 'silent revolution' through a new configuration of family arrangements and increasing participation in education and labour markets.[116] The changes are quite remarkable. Since 1991, women are already the majority in higher education, and there has been a steep increase in female enrolment in prestigious areas previously dominated by men, such as medicine, law and architecture.[117] Equality for women has improved more remarkably than that for Blacks and Browns,[118] though their income is still lower compared to men's.[119] Gay rights have also improved, especially in view of the recognition by the Supreme Court that same-sex couples have the same rights derived from civil unions,[120] later extended by the National Council of Justice (CNJ) to same-sex marriages.[121] The country has nevertheless endured a severe backlash by conservative, far-right and religious movements, and misogyny is still largely widespread.

This is the scenario of a country dealing with progressive movements towards gender equality but which is continuously challenged by longstanding and entrenched practices of gender discrimination. The rise of religious movements pushing politics to the Right by strengthening polarisation, placing gender and sexuality as a key 'democratic conflict in Brazil' and transforming it into 'culture wars' – a phenomenon converted into political capital by President Bolsonaro – is also noteworthy.[122] Backlash from religious, far-right and conservative organisations of all sorts have seized this moment to strengthen their agenda. As Debora Diniz argues, there is currently a 'new form of power at play', which 'besides the traditional colonial patriarchy that founded most of our institutions and laws' is basically 'online hate and disinformation movements that reach and engage

[112] Article 226, §§ 3, 5, 7.
[113] Article 7, XVIII, XIX, XX, XXV, XXX.
[114] Article 5, L.
[115] See Lei n. 14.188, de 28 de Julho de 2021; Lei n. 14.022, de 7 de Julho de 2020 (aimed at combatting domestic violence); Lei n. 11340, de 7 de Agosto de 2006 (so-called *Lei Maria da Penha*, also aimed at combatting domestic violence against women). See W Pasinato, 'The Maria da Penha Law: 10 Years On' (2016) 24 *SUR-International Journal of Human Rights* 155.
[116] Arretche (n 54) ix.
[117] ibid.
[118] Arretche (n 14) 333.
[119] Arretche (n 54) ix.
[120] STF, ADPF 132 (2011). See AJ Moreira, 'We Are a Family! Legal Recognition of Same-Sex Unions in Brazil' (2012) 60 *American Journal of Comparative Law* 1003; DW Arguelhes and LM Ribeiro, 'Courts as the First and the Only Legislative Chambers? The Brazilian Supreme Court and the Legalization of Same-Sex Marriage' (2017) 50 *Verfassung in Recht und Übersee* 281.
[121] CNJ, Res 175 (2013). See Arguelhes and Ribeiro (n 120).
[122] AE Smith, *Religion and Brazilian Democracy: Mobilizing the People of God* (Cambridge University Press, 2019) 3.

millions of people on a daily basis'.[123] What seemed until recently a progressive, though slow, path towards greater inclusion of such groups has proven a much longer and bumpier road given the last political and social developments in the country.

Some data help explain the gap between men and women in Brazil. According to the Brazilian Institute of Geography and Statistics (IBGE),[124] in 2019, women had an annual income which was 77.7 per cent of the equivalent male income. Moreover, even though they correspond to 52.4 per cent of the population in working age, 56.8 per cent of the working population were men (therefore, 43.2 per cent were women).[125] In the poorest regions, the numbers of working women among the working population were even lower: 38.7 per cent in the North and 41.8 per cent in the Northeast, but, interestingly, it is in the richest regions where the income gap between men and women was more pronounced (in the wealthier South, women earned 72.8 per cent of male salaries, while in the poorer North and Northeast, this number was 92.6 per cent and 86.5 per cent, respectively). 92.1 per cent of women and 78.6 per cent of men responded that they carried out household activities, and this gap increases when they are married or in a civil partnership but decreases when they move up the education ladder. On average, employed women dedicate 8.1 hours/week more to domestic activities than men, though this number is certainly higher in reality.[126] On the other hand, according to IBGE's 2018 data, women are becoming increasingly educated and are already among the majority of those who finish high school (49.5 per cent v 45 per cent, among men) and study at an university or have already obtained a university degree, (29.3 per cent v 21.2 per cent, among men).[127] Though more educated than men and in more prestigious and theoretically well-paid professions, women still lag far behind. According to 2015 data, women earned 62.2 per cent, 69.7 per cent and 81.1 per cent of male salaries if they hold a graduate, master or doctorate degree, respectively.[128] Moreover, if women hold a leadership position in Brazil's larger corporations, they earn, on average, 61.6 per cent of the equivalent male hourly wage.[129] More dramatic still is the female political representation. According to ECLAC's[130]

[123] E Bähre and D Diniz, 'Women's Rights and Misogyny in Brazil: An Interview with Debora Diniz' (2020) 36 *Anthropology Today* 18.

[124] 'PNAD Contínua' (*IBGE*, 2019) www.ibge.gov.br/estatisticas/sociais/trabalho/17270-pnad-continua.html?=&t=o-que-e.

[125] According to IBGE's gender classification.

[126] See n 124. See also L Pinheiro and M Medeiros, 'Desigualdades de Gênero em Tempo de Trabalho Pago e Não-Pago no Brasil' (2015) 33 *Revista Sociedade e Estado* 161.

[127] 'Pesquisa Nacional por Amostra de Domicílios Contínua: Educação' (*IBGE*, 2019) https://biblioteca.ibge.gov.br/index.php/biblioteca-catalogo?view=detalhes&id=2101657.

[128] See TTDRW Proni and MW Proni, 'Discriminação de Gênero em Grandes Empresas no Brasil' (2018) 26 *Revista Estudos Feministas* 1–21.

[129] See ibid 9; S Ben Yahmed, 'Formal but Less Equal. Gender Wage Gaps in Formal and Informal Jobs in Urban Brazil' (2018) 101 *World Development* 73.

[130] Economic Commission for Latin America and the Caribbean of the United Nations.

Gender Equality Observatory for Latin America and the Caribbean, women represented only 18.2 per cent of judges in the highest court, 15 per cent of the National Congress members, 15 per cent of state legislators, 13.5 per cent of city councillors, 4.9 per cent of ministers in the federal cabinet (the lowest in Latin America), 3.7 per cent of state governors (only one female governor among the 27 elected in 2018) and 11.6 per cent of elected mayors.[131]

Misogyny is also expressed in alarming numbers related to violence against women. According to ECLAC, Brazil had a rate of 1.8 feminicides per 100,000 women in 2019, but such a number is easily challenged due to under-reporting.[132] According to the *2021 Brazilian Yearbook of Public Security*, in 2020, there were 1,350 victims of feminicide (61.8 per cent of Black women). Moreover, there were 60,460 rapes reported in 2020, of which 60.6 per cent were of females under the age of 13.[133]

The nonobservance of basic reproductive rights also directly impacts vulnerable women. Though reducing by 9.5 per cent between 2008 and 2015, there were an average of 200,000 hospitalisations per year for procedures related to abortion, mostly due to unsafe abortions given Brazil's restrictive legislation on the matter.[134] According to the Ministry of Health, there was an average of 2.5 per cent of cases almost resulting in death among those hospitalised,[135] and, from 2006 to 2015, there were officially 990 deaths associated with abortion in the country,[136] not taking into account the no doubt higher number of cases that were not reported.[137] Inequality is highly visible as shown by these numbers: among those deaths, 68 per cent were single, 70.5 per cent Black and most had less than seven years of schooling.[138] Such findings confirm other impactful studies pointing out that 'in 2016, 1 in every 5 women had undergone at least one abortion by the age of 40',[139] which implies that, in average, 500,000 abortions are carried out yearly,[140] mostly on Black, Brown, or Indigenous women with

[131] See 'Gender and Equality Observatory for Latin America and the Caribbean' (*ECLAC*) https://oig.cepal.org/en/autonomies/autonomy-decision-making; See also F Biroli and LF Miguel, *Feminismo e Política* (Boitempo Editorial, 2015) 168; LF Miguel and F Biroli, 'Mídia e Representação Política Feminina: Hipóteses de Pesquisa' (2009) 15 *Opinião Pública* 55.

[132] See 'Gender and Equality Observatory for Latin America and the Caribbean' (*ECLAC*) https://oig.cepal.org/en/indicators/femicide-or-feminicide.

[133] 'Anuário Brasileiro de Segurança Pública 2021' (*Fórum Brasileiro de Segurança Pública*, 2021) 13–14, https://forumseguranca.org.br/wp-content/uploads/2021/07/anuario-2021-completo-v6-bx.pdf.

[134] BB Cardoso, FMDSB Vieira and V Saraceni, 'Aborto no Brasil: O Que Dizem os Dados Oficiais' (2020) 36 *Cadernos de Saúde Pública* 6.

[135] Anis – Instituto de Bioética, *Aborto: Por Que Precisamos Descriminalizar? Argumentos Apresentados ao Supremo Tribunal Federal na Audiência Pública da ADPF 442* (Letras Livres, 2019).

[136] Cardoso (n 134) 9.

[137] See Anis (n 135) 5.

[138] See Cardoso (n 134) 10.

[139] See D Diniz, et al., 'National Abortion Survey 2016' (2017) 22 *Ciência & Saúde Coletiva* 653.

[140] Anis (n 135) 1; Diniz et al (n 139) 656.

low educational levels from the poorest regions of the country.[141] Almost half of all abortions result in hospitalisations, but racism creates barriers for Blacks and Browns to deal with post-abortion care, resulting in a higher number of deaths among these groups.[142] It is therefore a common practice despite its prohibition in most cases and, because women have abortions in very unsafe conditions, it represents a serious public health problem[143] and an undeniable violence especially against vulnerable women.

As for the LGBTQIA+ community, though the world's imaginary picture of Brazil is of a country that recognises and even promotes gender diversity, the current reality is also very disturbing. It has never passed a legislation incriminating homosexuality since its independence from Portugal in 1824 and is marked by a historically strong activist movement for inclusion,[144] but discrimination is pervasive.[145] The institutional response to such an inclusive agenda has been ambiguous. On the one hand, gay rights have improved, especially in view of the recognition by the Brazilian Supreme Court that same-sex couples have the same rights derived from civil unions,[146] later extended by the National Council of Justice (CNJ) to same-sex marriages.[147] On the other hand, such progress is mainly through the judicial system and practically no federal legislation has been approved in this regard.[148] The country has also endured a severe backlash from conservative, far-right and religious groups, placing it in a very disturbing situation in comparison to some of its neighbours, such as Uruguay[149] and Argentina.[150] Omar Encarnación, by comparing Brazil to Argentina, for example, correctly points out that 'not only has this backlash effectively prevented the post-same-sex marriage gay rights boom witnessed in Argentina, but also it threatens gay rights already made, including same-sex marriage'.[151]

Violence against the LGBTQIA+ community is upsetting. Similar to data on inequality for this community, there is very little reliable information. As recently as 2019 the *Brazilian Forum on Public Security* began to compile data on violence against the LGBTQIA+ community from states' police reports,

[141] Diniz et al (139) 12.

[142] See EF Goes et al., 'Racial Vulnerability and Individual Barriers for Brazilian Women Seeking First Care Following Abortion' (2020) 36 Suppl 1 *Cadernos de Saúde Pública* e00189618.

[143] See Diniz et al (n 139) 659.

[144] See OG Encarnación, 'A Latin American Puzzle: Gay Rights Landscapes in Argentina and Brazil' (2018) 40 *Human Rights Quarterly* 195–96.

[145] See ARB Vianna and S Carrara, 'Sexual Politics and Sexual Rights in Brazil: A Case Study' in J Corrales and M Pecheny (eds), *The Politics of Sexuality in Latin America* (University of Pittsburgh Pre, 2010).

[146] STF, ADPF 132 (2011).

[147] CNJ, Resl. 175 (2013). See Arguelhes and Ribeiro (n 120).

[148] See Encarnación (n 144) 155.

[149] ibid 106. Uruguay was the first Latin American country to pass a nationwide legislation on gay civil unions in 2007.

[150] ibid.

[151] ibid 195.

though at that time only 38 per cent of states provided some data. There is an 'invisibility of the violence against the LGBTQIA+ community',[152] but the available data provided a dark picture. In the 10 respondent states, there were 99 and 109 homicides, and 704 and 713 cases of intentional physical injury against this group in 2017 and 2018, respectively. In the 2020 yearbook, 12 of the 27 federal units provided no data on LGBTQIA+ victims of homicide,[153] and, in 2021, eight units did not either, so the pattern remains.[154] In 2021, 1,169 cases of physical injury, 121 homicides, and 88 rapes among the LGBTQIA+ community were reported, an increase of 20.9 per cent, 24.7 per cent and 20.5 per cent, respectively, compared to 2020.[155]

Such numbers reveal two contrasting pictures: on the one hand, the country has democratised and some improvement has been made towards inclusion, following an international agenda pushing for public policies aimed at attacking such types of discrimination. On the other hand, the country has been struggling with conservative and far-right backlashes, some headed by very influential religious groups that are increasingly holding public offices, particularly in Congress and, now, in the presidency. Although up till now the Supreme Court has safeguarded and even expanded some such individual rights, Congress and the president have behaved as veto players when proposals are brought to deliberation. There is an institutionally difficult balance leading to deadlock for further inclusive policies, and the distrust in the capacity of institutions to overcome it has naturally impaired the rule of law in Brazil.

C. Indigenous People

In 1967, the so-called *Figueiredo Commission* provided a 7,000 page report exposing the reality of Indigenous communities in the country. The conclusions were shocking: various human rights violations against Indigenous people, such as mass killings, looting of Indigenous goods, illegal appropriation of resources, labour exploitation, enslavement, rape and torture, many of which with direct involvement of state officials, were standard practice. This report's conclusions were initially released to the press and then published in the Official Gazette. They also led to a parliamentary inquiry. However, the case was later closed following the Institutional Act n. 5, the most authoritarian Act passed during the Brazilian

[152] T Amparo, *Anuário Brasileiro de Segurança Pública 2019* (Fórum Brasileiro de Segurança Pública, 2019) 90.
[153] D Pacheco, *Anuário Brasileiro de Segurança Pública* 2020 (Fórum Brasileiro de Segurança Pública 2020) 111.
[154] D Pacheco, *Anuário Brasileiro de Segurança Pública 2021* (Fórum Brasileiro de Segurança Pública, 2021) 83.
[155] ibid 78.

civilian-military dictatorship (1964–85), and was kept closed for over 40 years.[156] The report, nevertheless, rapidly made international headlines at the time. *The New York Times* published, on the front page, the report *Twenty Years of Shame* by Paul L Montgomery, which, besides mentioning such findings, concluded that 'Indians have had little play in the depths of Brazilian civilization'.[157] More impactful still was Norman Lewis' *Genocide*, published by the British newspaper *The Sunday Times* and later in his book *A View of the World*,[158] in which he wrote in detail – 12,000 words – on the massacre of Indians, and how the Brazilian government was complacent about such crimes.

Such a depiction of the reality of Indigenous communities in Brazil is real and tragic, and it reflects a paradigm that is widespread all over Latin America: Indigenous communities have been forcefully assimilated and exterminated to a large extent.[159] Brazil is, however, not the worst case in the region: Uruguay, Argentina, and Chile, for instance, were 'particularly brutal'.[160] According to ECLAC,[161] by 2010, there were 826 Indigenous people and another 200 estimated to be voluntarily isolated in Latin America, comprising 45 million Indigenous people. Though Indians represent only a fraction of Brazil's population (0.5 per cent), due to its numerous population and large territory (especially in the Amazon region), Brazil features the greatest number of Indigenous communities: 305, amounting to approximately 900,000 Indians and 274 languages, among which 70 are in danger of physical or cultural disappearance.[162] The preservation of such communities in Brazil becomes then a fundamental concern by national and international organisations, all the more so because their preservation is also largely intertwined with environmental protection particularly in the Amazon forest.[163]

Until the 1980s, Brazil's public policies targeted these communities with the purpose of integrating them into general society. This scenario would only change with the emergence of movements for Indigenous rights all over Latin America

[156] MC Cunha, 'Povos da Megadiversidade: O Que Mudou na Política Indigenista no Último Meio Século (*Piauí*, January 2019), https://piaui.folha.uol.com.br/materia/povos-da-megadiversidade/.

[157] PL Montgomery, 'Twenty Years of Shame' *New York Times* (24 March 1968) 214, https://timesmachine.nytimes.com/timesmachine/1968/03/24/103470337.html?pageNumber=214.

[158] N Lewis, *A View of the World* (Eland Publishing, 2011).

[159] See AA Cave, 'Genocide in the Americas' in D Stone (ed), *The Historiography of Genocide* (Palgrave Macmillan, 2008) 273–95.

[160] DJ Yashar, *Contesting Citizenship in Latin America: The Rise of Indigenous Movements and the Postliberal Challenge* (Cambridge University Press, 2005) 37.

[161] 'Os Povos Indígenas na América Latina: Avanços na Última Década e Desafios Pendentes para a Garantia de Seus Direitos' (*ECLAC*, 2015) https://repositorio.cepal.org/bitstream/handle/11362/37773/1/S1420764_pt.pdf.

[162] 'O Brasil Indígena' (*IBGE*, 2010) www.gov.br/funai/pt-br/arquivos/conteudo/ascom/2013/img/12-dez/pdf-brasil-ind.pdf.

[163] See A Zhouri, '"Adverse Forces" in the Brazilian Amazon: Developmentalism Versus Environmentalism and Indigenous Rights' (2010) 19 *The Journal of Environment & Development* 252.

asking for recognition, which helped '[shape] the quality of democracy'.[164] Brazil, in particular, was strongly advanced in the protection of these minorities with the 1988 Constitution and an avant-garde legislation,[165] a context favoured by the intense participation of civil organisations dedicated to the Indigenous cause during the proceedings of the Constituent Assembly in 1987–88.[166] The new Constitution sets out clearly the recognition of Indigenous 'organisation, customs, languages, creeds, and traditions' and the 'original rights to the lands they originally occupy'.[167] Though the lands traditionally occupied by Indians belong to the Union,[168] Indians have 'permanent possession' and 'exclusive usufruct of the riches of the soil, the rivers and the lakes existing therein'.[169] Currently, there are approximately 110,000,000 hectares of Indigenous traditionally occupied lands in the country,[170] which correspond to 12.5 per cent of Brazil's territory.[171] The National Indian Foundation (FUNAI),[172] which is responsible for overseeing and enforcing protective policies toward Indigenous people,[173] is the federal institution that demarcates the Indigenous territories based on anthropological studies.[174]

Despite these achievements, the reality is, however, gloomier and the protection of such communities has significantly deteriorated during the Bolsonaro government. Land disputes, which were already widespread, intensified. Indigenous communities, whose lands help prevent deforestation due to their 'sustainable forest stewardship',[175] suffer the impacts of a federal policy aimed at exploring the Amazon Forest by encouraging farmers, miners and

[164] DL Van Cott, 'Latin America's Indigenous Peoples' (2007) 18 *Journal of Democracy* 127.

[165] See Lei n. 6.001, de 19 de Dezembro de 1973 (Indian Statute).

[166] See MCD Cunha, 'Índios na Constituição' (2018) 37 *Novos Estudos CEBRAP* 429.

[167] Article 231.

[168] Article 20, XI.

[169] Article 231, §2.

[170] According to the National Indian Foundation (FUNAI), there are 441 regularised Indigenous traditional lands amounting to almost 110,000,000 hectares. See www.funai.gov.br/index.php/indios-no-brasil/terras-indigenas.

[171] See M Vick, 'O Que São Terras Indígenas. E qual a Autonomia de seus Ocupantes' (*Nexo*, 27 May 2019) www.nexojornal.com.br/expresso/2019/01/11/O-que-s%C3%A3o-terras-ind%C3%ADgenas.-E-qual-a-autonomia-de-seus-ocupantes.

[172] For more information on the FUNAI's mission, see www.funai.gov.br/index.php/nossas-acoes/politica-indigenista#.

[173] FUNAI replaced the Indians Protection Service (SPI) in the aftermath of the report by the *Figueiredo Commission*. It was created by the Federal Law n. 5.371/1967.

[174] Bolsonaro government attempted to transfer the demarcation of Indigenous territories to the Ministry of Agriculture, but Congress and the Supreme Court stalled such a project. See STF, ADI 6172 (2019), 6173 (2019), 6174 (2019).

[175] See N Anderson, 'REDDy or Not? The Effects on Indigenous Peoples in Brazil of a Global Mechanism for Reducing Emissions from Deforestation and Degradation' (2009) 2 *Journal of Sustainable Development* 18; S Schwartzman and B Zimmerman, 'Conservation Alliances with Indigenous Peoples of the Amazon' (2005) 19 *Conservation Biology* 721.

ranchers to advance their personal economic interests even further. Along with the rising deforestation of the Amazon rainforest, Indigenous territories and their communities are continuously under attack caused by sheer greed and a longstanding mindset largely echoed by the military, economic elites and sectors of the government that regard Indigenous peoples, environmentalists and their allies as 'opponents to economic growth and barriers to development' and also as part of an 'international conspiracy to occupy the Amazon'.[176] Moreover, Indigenous communities have long suffered a process of acculturation by religious missionaries and, more currently, by rising neo-Pentecostal churches,[177] whose racism against such communities and their original culture is rampant.[178]

Such a mindset that sees environmentalists and Indigenous people as opponents of development, usually followed by acculturation discourses, challenges the pluralistic constitutional order[179] and the need for preservation of the socioenvironmental diversity that both the forest and these communities provide. President Bolsonaro's environmental and Indigenous policies encourage this mindset and its deleterious practices. They rolled back several achievements in the direction of greater inclusion and recognition of Indigenous people that had gained momentum since the 1980s. In his government, there has been a deliberated policy to stall the demarcation of Indigenous territories, encourage deforestation and dismantle the agencies aimed at protecting the Indigenous peoples and the environment, such as FUNAI and the Brazilian Institute of Environment and Natural Resources (IBAMA). Illegal mining and deforestation have significantly advanced into Indigenous territory. Such a policy was denounced as a crime against humanity and genocide in the International Criminal Court (ICC) in the Hague, and was reinforced by the way his government handled the COVID-19 crisis particularly with the Indigenous community.[180] President Bolsonaro went even further and vetoed emergency policies approved by Congress aimed at protecting such communities, such as access to hygiene parcels, drinking water and hospital beds.[181] The outcome could not be worse: according to the Articulation of Indigenous People of Brazil (APIB), an NGO, by February 2022,

[176] Zhouri (n 163) 252, 269.

[177] See R Wright, *Transformando os Deuses: Igrejas Evangélicas, Pentecostais e Neopentecostais entre os Povos Indígenas no Brasil* (Editora da Unicamp, 2004); A Vilaça and R Wright, *Native Christians: Modes and Effects of Christianity among Indigenous Peoples of the Americas* (Ashgate, 2009).

[178] See F Milanez et al, 'Existência e Diferença: O Racismo Contra os Povos Indígenas' (2019) 10 *Revista Direito e Práxis* 2174.

[179] Article 231 of the 1988 Constitution.

[180] See P Reeves, 'Brazil's Bolsonaro is Accused of Crime Against Humanity over Coronavirus "Neglect"' (*NPR*, 27 July 2020) www.npr.org/sections/coronavirus-live-updates/2020/07/27/895940087/brazils-bolsonaro-is-accused-of-crime-against-humanity-over-coronavirus-neglect.

[181] See R Pedroso and Z Rahim, 'Brazilian President Jair Bolsonaro Vetoes Covid-19 Protections for Indigenous People' (*CNN*, 8 July 2020) https://edition.cnn.com/2020/07/08/americas/brazil-jair-bolsonaro-coronavirus-intl/index.html.

there were already over 65,000 confirmed Indians with COVID-19, among whom 1,263 died in 162 distinct communities: a tragedy.[182]

D. Regional Inequalities

Inequality in Brazil is also regionalised. If in a megalopolis like São Paulo, lush richness and extreme poverty can be found side by side, Brazil's South and North represent such extremes at a macrolevel perspective. The Southeast region, the most populated, produces more than half of Brazil's gross domestic product (PNB). São Paulo is responsible for about one third of Brazil's PNB (29 per cent), followed by Rio de Janeiro (9 per cent) and Minas Gerais (8 per cent), all three states in the Southeast region.[183] São Paulo city, the capital of São Paulo state, concentrates alone 10 per cent of PNB, though it has 6 per cent of the population, which correspond to the same wealth produced by the sum of the 4,300 poorest municipalities and where approximately one quarter of Brazilians live.[184] The absolute majority of the top 500 richest/per capita cities are situated in the Southeast and South regions, while 90 per cent of the top 500 poorest/per capita cities are located in the Northeast region.[185] Brazil's average income is about twice – and São Paulo's is about three times – that of Maranhão, Brazil's poorest state. With the exception of the Federal District in the Midwest region, where Brasília, the federal capital, is located and there is a concentration of public servants (whose wages are much higher than the national average), the next top five richest states/per capita are in the Southeast or South region (São Paulo, Rio de Janeiro, Rio Grande do Sul, Santa Catarina, and Paraná). All Brazil's states in the North and Northeast regions have lower income/per capita than every single state in the South, Southeast, and Midwest.[186]

Such numbers reflect significant disparities in access to public services and goods. The table below provides an overview of this reality by comparing key data (in per cent) in Brazil, São Paulo (the richest state), and Maranhão (the poorest state).[187]

[182] 'Panorama Geral da COVID-19' (APIB), https://apiboficial.org.

[183] 'PIB 2019' (*IBGE*), www.ibge.gov.br/explica/pib.php.

[184] M Roubicek, 'O PIB dos Municípios Brasileiros. E as Discrepâncias Regionais' (*Nexo*, 1 January 2020) www.nexojornal.com.br/expresso/2020/01/01/O-PIB-dos-munic%C3%ADpios-brasileiros.-E-as-discrep%C3%A2ncias-regionais.

[185] ibid.

[186] M Roubicek, 'Qual Foi o Quadro da Renda dos Brasileiros nos Estados em 2019' (*Nexo*, 1 March 2020), https://www.nexojornal.com.br/expresso/2020/03/01/Qual-foi-o-quadro-da-renda-dos-brasileiros-nos-estados-em-2019.

[187] 'Pesquisa Nacional por Amostras de Domicílio 2015, Pesquisa Nacional por Amostra de Domicílios Contínua 2019 (*IBGE*, 2019) www.ibge.gov.br/estatisticas/sociais/trabalho/9171-pesquisa-nacional-por-amostra-de-domicilios-continua-mensal.html?edicao=30786&t=downloads.

Table 2.1 Access to Public Services and Goods in São Paulo, Maranhão and Brazil

	São Paulo	Maranhão	Brazil
Washing machine	83.4	20.9	61.1
Computer	60.9	18.3	46.2
Sewage	92.6	22.5	68.3
Internet Use	70.6	33.1	57.8
Cell phone	83.9	54.7	78.3
Garbage Collection	95	56.8	84.4
Water Supply Network	96.2	70.3	85.5
Automobile	63.2	18.9	49.2
Illiteracy	2.6	15.6	6.6
Illiteracy (>60 years old)	7.9	45.9	24.1
Schooling years (> 25 years old, in years)	10.5	7.6	9.4
Bolsa-Família benefit	5.5	35.2	13.5

These numbers reveal that Maranhão, one of the Northeastern states, lags far behind São Paulo – and Brazil's average – in social and economic development. If we extend such an analysis to other states, the reality might be a bit less shocking, but nevertheless still very unequal. Brazil's North and Northeast only began to achieve higher levels of basic public services once the other regions had already moved towards universalisation. While the Southeast region was already heading in this direction in the 1970s and early 1980s, the North and Northeast regions would only reach high coverage of such services in the 2010s.[188]

Despite the economic downturn of the last years,[189] Brazil's social development has improved over the years of democratic life. The Northeast and North regions, though still comparatively underdeveloped, have seen visible progress. According to the Municipal Human Development Index (MHDI),[190] the Northeast region had, in 1991, 99.2 per cent of its municipalities with very low human development. In 2010, only 0.8 per cent of its municipalities are still there, while 61.2 per cent are in the low human development, 36.1 per cent in the medium development, and 1.9 per cent are in the high development. Overall, all the Northeastern states are currently situated in the medium human

[188] Arretche (n 66) 139.

[189] See MC Neri, *Qual Foi o Impacto da Crise sobre a Pobreza e a Distribuição de Renda* (FGV Social, 2018).

[190] See 'Desenvolvimento Humano nas Macrorregiões Brasileiras' (*PNUD, IPEA, FJP*, 2016) http://repositorio.ipea.gov.br/bitstream/11058/6217/1/Desenvolvimento%20humano%20nas%20macrorregiões%20brasileiras.pdf.

development (0.663),[191] which is nevertheless still below the national average. In comparison, in the Southeast region, in 1991, 74.5 per cent of its municipalities had very low human development, 23.9 per cent low development, and 1.6 per cent medium development. In 2010, the majority of the cities are ranked as highly or very highly developed (52.2 per cent and 1.7 per cent, respectively), while 41.7 per cent have medium development and 4.4 per cent low development (there is no very low development anymore). The Southeast region is now ranked as highly developed (0.766).[192]

Poverty reduction effectively gained strength, but such progress has recently stalled or even reversed. World Bank's GINI Index, which measures income inequality (0 meaning perfect equality, while 100 implies perfect inequality), shows that Brazil, whose index was declining (63.3 in 1989; 51.3 in 2015), saw an increase from 2015 to 2019 (53.9).[193] This movement indicates that there has been a slight reduction of income/per capita and increase of poverty following the political and economic crisis that hit the country from 2014 onwards. Despite that, Brazil has kept advancing in development according to the Municipal Human Development Index, because, though income has decreased, education and longevity have improved, and it is hence ranked as having high human development (0.765).[194] When such a number is regionalised, there has been progress in development from 2010 to 2017: of all 27 Federal Units, only four states are ranked as medium human development (Maranhão, Alagoas, Piauí, and Pará), 20 states are classified as high human development, and two states (São Paulo and Santa Catarina) and the Federal District are qualified as very high human development.[195] The development gap between North/Northeastern and South/Southeastern regions, though reduced, is still significant.

Possibly more importantly for the rule of law, however, is that, overall, Brazil's welfare clearly improved also in the country's poorest regions. In the 1970s, basic services such as water, garbage collection, sewage and electricity were lacking in most cities, and the levels of education and healthcare were very deficient.[196] The numbers have since improved: in 2019, with the exception of sewage, which is moving slower (68.3 per cent of all households), basic services are reaching universalisation (99.5 per cent electricity, 85.5 per cent water

[191] The Municipal Human Development Index (MHDI) ranges from 0 (lowest development) to 1 (highest development).

[192] ibid 46.

[193] 'World Bank's GINI Index' (*The World Bank*) https://data.worldbank.org/indicator/SI.POV.GINI?locations=BR.

[194] See 'Human Development Data Center' (*United Nations Development Programme*) http://hdr.undp.org/en/data.

[195] 'Radar IDHM: Evolução do IDHM e de seus Índices Componentes no Período de 2012 a 2017' (*IPEA, FJP, PNUD* 2019) www.ipea.gov.br/portal/index.php?option=com_content&view=article&id=34682.

[196] Arretche (n 66) 138.

distribution, 84.4 per cent garbage collection). Illiteracy affects 6.6 per cent of Brazilians and 48.8 per cent of those over 25 years old finished at least basic education.[197] The North and Northeast regions, however, are still lagging far behind: daily water distribution (97 per cent in the South, 69 per cent in the Northeast, 89 per cent in the North); sewage system (88.9 per cent in the Southeast, 27.4 per cent in the North, 47.2 per cent in the Northeast); garbage collection (92.1 per cent in the Southeast, 72.4 per cent in the North, 70.8 per cent in the Northeast); illiteracy (3.3 per cent in the Southeast; 13.9 per cent in the Northeast, 7.6 per cent in the North); basic education (54.5 per cent in the Southeast, 39.9 per cent in the Northeast, 45.4 per cent in the North); years of study (10.1 in the Southeast, 8.1 in the Northeast and 8.9 in the North);[198] physicians/1000 inhabitants (3.15 in the Southeast, 1.30 in the North, 1.69 in the Northeast).[199] Yet, compared to what the situation was like in the 1970s, when such services were practically nonexistent in the poorest regions and very concentrated only in the Southeast and South,[200] there is some reason to celebrate.

Despite that, regional inequality has risen,[201] and the Northeast remains the poorest region. Nowadays the country's overall poverty has declined and few municipalities are extremely poor, but poverty has become even more territorially concentrated.[202] Successful programmes such as *Bolsa Família*, one of the world's largest conditional cash transfer programmes, have had a great impact on the reduction of poverty, mainly in Brazil's poorest regions, by providing some income to poor families while demanding school enrolment and regular medical check-ups.[203] However, the South and the Southeast regions saw an even stronger drop in their poverty from the 1970s onwards.[204] This is because the country is currently wealthier and, as Arretche argues, 'progress in the production of wealth tends to be accompanied by a reduction in the percentage of poor and by expansion in the supply of basic services'.[205] Therefore, though regional inequality is still rampant and extreme poverty is more concentrated in fewer areas, general welfare has improved following a massive poverty reduction and greater access to basic services.[206] Though such a phenomenon was faster in the affluent Southeast and South, and the divide between Southeast/South and

197 PNAD Contínua (IBGE, 2019).
198 ibid.
199 M Scheffer (ed), *Demografia Médica no Brasil 2020* (FMUSP, CFM, 2020) 48.
200 Arretche (n 65) 146.
201 ibid 145.
202 ibid 142.
203 See Campello and Neri (n 19); L Chitolina, MN Foguel and NA Menezes-Filho, 'The Impact of the Expansion of the Bolsa Família Program on the Time Allocation of Youths and their Parents' (2016) 70 *Revista Brasileira de Economia* 183–202; Fenwhick (n 85); Pereira (n 102).
204 Arretche (n 66) 142.
205 ibid 139.
206 ibid 145.

Northeast/North may be even more pronounced today, there has been a decrease in inequality of access to basic services.[207]

The rule of law is notably impacted by the level of economic and social development,[208] and it is negatively associated with inequality.[209] A society that has lower access to basic services, and thence lower levels of well-being, tends to have a higher distrust in institutions and feebler capacity to coordinate strategies to control state arbitrariness, corruption and violence.[210] It is no wonder that clientelism, corruption and violence gain traction in such areas. The lack of basic services and higher levels of unemployment and poverty are catalysts for this phenomenon as they can lead to a '*citizen* strategy of clientelism'.[211] Even a successful programme such as *Bolsa Família*, which is quite insulated from clientelism because of its decentralisation and direct cash transfer, is not the 'silver bullet'.[212] The so-called political families (usually from white elites) that have been in power for centuries are a common feature in the region – and corruption is widespread.[213] Finally, the North and Northeast are the regions with a higher number of homicides/per capita: while in 2019 in Sergipe state (in the Northeast) there were 42.33 homicides/100,000 inhabitants, this number was 7.32 in São Paulo.[214]

In a continental country with such contrasting realities, it is conceptually difficult to say that there is one single rule of law. The disparities are still significant in this divide between the North/Northeast and South/Southeast, and, despite some progress over the years of democratic life as regards greater welfare and lower poverty, the gap is still wide. Add to such a regional divide the inner inequalities in each municipality (race, gender, etc), and it is fair to say that, in Brazil, there are various degrees of commitment to the rule of law and distinct levels of institutional performance and accountability.

[207] ibid 159.

[208] See S Haggard, A MacIntyre and L Tiede, 'The Rule of Law and Economic Development' (2008) 11 *Annual Review of Political Science* 205; DC North, *Institutions, Institutional Change and Economic Performance* (Cambridge University Press, 1990); D Acemoglu and JA Robinson, *Why Nations Fail: The Origins of Power, Prosperity and Poverty* (Crown Business, 2012).

[209] See DL Bennett and B Nikolaev, 'Factor Endowments, the Rule of Law and Structural Inequality' (2016) 12 *Journal of Institutional Economics* 773.

[210] See D Acemoglu and JA Robinson, *The Narrow Corridor: States, Societies, and the Fate of Liberty* (Penguin, 2019).

[211] S Nichter, 'Political Clientelism and Social Policy in Brazil' in DA Brun and L Diamond (ed), *Clientelism, Social Policy, and the Quality of Democracy* (JHU Press, 2014) 147.

[212] ibid.

[213] See K Drybread, 'When Corruption Is Not a Crime: "Innocent" White Politicians and the Rationalization of Criminality in Brazil' (2018) 59 *Culture, Theory and Critique* 332 (arguing that 'In northeastern Brazil, a small number of political families have clung to power for centuries' and how they strategically blame the poor, and not them, for corruption); L Lewin, *Politics and Parentela in Paraíba: A Case Study of Family-Based Oligarchy in Brazil* (Princeton University Press, 2014).

[214] *Atlas da Violência* (IPEA, Forum Brasileiro de Segurança Pública, 2021) 18.

IV. INEQUALITY AND BRAZIL'S DECLINING RULE OF LAW

Inequality matters for democracy and the rule of law, and its impacts on both are well-documented in the literature.[215] An unequal country fails to provide a more robust system of impartial and formal norms that apply equally to all regardless of their social, political and economic status, while, at the same time, hindering coordination of concurrent interests to challenge state abuses. Inequality affects key choices of institutional design and functioning,[216] with long term effects. Unequal countries mutually reinforce inequality, mistrust and corruption, which are hard to eradicate given their intimate correlation with wealth distribution and society's culture.[217] The negative impacts of inequality on democratic consolidation – despite some controversy over its effects on democratisation – have been empirically demonstrated,[218] thereby greatly impacting the rule of law.[219] Democratisation itself may not necessarily diminish inequality – it may even increase it in some circumstances[220] – but inequality is certainly not a good companion for the rule of law.

Inequality, after all, hinders the development of formal and informal institutions aimed at effectively protecting constitutional rights and laws targeting those most in need,[221] while protecting elites from any radical change in their status quo, a phenomenon that also persists in democracies.[222] Democracies can be very unequal, as in Brazil, but their quality, measured according to distinct variables and methodologies, cannot be dissociated from inequality and its detrimental effect on the rule of law. Moreover, persistent inequality may also help explain some global movements toward democratic backsliding, rising polarisation and popular distrust in democratic institutions, which have gained expression with the populist narrative of a popular revolution against

[215] See Bennett and Nikolaev (n 209) 789; DM Brinks, 'Inequality, Institutions, and the Rule of Law: The Social and Institutional Bases of Rights' (2008) 351 Kellogg Institute Working Paper 1–32; EM Uslaner, *Corruption, Inequality, and the Rule of Law* (Cambridge University Press, 2008).

[216] See Beramendi and Rueda (n 25) 252.

[217] See Uslaner (n 215) 24.

[218] See C Boix, *Democracy and Redistribution* (Cambridge University Press, 2003) 3; D Acemoglu and JA Robinson, *Economic Origins of Dictatorship and Democracy* (Cambridge University Press, 2006) xiv; C Houle, 'Inequality and Democracy: Why Inequality Harms Consolidation but Does Not Affect Democratization' (2009) 61 *World Politics* 590; J Teorell, *Determinants of Democratization: Explaining Regime Change in the World, 1972–2006* (Cambridge University Press, 2010) 61.

[219] See Uslaner (n 215) 552; U Sunde, M Cervellati and P Fortunato, 'Are All Democracies Equally Good? The Role of Interactions between Political Environment and Inequality for the Rule of Law' (2008) 99 *Economics Letters* 552.

[220] See D Acemoglu et al, 'Democracy, Redistribution, and Inequality' in A Atkinson and F Bourguignon (eds), *Handbook of Income Distribution* (Elsevier, 2015) 1886.

[221] See Brinks (n 215).

[222] See S Haggard and RR Kaufman, *Dictators and Democrats: Masses, Elites, and Regime Change* (Princeton University Press, 2016) 222; M Albertus and V Menaldo, *Authoritarianism and the Elite Origins of Democracy* (Cambridge University Press, 2018).

the elites.[223] Brazil illustrates this phenomenon with the rise of President Bolsonaro.

Empirical data from renowned international institutes have shown that the quality of democracy and the rule of law in Brazil, which seemed until recently to move upwards, has gradually worsened, at least since 2015. Although such a decline is normally associated with some key junctures in the political realm, such as the impeachment of President Dilma Rousseff in 2016 and the election of President Jair Bolsonaro in 2018 (and, in particular, his pernicious government),[224] inequality and, especially, the worsening of social welfare are major structural factors impacting those numbers. It is no wonder that the *Latinobarómetro Informe 2021*, one of the most comprehensive surveys on the quality of democracy in Latin America, begins its report by pointing out that 'Latin Americans do not tolerate anymore governments that defend the interests of a few, the concentration of wealth … The abuse of power, the privileges, the restriction of pluralism are at the heart of the demand for equality before the law, respect, and dignity.'[225] Inequality matters a great deal for democratic crises, and Brazil is one major case among many others in the world as it has consistently seen its achievements in democracy and the rule of law being reversed in the last few years.

Some international indexers, such as Varieties of Democracy (V-Dem), the World Justice Project (WJP) Rule of Law Index, and The Economist Intelligence Unit's (EUI's) Democracy Index and surveys, such as *Latinobarómetro*, have clearly pointed out Brazil's downfall. The impact has been particularly felt by V-Dem, which possibly offers the most concerning analysis in this regard. Its 2021 report places Brazil among the top 10 autocratising countries and fourth among those whose numbers declined the most from 2010 to 2020.[226] Its various democracy indexes rank Brazil among the worst countries in South America.[227] The World Justice Project (WJP) Rule of Law Index 2021 also points out a worrying scenario for Brazil's rule of law. The country lost three positions in comparison with the previous year and is in 77th position among 139 countries examined and in 16th position in Latin America and Caribbean.[228] Such a decline was

[223] See S Levitsky and D Ziblatt, *How Democracies Die* (Crown, 2018); J-W Müller, *What Is Populism?* (University of Pennsylvania Press, 2016); A Huq and T Ginsburg, 'How to Lose a Constitutional Democracy' (2018) 65 *UCLA Law Review* 1; A Przeworski, *Crises of Democracy* (Cambridge University Press, 2019).

[224] See ch 4.

[225] 'Informe 2021' (*Corporación Latinobarómetro*, 2021) www.latinobarometro.org/latContents.jsp.

[226] 'Democracy Report 2021: Autocratization Turns Viral' (*V-Dem Institute*, 2021) 19.

[227] Brazil is ranked 56th in the 'liberal Democracy Index'; 56th in the 'Electoral Democracy Index'; 79th in the 'Liberal Component Index', 140th in the 'Egalitarian Component Index'; 63rd in the 'Participatory Component Index'; and 136th in the 'Deliberative Component Index'. See 'Democracy Report 2021' (n 226) 34.

[228] 'The World Justice Project Rule of Law Index 2021' (*World Justice Project*, 2021) 57.

found in all its markers, with the exception of 'order and security', but it was notably concentrated on 'constraints on government powers' (76th among the 139 countries), 'regulatory enforcement' (75th) and 'fundamental rights' (95th). Brazil, according to such an index, also features one of world's worst criminal justice systems (112th).[229] The Economist Intelligence Unit's (EUI's) Democracy Index 2020, even though providing a less grim picture of Brazil's 'flawed democracy', has graded Brazil below 7 (on a scale from 0 to 10) since 2015, coinciding with critical political events in the country. Brazil is ranked 49th after Uruguay (15th), Chile (17th), Costa Rica (18th) – the three Latin American full democracies – Panama (40th), Colombia (46th) and Argentina (48th). For *The Economist*, Brazil's democracy has certainly worsened, but it is not yet moving towards autocratisation. Finally, *Latinobarómetro* corroborates such conclusions and raises concerns about the 'deterioration' of Brazil's democracy under Bolsonaro.[230] Its numbers are indeed alarming: only 40 per cent of Brazilians support democracy (below the average of 49 per cent in the region), though 59 per cent reject a military regime and only 11 per cent support an authoritarian government.[231] Its numbers, in various segments, normally place Brazil in one of the most troublesome positions in Latin America. Key for such findings is, as expected, inequality: only 14 per cent of Brazilians responded that wealth distribution is fair, and merely 20 per cent answered that they enjoy equal social and economic opportunities, both the lowest numbers in Latin America.[232]

It is disturbing for any analysis of the health of Brazilian democracy and rule of law to see such numbers. On the one hand, the country has seen important improvements in its institutional capacities[233] and mechanisms of democracy.[234] On the other, such improvements have undergone serious setbacks and backlashes in the last years, placing the country in a peculiar position in Latin America despite the generalised democratic backsliding in most of the region and the globe. It is quite symptomatic to evince that Brazil is ranked, according to some such indexers, below other countries whose histories are marked by far more unstable political backgrounds, higher levels of poverty and economic underdevelopment and widespread disregard for the rule of law.

It should be noted that this is, however, a difficult moment in which to provide definite conclusions and a clear picture of the reality. Even if the most accurate methodologies were adopted, those numbers should always be taken with a pinch of salt and be accompanied by other contextual discussions. Latinobarómetro is particularly compelling, because it shows the vivid

[229] ibid.
[230] 'Informe 2021' (n 225) 9.
[231] ibid 37.
[232] ibid 60.
[233] See CR Sunstein and A Vermeule, 'Interpretation and Institutions' (2010) 101 *Michigan Law Review* 886.
[234] See A Vermeule, *Mechanisms of Democracy* (Oxford University Press, 2007) 1–273.

sentiment of a country undergoing a severe and generalised distrust in its democratic institutions, while delivering a fairly sharp picture of the reasons that led to the rise of President Bolsonaro. The other indexers, though having contrasting conclusions, point out that the country's democracy and the rule of law are in serious trouble. Brazil looked until a few years ago to be on the path to development, but it has systematically undervalued the perils of inequality and the authoritarian mindset that has strong ties with inequality. If this is the message the country's last developments get across, it should not be forgotten that it has also proven to be able to advance an agenda of social and institutional progress, even if only partially and gradually.

Those indexers and surveys raise rich debates by pointing out where the main problem may lie, but they are just the tip of the iceberg of a much more nuanced discussion. Large-N analyses, especially by comparing so many variables, are methodologically challenging and echo perceptions that may not be consensual at all. For instance, opinions on the subject range from largely pessimistic, such as Saad-Filho and Boffo's of a 'nation [that] is tearing itself apart',[235] or Bianchi, Rangel and Chaloub's Brazil's 'de-democratization',[236] to very optimistic ones, such as Marcus André Melo's emphasis on Brazil's 'enormous institutional improvements in governance' and 'the independence and overall effectiveness of the Brazilian web of accountability institutions … unparalleled in new democracies and probably even in a host of older democracies'.[237] Still, it is possibly Tom Gerald Daly who best interpreted the current scenario: 'Brazil has moved from a context of democratic decay to a context of democratic survival', but it does not follow that Brazil cannot be evidence of a case of 'democratic resilience'. As he says, 'many fundamentals of a healthy democracy remain in place: a significant swathe of the public remains committed to democratic rule, civil society is vibrant and robust, and the core constitutional institutions for defending democracy – independent (if highly imperfect) courts, rights protections, and a free media- remain in place'.[238]

The next chapters will delve into such a complex reality and explore some of the nuances that those indexers and surveys may only partially reach. First, though, we should look into the persistent authoritarian mindset in Brazil, which, alongside inequality, is the major factor undermining the country's rule of law.

[235] A Saad-Filho and M Boffo, 'The Corruption of Democracy: Corruption Scandals, Class Alliances, and Political Authoritarianism in Brazil' (2020) *Geoforum* 8.

[236] B Bianchi et al, 'De-Democratization in Contemporary Brazil: From 2015 to 2020' in B Bianchi et al (eds), *Democracy and Brazil: Collapse and Regression* (Routledge, 2020) 1–15.

[237] MA Melo, 'Latin America's New Turbulence: Crisis and Integrity in Brazil' (2016) 27 *Journal of Democracy* 63.

[238] Daly (n 6) 22.

3

The Authoritarian Mindset and the Rule of Law in Brazil

I. INTRODUCTION: HOBSBAWM'S OMEN AND THE AUTHORITARIAN MINDSET IN BRAZIL

In 1995, the English historian Eric J Hobsbawm was in Brazil for a conference at the Art Museum of São Paulo to discuss the main difficulties he encountered when writing his celebrated book *The Age of Extremes*.[1] His lecture, titled 'The Present as History: Writing the History of One's Own Times',[2] was a lesson for anyone coping with the difficulties of writing about the present. As he said, there are three problems in such an approach: 'the problem of the historian's own date of birth, or, more generally, of generations, the problem of how one's own perspective on the past can change as history proceeds, and the problem of how to escape the assumptions of the time which most of us share'.[3] His words certainly serve as a cautionary tale when a complex topic such as the rule of law faces a reality whose political and legal backgrounds are being currently lived by the writer, and, more seriously, change at a pace that seems faster than the writing itself.

Yet words, even when written in distinct contexts and times, can be resilient and have the power to predict a future that a writer could not expect at the time of his or her own writing. Hobsbawm himself could not foresee what Brazil would experience, but his diagnosis of a country that had just transitioned to a democratic regime is striking. In June 1988, in an interview for *O Estado de S.Paulo*, a newspaper, Paulo Sérgio Pinheiro, the interviewer and professor of political science at the University of São Paulo, asked him about his thoughts on the political and social situation of Brazil after the end of the civilian-military dictatorship, and Hobsbawm answered:

> … In this political situation, all I can say is that the transition seems to be taking too much time and, maybe, I could also say that it does not strike me as a good sign

[1] E Hobsbawm, *The Age of Extremes: A History of the World, 1914–1991* (Vintage, 1995).
[2] E Hobsbawm, 'The Present as History: Writing the History of One's Time' in D Bates, J Wallis and J Winters (eds), *The Creighton Century, 1907–2007* (University of London Press, 2002) 273–85.
[3] ibid 273.

> for the country's politics that at least two of the figures in the command of the next presidential elections were people or phenomena that I heard about 26 years ago, when I came to Brazil for the first time. It seems that figures of the past are not necessarily good for the future.[4]

'That figures of the past are not necessarily good for the future' was a good omen of the developments Brazil would endure in the years ahead. That constitutional transition, which was 'taking too much time', was itself a clash of narratives on the degree of influence the authoritarian past would have in the rising democratic regime. Such a clash had a substantial impact on the very understanding of that constitutional moment, and it is no wonder that Hobsbawm had his own concerns about the capacity of that moment to overcome a past symbolised by those 'people or phenomena that [he] heard about 26 years ago'. More dramatically, Hobsbawm's omen would prove true decades later, when such an authoritarian mindset seemed to regain strength after years of democratic life.

There was something unresolved in that transition that would charge a high price in the future. An authoritarian mindset, now re-contextualised for a more urban and democratic country, would reappear in the form of a leadership which would take advantage of the growing distrust in the political system and the economy that had left many behind. For many scholars and analysts, such a phenomenon would be evidence of the urgency of Hobsbawm's cautionary tale. After all, until recently, there was a general perception that Brazilian democracy would not experience an authoritarian revival. As Hobsbawm warned, however, such assumptions are often discredited by history, especially when the pace of change is nowhere near the pace of writing. Those 'figures of the past' have somehow reappeared – or more accurately never disappeared – in Brazil.

Bolsonaro, who was elected with 55 per cent of the valid votes in the second round in 2018, is symptomatic of the authoritarian mindset that has long played an impactful role in Brazilian political life, with detrimental effects on the rule of law. Bolsonaro's words and practices are a shock to anyone who cherishes the values of democracy,[5] and they certainly infer an authoritarianism among Brazilians that seemed tamed until recently. They are also shocking because they are explicit, straightforward, grotesque – which might seem strategically unwise as they foster a stronger social backlash and institutional reaction[6] – but they are not a novelty in Brazil. Such an authoritarian mindset has pervaded Brazilian history in different contexts and adapted itself in a way that challenges common wisdom.

[4] PS Pinheiro, 'Eric Hobsbawm: Um Espelho do Mundo em Mutação' (1989) 3 *Estudos Avançados* 86.

[5] See M Simões, 'Brazil's Polarizing New President, Jair Bolsonaro, in His Own Words' (*The New York Times*, 28 October 2018) www.nytimes.com/2018/10/28/world/americas/brazil-president-jair-bolsonaro-quotes.html.

[6] See JZ Benvindo, 'The Party Fragmentation Paradox in Brazil: A Shield Against Authoritarianism?' (*International Journal of Constitutional Law Blog*, 24 October 2019) www.iconnectblog.com/2019/10/the-party-fragmentation-paradox-in-brazil-a-shield-against-authoritarianism/.

Bolsonaro's election is also a symptom of a country that has not come to terms with its authoritarian past. Brazil has not really challenged its dictatorial years, as Hobsbawm's omen could foresee at the very moment of the democratic transition. For example, unlike its neighbours Argentina, Uruguay and Chile, where amnesty laws were reversed or judged unconstitutional by their Supreme Courts, Brazil kept granting de facto impunity to all those who perpetrated human rights violations during those dark years and had this understanding confirmed by its Supreme Court in a controversial ruling in 2010.[7] Although the political transition led to a constitutional transition in 1987–88, when the Constituent Assembly became the stage of effective participation of distinct sectors of civil society,[8] much of that past was kept virtually untouched in the new democratic regime. At other times, such authoritarianism became more explicit as is the case with President Bolsonaro, but his election, though helped by favourable circumstances, was no surprise in a country where different types of authoritarian behaviours are still rife.

This chapter aims to introduce the reader to a discourse that has long played a major role in shaping Brazilian political life, with serious impacts on the development of the rule of law. It is a brief genealogy of an authoritarian mindset whose origins go far beyond the scope of this book, but whose analysis, especially from the perspective of its growing presence in the country's democratic regime, is a prerequisite for understanding its formal and informal institutions,[9] the challenges to consolidate its democracy and the commitment to the rule of law, and the difficulties in overcoming extractive political and economic institutions[10] that have historically plagued the country's development. Deep-rooted in the country's rampant social inequality,[11] such an authoritarian mindset has proven strongly resilient even in circumstances where democracy

[7] See N Schneider, 'Impunity in Post-Authoritarian Brazil: The Supreme Court's Recent Verdict on the Amnesty Law' (2011) 90 *Review of Latin American and Caribbean Studies* 39; C Paixão, 'Past and Future of Authoritarian Regimes: Constitution, Transition to Democracy and Amnesty in Brazil and Chile' (2015) 30 *Journal of Constitutional History* 89; C Paixão, 'The Protection of Rights in the Brazilian Transition: Amnesty Law, Violations of Human Rights and Constitutional Form' (2014) *forum historiae iuris*; EPN Meyer, *Constitutional Erosion in Brazil: Progresses and Failures of a Constitutional Project* (Hart Publishing, 2021) 24–51; L Mallinder, 'The End of Amnesty or Regional Overreach? Interpreting the Erosion of South America's Amnesty Laws' (2016) 65 *International and Comparative Law Quarterly* 645; M Torelly, 'Assessing a Late Truth Commission: Challenges and Achievements of the Brazilian National Truth Commission' (2018) 12 *International Journal of Transitional Justice* 194.

[8] See L Barbosa, *História Constitucional Brasileira: Mudança Constitucional, Autoritarismo e Democracia no Brasil Pós-1964* (Biblioteca Digital da Câmara dos Deputados, 2012) 143–248; JZ Benvindo, 'The Forgotten People in Brazilian Constitutionalism: Revisiting Behavior Strategic Analyses of Regime Transitions' (2017) 15 *International Journal of Constitutional Law* 332.

[9] See G Helmke and S Levitsky, 'Introduction' in G Helmke and S Levitsky (eds), *Informal Institutions and Democracy: Lessons from Latin America* (The John Hopkins University Press, 2006) 1–30.

[10] See D Acemoglu and JA Robinson, *Why Nations Fail: The Origins of Power, Prosperity and Poverty* (Crown Business, 2012) 91–96.

[11] See ch 2.

seemed to be heading to a point of no return, where the future, despite the historical wrongs of Brazilian social life, would be increasingly inclusive and prosperous.

After having examined the impacts of inequality in the country, the next step in understanding the rule of law in Brazil is to explore some of the nuances of such an authoritarian mindset. This chapter delves into some of its core elements by stressing the efforts to provide a theoretical justification for authoritarianism that gained momentum in two particular periods of Brazilian history: the Getúlio Vargas' Estado Novo (1930–45) and the civilian-military dictatorship (1964–85). Both periods were the most repressive in Brazil's twentieth century, but both also aimed to furnish good reasons for such an authoritarian behaviour. Interestingly enough, several arguments raised during Vargas' dictatorship were renewed during the civilian-military dictatorship, showing that, despite changing realities, there is a continuity and preservation of that authoritarian mindset. This chapter ends by suggesting that the Bolsonaro presidency reassumed many of those justifications, though years of democracy and improved institutional framework have proven important barriers to some of his most authoritarian impulses. The question that lies ahead is how strong Brazilian institutions need to be to finally overcome such an authoritarian mindset and whether, in spite of the 'figures of the past' reappearing whenever the opportunity arises, Brazil will be able to look to the future at last.

II. THE THEORETICAL JUSTIFICATION OF THE AUTHORITARIAN MINDSET: THE THREE MAIN PILLARS

Brazil has a long history of a conflicting relationship with authoritarianism despite the years of democracy since the end of the last dictatorship in 1985. The whole of the twentieth century is a sequence of transitions between more democratic and more authoritarian governments. 'We can say that Brazil, in over one hundred years of republic, has a political, legal, and constitutional history permeated by regime changes, transitions, ruptures, and continuities', wrote Cristiano Paixão, adding to that the conclusion of the very 'complexity of such transformations, the capacity of keeping, in the new regime, components of the former order, and, above all, the impossibility of monocausal explanations'.[12] What is more, the authoritarian regimes had the support of distinct sectors of society.[13] There is, accordingly, a deep connection between, first, authoritarianism and continuity despite regime changes, and, secondly, between authoritarianism and popular support. Both perspectives go hand in hand.

[12] C Paixão, 'Direito, Política, Autoritarismo e Democracia no Brasil: da Revolução de 30 à Promulgação da Constituição da República de 1988' (2011) 26 *Araucária* 147.

[13] See D Rollemberg and SV Quadrat, 'Apresentação' in D Rollemberg and SV Quadrat (eds), *A Construção Social dos Regimes Autoritários: Legitimidade, Consenso e Consentimento no Século XX – Brasil e América Latina* (Civilização Brasileira, 2010) 25.

A diachronic analysis of how such authoritarian forces have organised themselves in distinct periods of Brazilian history is telling of its continuity through reinvention. Two periods of Brazilian history are particularly noteworthy for this purpose: Getúlio Vargas' Estado Novo (1937–45) and the civilian-military dictatorship (1964–85). In both periods, the demand for justification of authoritarian acts through the language of democracy gave rise to a genealogy of arguments that have reappeared in distinct contexts (the Bolsonaro presidency is just the most recent, albeit the most explicit, example).

Prominent scholars have pointed out three pillars sustaining such an authoritarian mindset. Silene de Moraes Freire stresses the depoliticisation of society through the 'construction of a modernity "from above" with no ruptures with the archaic foundations of Brazilian society and destructive to democratic possibilities'.[14] Boris Fausto connects the constitution of such an authoritarian mindset to Brazil's institutional framework: 'the authoritarian mindset gained considerable prestige, and the main ideologues of this current had a significant role in creating institutions and in the political life more broadly'.[15] Raymundo Faoro provides a more sociological viewpoint by stressing what he calls 'estamentos', as a 'social stratum with effective political authority within an order of aristocratic content',[16] which has long adopted diverse strategies to 'privatise' the state according to their interests and to disrupt the exercise of citizenship.

Briefly, from these three viewpoints, the main three pillars of the authoritarian mindset could be summed up as follows: (1) the depoliticisation of society, which is seen as still unprepared for dealing with the challenges of the country or as a player that should be tamed rather than regarded as an active participant of political life; (2) the institutionalisation of a technocracy that steadily deals with political, economic and legal elites in order to keep their privileges and benefits virtually untouched (which helps explain the high inequality); and (3) the strategic use of the legal framework for a symbiotic and clientelistic relationship between the private and public spheres. These three main pillars have seriously impacted the rule of law in Brazil, though their prevalence and influence over Brazil's institutions have obviously fluctuated over history.

III. THE REINVENTION OF THE AUTHORITARIAN MINDSET IN HISTORY

A. The Authoritarian Mindset in Authoritarian Regimes

If we look into the genealogy of such an authoritarian mindset, we should point to the beginning of the twentieth century, when authors such as Oliveira Vianna,

[14] SDM Freire, 'Pensamento Autoritário e Modernidade no Brasil' (2009) 6 *Revista da Faculdade de Serviço Social da Universidade do Estado do Rio de Janeiro* 205.

[15] B Fausto, *O Pensamento Nacionalista Autoritário* (1920–1940) (EPUB edn, Zahar, 2001) ch 3, para 1.

[16] R Faoro, *Os Donos do Poder: A Formação do Patronato Político Brasileiro* (Globo Livros, 2001) 830.

Azevedo Amaral and Francisco Campos gained prominence and influence over political life. These authors were fierce defenders of the need for an authoritarian regime as a way to transform Brazil into a nation, not a mere agglomerate of people, which could finally feature a national identity. A powerful, centralising and authoritarian regime would be justified as a necessary avenue to build that sought-after nation.[17] Oliveira Vianna said: 'I do not have any confidence in the procedures of direct democracy in our country.'[18] Azevedo Amaral stated that liberal democracy was an 'illusion' that meant the 'grotesque functioning of a simulacrum of a representative system that is … alien to our national realities',[19] so a new regime or a new 'national organisation' that is 'emancipated from the fictions and mistakes of the liberal-democratic ideology … is rigorously of an authentic democracy, which is founded upon the suppressed bases of our peculiar collective physiognomy'.[20] Francisco Campos, in turn, would defend even more directly that 'the political regime of the masses is dictatorship'.[21] This authoritarian mindset played a fundamental role during many years of the twentieth century and provided justifications for both the *Estado Novo* (1937–45) and the civilian-military dictatorship (1964–85).[22]

During the civilian-military dictatorship, when Brazil was urbanising fast,[23] once again the argument that Brazil needed a government that would be strong and relentless enough to combat the political crisis and the growth of social tensions reappeared. These were Cold War years and the perception that an authoritarian turn was needed, even one disguised as democratic, gained momentum. Those three characteristics – depoliticisation of society, the institutionalisation of a technocracy and the empowerment of clientelistic relationships between the private and public sectors – were reshaped for the new context. The enemies were also immediately labelled: 'communists', 'subversive political actors' and 'terrorists' who were – so the argument goes – causing serious threats to Brazil's 'democratic achievements'. When President João Goulart, whose government was leaning far to the Left according to that mindset, was toppled by a military coup on 31 March 1964, Brazilians were given a sense of urgency and salvation against the danger of following the path toward communism. This threat served as an 'anti-Goulart mobilizing cement' that would 'unify heterogeneous

[17] See Fausto (n 15) ch 3.

[18] FJ Oliveira Vianna, *Problemas de Política Objetiva* (Record Cultural, 1974) 191.

[19] AJD Azevedo Amaral, *O Estado Autoritário e a Realidade Nacional* (eBooksBrasil, CPDOC/FGV, 2002) 60.

[20] ibid 179.

[21] F Campos, *O Estado Nacional: Sua Estrutura, Seu Conteúdo Ideológico* (José Olímpio, 1940) 16.

[22] Francisco Campos was a very influential advisor of the governments of both periods. He was the Minister of Education and Health during Getúlio Vargas's dictatorship and was one of the authors of the first Institutional Acts (AI-1 and AI-2) that inaugurated the civilian-military dictatorship.

[23] According to the Brazilian Institute of Geography and Statistics (IBGE), in 1960, Brazil was 44.67% urban, but, at the end of the 1980s, it was about 70% urban. See IBGE Séries Históricas e Estatística, https://seriesestatisticas.ibge.gov.br/series.aspx?vcodigo=POP122.

sectors into a favourable front to topple the President'.[24] Although Brazil had been experiencing democratic, though very turbulent, years since the end of Estado Novo in 1945, Brazilians were strongly supportive of the civilian-military dictatorial regime.[25] Democracy was still a very short and conflictive reality for most Brazilians and it is no wonder that the idea of restoring law and order was embedded in the collective mindset, especially in an environment where social polarisation was reaching new highs. A technocracy associated with the military would be the best call for laying the groundwork for the development that had been severely hampered by such a conflictive background.

Moreover, the law should be respected but based on an ideology that strategically instrumentalised it to optimally function under an authoritarian government. The civilian-military dictatorship intensified one of the most perverse features of Brazilian legal history: it provided a veneer of democracy by claiming that it was committed to the rule of law, while twisting such a rule of law according to its own convenience. During the dictatorship, the Constitution would be presumably respected and its changes would follow the traditional procedures for constitutional change, even though, outside the Constitution, the regime began enacting the so-called Institutional Acts. Those Institutional Acts comprised, nevertheless, significant authoritarian content and could not be subject to constitutional review by the Supreme Court. By the same token, Brazil's National Congress would be seemingly operative during most of the dictatorial years and even feature an opposition party, the Brazilian Democratic Movement (MDB), although it could not really act as a check on the government since electoral rules were continuously altered to favour the ruling party, the National Renewal Alliance (ARENA). The Supreme Court would also look functional despite the fact that it was raised the number of justices from 11 to 16, determining the mandatory retirement of opposing justices, and constraining its capacity of granting habeas corpus and reviewing the Institutional Acts. As Leonardo Barbosa argued, 'the military regime kept the democratic institutions, for much of its period, under a kind of "monitored functioning" … controlling institutions was needed, but as long as they kept "functioning" for the regime, thus legitimising it'.[26]

The justification for this movement kept much of that mindset expressed by those prominent scholars from the beginning of the twentieth century, but they were readapted to the new context. The first Institutional Act, written by Francisco Campos and which inaugurated the dictatorship,[27] provides a rich

[24] RPS Motta, 'João Goulart e a Mobilização Anticomunista de 1961-64' in MDM Ferreira (ed), *João Goulart: Entre a Memória e a História* (FGV Editora, 2006) 146.

[25] See Rollemberg and Quadrat (n 13) (featuring a set of articles examining the popular support for dictatorships of the twentieth century in Brazil).

[26] Barbosa (n 8) 157–58.

[27] See MA Cattoni de Oliveira and RD Patrus, 'Constituição e Poder Constituinte no Brasil Pós-1964: O Processo de Constitucionalização Brasileiro entre "Transição e Ruptura"' (2016) 45 *Quaderni Fiorentini* 178–79 (showing how Francisco Campos gave a lecture on 'revolutionary constituent power').

overview of the narrative the government would then adopt. It was a strategic and well thought out plan to legitimise the coup d'état as a radical movement that was not only imperative and urgent, but also an unequivocal expression of democratic values against those who have long aimed to destroy them. Moreover, that coup d'état was itself a 'Revolution' expressing the 'will of the nation' and, as such, legitimised itself as a 'constituent authority'.[28]

It is striking how, from a true coup d'état, the dictatorship saw itself as the most legitimate movement to reconstruct Brazil and bestowed upon itself the powers of a 'constituent authority'.[29] That narrative was a perfect playbook of how to manipulate concepts for the masses by providing a veneer of democracy to an authoritarian regime. The new government is 'revolutionary', and, as 'the most expressive and most radical form of constituent authority, [it] establishes its own legitimacy'.[30] Although it kept most of the previous institutions working, like the National Congress, it made it clear that 'the revolution is not seeking to legitimise itself through Congress', but, rather, it is 'legitimised by this institutional act, the results of the exercise of the constituent authority inherent in all revolutions'.[31]

The following Institutional Acts adopted the same strategy of twisting concepts in order to justify, through a seemingly democratic narrative, a regime that was becoming more violent and increasingly perpetrating human rights violations. The Institutional Act No. 2 – which harshly tightened control over Congress by disfranchising political parties and opponents, and the judiciary by packing the Supreme Court and creating federal courts to rule on cases related to the regime – went even further with this plan. The argument was that the military government was essential to 'eliminate a situation and a government which were plunging the country into corruption and subversion'.[32] The fact that such a regime called itself a 'true revolution'[33] meant that it could last up until the country was able to overcome those threats: 'it is not stated that the revolution was, but that it is and that it will continue. Thus, its constituent authority has not been exhausted, since it is inherent in the revolutionary process, which must be dynamic in order to achieve its objectives'.[34] Democracy, though still defended as a feature of that regime, needed to be balanced with other values: 'democracy presupposes liberty, but it does not exclude responsibility or entail license to go against the very political will of the nation'.[35]

[28] See Ato Institucional n. 1, de 9 de abril de 1964. Translation by CW Guerchon, 'Institutional Acts of the Brazilian Government' (1971) 1 *International Journal of Politics* 258.

[29] ibid Preamble.

[30] ibid Preamble.

[31] ibid 259, Preamble.

[32] Ato Institucional n. 2, de 27 de outubro de 1965. Translation by Guerchon (n 28) 263.

[33] Ato Institucional, de 9 de abril de 1964. Translation by Guerchon (n 28) 258.

[34] Ato Institucional n. 2, de 27 de outubro de 1965. Translation by Guerchon (n 28) 263.

[35] ibid 264.

Finally, at the moment when the dictatorship witnessed its most atrocious human rights violations, the Institutional Act No. 5, once again, meant to justify itself on the basis of an urgent need to 'assure true democratic order, based on liberty, respect for the dignity of the human individual, the combatting of subversion and ideologies opposed to the traditions of our people, and the struggle against corruption …'.[36] The civilian-military dictatorship adopted this most blatant perversion of concepts in order to 'prevent the frustration of the higher ideals of the revolution, safeguarding order, security, calm, the economic and cultural development and political and social harmony of the country, which [were] threatened by subversive processes and revolutionary warfare'.[37] It was later revealed that those who subscribed were clearly aware of its undeniable dictatorial nature, but, as Jarbas Passarinho, Minister of Labour at that time, said: 'Screw up, Mr. President, at this moment, each and every scruple of conscience.'[38] Violence was indispensable for 'democracy' to thrive in the country.

These legal documents reveal that a key feature of Brazilian constitutionalism is its constant need for justification, even in circumstances of typical authoritarianism. One of the features of the Brazilian military regime – says Cristiano Paixão – was the concern with drafting legal norms upholding arbitrary measures.[39] Naturally those distinct justifications aimed at maintaining popular support strong while the regime was ruthless with those who opposed it. It is worth noting that the civilian-military dictatorship did not follow the path of simply overlooking the legal framework and implementing repressive actions without the burden of justifying them. After the transition to democracy in 1985, this narrative would naturally face new challenges, but it would not vanish. As has been the history of Brazil, those three features mentioned above – the depoliticisation of society, the institutionalisation of a technocracy and the empowerment of clientelistic relationships between the private and public sectors – would be readapted to new circumstances.

B. The Authoritarian Mindset in the Awakening of Democracy: A Clash of Narratives

The Constituent Assembly of 1987–88 is itself a clash of narratives, one that recalls those three features and one that attempts to overcome them by putting people themselves at the forefront of building the new constitutional order. On the one hand, that authoritarian mindset reappeared by claiming that

[36] Ato Institucional n. 5, de 13 de dezembro de 1968. Translation by Guerchon (n 28) 265.
[37] ibid 266.
[38] See E Gaspari, *A Ditadura Envergonhada* (Companhia das Letras, 2002) 337.
[39] Paixão (n 12) 158.

'drafting a constitutional text represents a highly technical task',[40] and should thus be made by a committee of experts with the necessary knowledge and wisdom. This thinking reflected the mindset of those who previously gave support to the civilian-military dictatorship and saw, when the transition to democracy became inevitable, the need to control the process in order to fend off more radical moves from popular movements that had been gaining ground at least since the 1970s. On the other hand, a distinct narrative from grassroots movements, professional organisations, the Catholic Church and organised civil society was gaining momentum and would directly impact the new democratic order.[41] The authoritarian mindset was still very widespread and influential during and after the Constituent Assembly, but the novelty was that, possibly for the first time in Brazilian history, it would be challenged by another increasingly powerful democratic mindset. The 1988 Constitution, which resulted from such a clash of mindsets, is itself also a clash of mindsets within its own text. It is very democratic by expanding individual and social rights as well as strengthening accountability and control institutions, but, at the same time, it keeps some of the authoritarian enclaves of the previous years virtually untouched.

The drafting of the 1988 Constitution is revealing of how the authoritarian mindset readapts to new contexts but keeps untouched much of that longstanding discourse that, first, disenfranchises the citizenry from their capacity to more directly participate in the political process; secondly, restricts such a capacity to technocrats associated with political elites; and thirdly, empowers private-public relationships designed to benefit clientelist practices. The military, which, since the end of the 1970s incrementally promoted a political opening of the regime,[42] was not disposed to dialogue with civil society. There was not, by any means, the acceptance that the people could somehow institutionalise their participation in the political arena.[43]

Even after the transition to the civilian government of President José Sarney in 1985, the armed forces were still very influential (Sarney was a former member of ARENA, the military's ruling party) and the political elites of those authoritarian years were largely present during the Constituent Assembly of 1987–88. Despite a proposal with such a purpose,[44] no exclusive Constituent Assembly elected with the sole goal of drafting the Constitution took place. Instead, the National Congress elected in 1986 played this role, though – it is worth noting – leaders from the opposition formed the majority. Moreover, the

[40] M Reale, 'Como Deverá Ser a Nova Constituição' (1985) 60/61 *Revista Brasileira Estudos Políticos* 11.

[41] See C Michiles, *Cidadão Constituinte: A Saga das Emendas Populares* (Paz e Terra, 1989); Barbosa (n 8) 149–53; Benvindo (n 8).

[42] See MJD Rezende, 'Raymundo Faoro e os Enigmas da Transição Política no Início da Década de 1980 no Brasil' (2008) 42 *Revista de Ciências Humanas* 184–85.

[43] ibid.

[44] See Barbosa (n 8) 193–204.

1988 Constitution resulted from a constituent amendment to the authoritarian 1967/1969 Constitution,[45] which led some scholars to argue that the new Constitution was nothing other than the product of a secondary constituent power.[46] In many respects, therefore, there were seemingly plausible arguments in favour of the prevalence of an authoritarian mindset during the Constituent Assembly, which could then stress that Brazil was in a typical transition with no rupture. As Paixão argues, 'between March 1985 and February 1987, it should be acknowledged that the military regime largely succeeded in its strategy of "safe, slow, and gradual opening"'.[47]

It is this conciliatory discourse that is beneath some authoritarian legacies in the constitutional text. They resulted from a series of pact-makings, compromises and bargains meant to protect, through legal means, privileges and benefits that certain segments of society have long enjoyed. The 1988 Constitution is what constitutional scholars call an evolutionary Constitution:[48] it resulted from a transition to a new regime, but the degree of rupture – or even whether it was indeed a rupture – with the previous authoritarian years is disputed among scholars and politicians. There are those who still defend it as a continuation of – or a conciliation with – that past[49] and those who are clearly critical of this position, pointing out the break with those authoritarian years as the hallmark of that moment.[50] Despite that, the argument for conciliation rather than rupture would be a remarkable success and impact the way bargains and compromises were set during the Constituent Assembly. For this account, it was not a 'new beginning', but a harmonisation of interests where, in the end, 'there [were] no winners or losers'.[51] One could argue that the final result of those bargains was a Constitution that is not very distinct from the previous one. In fact, according to Elkins, Ginsburg and Melton's similarity scores, the 1988 Constitution matched 77 per cent of the topics of the 1967/1969 Constitution.[52]

Moreover, for some, such a conciliatory transition would undermine the future of Brazilian democracy. Many analysts at that time were very critical of how the debates during the Constituent Assembly took place and the decisions

[45] Emenda Constitucional n. 26, de 27 de novembro de 1985.

[46] See MG Ferreira Filho, 'Nova Perspectiva do Processo Constitucional' (1985) 60/61 *Revista Brasileira de Estudos Políticos* 129. For a critical discussion of this debate, see JZ Benvindo, 'Brazil in the Context of the Debate over Unamendability in Latin America' in R Albert and B Oder (eds), *An Unamendable Constitution?* (Springer, 2018) 345–64; Barbosa (n 8) 185–237.

[47] C Paixão, 'Autonomia, Democracia e Poder Constituinte: Disputas Conceituais na Experiência Constitucional Brasileira (1964–2014)' (2014) 43 *Quaderni Fiorentini* 439.

[48] See Z Elkins, T Ginsburg and J Melton, *The Endurance of National Constitutions* (Cambridge University Press, 2009) 25.

[49] See MG Ferreira Filho, 'Significação e Alcance das "Cláusulas Pétreas"' (1995) 202 *Revista de Direito Administrativo* 11.

[50] See Barbosa (n 8) 143–248; Paixão (n 47); MA Cattoni de Oliveira, 'Democracia Sem Espera e Processo de Constitucionalização: Uma Crítica aos Discursos Oficiais sobre a Chamada "Transição Política Brasileira"' (2010) *Revista Anistia Política e Justiça de Transição* 200.

[51] AP Veiga, 'Diário do Congresso Nacional', 28 November 1985, p 2506.

[52] Elkins et al (n 48) 57.

that were made in respect of matters of great import for the future. For instance, Francisco Weffort stressed the maintenance of the status quo in a context of 'conversion' and 'continuity',[53] and Adriano Nervo Codato more directly pointed out that that the new constitutional order had 'no real replacement of the groups connected to the dictatorship, but rather a re-accommodation within the realm of the elites'.[54] These were also the main arguments that some foreign analysts raised at the exact moment when Latin America, and especially South America, was experiencing a series of regime transitions from dictatorship to democracy.[55]

Indeed, for some scholars, bargains and compromises that could somehow stabilise the transitional process[56] became, in the end, a serious threat to the consolidation of democracy. Frances Hagopian was particularly assertive on the subject: 'In Brazil, pacts did not broaden and deepen democracy, nor did the politicians who forged them create strong democratic institutions and resolve to adhere to democratic political practice. Elite pact making as practiced in Brazil does not produce "democracy by undemocratic means".'[57] The prospects were grim since those pacts were visibly aimed at keeping the status quo virtually untouched in an environment of deep inequality and a strong authoritarian mindset. Democracy was coming, but its conditions challenged the premise of a path toward a stable democracy. Weffort, in this regard, did not mince his words: Brazil was living a 'conservative transition'[58] that kept intact much of that authoritarian legacy and was still marked by high inequality, and, as such, would not be considered a consolidated democracy.[59]

[53] F Weffort, 'Novas Democracias. Que Democracias?' (1992) 27 *Lua Nova* 20.

[54] AN Codato, 'Political Transition and Democratic Consolidation in Brazil: A Historical Perspective' in AN Codato (ed), *Political Transition and Democratic Consolidation: Studies on Contemporary Brazil* (Nova Publishers, 2006) 18–19.

[55] See TL Karl, 'Dilemmas of Democratization in Latin America' (1990) 23 *Comparative Politics* 1; G O'Donnell, PC Schmitter and L Whitehead, *Transitions from Authoritarian Rule* (Johns Hopkins University Press, 1986); S Mainwaring and MS Shugart, *Presidentialism and Democracy in Latin America* (Cambridge University Press, 1997); TR Scully and S Mainwaring, *Building Democratic Institutions: Party Systems in Latin America* (Stanford University Press, 1995); B Loveman, '"Protected Democracies" and Military Guardianship: Political Transitions in Latin America, 1978–1993' (1994) 36 *Journal of Interamerican Studies and World Affairs* 105; J Higley and R Gunther, *Elites and Democratic Consolidation in Latin America and Southern Europe* (Cambridge University Press, 1992); J Grugel, 'Transitions from Authoritarian Rule: Lessons from Latin America' (1991) 39 *Political Studies* 363; A Przeworski, *Democracy and the Market: Political and Economic Reforms in Eastern Europe and Latin America* (Cambridge University Press, 1991); L Diamond, JJ Linz and SM Lipset, *Democracy in Developing Countries: Latin America* (London, Adamantine Press, 1999); JM Malloy and MA Seligson, *Authoritarians and Democrats: Regime Transition in Latin America* (University of Pittsburgh Press, 1987); F Hagopian, '"Democracy by Undemocratic Means"?: Elites, Political Pacts, and Regime Transition in Brazil' (1990) 23 *Comparative Political Studies* 147.

[56] See SP Huntington, 'Will More Countries Become Democratic?' (2016) 131 *Political Science Quarterly* 259.

[57] Hagopian (n 55) 166.

[58] Weffort (n 53) 21.

[59] ibid 30.

Despite all this, there was also something emerging whose potential could shake up those assumptions to some extent. Indeed, the transition was very conservative in many ways, but it also brought about changes that were in principle unexpected from the point of view of a typical controlled transition. The authoritarian mindset was still very much alive, but a sequence of events created an environment that led to a much greater participatory constitution-making process. The 1988 Constitution could therefore not be interpreted as a work of technocrats who did everything they could to avoid the participation of the public nor could it be summed up in merely clientelistic terms like the emphasis on bargains and compromises would suggest.[60]

In a sense, the 1988 Constitution resulted from the disruption of those longstanding three pillars that have long characterised Brazilian political life, without stating that they did not have an impactful influence on its text and, above all, on how it would be put into practice. Although this dispute of narratives has since affected the very meaning of the Constitution,[61] there is a consensus that, unlike the country's previous constitutional experiences, there was a momentum for change that brought together various segments of civil society. There was an explicit civilian counter-movement that not only pushed for, but also put in place principles that largely contrasted with the claim that the new document represented the final term of the 'revolutionary cycle', as some would argue.[62] Instead, a rupture with that past, though not obviously a total one, was clearly in the making.

During the works of the Constituent Assembly, distinct sectors of organised civil society, such as the Brazilian Bar Association (OAB), the Catholic Church and other religious groups, the Brazilian Press Association (ABI), labour unions, minority rights movements and federations from economic sectors (industry, agriculture, commerce, etc), among others, were very influential in a way that was unprecedented in Brazilian constitutional history.[63] This democratisation of constitution-making resulted from incremental, but effective, popular movements that, especially since the late 1970s, had become prominent as the dictatorship began coming to an end.[64] Moreover, some contingencies played an important role in defining a more democratic environment for

[60] See Benvindo (n 8).

[61] Paixão (n 47) 439–48.

[62] See AM Motta, *1964–31 de Março: O Movimento Revolucionário e a sua História* (Biblioteca do Exército, 2003); JC Moreira Alves, 'Diário da Assembleia Nacional Constituinte', 2 February 1987, 5 ('the final term of the transition which, with no constitutional rupture and through conciliation, the revolutionary cycle comes to an end').

[63] Many records of this social mobilisation can be found in the Coleção Memória da Constituinte (Memories Collection of the Constituent Assembly) at the Historical Archives of the Museum of the Republic in Rio de Janeiro. See MH Versiani, 'A Republic during the Constituent Assembly (1985–1988)' (2010) 30 *Revista Brasileira de História* 233; Michiles (n 41).

[64] See B Kucinski, *O Fim da Ditadura Militar* (Contexto, 2001).

constitution-making. For example, the Brazilian Democratic Movement Party (PMDB), the opposition party during the dictatorship (then called MDB), reached a comfortable majority in the congressional elections in 1986, thus becoming the majority during the Constituent Assembly. PMDB's President, Ulysses Guimarães, was also the Speaker of the House and, more importantly, the President of the Constituent Assembly, who personally engaged in laying the groundwork for a more democratic constitutional document.[65] Senator Mario Covas (PMDB), the leader of the majority, was a strong advocate of democracy and played a major role. Also, the fact that the Brazilian President at the time, José Sarney, who shared that authoritarian mindset, was seen as an illegitimate and weak figure – Brazil was enduring a severe economic and political crisis at that time[66] – helped configure an environment where the results of that constitution-making were largely unpredictable. During the Constituent Assembly, there was a significant fragmentation of the political leaderships and a clear conflict between progressive and backward mindsets. The deliberative procedures and the decentralised organisation of the works, whose functioning rules were very openly and publicly discussed,[67] facilitated the arrival of new players.

Yet, while this configuration permitted advancing a democratic agenda, it also made it more difficult to reach a consensus on matters that could more structurally affect the status quo. 'The Brazilian constituent process was an ambivalent moment of definition of the rules of the future democratic game at the same time when the game had already begun.'[68] By some means, this explains why, from such a melting pot of narratives, the 1988 Constitution represents a rupture with that past since it launches a democratic order and creates mechanisms[69] that would strengthen the rule of law over the following years.[70] At the same time, nevertheless, it kept some corporatist bargains, constitutional designs and formal and informal practices that have long hindered the consolidation of democracy in Brazil. It is a democratic document and is certainly the most inclusive and forward-looking document in Brazilian history. It features an extensive catalogue of both individual and social rights and defines policies targeted at consolidating a welfare state. It also strengthens mechanisms of accountability and transparency as well as laying down procedures of direct participation, such as popular legal – though not constitutional – initiatives,[71] plebiscites

[65] See Paixão (n 47) 444.

[66] LC Bresser Pereira, 'Ideologias Econômicas e Democracia no Brasil' (1989) 3 *Estudos Avançados* 47.

[67] See Barbosa (n 8) 217 ('No other Constituent Assembly in Brazil discussed its own functioning rules in such an open way').

[68] S Gomes, 'O Impacto das Regras de Organização do Processo Legislativo no Comportamento dos Parlamentares: Um Estudo de Caso da Assembléia Nacional Constituinte (1987–1988)' (2006) 49 *Dados-Revista de Ciências Sociais* 217.

[69] See A Vermeule, *Mechanisms of Democracy* (Oxford University Press, 2007).

[70] See Benvindo (n 8).

[71] Article 61, para 2.

and referenda.[72] It also provides for a greater participation of the citizenry in the administration of segments of the welfare state and public policies.[73]

However, the political system, either because of its design or because of the longstanding behaviours of political players,[74] suffers from a crisis of representation and entrenched corruption. Even those greater participatory mechanisms in the constitutional text have been rather unusual, with very few examples put into practice.[75] Leonardo Avritzer diagnoses it by saying that 'the institutions of semi-direct democracy, such as plebiscite, referendum, and popular initiative, have remained much more bound to the functioning of National Congress or the state legislatures than would be expected or what happens in other countries'.[76] The Constituent Assembly was therefore a participatory event and the Constitution certainly is a symbol of the serious attempt to overcome that past, but it does not necessarily follow from that moment of popular engagement that Brazilian constitutionalism would foster a permanent involvement of the citizenry in future political affairs. Indeed, though popular engagement has naturally increased, Brazil's case shows that the correlation between a participatory constitutional-making and a future participatory constitutional practice cannot be taken for granted.[77]

For this reason, the Constituent Assembly and the clash of narratives that marks it are central to understanding the rule of law in the country. Unlike some other experiences in Latin America – for example, in Chile, where the regime transition did not translate itself into a constitutional transition[78] – Brazil rapidly moved to drafting a new Constitution. Such a movement did not contradict the behaviour the country had until then traditionally adopted. In Brazil's history, regime transitions were followed by constitutional replacements[79] and it would not be different this time. What differed from previous experiences – and also from other Latin American ones[80] – was that the 1987/1988 Constituent Assembly had a direct presence of distinct groups of organised civil society

[72] Article 14. At the state and municipal levels, see Articles 27 and 29, XII and XIII.

[73] See Articles 194, VII; 294, III.

[74] See F Limongi and AC Fiegueiredo, 'A Crise Atual e o Debate Institucional' (2017) 36 *Novos Estudos CEBRAP* 96.

[75] See L Avritzer, 'Reforma Política e Participação no Brasil' in L Avritzer and F Anastasia (eds), *Reforma Política no Brasil* (Belo Horizonte, Editora UFMG, 2006) 35–45.

[76] ibid 41.

[77] See S Suteu, *Eternity Clauses in Democratic Constitutionalism* (Oxford University Press, 2021) ch 7.

[78] See T Ginsburg, '¿Fruto de la Parra Envenenada? Algunas Observaciones Comparadas sobre la Constitución Chilena' (2014) 133 *Estudios Públicos* 1.

[79] See JZ Benvindo, C Bernal and R Albert, 'Introduction: Facts and Fictions in Latin America Constitutionalism' in R Albert, C Bernal and JZ Benvindo (eds), *Constitutional Change and Transformation in Latin America* (Hart Publishing, 2019) 7.

[80] See J Couso, 'Trying Democracy in the Shadow of an Authoritarian Legality: Chile's Transition to Democracy and Pinochet's Constitution of 1980' (2013) 29 *Wisconsin International Law Journal* 393; Ginsburg (n 78); W Hunter, 'Negotiating Civil-Military Relations in Post-Authoritarian Argentina and Chile' (1998) 42 *International Studies Quarterly* 295.

interfering in the deliberation process. The uniqueness of this participatory constitution-making process would also be responsible for projecting the relative success of the 1988 Constitution in Brazilian life, 'up until this moment, the most successful from the institutional viewpoint and – why not say? – the most successful from the point of view of the rights and guarantees for the people'.[81] The remaining question is whether such a democratic, inclusive and forward-looking document has been able to challenge the preservationist provisions and practices that that very document also embraced. That clash of narratives, where the authoritarian mindset could find a rich environment to reinvent itself, would become the Achilles heel of Brazilian democracy, while those three pillars would find new ways to re-emerge. Though years have passed since the transition to democracy, the 'figures of the past' would still present themselves as the 'enabling' and 'necessary condition' of democracy. The question is, which democracy are they really striving for?

C. The Authoritarian Mindset and the Revival of the Military under Jair Bolsonaro

Among those 'figures of the past', there is possibly no other that has been more controversial than the military. Along with the rise of President Jair Bolsonaro, the military reappeared in political life as never before since the end of the civilian-military dictatorship in 1985. Marcelo Pimentel, a retired colonel, has repeatedly argued that Bolsonaro's government is, in reality, a 'true military government' or a 'government of generals' and that there is a 'military party' ruling the country.[82] Piero Leirner, a leading sociologist, states that Brazil is currently enduring a sort of 'hybrid warfare' unleashed by the military whose goal is to 'take over the government',[83] and, though the 'Project Bolsonaro is finite', it represents a 'project of reconfiguration of the state that has as main artificer the Armed Forces'.[84] Emílio Meyer and Ulisses dos Reis wrote a post to *Verfassungsblog* titled 'Brazilian Democracy under Military Tutelage', whose first words are quite strong: 'the relationship between the military and the civilian government is one that has defined the whole constitutional history of Brazil and could pave the way for a collapse of democracy'.[85] Some other scholars have

[81] Barbosa (n 8) 368.

[82] See JP Charleaux, 'Onde Estavam, Estão e Estarão os Militares em relação a Bolsonaro" (*Nexo*, 12 June 2021) www.nexojornal.com.br/expresso/2021/06/12/Onde-estavam-est%C3%A3o-e-estar%C3%A3o-os-militares-em-rela%C3%A7%C3%A3o-a-Bolsonaro.

[83] PC Leirner, 'Hybrid Warfare in Brazil' (2020) 10 *HAU: Journal of Ethnographic Theory* 48.

[84] See R Machado and PC Leirner, '"Projeto Bolsonaro" É Finito, Mas É Preciso Ficar Atento aos Militares. Entrevista Especial com Piero Leirner' (*Instituto Humitas Unisinos*, 25 June 2021) www.ihu.unisinos.br/159-noticias/entrevistas/610493-projeto-bolsonaro-e-finito-mas-e-preciso-ficar-atento-aos-militares-entrevista-especial-com-piero-leirner.

[85] EPN Meyer and ULS dos Reis, 'Brazilian Democracy under Military Tutelage' (*Verfassungsblog*, 19 February 2021) https://verfassungsblog.de/brazilian-democracy-under-military-tutelage/.

pointed out some other nuances of such a relationship between the military and President Bolsonaro,[86] but the consensus is quite widespread that Bolsonaro and the military are intrinsically connected and that the military saw, in Bolsonaro, the opportunity to regain relevance in national debates and to obtain further benefits.

This expresses the most explicit version of the authoritarian mindset. One of the most damaging legacies of the transition to democracy is that the military was not confronted with its past and the atrocities it had committed during the dictatorship. As with many other legacies of the Constituent Assembly, a compromise with the military would pay a high price a few decades later. Unlike in Argentina and Uruguay, where the military was in a weaker bargaining position during the transition to democracy, in Brazil it 'had allies in civil society who wished to limit change in the New Republic' and could '[retain] the ability to control its own affairs free from civilian interference'.[87] Despite some attempts to limit the military to external defence,[88] the 1988 Brazilian Constitution ended up not providing a design that could effectively help overcome the longstanding difficulty of providing full civilian control over the military. The compromise of the constitutional project was therefore to 'normalise' the relationship between civilians and the military, sweeping under the carpet the expected tensions that usually occur during regime transitions.

This 'normalisation' was defined by three mechanisms. First, some level of separation between the military and civilians was set in the constitutional text through the prohibition of political party affiliation and constraints on their participation in the civil administration, though not prohibiting it.[89] Such a separation would also imply a degree of non-encroachment on their benefits and guarantees (for example, a more generous pension system) that could not be found in any other civilian public career. It also meant the absence of civilian mechanisms for overseeing military activities, so Congress and the civilian judiciary have little or no authority to check the military.[90] Secondly, an agreement that what happened in the past remains in the past should be interpreted as virtually untouchable. Such an agreement was visible when the Supreme Court

[86] See JR Martins Filho (ed), *Os Militares e a Crise Brasileira* (Alameda, 2021).

[87] F Hagopian, '"Democracy by Undemocratic Means"?: Elites, Political Pacts, and Regime Transition in Brazil' (1990) 23 *Comparative Political Studies* 155. For a very interesting comparative analysis, see AC Stepan, *Rethinking Military Politics: Brazil and the Southern Cone* (Princeton University Press, 1988).

[88] Hagopian (n 87) 156.

[89] Article 142, II, III, V. A proposal for constitutional amendment that prohibits members of the Armed Forces from participating in civil administration is currently under analysis in Congress and has gathered the support of various congressmen and former Ministers of Defence. See Proposal for Constitutional Amendment n. 21/2021, www.camara.leg.br/proposicoesWeb/fichadetramitacao?idProposicao=2291133.

[90] The 1988 Constitution, Lei Complementar n. 97/1999 (which regulates the Armed Forces) and other legal provisions applicable to the military do not set civilian mechanisms of accountability over their activities.

ruled that the Amnesty Law,[91] which was passed during the civilian-military dictatorship, is constitutional under the new democratic regime,[92] unlike what had occurred in other countries in Latin America.[93] Thirdly, the new constitutional text allowed some leeway of interpretation of the false statement that the military are the 'protectors' or 'moderators' of democracy. In this regard, the Constitution prescribes that the military are responsible for not only defending the country, but also '[guaranteeing] the constitutional powers'.[94] More seriously, it says that, 'on the initiative of these', the Armed Forces is responsible for '[guaranteeing] ... law and order',[95] certainly an authoritarian legacy that could be wrongly interpreted as that any branch could unilaterally request the military for such a purpose without being checked or any authorisation by the other branches of power.[96]

That 'normalisation' could be preserved as long as such tensions could be kept under the radar, and the political realm would not dare to disrupt that fragile agreement and the compromises of the constitutional project. Those compromises seemed to be working properly as demonstrated by the fact that, since 1999, the Minister of Defence had been a civilian, not a member of the Armed Forces. This movement clearly signalled that some progress had been made in this relationship, and it looked like Brazil had finally achieved such a degree of civilian control over the military that, despite not being perfect, did not seem to be causing disruption. For various scholars during those years, the military was no longer of major concern and rarely appeared as a variable for political analyses.

However, the disruption did happen – and it happened fast. It first occurred when the Brazilian Military assumed the command of *Minustah*, the United Nations' Stabilisation Mission in Haiti in 2004, which laid the groundwork for the return of the military to Brazilian politics (many generals of that mission would later integrate the Bolsonaro government).[97] However, it was during the Dilma Rousseff presidency, a former victim of the dictatorship herself, that such a movement gained momentum. When she installed the National Truth Commission in 2011[98] as a means to make public the recognition by the state of the atrocities and crimes perpetrated by the military during the

[91] Lei n. 6.683, de 28 de Agosto de 1979.

[92] STF, ADPF 153 (2010); See n 7.

[93] See C Paixão (n 7); L Mallinder, 'The End of Amnesty or Regional Overreach? Interpreting the Erosion of South America's Amnesty Laws' (2016) 65 *International and Comparative Law Quarterly* 645.

[94] Article 142.

[95] ibid.

[96] See VAD Silva, *Direito Constitucional Brasileiro* (Editora da Universidade de São Paulo, 2021) 472.

[97] See AA Marques, 'A Conexão Porto Príncipe-Brasília: A Participação em Missões de Paz e o Envolvimento na Política Doméstica' in JRM Filho (ed), *Os Militares e a Crise Brasileira* (Alameda, 2021).

[98] Lei n. 12.528, de 18 de novembro de 2011.

civilian-military dictatorship (1964–85), the opposition from the Armed Forces was fierce.[99] There was also a growing resentment among members of the Armed Forces, who saw themselves left out of the country's major decisions during the democratic years,[100] a feeling that was aggravated by the fact that Brazil's history is marked by the constant involvement of the military in political affairs.[101]

The anti-corruption crusade[102] that gained impetus in the last years of President Dilma Rousseff being in office (2010–16) paved the way for the rapid revival of the military – a phenomenon that looked, until recently, largely improbable. As had happened in those past dictatorships, by pointing out that the political system is corrupt, the military seized the opportunity to reappear as essential players in the political realm. President Michel Temer, who succeeded President Dilma Rousseff after her impeachment, appointed several members of the military to key positions in his government and also appointed, for the first time since 1999, an army general as Minister of Defence. It was in the Bolsonaro administration, in any case, that such an association with the military hit new highs. The number of military figures in the government jumped from 2,765 in 2018 to 6,157 in 2020[103] and increased tenfold among those who command state-owned enterprises.[104] It was during his government that a set of benefits and privileges were granted to the military as never seen before since the transition to democracy,[105] in a clear movement of co-optation.

The 'equilibrium' between the military and civilians by 'normalising' their tensions would thus be severely disrupted to the point that the very idea of a coup d'état reappeared in political analyses, a shocking outcome if we look to what the country had already achieved over the years of democratic life. Several debates over the role of the military in politics and the risks involved in their close participation in the Bolsonaro administration took place, and comparisons with other countries such as Venezuela began to appear in the media.[106]

[99] See Meyer (n 7) 134–35; DDL Azevedo, *Espectros da Ditadura: da Comissão da Verdade ao Bolsonarismo* (Autonomia Literária, 2020).

[100] See N Viana, *Dano Colateral: A Intervenção dos Militares na Segurança Pública* (Companhia das Letras, 2021).

[101] See MJD Rezende, 'As Forças Armadas e a Reflexão de Raymundo Faoro sobre a Abertura Política, 1984' (2009) 43 *Revista de Ciências Humanas* 97; R Faoro, *Democratização e as Forças Armadas* (Ordem dos Advogados do Brasil, 1984).

[102] See ch 6.

[103] C Motta, 'Mais de 6 Mil Militares Atuam em Cargos Civis no Governo Jair Bolsonaro' (*Rede Brasil Atual*, 18 May 2021) www.redebrasilatual.com.br/politica/2021/05/militares-governo-bolsonaro-6-mil-cargos-civis/.

[104] C Seabra and D Garcia, 'Bolsonaro Multiplica por 10 Número de Militares no Comando de Estatais' (*Folha de S. Paulo*, 6 May 2021) www1.folha.uol.com.br/mercado/2021/03/bolsonaro-multiplica-por-10-numero-de-militares-no-comando-de-estatais.shtml.

[105] See A Shalders, 'Sob Bolsonaro, Benefícios a Militares e Policiais Vão Custar R$ 27,7 bi até 2022' (*Estado de S. Paulo*, 18 September 2021) https://politica.estadao.com.br/noticias/geral,sob-bolsonaro-beneficios-a-militares-e-policiais-vao-custar-r-27-7-bi-ate-2022,70003843456.

[106] See G Mendes, 'Pesquisadora Cobra Freio à Escalada Militar: "Estamos Virando Venezuela"' (*Congresso em Foco*, 7 June 2021) https://congressoemfoco.uol.com.br/temas/forcas-armadas/

Other discussions provided a more nuanced view of Bolsonaro as a phenomenon of our times. Sérgio Abranches, a leading political scientist, claimed that the country was enduring a 'hybrid coup' whereby 'Bolsonaro needs extra-parliamentarian resource [to enable] him to domesticate parliament and, therefrom, also subjugate the judiciary'.[107] In his view, since Bolsonaro had met with some institutional resistance to his authoritarian project and his popularity had plummeted, the military would thus function as a threatening force – an 'extra-parliamentarian resource' – aimed at subjugating the country's institutions to his purposes. Lilia Schwarcz, a prominent anthropologist and historian, maintained that Bolsonaro's government was, in reality, 'a state of coup', in which he '[did] not need to stage a coup, because, in his daily life, he [was] slowly building [that] coup'.[108] Brazil, in this regard, would be heading in the opposite direction to other cases of democratic crises in Latin America. In 2019, for example, Adam Przeworski argued, in his *Crises of Democracy*, that 'astonishingly [the military] is no longer a political actor, even in Latin America, and it all but disappeared from the pages of political science as well'.[109] This was the case in Brazil just a few years ago. After the Temer and especially the Bolsonaro administrations, it is not the case anymore, to the astonishment of both Brazilian and foreign analysts.[110]

The rise of the authoritarian mindset in its most explicit form is severely detrimental to the rule of law in Brazil. It is a symptom of Brazil's democratic crisis, and it becomes more dramatic still with this re-emergence of the military in this trade-off between granting benefits to the military and its politicisation in favour of the government. However, there should be some caution when Brazilian democracy, because of such recent movements, is depicted as being under the control of the military. If this argument prevails, it seems that Brazilian democracy, like many other episodes of the country's history, keeps being highly dependent on the movements of such an institution.[111] It is obviously a concern

pesquisadora-cobra-freio-a-escalada-militar-estamos-virando-venezuela/; M Sanches, '"Bolsonaro Adota Medidas do Manual de Chávez": Entenda Semelhanças e Diferenças entre Brasil e Venezuela' (*Terra*, 9 August 2021) www.terra.com.br/noticias/brasil/bolsonaro-adota-medidas-do-manual-de-chavez-entenda-semelhancas-e-diferencas-entre-brasil-e-venezuela,6300cb2ad77d720818ec0f882e0cd07csykkaoun.html.

[107] S Abranches, 'O Golpe Híbrido de Bolsonaro' (*Sérgio Abranches*, 15 August 2021) https://sergioabranches.com.br/politica/535-o-golpe-hibrido-de-bolsonaro.

[108] G Afiune and L Schwarcz, 'Entrevista Governo Bolsonaro é "Estado de Golpe", Afirma Historiadora Lilia Schwarcz (*Agência Púlbica*, 12 August 2020) https://apublica.org/2020/08/governo-bolsonaro-e-estado-de-golpe-afirma-historiadora-lilia-schwarcz/.

[109] A Przeworski, *Crises of Democracy* (Cambridge University Press, 2019) 140.

[110] JZ Benvindo, 'A "Hybrid Coup" in Brazil?: Bolsonaro in Desperation Mode' (*International Journal of Constitutional Law Blog*, 25 August 2021) www.iconnectblog.com/2021/08/a-hybrid-coup-in-brazil-bolsonaro-in-desperation-mode/.

[111] See JZ Benvindo, 'The Historian of the Future in Brazilian Democracy: The Challenges of Interpreting and Comparing Events of Our Time' (*International Journal of Constitutional Law Blog*, 24 February 2021) www.iconnectblog.com/2021/02/the-historian-of-the-future-in-brazilian-democracy-the-challenges-of-interpreting-and-comparing-events-of-our-own-time/.

that deserves close scrutiny from society. It is also a reminder that full civilian control over the military is not the reality, and certainly becoming less likely. More importantly, it should serve as a cautionary tale of the need to finally challenge the wrongs of such an authoritarian mindset that have simply been 'normalised' and swept under the carpet repeatedly in Brazilian history.

However, years of democracy, even if flawed, matter. Despite the 'normalisation', Brazil has undergone significant changes in society and largely improved its institutional framework[112] and mechanisms of democracy.[113] There is a self-correcting learning process[114] that should not be overlooked, and democracy, as regards both good and bad features, has the trend of preservation as a self-reinforcing process that makes any switching costs substantially higher over the years, which does not deny the power of contingencies.[115] Even if such an association with the government is very concerning, it should be noticed that it has not really strengthened the Bolsonaro government, but it has rather revealed his blatant weakness, while the military has been demoralised. It might be a sign of our times, and it may prove Przeworski's words to be partially redeemed. The military have not 'disappeared from the political scene',[116] but they do not look as threatening as they once did.[117]

The Bolsonaro presidency placed the military more than ever before on the radar of political analyses, and its revival is certainly deleterious to the rule of law. Yet, the fact that such a revival could not radically affect how traditional political forces behave – in fact, Bolsonaro's weakness increased the costs of political bargains, including patronage and corruption – is meaningful. Such signs should serve as a cautionary tale for analyses that look on such a revival as if the military of today had the strength they once had or Brazil's democracy featured the same vulnerabilities of the past. It should also be a cautionary tale for immediate comparisons with other cases of democratic backsliding.

Therefore, even though this book acknowledges the serious damage of such a revival of the military for the rule of law and the importance of the 'military issue' for Brazilian democracy, it assumes that the 'equilibrium' has already shifted to more nuanced and complex alliances at the institutional level than

[112] See LD Carson and MM Prado, 'Using Institutional Multiplicity to Address Corruption as a Collective Action Problem: Lessons from the Brazilian Case' (2016) 62 *The Quarterly Review of Economics and Finance* 56; MA Melo and C Pereira, *Making Brazil Work: Checking the President in a Multiparty System* (Palgrave Macmillan, 2013); TJ Power and MM Taylor (eds), *Corruption and Democracy in Brazil: The Struggle for Accountability* (University of Notre Dame, 2011); F Hagopian, 'Brazil's Accountability Paradox' (2016) 27 *Journal of Democracy* 119.

[113] See A Vermeule (n 69).

[114] See J Habermas, 'Constitutional Democracy: A Paradoxical Union of Contradictory Principles' (2001) 29 *Political Theory* 774.

[115] See P Pierson, *Politics in Time: History, Institutions, and Social Analysis* (Princeton University Press, 2004) 50.

[116] Przeworski (n 109) 140

[117] See Benvindo (n 8).

the traditional civilian-military relationships. The authoritarian mindset is still very much alive, but it goes far beyond the 'military issue' and is entrenched in the functioning of Brazilian institutions, now operating under democratic rule. It is beneath several dysfunctionalities of the rule of law in Brazil. The 'military issue' should justifiably be brought to everyone's attention, but it is the 'normalisation' of both the authoritarian mindset and inequality that may more accurately explain why Brazil still has a long way to go to overcome the pitfalls of the country's rule of law. Sometimes it is not the most visible nor the most ostensible examples of the authoritarian mindset that hold sway, but those that have repeatedly gone unscathed in Brazilian history.

IV. THE REINVENTION OF THE AUTHORITARIAN MINDSET AFTER YEARS OF DEMOCRATIC LIFE

This chapter has aimed to introduce some features of the authoritarian mindset that have been alive and active during central moments of Brazilian constitutionalism, particularly during the 1987–88 Constituent Assembly. As it has been a feature of Brazilian history, such a mindset has proven remarkably resilient and capable of successfully reinventing itself during democratic moments. The following chapters will explore further how Brazil has evolved amid this clash of narratives and how the rule of law has been entangled in such a reality. Brazil has since largely experienced improvements in the functioning of – and commitment to – the rule of law, but the gap between the new democratic reality and the longstanding practices that have hindered the consolidation of democracy will always clash with each other.

The political and judicial systems, which are some of the core legacies both in design and informal practices of that 'past', have proven rather dysfunctional in settling the conflicts that naturally emerge in a country that has gradually become more democratic. There is also, on the other hand, the backlash of that very authoritarian mindset as the country has begun assuming democratic principles as non-negotiable. The representation deficit of the political system, where the same 'figures of the past' keep exerting significant influence, is conspicuous. There lies much of the institutional portrayal of the gap between what that participatory environment of the Constituent Assembly of 1987/1988 aimed to achieve and what the same Constituent Assembly aimed to preserve. It is in this paradox that much of the country's constitutionalism would be shaped and the dilemmas for the rule of law would be found. If, during the Constituent Assembly, the clash of narratives played a fundamental role in the very drafting of the constitutional text, in the period that followed it such a clash had a decisive impact on how constitutionalism would be internalised as a standard practice. Constitutionalism in Brazil is a struggle for inclusion where exclusion has long been the rule, where institutions certainly matter but are simply not powerful enough to overcome entrenched and longstanding interests, and where the past is reinvented in every future.

This chapter began with Hobsbawm's omen and followed the route of a brief introduction to the authoritarian mindset as it has been coined, justified and reinvented with particular emphasis on the process that led to the country's current constitutionalism. However, it merely suggested some possible connections with recent events in the country, when Brazil was faced with an authoritarian mindset that, more than ever during democracy, reappeared in the figure of President Jair Bolsonaro and the revival of the military. From the drafting of the 1988 Constitution to today, nonetheless, there are many nuances the following chapters will further explore. In this analysis, there is evidently the risk of falling into anachronisms, when the past is portrayed as if it were the present and vice-versa. Yet, as this chapter emphasised, the argument here is not repetition, but preservation through reinvention. The authoritarian mindset has had a considerable capacity for reinventing itself over time. In fact, it is shocking to read analyses by prominent scholars written in the 2000s and compare them with their current insights about what the country has become and may become in the future, as it is also shocking to read analyses of prominent scholars during the transition to democracy and their insights about the country just one or two decades later. Many of those analyses might seem outdated today, and some written today might become outdated in the future. Hobsbawm's cautionary tale certainly applies here. Still, the consensus that Brazil has a conflictive relationship with its authoritarian past appears to be rather immune to change.

If Brazil ended up electing Jair Bolsonaro as President, such an outcome certainly frightened those who have long praised Brazil's democratic achievements, but it also confirmed a diagnosis that was certainly not new. While his election shook many of the traditional certainties about the Brazilian political system, as will be later discussed,[118] it also revealed how that authoritarian mindset Brazilians thought they had overcome is still very deeply rooted and pervasive. New strategies and new methods of representing it in a democratic environment have emerged, and it would not be a democratic constitution, a more inclusive constitutional design, and an improvement of institutional capacities[119] that alone would surmount centuries of extractive political institutions.[120] As Fernando Limongi and Angelina Cheibub Figueiredo correctly argued about the country's recent political crisis, '… the corruption and the crisis that the country has endured have little to do with institutional design. To recognise that institutions matter is not the same as saying that only institutions matter …'.[121] There are deeper sociological causes beneath the resilience of such an authoritarian mindset and the still deficient performance of the rule of law.

[118] See ch 4.

[119] See CR Sunstein and A Vermeule, 'Interpretation and Institutions' (2010) 101 *Michigan Law Review* 885.

[120] See Acemoglu and Robinson (n 10) 94 ('when both political and economic institutions are extractive, the incentives will not be there for creative destruction and technological change').

[121] Limongi and Figueiredo (n 74) 96.

The following chapters will explore such a clash of narratives in the very functioning of institutions, in the very commitment or not to the rule of law, and in the very practice of democracy as a continuous struggle for inclusion in a country with such high inequality. Gradually, the signs that led to the rise of a 'past figure' like Jair Bolsonaro and the military may become more visible, but such a narrative would be unsatisfactory if it were based on 'monocausal explanations'.[122] As has been the case in Brazil's history, the signs that have led to a vibrant democracy are also the signs that have led to its recurring disappointments. The question is whether, unlike the situation that has played out in Brazil's democracy and despite the natural institutional achievements of years of democratic life, Brazil will finally learn from its mistakes. Hobsbawm's omen is still very much true. But for how long?

[122] Paixão (n 12) 147.

4

The Rule of Law and Brazilian Political Institutions: A Reshaped 'Coalition Presidentialism'

I. INTRODUCTION: SOME CAUTIONARY REMARKS ABOUT THE BRAZILIAN POLITICAL SYSTEM

THERE IS A general perception that Latin America's political environment is structurally dysfunctional, with plenty of incentives for graft and deference toward private interests instead of the common good. Often, such a diagnosis comes with the conclusion that the legislative power is practically irrelevant and is basically there to endorse the president's agenda, with little capacity to seriously act as an effective check on presidential powers. This picture becomes even more dramatic because political scientists and constitutional lawyers have also historically depicted Latin America as a haven for strong presidents,[1] a region whose common past is there to prove that, with such an institutional arrangement, democracy has been the exception while dictatorships, in their distinct shapes and magnitudes, have prevailed. Institutional design leading to strong presidents and weak legislatures and constitutional courts is therefore the ideal scenario for transforming the rule of law into a subverted concept with little connection to reality. Adding to this context the dire numbers of social inequality, the authoritarian mindset and the various consequences thereof, the upshot is that the political system has long been strategically structured not to effectively change the reality: it has kept historical privileges and benefits to certain elites virtually untouched, while giving the false impression that it is working to gradually provide the population with some expected gains from a democratic society.

There is a lot of truth in such statements, but there is also a lot of simplification, generalisation, and many stereotypes. They simplify the reality, because

[1] See CS Nino, 'Transition to Democracy, Corporatism, and Presidentialism with Reference to Latin America' in D Greenberg et al (ed), *Constitutionalism and Democracy: Transitions in the Contemporary World* (Oxford University Press, 1993) 46–64; R Gargarella, *Latin American Constitutionalism, 1810–2010: The Engine Room of the Constitution* (Oxford University Press, 2013).

they assume beforehand that institutional design, although affecting how constitutionalism, institutions and individuals behave and operate in such a reality,[2] delivers more than it can, while perhaps placing too much emphasis on the path dependence argument:[3] because Latin American has been historically underdeveloped and its institutions have behaved extractively and not inclusively,[4] it is doomed to continuously repeat the errors of the past. They generalise Latin America as if it were a unique and homogeneous reality, when it has become increasingly diversified over the years despite the common origins and connections. Indeed, as we have argued elsewhere, 'it is long past time to move beyond the conventional wisdom that there exists a one-size-fits-all "Latin American constitutionalism"',[5] an argument that evidently extends to its several political systems. Finally, they reproduce stereotypes normally associated with the so-called 'global south',[6] a concept that explains very little and stigmatises even further variables that, when properly examined, may seriously challenge such characterisations of the region and reveal unexpected scenarios. In this regard, it is worth recalling Adam Przeworski's 'culture of lament'[7] associated with the continuous emphasis on Latin America's institutional deficiency, whereas, for him, 'there is absolutely no reason to think that horizontal accountability of the executive is less tight in Latin America than in "consolidated" democracies',[8] and, to state more broadly, '[he is] skeptical that the high degree of inequality and prevalence of poverty in Latin America are due to the weakness of accountability, electoral, horizontal, or social'.[9]

Interesting examples contrasting with those preconceptions include studies that stress that Latin America's political systems are not necessarily designed around strong and unchecked presidents. Scott Morgenstern argues, in this regard, that if Latin America's legislatures 'may not take the most prominent role in the policy process, democratic politics revolve around their most representative bodies'.[10] Cheibub, Elkins and Ginsburg, in turn, state that a constitutional design leading to strong presidents is not necessarily bad per se: '… prima facie …

[2] See A Vermeule, *The System of the Constitution* (Oxford University Press, 2011).

[3] See MDG Kinzo, 'A Democratização Brasileira: Um Balanço do Processo Político desde a Transição' (2001) 15 *São Paulo em Perspectiva* 3; P Pierson, *Politics in Time: History, Institutions, and Social Analysis* (Princeton University Press, 2004) 17–53.

[4] See D Acemoglu and JA Robinson, *Why Nations Fail: The Origins of Power, Prosperity and Poverty* (Crown Business, 2012) 79.

[5] See JZ Benvindo, C Bernal and R Albert, 'Introduction: Facts and Fictions in Latin America Constitutionalism' in R Albert, C Bernal and JZ Benvindo (ed), *Constitutional Change and Transformation in Latin America* (Hart Publishing, 2019) 12.

[6] See R Hirschl, *Comparative Matters: The Renaissance of Comparative Constitutional Law* (Oxford University Press, 2014) 207.

[7] A Przeworski, 'Self-Enforcing Democracy' in DA Wittman and BR Weingast (eds), *The Oxford Handbook of Political Economy* (Oxford University Press, 2006) 325.

[8] ibid 327.

[9] ibid 331.

[10] S Morgenstern, 'Towards a Model of Latin American Legislatures' in S Morgenstern and B Nacif (eds), *Legislative Politics in Latin America* (Cambridge University Press, 2002) 2.

democracy is not incompatible with expanded executive lawmaking … As a normative matter, then, we believe the Latin American presidential pattern is one to be celebrated rather than condemned'.[11] The same reasoning applies to courts, which will be further explored in the next chapter. The political system has been steadily more affected by the functioning and expanded powers of Latin American constitutional courts: 'this blend of more insulation from political pressure and a growing capacity to influence policy is considerably greater than what existed in the recent past'.[12] Therefore, despite the common origins and the various connections, there is no single narrative that could correctly portray the diversely rich political developments of the region.[13]

Latin America's political systems raise significant analytical challenges but, at the same time, offer a myriad of experiences that enrich comparative political and constitutional studies. Their constitutional histories, with over 200 years of political and constitutional breakdowns[14] and transitions from dictatorships to democracies and vice-versa, have an abundance of examples that certainly help explain some of the phenomena that the world is currently enduring, such as populisms,[15] increasing polarisation[16] and rising inequality.[17] Yet, although we have come a long way, particularly in view of social inequality and the still widespread authoritarian mindset,[18] from the 1980s onwards, most Latin American countries have undergone a process of consolidation of their democratic institutions and adopted strategies to cope with potential instabilities, such as more robust constitutional designs, stronger constitutional courts, a set of control and accountability agencies and mechanisms for popular engagement in political affairs.[19] Understanding Latin America is thus an immersion in the paradox

[11] JA Cheibub, Z Elkins and T Ginsburg, 'Latin American Presidentialism in Comparative and Historical Perspective' (2011) 89 *Texas Law Review* 1730.

[12] G Helmke and J Ríos-Figueroa, 'Introduction: Courts in Latin America' in G Helmke and J Ríos-Figueroa (eds), *Courts in Latin America* (Cambridge University Press, 2011) 2.

[13] See Benvindo et al (n 5) 18.

[14] See Gargarella (n 1).

[15] See J-W Müller, *What Is Populism?* (University of Pennsylvania Press, 2016); D Landau, 'Populist Constitutions' (2018) 85 *University of Chicago Law Review* 521; C de la Torre, 'Populism and the Politics of the Extraordinary in Latin America' (2016) 21 *Journal of Political Ideologies* 121; TG Daly, 'Populism, Public Law, and Democratic Decay in Brazil: Understanding the Rise of Jair Bolsonaro' (2019) *International Human Rights Researchers' Workshop: 'Democratic Backsliding and Human Rights*.

[16] See S Levitsky and D Ziblatt, *How Democracies Die* (Crown, 2018); A Huq and T Ginsburg, 'How to Lose a Constitutional Democracy' (2018) 65 *UCLA Law Review* 1; J McCoy and M Somer, 'Toward a Theory of Pernicious Polarization and How It Harms Democracies: Comparative Evidence and Possible Remedies' (2019) 681 *The Annals of the American Academy of Political and Social Science* 234.

[17] See T Piketty, *Capital in the Twenty-First Century* (Harvard University Press, 2017); L Cord et al, 'Inequality Stagnation in Latin America in the Aftermath of the Global Financial Crisis' (2017) 21 *Review of Development Economics* 157; PHG Ferreira de Souza, 'A History of Inequality: Top Incomes in Brazil, 1926–2015' (2017) 167 *Working Paper – International Policy Centre for Inclusive Growth (IPC-IG)*.

[18] See chs 2 and 3.

[19] See Benvindo et al (n 5) 3.

of development toward the future amidst the permanent and stubborn calls from the past, where democracy and authoritarianism clash with each other on various grounds, but also where the degree of such paradoxes and clashes is not linear and has been reshaped over the years.

Brazil's political system is part of this realm of paradoxes and clashes that have marked Latin America, and, as such, any analysis of how its political system deals with the rule of law should be followed by a cautionary tale of what can be overlooked when simplification, generalisation, and stereotypes dominate the discussion. The nuances of the Brazilian political system are not easily understood unless typical preconceptions are confronted with a reality that can reveal unlikely and unexpected outcomes, such as strong presidents who can rapidly become weak and constrained depending on the behaviours of other political and legal players, the fragmented and multiparty political system that can act as an effective check on the executive power[20] or the Supreme Court that can strategically make use of its dysfunctionalities to both position itself as a powerful political player and aggrandise itself as the final check on the other branches of power.[21] These and other particularities show much of how the political system understands its role under a framework that sometimes challenges the rule of law, but which also aims to comply, at least apparently, with the rule of law.

More specifically, the Brazilian political system cannot be easily examined according to the binary stability/instability that has been a mark of Latin American studies, but rather as one in which crises affecting presidents, at least since redemocratisation in 1985, have led to countless interpretations of the very meaning of instability. Presidential impeachments, for instance, which have since then taken place twice (Fernando Collor de Mello, in 1992, and Dilma Rousseff, in 2016), have been assessed as either part of the game, and thus as a constitutionally reactive stabilisation mechanism of a presidential regime,[22] or, on the other hand, as a contemporary form of coup d'état that, despite being a constitutional mechanism, goes against the rule of law more sharply.[23]

[20] See JZ Benvindo, 'The Party Fragmentation Paradox in Brazil: A Shield Against Authoritarianism?' (*International Journal of Constitutional Law Blog*, 24 October 2019) www.iconnectblog.com/2019/10/the-party-fragmentation-paradox-in-brazil-a-shield-against-authoritarianism/.

[21] See ch 5.

[22] See 'Brazil: The Great Betrayal' (*The Economist*, 23 April 2016) www.economist.com/leaders/2016/04/23/the-great-betrayal (calling it 'a shred of hope').

[23] See RMR Queiroz, 'Abuse of Rhetorical Power and Presidential Impeachment in Brazil: Reflections from Legal History' (2020) 40 *Journal of Constitutional History* 215; RMR Queiroz, *Como Remover um Presidente: Teoria, História e Prática do Impeachment no Brasil* (Zahar, 2021); T Ginsburg, A Huq and D Landau, 'The Comparative Constituitonal Law of Presidential Impeachment' (2021) 88 *The University of Chicago Law Reivew* 81. JZ Benvindo, 'Abusive Impeachment? Brazilian Political Turmoil and the Judicialization of Mega-Politics' (*International Journal of Constituitonal Law Blog*, 26 April 2016) www.iconnectblog.com/2016/04/abusive-impeachment-brazilian-political-turmoil-and-the-judicialization-of-mega-politics/.

Brazil is also a compelling case of a political framework whereby governance may reasonably function despite significant political fragmentation in Congress. Unlike distinct analyses that normally interpret strong presidentialisms as well as multiparty systems as reasons for institutional instability,[24] governance, at least up until quite recently, could be preserved, even if flawed in many respects. Despite the increasing fragmentation of the Brazilian party system, governments could, for most of the democratic years, build coalitions and pass their agenda in Congress.[25] Even if somewhat optimistically, Marcus André Melo and Carlos Pereira dedicated a seminal book to justify why 'Brazil has been the paradigmatic case of successful multiparty presidential democracy'.[26] Along with Chile, they both portrayed Brazil as a presidential country whose institutional design should be examined as a counter-example to many preconceptions related to multiparty presidential systems: 'Chile and Brazil have emerged as the successful models for governance in Latin American region. And both countries are multiparty presidential democracies whose presidents are among the strongest in the region'.[27] Most recently, Fernando Limongi and Angelina Cheibub Figueiredo focused on Brazil's political crisis and concluded that, even though political coalitions and corruption 'coexist … there is a huge distance from coexistence and causality' and that 'the crisis that the country is enduring has little to do with institutional design'.[28]

In addition, political and constitutional change in Latin America – and particularly in Brazil – can sometimes be so intense and deeply unexpected that bold and conclusive statements on stability and instability can rapidly be disputed. For example, in 2013, when Melo's and Pereira's book was published, Brazil would experience one of its most significant and consequential popular protests in recent history – one that would be a turning point in Brazilian politics and prompt the beginning of a dramatic backlash against the political class.[29] What had previously been a case of fairly functional governance and rather stable political performance turned itself into a series of acts and bargains that would

[24] See MS Shugart and JM Carey, *Presidents and Assemblies: Constitutional Design and Electoral Dynamics* (Cambridge University Press, 1992) 28–54.

[25] See F Limongi, 'A Democracia no Brasil: Presidencialismo, Coalizão Partidária e Processo Decisório' (2006) 76 *Novos Estudos CEBRAP* 23; AC Figueiredo and F Limongi, 'Political Institutions and Governamental Performance in Brazilian Democracy' in D de la Fontaine and T Stehnken (eds), *The Political System of Brazil* (Springer, 2016); FDBC Gomes, 'Cooperação, Liderança e Impasse entre o Legislativo e o Executivo na Produção Legislativa do Congresso Nacional do Brasil' (2012) 55 *Dados – Revista de Ciências Sociais* 911.

[26] MA Melo and C Pereira, *Making Brazil Work: Checking the President in a Multiparty System* (Palgrave Macmillan, 2013) 12.

[27] ibid 3.

[28] F Limongi and AC Figueiredo, 'A Crise Atual e o Debate Institucional' (2017) 36 *Novos Estudos CEBRAP* 95–96.

[29] See A Freitas and GPD Silva, 'Das Manifestações de 2013 à Eleição de 2018 no Brasil' (2019) 38 *Novos Estudos CEBRAP* 137; JZ Benvindo, 'The Seeds of Change: Popular Protests as Constitutional Moments' (2015) 99 *Marquette Law Review* 364.

not only lead to the impeachment of a president, but also lay the groundwork for a rising politician, then elected president in a political campaign that had no precedent whatsoever in Brazilian history. This scenario would baffle political scientists and constitutional lawyers in Brazil and elsewhere, and it certainly led to a deep reassessment of the many markers they usually adopt to value the quality and resilience of such a country's democracy.

Therefore, this chapter adopts a cautionary approach when examining the rule of law and the Brazilian political system. Brazil, like other Latin American countries, really deserves a thorough investigation of the variables and markers that are normally associated with the compliance of its institutions – and, in this chapter, of the political institutions – with the rule of law. The argument is not that that there is a unique and special Latin American constitutionalism, since it would also lead to the type of generalisation, simplification and stereotype that we aim to avoid. Nor does it seek to reveal, more specifically, the Brazilian uniqueness in a comparative perspective, as if it were not translatable into other contexts whatsoever. The purpose is merely to begin the investigation by assuming beforehand that, in such a rapidly changeable political environment, there is no argument that can be taken for granted, even if the years of democratic life have brought about some stabilisation of expectations and premises to evaluate how the rule of law performs in such a reality.

For argument's sake, it will discuss the Brazilian 'coalition presidentialism' by stressing whether Brazil features a strong presidentialism, introducing the main characteristics of such a political system, and discussing how party fragmentation and its oligarchical composition affect its compliance with the rule of law. It concludes by arguing that Brazil's 'coalition presidentialism' has been strongly reshaped, which, depending on how the political players behave in this new system, may probably lead the country's political crisis to be 'normalised' through preservation, accommodation and oblivion. 'It seems that the institutions that have governed Brazilian democracy for the past generation are likely to persist', correctly argued Matthew Taylor.[30] This was, after all, Brazil's political past, this has been Brazil's political present, and this will possibly be Brazil's political future.

II. THE BRAZILIAN POLITICAL SYSTEM: EFFICIENCY OR DEEP DYSFUNCTIONALITY?

A. A Strong Presidentialism?

Brazil follows the Latin American tradition of strong presidential systems, and the 1988 Constitution exacerbated such a feature even further. Though the concept

[30] MM Taylor, 'The Troubling Strength of Brazilian Institutions in the Face of Scandal' (2019) 15 *Taiwan Journal of Democracy* 111.

of strong presidentialism might be 'overstretched',[31] the 1988 Constitution has indeed expanded the executive powers in comparison to previous democratic constitutions, most notably the 1946 Constitution.[32] Moreover, the civilian-military dictatorship (1964–85) and the authoritarian 1967/1969 Constitution impacted the new presidential regime, so features that are normally associated with strong presidents are all there, such as the powers to: (a) initiate constitutional amendments,[33] (b) issue legislation (particularly, the so-called Medidas Provisórias,[34] a sort of provisional decree), (c) partially and totally veto bills,[35] (d) exclusively propose bills in certain areas (for example, the national budget), and (e) exert a substantial and centralised control over public spending, though recently mitigated by the so-called 'mandatory budget'.[36] Angelina Cheibub Figueiredo and Fernando Limongi, in this regard, contend that 'the 1988 Constitution strengthened the institutional fragmentation and the centrifugal forces of the Brazilian political system that was in force in the 1946 Constitution, while radically changing the balance among the powers as set out in the prior democratic Constitution by concentrating power on the Executive'.[37] It is a typical scenario that could lead to what Roberto Gargarella calls an '"unbalanced" version of the system of checks and balances',[38] and hence to a system that has little compliance with the rule of law.

Strong presidential powers, which tend to foster a national agenda, can, however, be a two-way street. While expanding presidential powers, the 1988 Constitution also improved checks and balances. Congress became more directly involved in the national agenda through enhanced powers (for example, a lower quorum to overturn presidential vetoes,[39] the need to approve or reject Medidas

[31] See Melo and Pereira (n 26) 4.

[32] In particular, under the 1946 Constitution, unlike the 1988 Constitution, presidents did not have power to propose constitutional amendments and there were no Medidas Provisórias (See Article 87 of the 1946 Constitution).

[33] Article 60, II, of the 1988 Constitution.

[34] Medidas Provisórias (Provisional Measures) are temporary legislation issued by the executive with immediate force of law, but which need to pass in Congress in 120 days or will become ineffective. According to Article 62 of the 1988 Constitution, 'in relevant and urgent cases, the President of the Republic may adopt provisional measures with the force of law; such measures shall be submitted immediately to the National Congress'. There are some areas which cannot be subject to provisional measures, such as electoral and criminal law, among others.

[35] Article 84, V, of the 1988 Constitution.

[36] See Emenda Constitucional n. 86, de 17 de Março de 2015; Emenda Constitucional n. 100, de 26 de Junho de 2019. See also NCB Santos and CE Gasparini, 'Orçamento Impositivo e Relação entre Poderes no Brasil' (2020) *Revista Brasileira de Ciência Política* 395 (The mandatory amendment means that it is 'mandatory to execute budget programming included by parliamentary amendments'.)

[37] AC Figueiredo and F Limongi, 'Instituições Políticas e Governabilidade: Desempenho do Governo e Apoio Legislativo na Democracia Brasileira' in C Ranulfo (ed), *A Democracia Brasileira: Balanços e Perspectivas para o Século 21* (Belo Horizonte, Editora UFMG, 2007) 1.

[38] R Gargarella, 'Latin America's Contribution to Constitutionalism' in R Sieder, K Ansolabeher and T Alfonso (eds), *Routledge Handbook of Law and Society in Latin America* (Routledge, 2019) 25.

[39] Article 66, § 4, of the 1988 Constitution.

Provisórias and to deliberate on any bill proposed by the executive power);[40] other control institutions became more robust, such as the audit courts and the Federal Revenue,[41] and more independent, such as the Judiciary and the Public Ministry,[42] responsible for 'defending the legal order, the democratic regime' and 'social and individual interests'.[43] By the same token, federalism, even though concentration is still the rule, constrains presidential powers. Finally, the very fragmentation of the political system significantly increases the need to negotiate and build coalitions in Congress, which have not always proven feasible (the two presidential impeachments in 1992 and 2016 are evidence of what can happen when things go terribly wrong).

Presidents (along with vice-presidents) are elected for a four-year term if they obtain the absolute majority of the valid votes.[44] Brazil adopts a second round system between the two most voted candidates in case no one reaches the absolute majority in the first ballot.[45] Since democracy was reinstated in 1985, all but the 1994 and 1998 presidential elections had a run-off and, with the exception of the 1989 and the 2018 elections, the disputes in the run-off were always between the centre-left Worker's Party (PT) and the centre-right Brazilian Social Democracy Party (PSDB), which formed large coalitions amid the highly fragmented party system. In addition, after the Constitutional Amendment n. 16/1997[46] introduced the possibility of subsequent re-election for presidents, governors, and mayors – an innovation in Brazilian political history –[47] all presidents who ran for re-election were re-elected: Fernando Henrique Cardozo (1998), Luiz Inácio Lula da Silva (2006) and Dilma Rousseff (2014).

Until 2014 at least, relatively normal elections took place despite the increasing polarisation between PSDB and PT over the years, which was a relevant sign of the growing maturity and institutionalisation of the Brazilian political system.[48] Moreover, Brazil, despite vast party fragmentation, had its most consolidated political parties as the major contenders, with little space left for new parties and outsiders[49] and a relatively stable political competition.[50]

[40] In the 1967/1969 Constitution, if a bill or even a constitutional amendment was not approved in due time, it was considered tacitly approved (Article 54, §§ 1, 2).

[41] See ch 6.

[42] See ch 5.

[43] Article 127 of the 1988 Constitution.

[44] Article 77, § 2, of the 1988 Constitution.

[45] Article 77, § 3, of the 1988 Constitution.

[46] Emenda Constitucional n. 16, de 4 de Junho de 1997.

[47] Brazilian Constitutions had until then never authorised re-election for subsequent terms. However, they never prohibited the election of former presidents, governors and mayors, if their terms were not subsequent.

[48] See S Mainwaring, 'Introduction' in S Mainwaring (ed), *Party Systems in Latin America: Institutionalization, Decay, and Collapse* (Cambridge University Press, 2018) 11.

[49] See S Mainwaring, F Bizzarro and TJ Power, 'The Uneven Institutionalization of a Party System: Brazil' in Mainwaring (n 48) 171.

[50] ibid.

It was a comparatively unique scenario. Mainwaring, Power, and Bizzarro, for instance, contended that 'this combination of an exceptionally fragmented party system in congress and the consistent dominance of the same two parties over many (six) presidential elections is rare and perhaps unique in the history of presidential democracies'.[51] Brazil seemed to have then reached a point of no return in its electoral process, in which multiple political parties normally built coalitions with moderate positions both in the Right and the Left. Governance could flow through such channels fairly efficiently, and presidents were able to advance their agenda with high rates of success despite their strong dependence on the discipline of the political coalitions,[52] whose majorities in Congress tend to be more unstable than if they were originally reached among members of one single party.[53]

Nevertheless, such a moderate mood among Brazilians clearly started to show signs of disruption in the 2014 elections, when Aécio Neves (PSDB), who lost the presidential election for Dilma Rousseff (PT) by the small margin of 51.64 per cent v 48.36 per cent in the second round, challenged the electoral result by filing a petition in the Superior Electoral Court demanding an audit of the polls.[54] A distinct paradigm in comparison to previous elections seemed to gain strength at that point in history, and the years ahead would prove that what was once a pretty stable political environment would turn into one of the most radicalised and polarised in Brazilian democracy. The 'coalition presidentialism'[55] would reveal itself to be quite vulnerable once the incentives for stabilising the political system fail.[56] In the middle of her second term in 2016, President Dilma Rousseff would undergo a traumatic impeachment based on flimsy charges – the manipulation of the national budget[57] – though the actual reason was the serious disarrangement of her political coalition in Congress.[58] It was a considerable breakdown of Brazilian 'coalition presidentialism', but not the last nor possibly the most impactful one. It opened, however, Pandora's box in the Brazilian political system, revealing many of its structural dysfunctionalities that Brazil would pay a high price for in the following years.

[51] ibid 174.

[52] See Limongi (n 25).

[53] See S Abranches, 'Presidencialismo de Coalizão: O Dilema Institucional Brasileiro' (1988) 31 *Dados – Revista de Ciências Sociais* 5 (arguing that 'the likelihood of instability and the complexity of the negotiations are much higher [in this system]'). See also VA da Silva, 'Review: Making Brazil Work: Checking the President in a Multiparty System' (2017) 15 *International Journal of Constitutional Law* 519.

[54] See A Matais, V Rosa and B Bulla, 'PSDB de Aécio Neves Pede Auditoria na Votação' (*Estado de S. Paulo*, 30 October 2014) https://politica.estadao.com.br/noticias/geral,psdb-de-aecio-neves-pede-auditoria-na-votacao,1585755.

[55] Abranches (n 53).

[56] See Silva (n 53).

[57] See Benvindo (n 23).

[58] See F Macaulay, 'Dilma Rousseff (2011–2016): A Crisis of Governance and Consensus in Brazil' in V Montecinos (ed), *Women Presidents and Prime Ministers in Post-Transition Democracies* (Palgrave Macmillan, 2017) 123–40.

Beneath such a disruption to 'coalition presidentialism', a growing movement against the political system, and, more specifically, the Worker's Party (PT), which had then been in office for over 13 years (2003–16), gained traction. Largely catalysed by the so-called 'Operation Car Wash', a massive corruption probe involving various politicians, CEOs and CFOs of the biggest Brazilian construction companies and Petrobras, the Brazilian state-owned oil company,[59] protesters thronged the streets of several cities in the country demanding a radical shift in national politics.[60] Those protests, however, also revealed the polarisation in Brazilian society.

President Dilma Rousseff's impeachment was a symptom of the political crisis that had been gaining shape even before her re-election in 2014[61] and a cause for an even sharper destabilisation of the political system, which reflected immediately on the 2018 elections. Jair Bolsonaro, a far-right populist, would take advantage of – and exacerbate even further – the political polarisation with the Worker's Party (PT), and, in contrast to various forecasts,[62] win the election against Fernando Haddad (PT) by 55.13 per cent v 44.87 per cent in the second round. His election was unprecedented: Bolsonaro came from an originally marginal political party (PSL – Social Liberal Party) which had not built coalitions with any other major political party and could not draw on hardly any resources (either public funding or advertising campaign in the media) for pursuing a political campaign with any real chance of success.[63] He brought home a powerful message, though: he was the symbol of anti-politics and, more specifically, embodied the so-called '*antipetismo*' which, amidst President Dilma Rousseff's impeachment and 'Operation Car Wash', was widespread in the country. He was successfully strategic in the use of social media to attack PT's supporters.[64]

A new way of running elections in the context of a highly polarised society would directly shake the basis of Brazil's 'coalition presidentialism'. In his first

[59] See J Watts, 'Operation Car Wash: Is This the Biggest Corruption Scandal in History?' *The Guardian* (1 June 2017) www.theguardian.com/world/2017/jun/01/brazil-operation-car-wash-is-this-the-biggest-corruption-scandal-in-history; PF Lagunes and J Svejnar, *Corruption and the Lava Jato Scandal in Latin America* (Routledge, 2020).

[60] JZ Benvindo, 'The Mass Protests of March and April 2015 in Brazil: A Continuation of June 2013?' (*International Journal of Constitutional Law Blog*, 29 April 2015) www.iconnectblog.com/2015/04/the-mass-protests-of-march-and-april-2015-in-brazil-a-continuation-of-june-2013/.

[61] See Benvindo (n 29); A Saad-Filho, 'Mass Protests under "Left Neoliberalism": Brazil, June-July 2013' (2013) 39 *Critical Sociology* 657.

[62] See, for example, Mainwaring et al (n 49) 195 (arguing that, given the context in 2017, they '[did] not expect radical deinstitutionalization, much less a collapse … even if citizens repudiate the existing parties, they have little choice but to vote for existing organizations because the rules of the game create high barriers to new parties and outsiders'.)

[63] The Brazilian electoral system sets out the distribution of public resources and campaign time in the media based on the number of seats each party has in Congress.

[64] See W Hunter and TJ Power, 'Bolsonaro and Brazil's Illiberal Backlash' (2019) 30 *Journal of Democracy* 68; EPN Meyer, *Constitutional Erosion in Brazil: Progresses and Failures of a Constitutional Project* (Hart Publishing, 2021) 176–98.

year in office, President Bolsonaro kept the same strategy of confronting what he called 'old politics' by linking it with graft and clientelism and appointed mostly non-partisan ministers to his cabinet.[65] Moreover, in a movement that broke the tradition of the military not getting directly involved in politics that had prevailed since the transition to democracy,[66] he appointed approximately 100 members of the armed forces, both retired and active, to high-ranking positions in his administration, among them seven ministers.[67] His confrontational behaviour sparked a backlash in Congress and some of his agenda faced difficulties in obtaining Congress' approval.[68] Once his popularity began to fall and his weakness became more apparent in his second year, Bolsonaro embraced, more than any other president before him, the 'old politics' as a strategy to remain in power and fend off impeachment, so pork-barrel and corruption became a desperate trade-off with Congress to build a political coalition, though a very volatile one.[69] President Bolsonaro might have been successful in disrupting the electoral process as it used to be, but he was not capable of disrupting the core of the Brazilian political system, fundamentally based on 'coalition presidentialism'. His chaotic behaviour and political weakness, nevertheless, laid the groundwork for reshaping such a system – and for much worse.[70]

There is no way to understand the Brazilian political system, with all its positive and negative features, without acknowledging the implications of a presidential regime whose legal design and longstanding practices made it largely dependent on the president's capacity for building firm and disciplined coalitions in Congress. President Dilma Rousseff, for example, had the majority in the beginning of her government, but along with the political crisis that afflicted her government following 'Operation Car Wash', her popularity plummeted, the economy stagnated and the discipline of her political coalition fell significantly.[71] On the other hand, presidents who could keep a well-functioning political coalition, even in circumstances of low popularity,[72] could advance

[65] See B Federowski and C Mandl, 'Brazil's Far-Right Bolsonaro: No Coalition Politics in Picks' (*Reuters*, 9 October 2018) www.reuters.com/article/us-brazil-election/brazils-far-right-bolsonaro-no-coalition-politics-in-cabinet-picks-idUSKCN1MJ27U.

[66] See ch 3.

[67] See M Pimentel, 'O Novo Ministro. E os Militares da Ativa e da Reserva no Governo' (*Nexo*, 14 June 2019) www.nexojornal.com.br/expresso/2019/06/14/O-novo-ministro.-E-os-militares-da-ativa-e-da-reserva-no-governo.

[68] See JZ Benvindo, 'Populism Meets Congressional Backlash in Brazil: Recasting Executive-Legislative Relations?' (*Constitutionnet*, 4 July 2019) http://constitutionnet.org/news/populism-meets-congressional-backlash-brazil-recasting-executive-legislative-relations.

[69] See JZ Benvindo, 'A "Hybrid Coup" in Brazil? Bolsonaro in Desperation Mode' (*International Journal of Constitutional Law Blog*, 25 August 2021) www.iconnectblog.com/2021/08/a-hybrid-coup-in-brazil-bolsonaro-in-desperation-mode/; Benvindo (n 20).

[70] See sections II(C) and III.

[71] See Silva (n 53) 66–68.

[72] President Michel Temer, who took office after President Rousseff's impeachment and whose popularity was well below the average when leaving office (62% rejection according to Datafolha) is an interesting case. See 'Após Reprovação Recorde, Temer Encerra Governo com Rejeição em Queda,

their agendas quite successfully.[73] There is a strong correlation between building strong and disciplined political coalitions and stable and effective government in Brazil.

Brazilian presidentialism can therefore only be called strong if we add the variable of capacity of setting well-coordinated cooperation with Congress. It is a two-way interaction between presidents and Congress, which can be interpreted as nothing other than traditional politics (including clientelism and pork-barrel), but it can also mean a form of check on the executive and power-sharing. Depending on how one interprets this relationship, the conclusions on whether 'coalition presidentialism' is fundamentally flawed and detrimental to the rule of law or is, rather, a system that makes potentially strong presidents more accountable and checked by requiring them to negotiate and share power with other branches, are all up for discussion.

B. A Highly Fragmented and Oligarchical Congress

'Coalition presidentialism' already suggests a complex scenario of continuous negotiation, bargains and potential clashes with Congress, but other properties of the Brazilian political framework add even greater difficulties to this equation. When the Brazilian political scientist Sérgio Abranches coined the concept 'coalition presidentialism' in 1988,[74] he was aware that Brazil features a singular blend of variables that represent the large heterogeneity, ambiguity and contradictions of Brazilian society.[75] By comparing Brazil with the political systems of several other countries, he asserted that 'Brazil is the only country which, aside from combining proportionality, multiparty system, and "imperial presidentialism",[76] organises the executive on the basis of broad coalitions'.[77] His diagnosis would prove correct, as he pointed out that one side effect of such a system, which is largely dependent on both political parties and regional alliances,[78] is the tendency for coalitional governments 'with relatively high rates of governmental fragmentation'.[79]

The National Congress comprised over 20 political parties after the 2018 elections.[80] It became the most fragmented ever in Latin American history and

Mostra Datafolha' (*Folha de S. Paulo*, 27 December 2018) www1.folha.uol.com.br/poder/2018/12/apos-reprovacao-recorde-temer-encerra-governo-com-rejeicao-em-queda.shtml.

[73] See Figueiredo and Limongi (n 37).

[74] See Abranches (n 53).

[75] ibid 32.

[76] ibid 22 ('"imperial presidentialism" means a political system that is based on the independence of powers, if not on the executive's hegemony, and which organises the cabinet as broad coalitions').

[77] ibid 21.

[78] ibid 22.

[79] ibid 32.

[80] See Chamber of Deputies, www.camara.leg.br/Internet/Deputado/bancada.asp; Federal Senate, www25.senado.leg.br/web/senadores/em-exercicio/-/e/por-partido;.

certainly one of the most fragmented worldwide.[81] The reasons for such a fragmentation, which have increased over the years, are many and are intimately connected to constitutional design, longstanding political practices and regional heterogeneity and inequality that are reflected upon the country's federal regime.

Brazil has been a bicameral country at the federal level[82] since its first Constitution of 1824.[83] The National Congress is composed of 513 federal deputies[84] and 81 senators, elected in 27 electoral districts (26 states and the Federal District).[85] There is no artificial electoral district in Brazil, so the correspondence between federal units and electoral districts is perfect at both the state and municipal levels.[86] As a federal country, senators are expected to represent the federal states in Congress, whereas federal deputies are the representatives of the people, though, in practice, both houses follow mostly partisan leaderships.[87] Federalism impacts significantly on the political system, and, although senators are elected through a plurality (first-past-the post) voting system – which favours individualism – it is in the Chamber of Deputies where we can observe the main reasons for such a high level of fragmentation.

States and the Federal District each elect three senators for an eight-year term, alternating one or two senators elected in national elections that take place every four years.[88] In the Chamber of Deputies, where federal deputies are elected for a four-year term, the premise of popular representation is deliberately distorted based on the minimum of eight and the maximum of 70 federal deputies for each federal unit.[89] Therefore, a populous state like São Paulo, with over 46 million inhabitants,[90] elects 70 federal deputies. Acre, a northern state of approximately 900,000 inhabitants (Brazil's third least populated), elects 8 federal deputies.[91] In São Paulo, there is one deputy for approximately 657,000 inhabitants, whereas, in Acre, this proportion is of just 112,500 inhabitants, which means that one vote from Acre corresponds to almost six votes from São Paulo. This so-called malapportionment of the Brazilian political system has been interpreted both as justifiable based on the country's regional inequalities[92] or, on the contrary, as an obstacle to the development of the beneficiary regions.[93]

[81] See Mainwaring et al (n 49) 176.

[82] At the state and municipal levels, the legislatures feature one single chamber.

[83] Article 14 of the 1824 Imperial Constitution.

[84] See Lei Complementar n. 78, de 30 de Dezembro de 1993.

[85] Article 46, §1, of the 1988 Constitution.

[86] See J Nicolau and J Stadler, 'The Brazilian Electoral System' in D de la Fontaine and T Stehnken (eds), *The Political System of Brazil* (Springer, 2016) 105.

[87] See M Arretche, 'Federalism, Bicameralism, and Institutional Change: General Trends and One Case-Study' (2010) 4 *Brazilian Political Science Review* 11; AC Figueiredo and F Limongi, 'Presidential Power, Legislative Organization, and Party Behavior in Brazil' (2000) 32 *Comparative Politics* 151.

[88] Article 46 of the 1988 Constitution.

[89] Article 45, §1, of the 1988 Constitution.

[90] See IBGE Census, https://cidades.ibge.gov.br/brasil/sp/panorama.

[91] ibid.

[92] See Arretche (n 87) 589

[93] See T Hiroi, 'Paradox of Redistribution: Legislative Overrepresentation and Regional Development in Brazil' (2018) 49 *The Journal of Federalism* 642.

Federal deputies (and also state deputies and town council representatives) are elected according to the proportionality method, according to which seats are first distributed based on the total number of votes the party (or, before 2020, the coalition)[94] obtained and only then allocated among the members of the party (or coalition) who achieved the largest number of votes.[95] Therefore, even if a candidate attains alone a larger number of votes, but his or her party does not reach the electoral quota for securing one seat in the Chamber of Deputies, he or she will not be elected. It is worth mentioning, however, that the electoral quota, according to Brazilian law, has a distinct meaning from what is normally understood as electoral threshold, which only since 2018 has Brazil begun to gradually adopt.[96] The electoral quota is estimated by the division of the total number of valid votes by the total number of seats in Congress. Therefore, the number of seats a party will secure in Congress is calculated by dividing the votes that party obtains by the electoral quota. If that quota is not even reached, the party cannot secure any seat in Congress.[97] The electoral threshold, on the other hand, is very unconventional, since it does not prevent parties from securing their seats in Congress but, rather, raises some barriers for public funding and media campaigns, among other constraints.[98]

Along with proportionality, Brazil also adopts open-list in its proportional representation, which means that the party members are ranked in the list based on the number of votes they individually attain in the elections, not on the party's previously elaborated ranking. An open-list proportional representation also has a bearing on party fragmentation, because it tends to foster individualism over party identification. A symptom of such a behaviour is found, for example, in how Brazilians identify themselves with the political parties. Unlike most candidate-centric electoral systems,[99] Brazilians can vote either for the party or the candidate (though the vote will count first for the party and only later for the most voted candidates). Evidence has shown, nevertheless, that about 90 per cent of the electorate vote for individual candidates,[100] which suggests

[94] With the introduction of the Constitutional Amendment n. 97/2017, party coalitions were forbidden for proportional elections from 2020 elections onwards. This change is aimed at reducing party fragmentation. See A Borges, 'Razões da Fragmentação: Coligações e Estratégias Partidárias na Presença de Eleições Majoritárias e Proporcionais Simultâneas' (2019) 62 *Dados – Revistas de Ciências Sociais* 1–37; IB de Souza Neves, 'Fragmentação Partidária e a Cláusula de Desempenho da Emenda Constitucional n. 97/2017: Uma Análise dos Aspectos Ideológicos dos Estatutos Partidários' (2021) 23 *Confluências Revista Interdisciplinar de Sociologia e Direito* 153.

[95] See Article 45 of the 1988 Constitution.

[96] See Emenda Constitucional 97, de 4 de Outubro de 2017; Lei n. 13.487, de 6 de Outubro de 2017; Lei n. 13.488, de 6 de Outubro de 2017.

[97] See Nicolau and Stadler (n 86).

[98] A previous attempt to set up an unconventional electoral threshold (Article 13 of the Law n. 9096/95) was declared unconstitutional by the Supreme Court in 1996 on the grounds that it was detrimental to small parties. See STF, ADI 1351, 1354 (2006).

[99] See DJ Samuels, 'Incentives to Cultivate a Party Vote in Candidate-Centric Electoral Systems: Evidence from Brazil' (1999) 32 *Comparative Political Studies* 488.

[100] See Nicolau and Stadler (n 86) 106.

that party identification is not a solid element of the Brazilian political system. In fact, with the exception of the Worker's Party (PT), which has since the 1980s built up a broad support base, Brazilians have historically had scant identification or loyalty with any political party.[101]

In addition to being largely fragmented and malapportioned, the Brazilian National Congress is also known for electing some influential oligarchical groups, whose clientelist behaviour has long impaired the rule of law in the country. The presence of oligarchical elites in national politics is a common feature in Latin America,[102] and Brazil does not differ from such a pattern.[103] The political system creates incentives to perpetuate entrenched practices that keep benefits for political groups or newcomers who eventually come to power virtually untouched.[104] It is a historical component of Brazilian politics, which is deeply rooted in the authoritarian mindset and inequality as we previously discussed.[105] In a way, Brazil is still plagued by the 'privatisation' of the public sphere – a diagnosis Raymundo Faoro brilliantly portrayed in the late 1950s in his book *Os Donos do Poder* (*The Owners of Power*) by referring to the so-called '*estamentos*'[106] in Brazilian institutions, a phenomenon, by the way, that has come to the attention of prominent scholars worldwide.[107]

'Coalition presidentialism' and a highly fragmented Congress seem to be the perfect context for creating incentives for clientelism, mainly when the oligarchical structure has a significant bearing on how negotiations and bargains take place for governance. It is a widespread feeling among Brazilians that their political system is rotten, and clientelism has been interpreted as the trade-off for any government to advance its agenda. Empirical evidence has also shown that, despite the growing 'popularisation of the political representation'[108]

[101] See Mainwaring (n 48) 165.

[102] See MA Cameron, 'The Return of Oligarchy? Threats to Representative Democracy in Latin America' (2021) 42 *Third World Quarterly* 775; C de la Torre, 'Populism in Latin America' in CR Kaltwasser et al (eds), *The Oxford Handbook of Populism* (Oxford University Press, 2017) 195–213; D Acemoglu and JA Robinson, 'De Facto Political Power and Institutional Persistence' (2006) 96 *American Economic Review* 325.

[103] See F Hagopian, 'The Politics of Oligarchy: The Persistence of Traditional Elites in Contemporary Brazil' (PhD Thesis, Massachusetts Institute of Technology, 1986); R Gay, 'The Even More Difficult Transition from Clientelism to Citizenship: Lessons from Brazil' in P Fernández-Kelly and J Shefner (eds), *Out of the Shadows: Political Action and the Informal Economy in Latin America* (The Pennsylvania State University Press, 2006) 195–218; B Ames, *The Deadlock of Democracy in Brazil* (University of Michigan Press, 2001).

[104] See Acemoglu and Robinson (n 102) 329.

[105] See chs 2 and 3.

[106] See R Faoro, *Os Donos do Poder: A Formação do Patronato Político Brasileiro* (Globo, 2001) 830.

[107] See Hagopian (n 103) 4; JDS Martins, 'Clientelism and Corruption in Contemporary Brazil' in W Little and E Posada-Carbó (eds), *Political Corruption in Europe and Latin America* (Palgrave Macmillan, 1996) 195–218;

[108] LM Rodrigues, *Mudanças na Classe Política Brasileira* (Centro Edelstein de Pesquisas Sociais, 2009) 9.

and the 'gradual process of diversification'[109] in the legislatures, Brazilian politicians still mostly originate from high social and economic strata,[110] and the correlation between the presence of traditional families and the adoption of pork-barrel politics is still high.[111] Newcomers from diverse origins, such as religious groups, security forces and the rural sector as well as bureaucrats and businesspeople have increasingly been elected as congresspeople, instead of those traditionally locally-oriented politicians,[112] but such changes in the politicians' backgrounds have not necessarily reflected on a nationally-oriented agenda, and many newcomers have been 'gradually "socialized" into veteran's campaign tactics'.[113]

Moreover, despite expanding urbanisation and the regional trend in favour of a larger share of female representation in parliament,[114] Brazil is ranked among the countries with the lowest number of congresswomen in the world (132nd among 193 countries by February 2019, according to the Inter-Parliamentary Union[115]), a phenomenon that Kristin N Wylie directly associates with the weak institutionalisation of the party system in Brazil and may help explain the under-representation of other marginalised social groups.[116] It is also worth noticing that the open-list proportional electoral system, which privileges individual success over party identification, and a biased candidate selection by party leaderships, can be largely detrimental to those marginalised groups in politics, especially in a context where inequality at all levels (economic, gender, racial, etc) is high and an authoritarian mindset is still deep-rooted in society.[117] In such a system, even the adoption of quotas, as Brazil has done since 1997,[118] may prove much less effective than expected.[119]

[109] RMD Mucinhato, 'Quem São os Deputados Brasileiros? Um Balanço do Perfil Biográfico de 1986 a 2012' in JÁ Moisés (ed), *O Congresso Nacional, os Partidos Políticos e o Sistema de Integridade: Representação, Participação e Controle Institucional no Brasil Contemporâneo* (Konrad Adenauer Stiftung, 2014) 83.

[110] ibid 82 (showing that, on average, a congressperson in Brazil has a university degree, a considerable estate and had previously worked in well-paid professions).

[111] See Ames (n 103) 271; RCD Oliveira, *Na Teia do Nepotismo: Sociologia Política das Relações de Parentesco e Poder Político no Paraná e no Brasil* (Insight, 2012).

[112] See Ames (n 103) 271.

[113] ibid.

[114] Currently, in Cuba, Bolivia, Mexico, Costa Rica, Nicaragua, Argentina, Ecuador, El Salvador and Peru, women represent at least 30% of congresspeople. Brazil, on the other hand, ties with Paraguay as the country with the lowest female representation in parliament in Latin America. Currently, women represent only 15% of federal deputies and 20% of senators.

[115] 'Women in National Parliaments' (*Inter-Parliamentary Union*, 1 February 2019) http://archive.ipu.org/wmn-e/classif.htm.

[116] See KN Wylie, *Party Institutionalization and Women's Representation in Democratic Brazil* (Cambridge University Press, 2018) 2.

[117] See chs 2 and 3.

[118] According to Law n. 9.504/97, Article 10, §3, ('each party or coalition will fulfil the minimum of 30% and the maximum of 70% for the candidacies of each sex').

[119] See LF Miguel, 'Political Representation and Gender in Brazil Quotas for Women and their Impact' (2008) 27 *Bulletin of Latin American Research* 197; C Araújo and JED Alves, 'Impactos de Indicadores Sociais e do Sistema Eleitoral sobre as Chances das Mulheres nas Eleições e suas

Therefore, the political-economic scenario has indeed changed and Brazil has certainly developed and democratised since the transition to democracy. Nonetheless, the relationship between 'coalition presidentialism' and a fragmented Congress operating through clientelism and pork barrel still plays the cards of Brazilian politics, with detrimental consequences for the rule of law.[120] That said, it does not necessarily follow that the political system is fully dysfunctional and checks and balances are not working at all. As previously mentioned, the risk of falling into simplifications, generalisations and stereotypes is considerable. Sérgio Abranches, for example, acknowledges the various defects of Brazil's political system, especially the way coalitions are illegitimately negotiated and built, but he is emphatic when arguing that the problem is not 'coalition presidentialism' itself, which can legitimately succeed, but other causes that are deep-rooted in Brazilian society and whose origins transcend this system.[121] 'Coalition presidentialism' and the features of the Brazilian political system have, for this reason, provided one of the richest discussions among political scientists in Latin America, and it is no wonder that controversies have long persisted. More interestingly, the recent political events have added further complexity to such a debate. The next section seeks to discuss further the difficulties, controversies, and particularities of this system for the rule of law.

C. Clientelism and 'Coalition Presidentialism': A Necessary Correlation?

The political system in Brazil, with this particular configuration, has been a subject of rich debates, and opinions on its quality for Brazilian democracy and the impacts on the rule of law vary significantly among scholars. Divergent prominent voices have argued that Brazil's political system is either highly dysfunctional with incentives to graft, patronage and a low degree of party institutionalisation, or operates quite efficiently despite its natural flaws. The scenario is currently more confusing because, although the country had gone through years of rather stable governments, the last events were nothing short of critical. They include, for instance, a massive corruption probe reaching several political bigwigs, a presidential impeachment and the election of a far-right president who continuously attacks Brazil's democracy. Interestingly enough, those disagreements, some expressed prior to the recent political developments,

Interações com as Cotas' (2007) 50 *Dados – Revista de Ciências Sociais* 535; Wylie (n 116); K Wylie and P dos Santos, 'A Law on Paper Only: Electoral Rules, Parties, and the Persistent Underrepresentation of Women in Brazilian Legislatures' (2016) 12 *Politics & Gender* 415; PAGD Santos and K Wylie, 'The Representation of Women' in B Ames (ed), *Routledge Handbook of Brazilian Politics* (Routledge, 2019) 57–72.

[120] See S Abranches, *Presidencialismo de Coalizão* (Kindle edn, Companhia das Letras, 2018) position 53.

[121] ibid position 55.

have nowadays become more necessary. What was once argued during the transition to democracy in the 1990s and early 2000s – and whose findings were later challenged by a sequence of rather stable governments – now regains strength and relevance with those recent events. Brazil has indeed changed and its political system may have proven less flawed than first depicted. It does not follow, however, that many of its original dysfunctionalities have disappeared and may even explain why the country has moved backwards in democratic credentials and in compliance with the rule of law over the last few years.

The Brazilian political system has attracted the attention of some leading north-American political scientists. Scott Mainwaring's 'Dilemmas of Multiparty Presidential Democracy: The Case of Brazil' (1992)[122] and *Rethinking the Party Systems in the Third Wave of Democratization: The Case of Brazil* (1999),[123] as well as Barry Ames' *The Deadlock of Democracy in Brazil* (2001),[124] are certainly amongst the most critical and impactful analyses of the Brazilian political regime, and their findings stress some fascinating convergent points. Both explore what lies beneath this system and plays a major role for its malfunctioning, such as its exclusionary behaviour, the control of local political elites and individuals over the national parties[125] and the still pervasive clientelism and pork-barrel.[126]

The main word here is 'gridlock'. Mainwaring says that 'the situation of permanent minority presidentialism easily leads to executive/legislative stalemate resulting in political immobilism',[127] with serious impacts on pursuing a national agenda and high incentives for patronage.[128] Barry Ames, who explores these features in more detail with an impressive set of analytical tools (especially rational choice) and empirical data, also argues that the Brazilian political system, as designed, is doomed to gridlock because of the 'large number of veto players' that hinder the production of 'innovative policies'.[129] Federalism, on the one hand, and patronage and pork-barrel, which are aggravated by an open list proportional representation system, on the other hand, have all shaped the relationship between presidents and Congress,[130] and it is no wonder that incentives

[122] S Mainwaring, 'Dilemmas of Multiparty Presidential Democracy: The Case of Brazil' (1992) 174 Kellog Institute Working Paper, https://kellogg.nd.edu/documents/1409.

[123] S Mainwaring, *Rethinking Party Systems in the Third Wave of Democratization: The Case of Brazil* (Stanford University Press, 1999).

[124] Ames (n 103).

[125] Mainwaring (n 123) 63; Ames (n 103) 17–18.

[126] Ames (n 103) 17–18; Mainwaring (n 123) 13, 39.

[127] Mainwaring (n 123) 2.

[128] ibid 13, 39.

[129] Ames (n 103) 12.

[130] Federalism and the pervasiveness of patronage and pork have been particularly important in shaping institutional choices, and certain historical events have locked Brazil into particular institutional patterns through a series of self-reinforcing processes. See P Pierson, *Politics in Time: History, Institutions, and Social Analysis* (Princeton University Press, 2004) 17–53.

for corruption are also high.[131] The political system is designed to foster fragmentation over coordination, weak parties and particularistic behaviours over 'significant legislation' and policies oriented to the common welfare. Both Mainwaring and Ames conclude that there is indeed a problem of governance,[132] and, in addition to sociological and historical causes, institutional design plays a major role in this respect: 'Brazil's political institutions not only matter a great deal but are at the heart of the nation's crisis of governability.'[133]

Interestingly enough, both authors wrote some of their conclusions after a turning point in Brazilian political science which occurred as a result of Angelina Cheibub Figueiredo's and Fernando Limongi's impressive and influential paper 'Partidos Políticos na Câmara dos Deputados 1989–1994' ('Political Parties in the Chamber of Deputies 1989–1994').[134] Unlike the mainstream literature, Figueiredo and Limongi, who examined 221 roll-call votes from 1988 to 1994 in the Chamber of Deputies, argued that 'the parties present a considerable average cohesion[135] in the period as a whole, much higher than the acceptable one …' and that there is a 'pattern of party coalitions that is consistent with the disposition of parties in an ideological continuum'.[136] Their data showed that party discipline has prevailed over individualism:[137] among the deputies from the biggest seven parties there is a percentage of discipline that is over 80 per cent. 'The plenary is, unquestionably, disciplined'[138] they concluded. In another paper published in 2001, they expanded their analysis to governance. They claim that 'the recent presidential experience in Brazil reveals that Congress is not an institutional veto player to the executive's agenda'.[139] On the contrary, the executive has effectively controlled the legislative agenda: 'under the 1988 Constitution, the executive emerged as the main de jure and de facto legislator', because of its 'constitutionally guaranteed capacity to control the agenda – the timing and the content – of the legislative works'.[140] Based on their view, it would be misleading to conclude that there is a crisis of governance in Brazil.

[131] Ames (n 103) 268.

[132] ibid 222; Mainwaring (n 123) 6.

[133] ibid 292.

[134] F Limongi and AC Fiegueiredo, 'Partidos Políticos na Câmara dos Deputados: 1989–1994' (1995) 38 *Dados – Revista de Ciências Sociais* 497.

[135] According to them, cohesion, measured according to the Rice Index, is significantly high. Based on their analysis of 221 roll-call votes from 1988 to 1994, they concluded that the 'average Rice of each one of the seven big parties was always higher than 70. This means that, for any roll-call vote, one can expect that 85% of the members of any of those big parties will be voting in the same way'. Limongi and Figueiredo (n 134) 506.

[136] ibid 500, 503 (arguing that, in practice, there would be not only party discipline (or cohesion, as they call it) but also predictability in how party members behave based on the recommendations made by party leaders and also on the connection with one of the three ideological blocs they could identify: right, centre, and left-wing blocs).

[137] See AC Figueiredo and F Limongi, *Executivo e Legislativo na Nova Ordem Constitucional* (Editora FGV, 2001) 11.

[138] Limongi and Figueiredo (n 134) 512.

[139] Figueiredo and Limongi (n 137) 9.

[140] ibid 11.

More enthusiastically, Marcus André Melo and Carlos Pereira are also two leading political scientists who advocate that the Brazilian political system is functional and accountable. Their book *Making Brazil Work: Checking the President in a Multiparty System*[141] contrasts with the mainstream literature[142] and reveals a much more positive outlook on the Brazilian system than most scholars have ever had. Their argument is that strong presidents and multiple parties can work well together if there is a 'set of institutionalized and effective checks … in place in order to constrain the president's action'.[143] According to them, strong presidents are needed for a successful coordination of interests with Congress, because presidents with expanded powers own a set of 'tradable coalition goods'[144] that enable negotiations with Congress.[145] Both authors acknowledge that such a system creates incentives for pork-barrel[146] and even graft as a trade-off for approving the presidential agenda, but they also sustain that it also creates 'contestability in the political markets' through strong opposition parties or coalition, which is 'key to prevent the political system from degenerating into dysfunctional clientelism and corruption'.[147]

Moreover – and this is possibly the most innovative part of their analysis – they dedicate various chapters of their book to prove that the network of accountability institutions in Brazil is quite robust and designed for – as the title of their book suggests – 'making Brazil work', such as Congress' high oversight capacities over executive actions and its effectiveness in law-making,[148] the judiciary's strong autonomy,[149] the independent and diversified media,[150] the mechanisms for boosting transparency,[151] independent regulatory agencies,[152] etc. The contrast with the mainstream literature could not be more direct as they emphasise the crucial role of constitutional design for such a positive scenario: 'the new Constitution of 1988 should, therefore, be viewed as the foundational moment or critical junction that defined the political institutions in Brazil and the powers of the political actors. It provided the institutional fertile terrain for political cooperation to take place'.[153]

[141] Melo and Pereira (n 26).
[142] See Gargarella (n 1); Nino (n 1); CS Nino, 'The Debate over Constitutional Reform in Latin America' (1992) 16 *Fordham International Law Journal* 635; JJ Linz and A Valenzuela, *The Failure of Presidential Democracy* (John Hopkins University Press, 1994); S Mainwaring and MS Shugart, *Presidentialism and Democracy in Latin America* (Cambridge University Press, 1997); JJ Linz, 'The Perils of Presidentialism' (1990) 1 *Journal of Democracy* 51.
[143] Melo and Pereira (n 26) 6.
[144] ibid 4.
[145] ibid.
[146] ibid 22.
[147] ibid 10.
[148] ibid.
[149] ibid. See also G Helmke and J Rios-Figueroa, 'Introduction' in G Helmke and J Rios-Figueroa (eds), *Courts in Latin America* (Cambridge University Press, 2011) 1–26.
[150] Melo and Pereira (n 26) 11.
[151] ibid 19.
[152] ibid 97.
[153] ibid 13.

It is symptomatic that the disputes over the main attributes of the Brazilian political system point to such diverse directions, even though they may have more connections than first seen. The studies focusing on the Brazilian political reality[154] some years after the transition to democracy are telling of how intricate it is to bring a narrative that could definitely describe and explain such a changing context. Some more critical and pessimistic arguments needed to be calibrated with important developments over the years and what was largely thought to be a very likely outcome proved much more nuanced. Those who ranked among the optimistic had also reviewed their main theses as the country was enduring a radical shift in its political spectrum, lately culminating in the election of President Bolsonaro.

It is not the purpose of this chapter to explore this endless debate much further. Yet, by placing these distinct perspectives side by side and adding the variable of the political developments that have taken place since they were written, there seems to be a confluence of some consensual points that are relevant to understand why the system has not been in gridlock as portrayed, yet it has borne a high level of dysfunctionality that is also detrimental to governance and the rule of law more broadly. If it has performed better than first expected, it does not follow that the system has reached a high degree of institutionality and that the rule of law has been preserved. There are evident signs that reforms are needed and empirical evidence has shown that, despite the promising signs in some areas (for example, the large network of accountability institutions), the political system has numerous shortcomings (for example, party fragmentation, clientelism, corruption and low representation of minorities).

In any case, it is encouraging to see that Scott Mainwaring was, a few years ago, somehow less critical of Brazil's political system and said that the country was among the 'stable democracies with shortcomings'.[155] An important reason for that lay in a more positive functioning of its political system and a better degree of institutionalisation of Brazil's political parties. In a paper written with Aníbal Pérez-Liñán, Mainwaring argued that Brazil has 'institutionalized party systems that enable citizens to choose among sharp programmatic differences – a potent shield against the rise of antisystem outsiders'.[156] In a more recent chapter, co-written with Timothy J Power and Fernando Bizzarro, he argued that 'along with El Salvador and Panama, Brazil is one of the few Latin American countries that have more institutionalized party systems today than a generation ago'.[157] Yet, criticism is still there. Brazil's party system has indeed

[154] See O Amorim Neto, 'Presidential Cabinets, Electoral Cycles, and Coalition Discipline in Brazil' in S Morgenstern and B Nacif (eds), *Legislative Politics in Latin America* (Cambridge University Press, 2002); TJ Power, *Political Right in Postauthoritarian Brazil: Elites, Institutions, and Democratization* (Penn State Press, 2010).

[155] S Mainwaring and A Pérez-Liñán, 'Cross-Currents in Latin America' (2015) 26 *Journal of Democracy* 120.

[156] ibid.

[157] Mainwaring et al (n 49) 164.

been institutionalised, but in an 'uneven and thin'[158] way. Years of economic stabilisation and socioeconomic advances, new legislation on party discipline and a 'high election-to-election stability of significant contenders in both presidential and lower chamber elections'[159] improved the quality of Brazil's political system, but the high party fragmentation and the still existing volatility in the election of governors were signs for concern.[160] More importantly, the recent corruption scandals that largely affected the Worker's Party (PT), Brazil's most organised party and 'in important ways … a central pillar of the system',[161] would perhaps lead to an inflection point in Brazilian politics. Mainwaring, Power, and Bizzarro could not be more assertive as history would be evidence of their prognosis just a few months later.

On the other hand, Barry Ames' persistent critical view of Brazil's political system serves as a cautionary tale. In his introduction to the *Routledge Handbook of Brazilian Politics*, he associated the recent political crises and corruption scandals with governmental gridlock. According to him, they are consequences of a system that promotes pork and patronage as a path for governance, in a trade-off that has made 'Brazil's democracy [seem] a bit less robust than it did just a few years ago'.[162] The signs of democratic decay are everywhere, such as the reduced support for democracy,[163] the increased negative partisanship, especially against the Worker's Party (PT) (the so-called '*anti-petismo*'), the rise of an authoritarian strand of the Right, and the growing polarisation and intolerance.[164]

The 2018 presidential elections were a turning point in that they profoundly harmed the country's 'coalition presidentialism' as had been operating since the 1990s. Sérgio Abranches, for example, argues that the 2018 general elections may have 'ended the political cycle that organised the Brazilian coalition presidentialism in the last 25 years …'[165] which 'opened a transitional period to a new political cycle and a new conformation of the party system'.[166] The reasons for such a shift, according to him, reside in the low quality of public policies, the disconnection of the parties with society, and – which Bolsonaro's political campaign took advantage of – 'the general contamination of the political system with corporate-party corruption'.[167] Though the empirical data have shown an increase in party institutionalisation and a more stable political system,[168]

[158] ibid.
[159] ibid 171.
[160] ibid.
[161] ibid 166.
[162] Ames (n 103) 11.
[163] See ch 2.
[164] Ames (n 103) 11.
[165] S Abranches, 'Polarizaçao Radicalizada e Ruptura Eleitoral' in S Abranches et al (eds), *Democracia em Risco? 22 Ensaios sobre o Brasil Hoje* (Companhia das Letras, 2019) 7.
[166] ibid 14.
[167] ibid 8.
[168] See Mainwaring (n 48).

the last events have raised the awareness that such institutionalisation is fragile and can be rapidly reversed. They have also helped strengthen the association of this political system with clientelism and corruption, which may confirm those pessimistic analyses that have long pointed out such a feature as ingrained in the Brazilian political system. In a way, the new cycle that Bolsonaro's election inaugurated would function as the disclosure of this system's mostly structural dysfunctionalities.

This is the reason why Bolsonaro's election deeply affects some discussions of the positive and negative features of Brazil's 'coalition presidentialism'. His election was indeed disruptive to the electoral process,[169] but his government would rapidly weaken as his confrontational behaviour with such a system began to charge a high price. As a trade-off for keeping his mandate safe from impeachment, he needed to enhance mechanisms of co-optation in Congress by spreading and increasing pork-barrel, clientelism and corruption. In the end, Bolsonaro would be influenced by the most deleterious features of 'old politics' that he previously had so emphatically attacked, suggesting thereby that the political system is not that easy to beat. However, a weak presidency, by losing its capacity of coordinating conflicting interests in Congress, encourages parochial and individualist agendas, which will struggle to obtain benefits in the costly market of fragmented politics. In the end, there remains nothing but bad governance, locally-oriented rather than nationally-oriented policies, in which centripetal and longstanding forces that have successfully operated inside Brazil's institutions dominate.[170]

Moreover, a weak president lays the groundwork for Congress to strengthen its grip on the national budget, whose grants are distributed according to pragmatic strategies of political survival and co-optation. What is more, particularly during his government, Congress advanced its control over such a distribution by vigorously adopting the so-called 'mandatory budget',[171] which imposes the mandatory execution of parliamentary amendments, and other far less transparent avenues for transferring public resources to lawmakers, such as the so-called 'secret budget', whose grants are unequally distributed among lawmakers in exchange for supporting the government without disclosing details of such operations.[172] Some such operations have since been under scrutiny by the

[169] Abranches (n 165) 7.

[170] See JZ Benvindo, 'The Paradoxical Nature of the "Ways of Moderation" in Brazilian Democracy' (*The International Journal of Constitutional Law Blog*, 13 November 2020) www.iconnectblog.com/2020/11/the-paradoxical-nature-of-the-ways-of-moderation-in-brazilian-democracy/.

[171] See Emenda Constitucional n. 86, de 17 de Março de 2015; Emenda Constitucional n. 100, de 26 de Junho de 2019. See also Santos and Gasparini (n 36).

[172] See 'Bolsonaro's Secret Budget for Parliamentarians Can Be Investigated' (*Prime Time Zone*, 11 May 2021) https://primetimezone.com/world/bolsonaros-secret-budget-for-parliamentarians-can-be-investigated/; B Rey, 'Understanding Bolsonaro's "Secret Budget" Scandal (*The Brazilian Report*, 17 May 2021) https://brazilian.report/power/2021/05/17/bolsonaro-secret-budget-scandal/. The newspaper *Estado de S. Paulo* published a series or reports on the 'secret budget' at: https://politica.estadao.com.br/noticias/geral,leia-todas-as-reportagens-sobre-o-orcamento-secreto,70003719972.

Federal Audit Court (*Tribunal de Contas da União*) and the Supreme Court,[173] but, until a decision is effectively made against such a practice, lawmakers and the government have largely adopted them as a means of co-optation. Even with such resources, however, gridlock, as some previous analyses point out, has become more frequent, while the government saw many of its legal proposals and *Medidas Provisórias*[174] being ultimately struck down in Congress.[175]

The upshot is that, due to increasing political fragmentation and polarisation, a weak and disruptive presidency and a Congress eager for resources and power, Brazil's 'coalition presidentialism' is no longer exactly what those previous discussions depicted. The relationship between the executive and parliament has become far less coordinated, so party discipline and the executive dominance over legislation[176] have decreased significantly, while the costs of political bargains have become notably higher. 'Coalition presidentialism' is therefore heading toward a new design and function, which features Congress as a more prominent player. As such, not only has it raised the costs of co-optation, which has negatively impacted governance and a national agenda, but also Congress itself could advance some policies at the national level despite such a disruptive government.[177] In the case of a would-be autocrat such as Bolsonaro, this may have paradoxically helped protect democracy, while also lowering its quality as it has prompted clientelism, pork-barrel, and corruption.[178] This may help explain why Brazil's democracy and rule of law has historically been a glass half full and a glass half empty.[179]

III. A RESHAPED 'COALITION PRESIDENTIALISM'

If the defects of 'coalition presidentialism' are now more explicit than ever, it does not follow that the institutional achievements related to the Brazilian

[173] STF, ADPF 850, 851. The Supreme Court had first suspended such operations, but later authorised them on the condition that Congress adopted transparency measures, which have since not been effectively implemented. See B Pires and A Shaudlers, 'Orçamento Secreto: Parlamentares Ignoram Determinação do STF por Transparência a Emendas' (*Estado de S. Paulo*, 5 February 2022); B Pires, 'TCU Diz que Orçamento Secreto Trouxe "Perplexidades", Mas Aprova Contas do Governo' (*Estado de S. Paulo*, 30 June 2021) https://politica.estadao.com.br/noticias/geral,tcu-diz-que-orcamento-secreto-trouxe-perplexidades-mas-aprova-contas-do-governo,70003764554.

[174] See n 34.

[175] See D Guilino and A Mendes, 'Bolsonaro Edita Mais MPs que Outros Presidentes, Mas Taxa de Aprovação É Menor' (*O Globo*, 26 December 2020) https://oglobo.globo.com/politica/bolsonaro-edita-mais-mps-que-outros-presidentes-mas-taxa-de-aprovacao-menor-24812510.

[176] See Figueiredo and Limongi (n 87) 163 (arguing that, in 2000, the 'level of executive dominance over legislation resembles that found in parliamentary regimes').

[177] Some important examples were the emergency basic income during the COVID-19 crisis and the pension reform, both approved according to Congress's formulations. See A Coelho, 'Brazil: The National Senate Approves Emergency Basic Income' (*BasicIncome*, 7 April 2020) https://basicincome.org/news/2020/04/brazil-the-national-senate-approves-emergency-basic-income/.

[178] See Benvindo (n 170); Benvindo (n 20).

[179] ibid.

political system should be ignored. Brazil's 'coalition presidentialism' could perform quite efficiently up until some years ago, at least according to Figueiredo and Limongi's and Melo and Pereira's arguments above, mostly because there was a high dependence of the legislative power on presidential incentives,[180] from cabinet offices to pork-barrel politics, in a negotiation that can be legitimate in most cases, but which can also lead to patronage and graft. Functional political regimes normally have the executive and legislative powers working in a symbiotic manner, and the executive is expected to have strong control over the legislative agenda,[181] but they also provide a set of tools to make such negotiations more transparent and accountable. The question that is now clearly on the table is whether such a system, which could preserve some governability and stability for many years, did so by empowering or constraining the capacity of Congress to act as a powerful check on the executive power. It is also whether such a system can provide a set of tools that makes it more prone to operating according to the rule of law.

These questions are not easy to answer, especially now that Brazil's 'coalition presidentialism' seems to be going through a transitional moment, and the first signs are pointing toward a more clientelist Congress, not a more accountable one. On the other hand, the system could prove fairly resilient against a would-be autocrat such as Bolsonaro, despite all the means of co-optation he so fiercely embraced. Fernando Limongi, who continuously expresses his concern with the sequence of political events that struck the country and the risk of an authoritarian regression – 'this genie that is leaving the bottle you do not put it back'[182] – argued that the Brazilian political system is clearly not compatible with a president who governs chaotically.[183] The strategy of continuously confronting the institutions does not play well in a system that is largely dependent on politics and on the ability of the executive to negotiate with Congress, especially in such a fragmentary party configuration.[184] Even if, in the end, Bolsonaro reverted to the most blatant 'old politics', he was never regarded as a normal president, but as an 'incidental' one, whose coalitions in Congress were improvised and precarious,[185] and an 'unlikely'[186] one, whose election was only possible due to a set of critical junctures that would not be easily repeated in the future.

[180] See Figueiredo and Limongi (n 137) 41.

[181] See AC Figueiredo and F Limongi, 'Constitutional Change, Legislative Performance and Institutional Consolidation' (2000) Special Issue No. 1 *Brazilian Review of Social Sciences* 1.

[182] C Jiménez, 'Limongi: "Líderes Responsáveis Não Têm o Direito de se Isentar da Insanidade de Bolsonaro"' (*El País*, 11 October 2018) https://brasil.elpais.com/brasil/2018/10/10/politica/1539187153_593055.html.

[183] F Betim, 'Bolsonaro Não Tem Inteligência Política, ou a Estratégia É Confrontar as Instituições?' (*El País*, 18 May 2019) https://brasil.elpais.com/brasil/2019/05/16/politica/1557961056_660775.html.

[184] See Benvindo (n 20).

[185] S Abranches, 'Governantes Incidentais' (*Sérgio Abranches*, 29 July 2019) https://sergioabranches.com.br/politica/336-governantes-incidentais.

[186] MHT de Almeida and FH Guarnieri, 'The Unlikely President' (2020) 1 *Revista Euro Latinoamericana de Análises Social y Político* 139.

Moreover, there are some positive signs that will perhaps make this system more functional. Mechanisms to make it less fragmentary have been approved in Congress, such as the prohibition of electoral coalitions and an electoral threshold for political parties,[187] meaning one of the main reasons for it being derailed may weaken. In addition, some signs that have led to the disruption of the political system seem to be fading away: the municipal elections in 2020, for instance, were much more conventional, with traditional parties regaining some ground even if leaning to the Right[188] (but not far-right, which was interpreted as a Bolsonaro defeat),[189] and civil society has increasingly shown its deep rejection of a government that has continuously attacked the country's institutions and whose series of mismanagements have impoverished Brazilians.[190]

It looks increasingly likely that the political wave and set of junctures that led to the rise of such an 'incidental' and 'unlikely' president are going away, so the political system may be able to recover from such turbulent years, even though some of its major dysfunctionalities – notably, clientelism, fragmentation, polarisation, lack of transparency and accountability, lack of representation of minorities – are still very present and, in some respects, became worse. What lies ahead is whether the Brazilian political system, after such disruptive years, will learn from its recent past and challenge some of its longstanding wrongs that have so directly contributed to such a scenario. As with many of the features of Brazilian constitutionalism, its political system cannot simply sweep this recent past under the carpet. Yet, as has been the rule in Brazilian constitutionalism, preservation, accommodation and oblivion tend to prevail in the end. In a way, the rule of law in Brazil has been continuously challenged by that other rule – the political system just makes it more visible than any other Brazilian institution.

[187] See n 94.

[188] See 'Para Analistas, Eleitor Priorizou Política Tradicional em 2020' (*Senado Notícias*, 16 November 2020) www12.senado.leg.br/noticias/materias/2020/11/16/para-analistas-eleitor-priorizou-politica-tradicional-em-2020.

[189] BH Bradlow, 'Brazilians Firmly Rejected Many Local Candidates their President Had Backed' (*The Washington Post*, 9 December 2020) www.washingtonpost.com/politics/2020/12/09/brazilians-firmly-rejected-many-local-candidates-their-president-had-backed/.

[190] See Benvindo (n 69); 'Quaest/Genial: Rejeição Popular ao Governo Bolsonaro Cresce Cinco Pontos e Vai a 53%' (*Carta Capital*, 5 October 2021) www.cartacapital.com.br/cartaexpressa/quaest-genial-rejeicao-popular-ao-governo-bolsonaro-cresce-cinco-pontos-e-vai-a-53/.

5

The Rule of Law and Brazil's Politicised Judicial System

I. INTRODUCTION: THE JUDICIARY IN A COUNTRY IN CRISIS

IT WOULD NOT be an overstatement to argue that the Brazilian judiciary is behind the most recent critical events in Brazil's political landscape, interfering directly in the pace and intensity of the crisis that led to the impeachment of a President (Dilma Rousseff), the imprisonment of a former President (Lula da Silva) and the rise of a far-right President (Jair Bolsonaro), severely undermining the political electoral stability that had prevailed in the country for over 25 years.[1] It is also the judiciary that possibly provided one of the world's most impactful cases of lawfare[2] in the so-called 'Operation Car Wash' that implicated former President Lula da Silva, who was not only arrested but also banned from running in the 2018 presidential elections.[3] This event ended up significantly contributing to Jair Bolsonaro's victory.[4] 'Operation Car Wash', presumably the most impactful and overarching case of white-collar crime in Latin America's history, was nothing short of a cataclysm: the effects on the political, economic, and legal realm were staggering and incalculable.[5] It revealed how corruption operates through various strategies to defraud public contracts, and important figures in the political and business sectors were

[1] See S Abranches, *Presidencialismo de Coalizão* (Companhia das Letras 2018). See also ch 4.

[2] See JT Esteves and C Cosentino, 'The Conviction of Former President Lula as the Maximum Expression of the Exercise of Lawfare' in C Proner et al (eds), *Comments on a Notorious Verdict: The Trial of Lula* (CLACSO, 2018) 117–21.

[3] D Phillips, 'Brazilian Court Bars Lula from Presidential Election' *The Guardian* (1 September 2018) www.theguardian.com/world/2018/sep/01/brazilian-court-bars-lula-from-presidential-election.

[4] Until his arrest, Lula was the frontrunner in the 2018 elections. However, with his arrest, Jair Bolsonaro became the frontrunner. See '39% Votariam em Lula; Sem Petista, Bolsonaro Lidera Disputa Presidencial' (*Datafolha*, 22 August 2018) https://datafolha.folha.uol.com.br/eleicoes/2018/08/1979559-39-votariam-em-lula-sem-petista-bolsonaro-lidera-disputa-presidencial.shtml.

[5] See PF Lagunes and J Svejnar, *Corruption and the Lava Jato Scandal in Latin America* (Routledge, 2020); E Valarini and M Pohlmann, 'Organizational Crime and Corruption in Brazil: A Case Study of the "Operation Carwash" Court Records' (2019) 59 *International Journal of Law, Crime and Justice* 100340; AS Katz, 'Making Brazil Work? Brazilian Coalitional Presidentialism at 30 and Its Post-Lava Jato Prospects' (2018) 5 *Revista de Investigações Constitucionais* 77. See also ch 6.

incriminated and arrested. Such positive outcomes notwithstanding, 'Operation Car Wash' became an example of judicial corruption. The deep violations of basic constitutional guarantees for political and personal gains, as later acknowledged by the Supreme Court in reference to judge Sérgio Moro and the federal prosecutors in the cases involving former President Lula da Silva,[6] turned that operation upside down. It also revealed how far the Brazilian judiciary was, from the lowest to the highest courts, overwhelmed by sheer politics.

These recent events are the culmination of years in which the Brazilian judiciary has become much stronger but still features low levels of transparency and accountability. They are evidence of how unchecked powers and political calculations can severely undermine political institutions which, despite their ups and downs, had until then functioned with relative stability.[7] History may take time to shrug off the variables that led to the political crisis that resulted in the election of the far-right President Jair Bolsonaro in 2018, but it is very likely that, were it not for 'Operation Car Wash', the current political landscape would look less gloomy. Such a judicial impact on the political landscape is nowhere to be found in Brazilian history, but it is striking that it took place exactly when Brazil was going through its longest and most fruitful experience of democratic life. There is no other institution that represents the paradoxical nature of the democratisation process in Brazil: the judiciary is the branch of power that more visibly merges the country's past with its future in the development of the rule of law.

The rising of the Brazilian judiciary, and particularly the Brazilian Federal Supreme Court (henceforth STF), in the democratisation process is nothing short of impressive. It was a very restrained judiciary during the civilian-military dictatorship (1964–85), when the STF was 'threatened, diluted, and, five years after having legitimised the coup, violated by the expulsion of three of its members'.[8] The judiciary also validated a series of human rights violations and did not directly challenge many of the authoritarian acts[9] despite some judicial resistance.[10] There was some autonomy, but, paradoxically, such autonomy also translated itself into complacent behaviour toward the dictatorship,[11] as if not challenging it was the best strategy to avoid attacks on its status quo.

[6] See Proner et al (n 2); N Bourcier and G Estrada, '"Lava Jato", the Brazilian Trap' (*Le Monde*, 11 April 2021) www.lemonde.fr/international/article/2021/04/11/lava-jato-the-brazilian-trap_6076361_3210.html.

[7] See ch 4.

[8] See F Recondo, *Tanques e Togas: O STF e a Ditadura Militar* (epub edn, Companhia das Letras, 2018) Introduction, para 1.

[9] VD Schinke and RS Castro, 'O Relatório da Comissão Nacional da Verdade: O Capítulo sobre a Atuaçao do Poder Judiciário durante a Ditadura' (2017) 18 *Espaço Jurídico Journal of Law* 143.

[10] See MJ Osiel, 'Dialogue with Dictators: Judicial Resistance in Argentina and Brazil' (1995) 20 *Law & Social Inquiry* 481.

[11] See HF Câmara (2017), 'STF na Ditadura Militar Brasileira: Um Tribunal Adaptável?' (PhD Thesis, Federal University of Paraná 2017) 240.

During the democratic transition, notably during the Constituent Assembly (1987–88), the judiciary was one of the major beneficiaries by expanding its powers through enhanced administrative, functional and budgetary autonomy,[12] and it has been since qualified as one of the most autonomous in Latin America.[13] The judiciary has undergone an intense transformation in its institutional capacities and become a key player in the Brazilian legal and political landscapes. Most strikingly, the STF has transitioned from a very restrained, bureaucratic and formalistic court in the beginning of the new democratic order – a legacy of the authoritarian years[14] – into possibly one of the world's most intervenient courts in political affairs, with a significant impact on Brazilian democracy. Interestingly, the Court's behaviour of intervening in political affairs is fostered by the very political system, in an 'institutional mutualism' that generates benefits both for the Court and the political parties.[15] The STF has therefore not exactly challenged the political class, but strategically interacted with it in a 'symbiotic' manner: the Court sees its political clout increase, whereas the political class finds an avenue to defend its interests outside the traditional political realm.[16]

Strong and independent courts in a democracy tend, at least in theory, to imply a more robust system of checks and balances and a more consistent web of protection of constitutional rights. In Brazil, the judiciary has surely improved its capacities of constraining the other branches of power, and the STF has been empirically portrayed as one of Latin America's most effective courts in settling interbranch disputes[17] and possibly 'one of the most powerful courts in the world'.[18] It has also been amongst the most stable courts in the region over history, which helps explain its resilience against executive control and its higher autonomy.[19] However, it lags behind some of its Latin American counterparts

[12] See A Koerner and LBD Freitas, 'O Supremo na Constituinte e a Constituinte no Supremo' (2013) 88 *Lua Nova* 145 (arguing that 'the Constituent Assembly appeared as an opportunity to promote the strengthening of the judiciary ...').

[13] See G Helmke and J Rios-Figueroa, 'Introduction' in G Helmke and J Rios-Figueroa (eds), *Courts in Latin America* (Cambridge University Press, 2011) 19; S Voigt, J Gutmann and LP Feld, 'Economic Growth and Judicial Independence, A Dozen Years On: Cross-Country Evidence Using an Updated Set of Indicators' (2015) 38 *European Journal of Political Economy* 197 (showing that Brazil scores quite high in de jure and, more importantly, de facto judicial independence (0.712 and 0.825 out of 1.0, respectively).

[14] OV Vieira, Supremo Tribunal Federal: Jurisprudência Política (Revista dos Tribunais, 2002).

[15] See D Bogéa, *Partidos Políticos e STF: Decifrando a Simbiose Institucional* (Appris, 2021) 172.

[16] ibid 27.

[17] See D Kapiszewski, 'Power Broker, Policy Maker, or Rights Protector? The Brazilian Supremo Tribunal Federal in Transition' in G Helmke and J Rios-Figueroa (eds), *Courts in Latin America* (Cambridge University Press, 2011) 154.

[18] KS Rosenn, 'Recent Important Decisions by the Brazilian Supreme Court' (2013) 45 *University of Miami Inter-American Law Review* 298.

[19] See A Pérez-Liñan and A Castagnola, 'Presidential Control of High Courts in Latin America: A Long-Term View (1904–2006)' (2009) 1 *Journal of Politis in Latin America* 108 (pointing out that 'Court in Brazil, Costa Rica, and Chile have been at least as stable as the U.S. Supreme Courts' from 1904–2006).

when it comes to enforcing social and economic rights, and even individual rights only began to gain some importance by the mid-2000s.[20] Overall, the judiciary has been a major player in Brazil's democracy, and its increased capacities have been portrayed as one of the most significant improvements in Brazil's web of accountability. However, this is only one side of the story.

A democratic environment provides courts with the tools to more consistently check the other branches of power and to enforce constitutional rights. The Brazilian judiciary thus has the potential to more seriously engage in fostering the rule of law, but, for this purpose, it needs to attack some of its cross-institutional deficiencies, legal design flaws and longstanding and entrenched practices. It is the paradox of a rather strong and independent judiciary that, by exerting a power intimately mediated by political calculations, has seen its own strength and independence being seriously questioned. The STF in particular has certainly provided some landmark decisions in numerous subjects and has exerted an important role in enforcing the Constitution and protecting democracy, but it has also behaved very controversially in other political matters. More importantly, the more the judiciary has let sheer politics be translated into the language of law, the less it has been regarded as a respectful and independent power. Recent events, such as those of 'Operation Car Wash', are just the culmination of a long and bumpy process.

This chapter explores the rising influence of the judiciary and the Supreme Court over political life and how such an influence has affected its role of protecting constitutionalism and fostering the rule of law. The first section is aimed at examining the judiciary's structure and discussing its independence and increasing 'symbiosis'[21] with the political system. The second section is aimed at stressing how it has behaved as a powerful corporation with its privileges and benefits virtually untouched. The chapter ends by analysing the judicial criminal system, which has proven very inefficient and indeed strengthened violence (eg, the shocking levels of police killings) amid the still high rates of social inequality in the country.

II. THE JUDICIARY'S CONSTITUTIONAL DESIGN

A. The Federal, State and Specialised Courts

The judicial system in Brazil does not seem, in principle, very distinct from other countries. As a federation, Brazil features both federal and state courts,

[20] See Kapiszewski (n 17); DW Arguelhes, 'Poder Não É Querer: Preferências Restritivas e Redesenho Institucional no Supremo Tribunal Federal Pós-Democratização' (2014) 25 *Universitas Jus* 25; AA Costa and JZ Benvindo, 'A Quem Interessa o Controle Concentrado de Constitucionalidade? O Descompasso entre Teoria e Prática na Defesa dos Direitos Fundamenetais' (2014) *University of Brasília Working Paper*, https://papers.ssrn.com/sol3/papers.cfm?abstract_id=2509541.

[21] See Bogéa (n 15).

but also some specialised courts in areas such as electoral, labour and military law. There are no administrative courts in Brazil, and administrative cases can be filed in state or federal courts depending on whether it is a state or federal matter or whether a state (or state institutions) or the Union (or federal institutions) is involved.[22] State courts deal with most cases, representing 64.5 per cent of all first instance courts in the country,[23] and are spread across every one of the 26 states and the Federal District. Cases judged by first instance state judges can reach State Appellate Courts (*Tribunais de Justiça*). Their jurisdiction is residual, reaching every case that is not deemed federal[24] or specialised (labour, electoral or military law). The federal judicial system consists of first instance federal courts in every state and the Federal District and six Federal Regional Courts (*Tribunais Regionais Federais*), each with jurisdiction over a variable number of states. At the highest level lie the superior courts, such as the Superior Court of Justice (STJ), which decides cases both from State Appellate Courts and Federal Regional Courts with the goal of setting precedents nationwide in basically all cases involving statutory interpretation that are not deemed constitutional or specialised. The specialised jurisdiction also features superior courts: the Superior Labour Court (TST), the Superior Electoral Court (TSE) and the Superior Military Court (STM). At the apex of the judicial system lies the Supreme Federal Court (*Supremo Tribunal Federal* (STF)), which is responsible for consolidating precedents on constitutional matters and, more broadly, to act as the 'guardian of the Constitution'.[25]

The Superior Court of Justice (STJ) is composed of 33 justices appointed by the President of the Republic and nominated after the Senate's approval. The presidential discretion in such an appointment is, however, limited. All justices must originate from the Federal Regional Courts (1/3), State Appellate Courts (1/3), or be chosen, in equal parts, among lawyers or members of the Federal, State or Federal District Public Ministries (1/3).[26] The STJ then provides a list of three names, approved after internal voting, to be submitted to the president.[27] The STJ can be reached through the so-called 'special appeal' (*recurso especial*) filed in State Appellate Courts or Federal Regional Courts 'when the decision appealed: a) is contrary to a treaty or a federal law, or denies it effectiveness; b) considers valid an act of a local government challenged in the light of a federal law; c) confers upon a federal law an interpretation different from that which has been conferred upon it by another court'.[28] It also has original jurisdiction, among other matters, over common crimes and *habeas corpus* involving state

[22] See Article 109 of the 1988 Constitution.
[23] *Justiça em Números 2020* (Conselho Nacional de Justiça, 2020) 31.
[24] Article 109 of the 1988 Constitution.
[25] For further details on Brazil's judiciary framework, see VA da Silva, *The Constitution of Brazil: A Contextual Analysis* (Hart Publishing, 2019) ch 4.
[26] Article 104 of the 1988 Constitution.
[27] Article 94 of the 1988 Constitution.
[28] Article 105, III, of the 1988 Constitution.

governors and some other authorities, *writs of mandamus* and *habeas data* against an act of a state minister, and conflicts of jurisdiction between courts (except those in which superior courts are involved).[29] It is also responsible for 'the homologation of foreign courts decisions and the granting of exequatur to letters rogatory'.[30]

Among the specialised courts, the most similar to the STJ is the Superior Labour Court (TST), which is composed of 27 justices also appointed by the President of the Republic and nominated after approval by the Senate. Also, here the presidential discretion is limited: all justices must be chosen among judges from the Regional Labour Courts (4/5) or among lawyers or members of the Labour Public Ministry (1/5). The TST then provides a list of three names, approved after internal voting, to be submitted to the president. Such a specialised Court decides cases that address labour conflicts, the right to strike and collective negotiations.[31] It does not reach, however, public servants hired through administrative law, whose cases are either decided by state or federal courts. The TST, as the apex labour court, harmonises precedents in labour law nationwide.

The specialised electoral judicial system oversees all elections for municipalities, states and the Union. Its structure is rather distinct from the other spheres of the judiciary, since its members exert a mandate for a limited term. The Superior Electoral Court (TSE) is composed of members of other courts and lawyers, who exert their mandate for a two-year term, which can be renewed once.[32] Five of its seven members are elected, by secret vote, among three justices of the Supreme Court (STF) and two justices of the Superior Court of Justice (STJ). The other two justices are appointed by the president among lawyers of 'notable juridical learning and good moral repute', who are then nominated by the STF.[33] The TSE harmonises precedents in electoral law nationwide and is the original jurisdiction for cases involving the election of the president and vice-president of the Republic as well as the registration and nullification of political parties. At the state level, the Regional Electoral Courts are composed of seven judges with a temporary mandate and have authority over cases of candidates for Governor and Vice-Governor as well as members of the National Congress elected in that state and the state Legislative Assemblies. They also judge appeals from decisions made by first instance judges or electoral boards.[34]

The specialised military judicial system is the least known among all spheres of the Brazilian judiciary and is an authoritarian legacy. The 1988 Constitution left it practically untouched despite the years of military rule and the atrocities

[29] Article 105, I, of the 1988 Constitution.
[30] Article 106, I, i, of the 1988 Constitution.
[31] Article 114 of the 1988 Constitution.
[32] Article 121 of the 1988 Constitution.
[33] Article 119 of the 1988 Constitution.
[34] Articles 120, 121 of the 1988 Constitution.

committed by the military during the civilian-military dictatorship (1964–85).[35] Its structure differs from the pattern of the Brazilian judiciary. The Superior Military Court (STM), whose origins date back to 1808 – the oldest superior court in the country[36] – is part of the federal system and is composed of 10 general-officers from the highest ranks of the three forces and five civilian judges, who enjoy life tenure and are appointed by the President of the Republic and nominated after the Senate's approval. However, unlike the other superior courts, it behaves basically as an appellate court since there are no second instance courts at the federal level.[37] More curious still, there is a parallel military judicial system at the state level, whose first instance is a military court, but the second instance can be either a Military Appellate Court, in states where more than 20,000 militaries are based, or the State Appellate Court (*Tribunal de Justiça*), where such a figure is not reached. Moreover, appeals from the state military judicial system reach the STJ, not the STM. The military judicial system, either at the federal or state level, addresses military crimes, but the 1988 Constitution leaves this definition to ordinary legislation,[38] such as the Military Criminal Code,[39] drafted during the civilian-military dictatorship (1964–85). This framework provides vast incentives for corporatist behaviour and protection of wrongdoings, which is aggravated by the fact that the military in Brazil encompasses members of the Armed Forces, at the federal level, and also the military police, at the state level.

The hierarchical configuration of Brazil's judiciary looks rather intuitive, but how it operates is not. For example, a case decided by a State Appellate Court or Federal Regional Court will very likely reach both the STJ and the STF, the first focusing on statutory provisions and the latter on the Constitution. It could even happen that, from a decision by the STJ, the case can be appealed to the STF based on a constitutional controversy from that decision. In the end, it could be said that a case could be decided by four instances, even though the access to both the STJ and STF is more restrictive. At the labour courts, a case, after being decided by first and second instance courts, can reach the TST, whose decision by one of its chambers can be appealed to one of the Court's higher chambers (called *Seções*) and, then, to the STF, if there is a constitutional matter under discussion. This configuration could imply that, in the end, five distinct judicial bodies examined the case.

Based only on these examples, it could already be anticipated that Brazil's judicial design is rather confusing, bureaucratic and slow, and such

[35] See J Zaverucha, 'Relações Civil-Militares: O Legado Autoritário da Constituição Brasileira de 1988' in E Teles and V Safatle (eds), *O Que Resta da Ditadura: A Exceção Brasileira* (Boitempo, 2010) 45.

[36] M Kornis and E Junqueira, 'Superior Tribunal Militar (STM)' (*FGV CPDOC*) www.fgv.br/cpdoc/acervo/dicionarios/verbete-tematico/superior-tribunal-militar-stm.

[37] See Article 6, Lei n. 8.457, de 4 de Setembro de 1992.

[38] Article 124 of the 1988 Constitution.

[39] Decreto-Lei n. 1001, de 21 de Outubro de 1969.

dysfunctionalities can naturally be subverted in favour of lawyers' and judges' own interests and strategies. Even though there have been incremental constraints on appeals to superior courts and the STF, the reality is that judges have to deal with a caseload that challenges quality and transforms their chambers into production-oriented organisations.

B. The Federal Supreme Court

The Federal Supreme Court (STF), created in 1890[40] just a few months after Brazil's transition to a republic, is the apex court of the Brazilian judicial system and is routinely in the spotlight. However, before the transition to democracy in 1985 and some structural and behavioural changes that took place with the new constitutional order, the Court would not appear in Brazil's major historical developments, unlike presidents and Congress. It has been – possibly also due to this rather restrained behaviour – the most stable institution throughout the country's history, showing a level of stability that is considerable by Latin America standards.[41] It has also presumably been the most successful branch in preserving its prerogatives, corporatist interests and structure over history. There were naturally some moments of crisis, such as during the civilian-military dictatorship (1964–85),[42] when three justices were expelled and two other retired in protest. The Court was then packed by increasing the number of justices from 11 to 16,[43] and it could not review typical authoritarian legislation, such as the Institutional Acts[44] and *habeas corpus* for political crimes.[45] It was also the period when its independence was visibly undermined.[46] Still, all in all, the Court has been mostly preserved.

During the transition to democracy, this high capacity of self-preservation would show its cards again: the STF's justices intensively lobbied to keep the Court's same structure and composition of the previous years, while expanding its powers even further in the new constitutional order. More than before, the STF would present itself as the 'guardian of the Constitution': while its authority over statutory interpretation was transferred to the STJ, new constitutional tools, such as a better structured abstract system of judicial review, were added to its repertoire. However, the STF remained as the apex Court of the traditional

[40] Article 54, Decreto n. 510, de 22 de Junho de 1890.

[41] See Pérez-Liñán and Castagnola (n 19) 96.

[42] See Câmara (n 11) 131–41.

[43] Article 6, Ato Institucional n. 2. de 27 de Outubro de 1965.

[44] The so-called *Atos Institucionais (Institutional Acts)* were a sort of authoritarian and repressive acts by the executive during the civilian-military dictatorship (1964–85). See CW Guerchon, 'Institutional Acts of the Brazilian Government' (1971) 1 *International Journal of Politics* 258.

[45] See Article 10, Ato Institucional n. 5, de 13 de Dezembro de 1968.

[46] See ADZD Carvalho, 'Entre o Dever da Toga e o Apoio à Farda: Independêncica Judicial e Imparcialdiade no STF durante o Regime Militar' (2017) 32 *Revista Brasileira de Ciências Sociais* 1.

and concrete system of judicial review, according to which appeals from the lower courts can reach the STF through the so-called extraordinary appeal (*recurso extraordinário*) if they feature a constitutional matter in dispute. It is also the Court originally responsible for deciding some conflicts among the units of the federation and criminal cases involving high-ranking authorities, such as members of Congress and the president.

Interestingly enough, Brazil could have left the Constituent Assembly with a distinctly designed constitutional court. A proposal for the creation of a constitutional court with exclusive authority over constitutional matters composed of justices with a limited term in office gathered large support especially from left-wing parties, but it did not prevail in the end.[47] Moreover, other proposals that aimed to enfranchise any citizen to file an abstract action of unconstitutionality (ADI), the major action in the abstract system of judicial review, lost to other proposals that kept such an avenue far more restrictive.[48] The STF behaved as a key player in the Constituent Assembly to preserve its own interests, while also working as a shield to block some constitutional innovations,[49] in a clear association with conservative politicians and movements[50] that saw themselves threatened by that democratic momentum.[51] As a court from the past in the new democratic order, which managed to 'rapidly transform the [constitutional] text into something much closer to the spirit of the previous constitutional order',[52] it seldom challenged the government[53] and, as Marcos Faro de Castro puts it, 'largely refrained from resorting to available remedies in order to expand its power by the cumulative articulation of substantive doctrine in case law'.[54] Many of its decisions at that time adopted a very formalist and self-restrained

[47] See Koerner and Freitas (n 12) 162–64.

[48] ibid 165.

[49] See, for instance, how the STF blocked the *Mandado de Injunção*, a new tool aimed at filling legislative gaps. See JZ Benvindo and F Acunha, 'Tempos na Atuação da Jurisdição Constitucional: A Interpretação Inicial do STF a respeito do Mandado de Injunção e as Oportunidades que Não Voltam' in A Martins, CR Roesler and C Paixão (eds), *Os Tempos do Direito: Diacronias, Crise e Historicidade* (Max Limonad, 2020) 93–108; DW Arguelhes and MM Prado, '"Resistance by Interpretation": Supreme Court Justices as Counter-Reformers to Constitutional Changes in Brazil in the 90s' in R Albert, C Bernal and JZ Benvindo (eds), *Constitutional Change and Transformation in Latin America* (Hart Publishing, 2019) 167–88.

[50] See Koerner and Freitas (n 12) 181 ('… the very insistence by the justices in the STF's institutional preservation expressed its alliance with the conservatives').

[51] On the democratic feature of the Constituent Assembly, see JZ Benvindo, 'The Forgotten People in Brazilian Constitutionalism: Revisiting Behavior Strategic Analyses of Regime Transitions' (2017) 15 *International Journal of Constitutional Law* 332; L Barbosa, *História Constitucional Brasileira: Mudança Constitucional, Autoritarismo e Democracia no Brasil Pós-1964* (Biblioteca Digital da Câmara dos Deputados, 2012) 143–248.

[52] See DW Arguelhes, 'La Moderación Judicial como Legado Constitucional Autoritario: El Supremo Tribunal Federal Brasilero y las Facultades Legislativas Presidenciales' (2020) 24 *Discusiones* 172.

[53] See Vieira (n 14). See also MFD Castro, 'The Courts, Law, and Democracy in Brazil' (2009) *International Social Science Journal* 241.

[54] Castro (n 53) 243.

approach that recalled its behaviours during the dictatorial years,[55] whose precedents would naturally not fit well in the new democratic regime. Moreover, such a preservationist behaviour also meant blocking the most progressive agenda of the new regime while paving the way for 'the constitution of a liberalising regime' that matched the governmental agenda.[56]

The STF left the Constituent Assembly stronger, but with very limited changes in its design and composition (even the justices were the same from the prior regime). It kept the number of 11 justices,[57] all appointed by the President of the Republic and nominated after the Senate's approval. The confirmation hearings in the Senate have since basically functioned as a rubber stamp of the executive, though naturally political negotiations and a fierce lobby for the potential appointees kept occurring behind the scenes.[58] According to the Constitution, justices must be native Brazilians and over 35 and under 65 years old, chosen among those with 'notable juridical learning and spotless reputation'.[59] There is no fixed term for the STF's justices, who can serve until the mandatory retirement of 75 years old. The possibility that justices can serve for such a long time has boosted the Court's preservationist nature,[60] though the correlation between the justices' decisions and the political inclinations of those presidents who appointed them is empirically inconsistent.[61] The Court's model of deliberation also followed the same pattern of the prior regime, but since 2002 the hearing sessions, which were already public, have been broadcast nationwide. The *seriatim* deliberative model, according to which justices render their opinion in a sequence (in the case, based on their seniority in office), aggravates the STF's lack of effective collegiate deliberation and even its unequal model of decision-making.[62] The final result is basically the sum of each opinion, which is not easily translatable into an opinion of the Court.[63] This model

[55] See Arguelhes (n 52); Arguelhes and Prado (n 49).

[56] See Koerner and Freitas (n 12) 80.

[57] The Institutional Act n. 6, in 1969, reduced the number of justices from 16 to 11, which was the number before the court-packing of the Institutional Act n. 2. It took advantage of the fact that five justices had then left the Court. See Article 1, Ato Institucional n. 6, de 1° de Fevereiro de 1969.

[58] Most recently, the confirmation hearing of Justice André Mendonça, an Evangelical pastor who is President Bolsonaro's second pick for a spot on the Supreme Court, was met with high opposition in the Senate, but was voted in by 47 in favour and 32 against. See 'Brazil's Senate Approves Bolsonaro's Supreme Court Pick' (*Reuters*, 1 December 2021) www.reuters.com/world/americas/brazils-senate-approves-bolsonaros-supreme-court-pick-2021-12-01/.

[59] Article 101 of the 1988 Constitution.

[60] See R Hirschl, *Towards Juristocracy: The Origins and Consequences of the New Constitutionalism* (Harvard University Press, 2004).

[61] See JM Silva, 'Mapeando o Supremo: As Posições dos Ministros do STF na Jurisdição Constitucional (2012–2017)' (2018) 37 *Novos Estudos CEBRAP* 52 ('the justices' few dissenting opinions do not bear a relationship with the political origins or their appointments.').

[62] See VA da Silva, 'Deciding without Deliberating' (2013) 11 *International Journal of Constitutional Law* 571; CH Mendes, *Constitutional Courts and Deliberative Democracy* (Oxford University Press, 2013) 142–75.

[63] ibid.

has also prompted a higher level of politicisation based on the fact that justices read their opinions to be also broadcast live on *TV Justiça*.[64]

The new constitutional order strengthened the abstract system of judicial review while basically keeping the concrete one untouched. The concrete system, which dates back to 1890, is inspired by the US Supreme Court's model and basically means that a case can reach the STF through appeals from the lower courts whenever there is an alleged violation of the constitution.[65] It always refers to a concrete case, and every single judge, even from lower courts, can declare that a legal norm is unconstitutional. The case can reach the Court especially through the extraordinary appeal (*recurso extraordinário*), but the 1988 Constitution has not laid down any specific mechanism for the STF to exert a more discretionary power in accepting or rejecting those appeals.

The 2004 Judicial Reform (constitutional amendment n. 45/2004) introduced the 'general repercussion' (*repercussão geral*), which was implemented by the Court in 2007: every extraordinary appeal since has to 'demonstrate the general repercussion of the constitutional issues discussed in the case', but it set the high quorum of two thirds of the justices to reject it.[66] Such a change has indeed impacted the Court's caseload,[67] which previously comprised mostly cases with identical constitutional controversy. With this mechanism, the STF basically selects one single paradigmatic case and the lower courts replicate that precedent in other cases with identical constitutional controversy. Therefore, such cases are retained by the lower courts until the STF's precedent is issued, thereby reducing the number of cases reaching the STF. It does not follow that such a mechanism has changed the Court's willingness to exert its discretion, though rejections have been significantly low.[68] The upshot is that the STF still keeps deciding a similar number of constitutional controversies, but now it is not just the Court itself that replicates the precedents in other cases with identical controversy.

A reinforced abstract system of judicial review seemed to be a radical revamp of Brazil's judicial review system. Unlike the 'representation of unconstitutionality' (*representação de inconstitucionalidade*) of the previous constitutional order that was an exclusive initiative of the Attorney-General of the Republic

[64] See FDM Lopes, 'Television and Judicial Behavior: Lessons from the Brazilian Supreme Court' (2018) '9 *Economic Analysis of Law Review* 47; Silva (n 62) 580–83.

[65] Article 102, III, of the 1988 Constitution.

[66] Article 102, §3, of the 1988 Constitution.

[67] In 2007, there were approximately 120,000 extraordinary appeals; in 2020, such a number dropped to roughly 13,000, a reduction of about 80%. See 'Aplicação da Repercussão Geral Reflete na Diminuição Expressiva do Acervo no STF' (*STF*, 3 May 2021) http://portal.stf.jus.br/noticias/verNoticiaDetalhe.asp?idConteudo=465224&ori=1.

[68] See LR Barroso and FM Rego, 'Como Salvar a Repercussão Geral: Ideias Simples para Reverter o Fracasso' (*Migalhas*, 21 February 2018) www.migalhas.com.br/depeso/274826/como-salvar-a-repercussao-geral-ideias-simples-para-reverter-um-fracasso (from its implementation in 2007 to the end of 2017, the Court only declared as not having general repercussion 317 constitutional controversies).

(*Procurador-Geral da República*),[69] the direct action of unconstitutionality (*ação direta de inconstitucionalidade* or simply ADI) of the new constitutional order can be filed by the President of the Republic, the directing board of the Federal Senate and the Chamber of Deputies, the directing board of a State Legislative Assembly or of the Federal District Legislative Chamber, state Governors or the Governor of the Federal District, the Attorney-General of the Republic, the Federal Council of the Brazilian Bar Association, a political party with representation in the National Congress, and a confederation of labour unions or a professional association of a nationwide nature.[70] It is not the wide enfranchisement that was first planned during the Constituent Assembly,[71] but it is far more inclusive than the previous model. Each of these persons and institutions can directly file an ADI to question the constitutionality of a federal or state law or normative act.[72]

Though rare, it is also possible to file an ADI in cases of legislative omission (ADI-O), when the unconstitutionality is due to a 'lack of a measure to render a constitutional provision effective'.[73] In this situation, the decision implies the notification of the competent power to adopt 'the necessary actions and, in case of an administrative body, to do so within thirty days'.[74] Other actions in the abstract system of judicial review are the declaratory action of constitutionality (*ação declaratória de constitucionalidade* or simply ADC), whose goal is to harmonise and bind the declaration of constitutionality of a statute nationwide if lower courts are interpreting it otherwise, and the 'claim of non-compliance with a fundamental precept' (*arguição de descumprimento de preceito fundamental* or ADPF). This last action, which was only implemented in 1999,[75] has in practice served as a subsidiary action for situations in which ADIs are not allowed, such as federal and state statutes enacted before the 1988 Constitution or in cases of municipal statutes.

Notwithstanding this mixed system of constitutional review, which apparently provides the Court with a set of tools for exerting its role of 'guardian of the Constitution', the STF cannot really be deemed a model of constitutional court. This system rather exacerbates its structural dysfunctionalities. There is no discretionary refusal of cases, such as the *writ of certiorari* of the US Supreme Court, thus every case requires a decision, even if it is a very standard one. The numbers are staggering: on average, the STF provides a final decision in approximately 100,000 cases/yearly (98,196 in 2021, 99,659 in 2020, 115,886 in 2019, 126,743 in 2018), but the vast majority are not collegiate: in 2021, for

[69] Emenda Constitucional n. 16, de 12 de junho de 1965.
[70] Article 103 of the 1988 Constitution.
[71] See Koerner and Freitas (n 12) 165.
[72] Article 102, I, a, of the 1988 Constitution.
[73] Article 102, §2, of the 1988 Constitution.
[74] ibid.
[75] Lei n. 9.882, de 3 de dezembro de 1999.

instance, only 15.7 per cent of the cases were decided by the STF's collegiate bodies.[76] Many decisions basically replicate precedents, but, nevertheless, this impressive caseload creates some serious barriers to research. It also serves to justify the justices' excessive individual powers, as if the reasons for retaining such powers were merely procedural, not strategic. On the other hand, the abstract system of judicial review, which has been claimed as 'an instrument to protect the objective order and to defend subjective rights',[77] has not effectively served for this purpose. Most cases in the abstract system of judicial review judged so far targeted other issues such as federal and interbranch conflicts, but not basic rights.[78]

It took some years until a radical shift began to take root and transform the Supreme Court into a key player in Brazil's democracy.[79] It first saw a renovation of its justices as the former ones were retiring – a movement that gained pace during the centre-left government of President Lula da Silva (2003–10). Some structural reforms, such as the 2004 Judiciary Reform,[80] which strengthened the abstract system of judicial review, inaugurated the National Council of Justice (the oversight body of the judiciary) and launched the *TV Justiça*, laid the groundwork for a more visible and politicised STF.[81] Yet, perhaps more importantly, there was a shift in the way the STF embraced its interpretative role of the Constitution. It was when the Court began adopting a more flexible interpretation of rules and principles[82] as well as malleable methodologies, such as the principle of proportionality,[83] which helped empower the Court to advance in areas of moral disagreement[84] or in those traditionally depicted as part of legislative or executive discretion and convenience.[85] The change was significant and more confrontational to certain segments of society and politics. It did not take long until a backlash would become more tangible.

The first visible shift was a higher focus on certain individual rights that brought wider attention to the Court. Although the Court has since not significantly changed its behaviour in areas of social and economic rights,[86] it has

[76] For detailed statistics of the STF's caseload, see http://portal.stf.jus.br/estatistica/.

[77] G Mendes, 'New Challenges of Constitutional Adjudication in Brazil' (2008) Brazil Institute Special Report 1.

[78] See Costa and Benvindo (n 20).

[79] See Koerner and Freitas (n 12).

[80] Emenda Constitucional n. 45, de 30 de Dezembro de 2004.

[81] For more on the STF's activism, see JZ Benvindo, *On the Limits of Constitutional Adjudication: Deconstructing Balancing and Judicial Activism* (Springer, 2010); Silva (n 25) pos. 2861, Kindle Edition.

[82] M Neves, *Constitutionalism and the Paradox of Principles and Rules: Between the Hydra and Hercules* (Oxford University Press, 2021).

[83] See Benvindo (n 81).

[84] See J Waldron, *Law and Disagreement* (Oxford University Press, 1999).

[85] See A Koerner, 'Ativismo Judicial? Jurisprudência Constitucional e Política no STF Pós-88' (2013) 96 *Novos Estudos CEBRAP* 69.

[86] See Kapiszewski (n 17) 161.

increasingly advanced in some sensitive subjects of individual rights that challenge the rising conservative and religious mindset in the country. This clash of narratives – the STF defending individual rights and conservative and religious movements as well as politicians arguing that such subjects are under legislative exclusive authority – brought the Court into the spotlight as never before. Decisions such as the one that recognised same-sex civil unions[87] (paving the way for same-sex marriages),[88] criminalised homophobia and transphobia,[89] declared unconstitutional municipal laws prohibiting gender and sexual education in schools,[90] or expanded the scope of legal abortions to cases of anencephaly[91] sparked a severe backlash from some conservative sectors of society and Congress. Petitions aiming to contest Brazil's restrictive legislation on abortion[92] have been received and challenged by those sectors with fierce opposition, even when there is not yet a Court's decision.[93] Other cases triggered some reaction from middle-class and rich segments of society, such as the one that declared constitutional quotas for Black people to access public universities.[94] However, despite those cases above and others on individual rights (for example, freedom of speech,[95] academic freedom,[96] embryonic stem-cells research[97] and presumption of innocence),[98] the same reasoning could not be extended to social and economic rights, with the exception of some relevant cases on the right to health (distribution of high-cost medicines by Brazil's universal health system,[99] or, more recently, on COVID-19 governance).[100]

More radical still is the STF's behavioural change in matters of sensitive political affairs, economic governance and interbranch conflicts.[101] That discrete, non-confrontational and self-restrained Court of the beginning of the democratic years, when it was 'relatively impervious to pressures for the expansion of judicial power',[102] does not exist anymore. On several occasions, the STF

[87] STF, ADI 4277 (2011).
[88] CNJ, Res. 175 (2013).
[89] STF, ADO 26 (2020).
[90] STF, ADPF 467 (2020).
[91] STF, ADPF 54 (2013).
[92] In Brazil, abortion is only allowed by law in two circumstances: (1) risk to woman's life; and (2) rape. The STF extended it to cases of anencephaly in 2013.
[93] STF, ADPF 442 (pending) (the petition is aimed at declaring the crime of abortion unconstitutional if the procedure is made in the first 12 weeks of pregnancy).
[94] STF, ADPF 186 (2014).
[95] STF, HC 82424 (2004).
[96] STF, ADPF 548 (2020).
[97] STF, ADI 3510 (2010).
[98] STF, ADC 43, 44, 54 (2019).
[99] See STF, STA -AgR 175 (2010), 211 (2017); RE 657.718 (2019). See also *Case Law Compilation: Covid-19* (STF 2021) http://portal.stf.jus.br/noticias/verNoticiaDetalhe.asp?idConteudo=466533&ori=1.
[100] See STF, ADI 6341 (2020), ADPF 690 (2021); ADPF 709 (2020), ADI 6586 (2020), ADI 6587 (2020).
[101] See Kapiszewski (n 17) 161.
[102] Castro (n 53) 246.

astonished the legal community with decisions that feature a degree of encroachment on the other powers that is rarely found in comparative law. For instance, the STF, either by one single justice[103] or one of its organs, suspended the President of the Federal Senate[104] and the President of the Chamber of Deputies from their duties;[105] declared unconstitutional the re-election of the Presidents of the Chamber of the Deputies and the Senate;[106] and even determined how the pace of legislative deliberations should occur.[107] Its decisions significantly rearranged the electoral competition by declaring electoral thresholds unconstitutional (then leading to growing party fragmentation),[108] prohibiting corporate campaign-finance contributions[109] and banning candidates from running in elections.[110] Even if one could argue that some such decisions were constitutionally justified, they nevertheless challenged previously adopted arguments in those circumstances, such as the *interna corporis doctrine* or the *administrative merits doctrine*, which claim that those subjects are respectively part of the parliament's or the executive's discretionary power.

As a major political player, it has nevertheless conducted itself very inconsistently. Its decisions often challenge well-established precedents and even internal procedural norms. The Court's high level of inconsistency and uncertainty is also aggravated by failures of institutional design and practice. The Court should decide by expressing the opinion of the Court, but, as seen, only a fraction (roughly 10–20 per cent) of decisions are decided by one of its collegiate bodies (two panels, composed of five justices each, or the plenum, composed of all 11 justices). Even though in most controversial and landmark cases the Court tends to decide them through one of these bodies, it does not rule out the possibility that the rapporteur issue a preliminary injunction, which may take time until it is confirmed (or not) by one of those collegiate bodies. The Court has adopted strategic manoeuvres that expose the politicisation of decision-making in several ways. Not only have justices calibrated their powers in order to control external factors that could destabilise the Court,[111] but they have also increasingly adopted design loopholes for their benefit. Informal mechanisms of timing

[103] See DW Arguelhes and IA Hartmann, 'Timing Control without Docket Control' (2017) 5 *Journal of Law and Courts* 105.

[104] STF. ADPF 402 (2016). A temporary injunction was issued by Justice Marco Aurélio de Mello but was later reversed by the plenum.

[105] STF, AC 4070 (2016).

[106] STF, ADI 6524 (2020).

[107] STF, MS 31816 MC-AgR (2013).

[108] STF, ADI 1351 (2006), 1354 (2006).

[109] STF, ADI 4650 (2015). See JZ Benvindo, 'Constitutional Design, Institutional Strategy, and Corporate Campaign Contributions in Brazil' (*International Journal of Constitutional Law Blog*, 30 October 2015) www.iconnectblog.com/2015/10/constitutional-design-institutional-strategy-and-corporate-campaign-contributions-in-brazil/.

[110] RE 630147 (2010); PET 7848 (2018).

[111] See Arguelhes (n 20).

control,[112] excessive individual judicial powers[113] and strategic collaboration with the press (often implying the anticipation of an opinion)[114] – just to name a few – have become normal decision-making strategies.

Pushed by the STF's unorthodox behaviours and structural dysfunctionalities, the whole judiciary has been impacted by a great influx of potential politicisation of its decisions. It is not that comparable moves are not found elsewhere, but they clearly point out that Brazil's empowered Supreme Court is also a consequence of its capacity for transforming entrenched interests and self-reinforcing processes[115] into a window to bypass potential constraints on its powers, also by 'mutually' bargaining with the political system.[116] The new constitutional order and the international trend toward more accountable and active constitutional courts have served well the purpose of justifiably placing the STF in the middle of the most challenging democratic debates in Brazil. In this regard, the STF has indeed behaved as an important player of Brazil's democracy, with all the ups and downs that such a role implies. It has also behaved as a relevant shield for democracy by blocking or constraining some authoritarian acts that have gained momentum, especially during the Bolsonaro presidency. Examples are the STF's prohibition of production and sharing of intelligence reports against critics of the government,[117] the investigation of those who attack the Court and its members through fake news and threats[118] and the investigation of whether President Bolsonaro interfered in the federal police for personal purposes.[119]

Based on these criteria, it could be argued that the Court, at least up until now, enjoys a reasonable level of autonomy that has proven more and more vital for the health of Brazil's democracy. However, unless such institutional designs and practices are significantly overhauled, Brazil's STF will keep presenting itself as a Court of 11 minds in continuous disputes, be they legitimate, well-founded or a sheer exercise of strategic and political calculations. The impacts on the rule of law are significant: a powerful, but rather dysfunctional and unaccountable Court may provide some leading and landmark decisions here and there,[120]

[112] See Arguelhes and Hartmann (n 103).

[113] See DW Arguelhes and LM Ribeiro, ''The Court, It is I'? Individual Judicial Powers in the Brazilian Supreme Court and their Implications for Constitutional Theory' (2018) 7 *Global Constitutionalism* 236.

[114] See DW Arguelhes and LM Ribeiro, 'O Supremo Individual: Mecanismos de Atuação Direta dos Ministros sobre o Processo Político' (2015) 46 *Revista Direito, Estado e Sociedade* 129–34.

[115] See P Pierson, *Politics in Time: History, Institutions, and Social Analysis* (Princeton University Press, 2004) 10.

[116] See Bogéa (n 15).

[117] STF, ADPF 722/MC (2020).

[118] STF, INQ 4781 (2021), ADPF 572 (2021).

[119] STF, INQ 4831(pending).

[120] The I-CONnect-Clough Center publishes yearly the *Global Review of Constitutional Law*, where selected leading cases and the country's constitutionalism are briefly discussed. See JZ Benvindo and A Osorio, 'Brazil' in R Albert et al (eds), *2020 Global Review of Constitutional Law* (I-CONnect-Clough Center, 2021) 43–48.

but it will be a court whose powers and institutionality will be consistently challenged for good and not so good reasons.

C. The 'Ancillary' Institutions of Justice: The Public Ministry, the Advocacy-General of the Union and the Public Defender's Office

The 1988 Constitution also empowered some ancillary institutions of justice, notably the Public Ministry (*Ministério Público*), the Public Defender's Office (*Defensoria Pública*) and the Advocacy-General of the Union (*Advocacia-Geral da União*) (and their counterparts in the federal states). The *Ministério Público*, though normally translated as Prosecutor's Office or Public Prosecution, should be more accurately translated simply as Public Ministry, because its scope goes far beyond criminal prosecution. It is a remarkably powerful institution, which is endowed with substantial institutional autonomy[121] and constitutional guarantees that are comparable to those of the judiciary. It is deemed by some to be a fourth branch of power[122] and is thereby not exactly a typical institution of justice despite the fact that its activities are mostly concentrated in the judicial system.

In the prior regime, the Public Ministry was the legal representative of the federal executive power, but the new constitutional order transferred such a role to the Advocacy-General of the Union. With the 1988 Constitution, the Public Ministry's design was radically revamped and its powers were so deliberately enhanced that its general duties would be described as '[defending] the juridical order, the democratic regime, and the inalienable social and individual interests'.[123] This vague constitutional clause combined with the Public Ministry's high degree of autonomy and vast guarantees implies that this institution features substantial powers to defend the rule of law and Brazil's democracy. It does prosecute crimes of all sorts, including cases of corruption, but it can also file Public Class Actions (*Ação Civil Pública*) to defend diffuse (for indeterminate persons) and collective rights (for persons with some legal connection),[124] in areas such as environmental, consumer and Indigenous rights. The scope can be much broader since the Constitution states that it can 'exercise other functions which may be conferred upon it, provided that they are compatible with its purpose(…)'.[125] It is also an external body to oversee the police,[126] even though

[121] Article 127, §2, of the 1988 Constitution.

[122] See RB Arantes and TMQ Moreira, 'Democracia, Instituições de Controle e Justiça sob a Ótica do Pluralismo Estatal' (2019) 25 *Opinião Pública* 110.

[123] Article 127 of the 1988 Constitution.

[124] See RB Arantes, 'The Federal Police and the Ministério Público' in TJ Power and MM Taylor (eds), *Corruption and Democracy in Brazil: The Struggle for Accountability* (University of Notre Dame, 2011) 187.

[125] Article 129, IX, of the 1988 Constitution.

[126] Article 129, VII, of the 1988 Constitution.

it has exerted such a role far less effectively than it should.[127] Finally, the Public Ministry is called to manifest its opinion in every case in the abstract system of judicial review, and the Attorney-General of the Republic (the highest authority of the Federal Public Ministry), can file Direct Actions of Unconstitutionality in the Supreme Court,[128] even though it has done so largely in favour of the Public Ministry's institutional interests rather than to effectively defend basic rights.[129]

The Public Ministry spreads across all the 26 states and the Federal District and also follows the specialisation of the judicial system (labour, electoral and military courts). There is also a specialised Public Ministry acting directly in the Federal Audit Court (TCU) (and its state and even municipal counterparts), though such accounting tribunals are part of the legislative body, not the judiciary. The members of the Public Ministry are admitted after successfully passing rigorous entrance examinations and, like judges, earn the highest salaries in Brazil's public sector. The argument for such high salaries has been based upon the maintenance of their autonomy, but the constitutional text contains a serious design flaw: the Attorney-General of the Republic is the only authority who can prosecute the President of the Republic for ordinary crimes by filing a criminal complaint directly in the Supreme Court, which then requests the Chamber of Deputies' authorisation.[130] However, the only constraints for appointing the Attorney-General of the Republic for a two-year term are that he or she is: (1) over 35 years old; (2) a career member of the Public Ministry; and (3) approved by the Federal Senate,[131] which has historically not exerted such a control. During President Lula da Silva (2003–10) and Dilma Rousseff's (2011–16) presidencies, the Attorney-General of the Republic was the one that had won the internal election among the members of the Federal Public Ministry in an internal election. President Michel Temer (2016–18) broke such a tradition and appointed the runner up. President Jair Bolsonaro (2019–22) disregarded this convention and appointed Augusto Aras, who was not among the most voted. The consequence is that, during the Bolsonaro administration, investigations against the President and his entourage did not make any effective progress.[132]

[127] For data on the Public Ministry's oversight over police activities, see 'Controle Externo da Atividade Policial em Números: Delegacias de Polícia Civil' (*Conselho Nacional do Ministério Público*) www.cnmp.mp.br/portal/transparencia/relatorios-em-bi/11796-controle-externo-da-atividade-policial-em-numeros-delegacias-de-policia-civil.

[128] Article 129, IV, of the 1988 Constitution.

[129] See Costa and Benvindo (n 20) 76 (arguing that the Public Ministry has acted below the average in matters of basic rights). See also KO Gomes, 'Em Defesa da Sociedade? Atuaçãoda Procuradoria Geral da República em Controle Concentrado de Constitucionalidade (1988–2012)' (MsC Dissertation, University of Brasília, 2015).

[130] Article 86 of the 1988 Constitution.

[131] Article 52, II, XI, of the 1988 Constitution.

[132] See CH Mendes, 'Arquitetura da Omissão' (*Folha de S. Paulo*, 2 June 2021) www1.folha.uol.com.br/colunas/conrado-hubner-mendes/2021/06/arquitetura-da-omissao.shtml; CH Mendes, 'Aras é a Antessala de Bolsonaro no Tribunal Penal Internacional' (*Folha de S. Paulo*, 26 January 2021) www1.folha.uol.com.br/colunas/conrado-hubner-mendes/2021/01/aras-e-a-antessala-de-bolsonaro-no-tribunal-penal-internacional.shtml.

Therefore, despite the Public Ministry's extensive powers, there is still a significant gap between its potential and its real performance in strengthening the rule of law. As it happens with the judiciary, its high autonomy has also raised the strategy of excluding itself from mechanisms of vertical and horizontal accountability,[133] and its members have also intensely lobbied to keep their corporatist interests untouched. Their mindset is also marked by what Rogério Arantes calls 'political voluntarism', that is, the Public Ministry behaves as if it were the only institution that can defend the interests of a 'weak society' in a country whose political institutions are portrayed as 'corrupt and/or unable to fulfil their duties'.[134] Such unconstrained behaviour has led the Public Ministry to present itself as the major player in combatting corruption, but it has in some cases overstepped the boundaries of due process of law, mainly by galvanising support of the media and large sectors of society. The politicisation of the Public Ministry has been pronounced in some leading cases – the most recent are those connected to 'Operation Car Wash'[135] – but the response from the internal and external bodies which oversee the Public Ministry, notably the National Council of the Public Ministry (CNMP), has been rather weak.[136]

The Public Defender's Office (*Defensoria Pública*) is, according to the Constitution, 'an essential institution to the jurisdictional function of the State and is responsible for the judicial guidance and defence, in all levels, of the needy under the terms of Article 5, LXXIV', which, in turn, says that 'the State shall provide full and free-of-charge assistance to all who prove insufficiency of funds'.[137] The Public Defender's Office is, therefore, the institution whose role is to defend those who cannot afford legal representation and, as such, is a major player in broadening access to the judiciary and democratising justice. Its consolidation as an important player in Brazil's judiciary, however, has been bumpier than the constitutional text points out: due to the lobby of other legal careers during the Constituent Assembly, some of which exerted that type of representation in various federal states, the effective implementation of the Public Defender's Office took some years[138] and only in 1994 was a supplementary law enacted organising the Federal Public Defender's Office and prescribing general rules for the State Public Defender's Offices.[139] The 2004 Judicial Reform enhanced its functional and administrative autonomy and, in 2009, Congress

[133] See Arantes (n 124) 188.

[134] ibid 188. See also L Avritzer and M Marona, 'A Tensão entre Soberania e Instituições de Controle na Democracia Brasileira' (2017) 60 *Dados – Revista de Ciências Sociais* 363.

[135] The STF has decided that the judge presiding over that operation acted with partiality, but it also stressed that the Public Ministry overstepped the boundaries of the due process of law. See n 5.

[136] See next section.

[137] Article 134 and Article 5, LLXXIV of the 1988 Constitution.

[138] See RB Arantes and TMQ Moreira, 'Democracia, Instituições de Controle e Justiça sob a Ótica do Pluralismo Estatal' (2019) 25 *Opinião Pública* 112.

[139] Lei Complementar n. 80, de 12 de Janeiro de 1994.

passed a new supplementary law that granted further powers to this institution, such as '[promoting] human rights' and 'defending ... individual and collective rights'.[140]

In the last few years, the Public Defender's Office has visibly gained strength. It is still much associated with the legal representation of defendants in the criminal judicial system, but it has appeared more frequently as a leading player in some cases that go far beyond criminal justice, sometimes even competing with the Public Ministry's expected role of protecting diffuse and collective rights. The Supreme Court has recognised that the Public Defender's Office can defend collective and diffuse rights of the needy and even file Public Class Actions (*Ações Civis Públicas*)[141] in areas such as consumer, housing, prisoners' rights and reproductive and sexual rights.

Finally, the Advocacy-General of the Union (and its counterparts in the states and some municipalities, normally called *procuradorias*) is the institution that represents the Union (or the states and municipalities) judicially or extrajudicially.[142] At the federal level, it is a new institution, created by the 1988 Constitution as a consequence of the Public Ministry's autonomous role as a defender of the society's interests and the legal order, which may not be in line with that of the federative unit. Therefore, in cases in which the interests of the Union (or of the states and municipalities) are at stake, it is the Advocacy-General of the Union (or *procuradorias*) that provides legal representation as well as works as a legal advisory board. It is also the institution that defends the legal norms that are questioned in the Supreme Court through judicial review.[143]

As with the members of the Public Ministry and the Public Defender's Office, the lawyers of the Advocacy-General of the Union are selected after rigorous entrance examinations, but, unlike those institutions, its head, the Advocate-General of the Union, is 'freely appointed by the President of the Republic from among citizens over thirty-five years of age, of notable juridical learning and spotless reputation'.[144] Even though most of its members are experts in their field and are highly qualified, the very nature of this institution makes it far less autonomous than the Public Ministry and the Public Defender's Office.

III. A MORE ACCESSIBLE, THOUGH STILL UNACCOUNTABLE, JUDICIARY AND THE INCREASING CULTURE OF RIGHTS

In the wake of the 1988 Constitution, one of the major discussions among legal sociologists and constitutional lawyers was how to enforce the vast array of

[140] Article 1, Lei Complementar n. 132, de 7 de Outubro de 2009.
[141] STF, ADI 3.943 (2015); RE 733.433 (2016).
[142] Article 131 of the 1988 Constitution.
[143] Article 103, §3, of the 1988 Constitution.
[144] Article 131, § 1, of the 1988 Constitution.

basic rights of the new constitutional order. It was a catharsis of expectations of a rising democracy after years of dictatorial rule, which intensified because Brazil had gone through both a regime transition and a constitutional transition. A new culture of rights, following such a momentum, was gaining traction, and the immediate consequence was that the judiciary was markedly impacted by new types of demands. Unlike, for example, what took place in Chile, where the transition to democracy kept alive a Constitution – drafted during Pinochet's rule – that was a 'sweeping experiment with University of Chicago-style "free" market economics',[145] the Brazilian Constitution pointed to a social welfare state,[146] where health, education, and social security and assistance were not deemed merely a right but also a 'duty of the State'.[147]

This protective framework led to a high constitutionalisation of demands in the judiciary, which, little by little, began issuing decisions that either embraced such protections, particularly in the lower courts, or constrained them in the higher courts.[148] These two movements – lower courts exerting a sort of activism and higher courts providing a shield against such moves – led to a growing frustration in society. Even though some lower courts decided favourably on the need for governmental public policies and economic programmes to be implemented, the final say by the higher courts was mostly preservationist. Social and economic rights require significant state funding and an effective governance against social inequality to become reality. Brazil was economically fragile – a series of crises and policies to combat inflation were the mark of the late 1980s and early 1990s – and social inequality, though increasingly targeted, was not treated with the urgency and effort it required.

However, years of democratic life have since provided a more robust awareness of the need to transform the judiciary into a more inclusive institution, where popular demands can more easily reach the courts and courts, in turn, can enforce rights and constrain the government when needed. The massive caseload and backlog of unresolved cases[149] as well as the bureaucratic structure of the judiciary have nevertheless limited such movements and even been strategically used as a means to reverse potential inclusive gains of the new Constitution. The advent of the 1988 Constitution has led to an 'explosion of litigations',[150] and the judiciary has been called upon to assure the web of social protection of the Constitution, but it has, in comparison to other judiciaries in Latin America,

[145] JM Cypher, 'Pinochet Meets Polanyi? The Curious Case of the Chilean Embrace of "Free" Market Economics' (2004) 38 *Journal of Economic Issues* 527.

[146] Article 194 of the 1988 Constitution.

[147] Article 196, 205, 208, of the 1988 Constitution.

[148] See Benvindo (n 81) 93–97.

[149] See L Da Ros and M Taylor, 'Opening the Black Box: Three Decades of Reforms to Brazil's Judicial System' (2017) School of International Service Research Paper 5, https://papers.ssrn.com/sol3/papers.cfm?abstract_id=3028731.

[150] JE Faria, 'O Sistema Brasileiro de Justiça: Experiência Recente e Futuros Desafios' (2004) 18 *Estudos Avançados* 105.

lagged behind in enforcing them.[151] There have been some important movements to bring the judiciary closer to the population, such as the introduction of the small claims courts (*juizados especiais*),[152] where individuals, even with no representation by a professional lawyer, can access the judiciary and obtain expedited decisions; the creation of the Public Defender's Office (*Defensoria Pública*); and the adoption of alternative dispute resolution mechanisms (ADRs) such as mediation and conciliation in various types of procedures[153] and the creation of mediation and conciliation centres, even at the Supreme Court.[154] Moreover, the 2004 Judicial Reform provided some innovations such as the introduction of the *amicus curiae* in public audiences,[155] the financial and administrative autonomy of the Defender's Public Office, the National Council of Justice (CNJ) and the National Council of the Public Ministry (CNMO) as bodies to oversee the Judiciary and the Public Ministry, and new procedural rules aiming at speeding up and harmonising conflict resolutions.[156]

The Constitution of 1988 features a comprehensive set of open and vague clauses in matters of basic rights, which boost the judiciary's interpretative powers. The expanded capacity of the Public Ministry and the Public Defender's Office to file actions in matters of diffuse and collective rights as well as a set of new legislation on collective rights also prompt a more active judiciary in rights protection.[157] The new constitutional design fosters, therefore, a more active judiciary, but it does so without providing it with robust mechanisms for coherence in decision making. The non-existence of a tradition of binding precedents combined with an excessive protection of judges' autonomy,[158] even after the introduction of the 'general repercussion' requirement[159] and a more emphatic reference to precedents in the new Civil Procedural Code,[160] creates an environment where individuals may find distinct decisions for identical controversies even in the same court. This situation is aggravated by the length of time the cases are kept unresolved.

Overall, however, the judiciary has behaved more favourably in protecting civil-political rights over social and economic ones, but even those first-generation

[151] See Helmke and Ríos-Figueroa (n 13) 9.

[152] Lei n. 9.999, de 26 de Setembro de 1995; Lei n. 10.259, de 12 de Julho de 2001.

[153] See HDB de Pinho and MP Paumgarten, 'The Challenges of Court Mediation from the Brazilian Perspective' (2015) 5 *International Journal of Procedural Law* 301.

[154] See 'Brazil: Federal Supreme Court Implements Mediation and Conciliation Center' (Library of Congress, 25 February 2021) www.loc.gov/law/foreign-news/article/brazil-federal-supreme-court-implements-mediation-and-conciliation-center/.

[155] See MG Godoy, 'As Audiências Públicas e os Amici Curiae Influenciam as Decisões dos Ministros do Supremo Tribunal Federal' (2015) 60 *Revista da Faculdade de Direito UFPR* 137.

[156] Emenda Constitucional n. 45, de 30 de Dezembro de 2004.

[157] See RB Arantes and MT Sadek, *Ministério Público e Política no Brasil* (Sumaré, 2002); RB Arantes, 'Judiciário: Entre a Justiça e a Política' in L Avelar and AO Cintra (eds), *Sistema Político Brasileiro: Uma Introdução* (Konrad-Adenauer-Stiftung, 2007) 79–108.

[158] Da Ros and Taylor (n 149) 7.

[159] See Section II(B).

[160] See Civil Procedural Code (Law n. 13.105/2015, Articles 926, 927).

rights are, as expected, unequally enforced depending on the claimant. The inequality of treatment, especially in the criminal justice system, between whites and Blacks, rich and poor, is shocking.[161] Social and economic rights, which largely impact the underprivileged segments of society, are often balanced with the general claim of 'governability', without specifying what such a 'governability' actually means. In principle, such rights can only be enforced insofar as they do not yield 'insupportable' costs to the government. Usually they are dubbed 'programmatic clauses',[162] depending on infra-constitutional regulation and on the government's definition of public policies according to the economic context.[163] The prevalence of economic reasoning – besides political calculations – in decision-making has been a crucial tone of Brazil's judiciary and of its strategic position in the political realm,[164] in a coordination with the political system[165] that speaks volumes about this behaviour. The high deficit of judicial response to such claims, the labyrinthine procedures and laws, the excessive delays, the unequal treatment and the uncertainty derived from inconsistent and incoherent decisions have brought about a lack of confidence in the judiciary (even though still greater than in other powers)[166] and a negative perception of its public image.[167] More importantly, its insulation from the real world has weakened its ability to behave as a catalyst of social justice.[168] Its preservationist conduct has rather exacerbated the fact that the judiciary can be both the most blatant illustration of inequality and a promoter of inequality.

IV. PRIVILEGES AND THE JUDICIAL SYSTEM: THE JUDICIARY AS A BLATANT ILLUSTRATION OF BRAZIL'S INEQUALITY

The system of justice and its 'ancillary' institutions are themselves a blatant illustration of Brazil's inequality. Their members are the best paid public officials in Brazil, whose salaries are comparable with or even higher than those of much wealthier nations and whose privileges are not found in any other public

[161] See ASA Guimarães, *Preconceito e Discriminação: Queixas e Ofensas e Tratamento Desigual dos Negros no Brasil* (Editora 34, 2004); MJ Mitchell and CH Wood, 'Ironies of Citizenship: Skin Color, Police Brutality, and the Challenge to Democracy in Brazil' (1999) 77 *Social Forces* 1001; L Wacquant, 'Toward a Dictatorship over the Poor? Notes on the Penalization of Poverty in Brazil' (2003) 5 *Punishment & Society* 197.

[162] See JAD Silva, Aplicabilidade das Normas Constitucionais (Malheiros, 2008).

[163] See Arantes (n 157); Faria (n 150).

[164] See Faria (n 150).

[165] See Bogéa (n 15).

[166] See LDO Ramos et al, *Relatório ICJ Brasil 2021* (Fundação Getúlio Vargas – FGV, 2021) 11 (40% confidence in the judiciary; 29% in the presidency; 12% in the National Congress).

[167] See FD Sá e Silva, 'SIPS Justiça: Opinião Pública, Pesquisa Aplicada e Reforma da Justiça: Contribuições e Desafios, Polítiticos e Analíticos' in F Schiavinatto (ed), *Sistema de Indicadores de Percepção Social (SIPS)* (IPEA, 2011) 17–42.

[168] See Arantes (n 157) 106.

career. The new constitutional order strengthened the judiciary's guarantees, especially its independence, but it has done so by providing it with a substantial budget and ample autonomy over its spending. According to the National Council of Justice (CNJ), the judiciary's total expenditure in 2020 corresponded to 1.3 per cent of Brazil's GDP or 11 per cent of all expenditures by the Union, the states, the Federal District and the municipalities combined.[169] The average monthly expenditure of every single judge was R$ 48,160 (roughly U$ 9,000.00),[170] including all sorts of compensations, benefits, and subsidies they earn, compared with the average salary of R$ 33,400 (roughly U$ 6,500.00).[171] Moreover, a newly-hired judge earns 81 per cent of a Supreme Court justice. *Piauí*, a magazine, published a series of comparisons showing that Brazil's judiciary proportionally costs three times more than the Spanish judiciary (1.5 per cent v 0.47 per cent of their GDPs),[172] and that, considering only the basic salary (not supplementary benefits), state judges earn three times more than a court clerk, five times more than a social worker, and 12 times more than a nursing assistant.[173] The whole judiciary, including judges and public servants, has an average income that is twice that of parliament and three times more than that of the executive.[174] The inequality is glaring both by domestic and international standards. As Luciano Da Ros and Matthew Taylor empirically prove, 'Brazil has the highest judicial budget in purchasing power parity terms per inhabitant of all the federal systems in the Western hemisphere'.[175]

Justa, a research project, organised some data furnished by the National Council of Justice (CNJ) that reveal a shocking amount of inequality in the judicial system: 51 per cent of Brazilian judges come from the upper social classes and are among the 0.08 per cent of Brazil's wealthiest people. By cross-examining various data on race and gender, the outlook is also disturbing: there are 7.4 times more white male judges than Black female judges. Based on the 2010 Brazilian demographic census, which points out a slight majority of Black people (*pretos* and *pardos*) in society (51 per cent), *Justa* concludes that 'white men are 37.8 times more likely than black women to become appeals court judges, 8.2 times more likely than black women to become judges [and] 4.6 times more likely than black female judges to become appeals court judges'.[176]

[169] CNJ, *Justiça em Números 2021* (CNJ, 2021) 77.

[170] The currency conversion from Brazilian Reais to US Dollars should be taken with a pinch of salt. In 2020 and 2021, Brazilian Real was one of the world's most devaluated currencies due to the political instability and economic downturn, so such values can change quite significantly from one year to the next.

[171] ibid 91.

[172] L Mazza, P Lopes and R Buono, 'Os Privilégios da Toga' (*Piauí*, 7 September 2020) https://piaui.folha.uol.com.br/os-privilegios-da-toga/.

[173] ibid.

[174] F Lopes and E Guedes, 'Três Décadas de Evolução do Funcionalismo Público no Brasil (1986–2017)' in *Atlas do Estado Brasileiro* (IPEA, 2020) www.ipea.gov.br/atlasestado/indicadores.

[175] Da Ros and Taylor (n 149) 5.

[176] See *Justa Report: Judges Are Among the Richest People in Brazil* (Justa, 2021) http://justa.org.br/wp-content/uploads/2019/06/1_4924989468760342688.pdf.

Also shocking is how the judiciary is overfinanced when compared to other basic services. In São Paulo, Brazil's wealthiest state, state courts consumed about 5 per cent of all the annual budget from 2013 to 2018, more than 10 distinct basic services combined, including housing, social programmes, energy, communication, citizen rights and sanitation. More importantly, this number has risen significantly: whereas the state budget rose 22 per cent in 2018 compared to 2013, the judiciary's budget increased 45 per cent (the rise was also considerable for the state Public Ministry – 52 per cent – and the Public Defender's Office – 40 per cent). Most of this growth is due to payments of staff and salaries, while investments in programmes aimed at promoting rights and citizenship as well as custody and social reintegration were mostly neglected.[177] A similar outcome could also be found in other Brazilian states.[178]

If the judiciary as a whole has been growing hungrier for resources, it has nevertheless fiercely combatted attempts to improve mechanisms of horizontal accountability. Members of the system of justice and its ancillary institutions are selected after having passed rigorous entrance exams, but those exams are self-reinforcing in that members of that very judicial system are usually the ones who design those exams, with little input from academia or other social movements. Inclusiveness has been also deficient: only recently have such exams begun adopting quotas for Black candidates.[179] The consequence is that, once recruited, members of the judiciary (and also the other institutions of the judicial system) reproduce a 'peculiar condition of an aristocratic body'[180] to fend off any effective control over its activities and advance its corporatist agenda.

Such corporatist agendas have led to a type of corruption that is deeply institutionalised and distorts the language of democracy, such as the principles of separation of powers and judicial independence, to obtain budgetary gains, increased salaries and strengthened prerogatives, while shielding the judiciary from external oversight.[181] The creation of the National Council of Justice (CNJ) and the National Council of the Public Ministry (CNMP) through the 2004 Judicial Reform[182] originally suffered fierce opposition, and, once installed, their role of overseeing has been very limited – not to say *strategically* limited. They are not in reality external oversight bodies, as they are mostly staffed by judges or members of the Public Ministry, so, even though seemingly providing some accountability, the defence of corporatist interests tends to prevail in

[177] ibid.

[178] The research also examined this development in the states of Ceará and Paraná.

[179] See 'Cotas para Negros em Concursos para Juiz São Adotadas em Quase Todo o País' (*CNJ*, 24 February 2017) www.cnj.jus.br/cotas-para-negros-em-concursos-para-juiz-sao-adotadas-em-quase-todo-pais.

[180] Arantes (n 157) 106.

[181] See R Albert et al, 'Constitutional Reform in Brazil: Lessons from Albania?' (2017) 4 *Revista de Investigações Constitucionais* 12.

[182] Emenda Constitucional n. 45, de 30 de Dezembro de 2004.

the end.[183] There has been, in any case, some progress especially in tackling ordinary corruption in the judicial system such as embezzlement, bribery, nepotism, and to foster greater transparency and efficiency, but the results up until now have been rather modest.[184] The CNJ and CNMP publish information on budgetary data, public procurements and salaries as well as reports and databanks providing data on judicial productivity, human resources, finance and bottlenecks in the judicial process, all available on the internet. Yet, when it comes to effective punishment, the numbers are rather disappointing. For instance, from 2004 to 2019, the CNJ only applied some sort of punishment in 118 cases, most of which (66) were mandatory retirement,[185] which looks more like a reward than a penalty.[186]

The system of justice has therefore been very successful in preserving its benefits, structures, and practices in the new democratic order, and its enhanced constitutional guarantees have been strategically adopted as a potent shield against any attempt to change this scenario. The upshot is that Brazil's system of justice ends up being less of a model for the rule of law if its improved institutional capacities are used in such a convenient way for their own political manoeuvres and strategic interests. Its self-enforcing processes, which have not significantly changed after the transition to democracy, leave little room for making the judiciary and the ancillary institutions of the system of justice more accountable and responsive to the demands of a highly unequal society. This symptom is well portrayed in the still low levels of enforcement of rights, particularly social and economic ones, as well as in the highly inefficient criminal justice system. It is also found in the challenges of balancing its reasonable levels of independence with the risks of excessive politicisation.

V. CRIMINAL JUSTICE AND POLICE FORCES

If there is a sector that suffers from severe dysfunctionality in Brazil's judicial system, it is criminal justice. In theory, however, it does not look very problematic. Its procedure is quite straightforward: once the investigation by the police (and/or the Public Ministry) concludes that there is a crime, the Public

[183] See Costa and Benvindo (n 20) (showing how the judiciary has been a successful player in advancing its agenda through the system of abstract judicial review in the Supreme Court); See also Albert et al (n 181) 15–19.

[184] See Albert et al (n 181) 18.

[185] This punishment is a vestige of the 'Organic Law of the Magistrature' (Lei Complementar n. 35, de 14 de Março de 1979), drafted during the civilian-military dictatorship, which prescribes a series of prerogatives and benefits not found in any other public career.

[186] See N Victor, 'Em 15 Anos, CNJ Aplicou 118 Punições a Integrantes do Judiciário (*Poder 360*, 1 August 2020) www.poder360.com.br/justica/em-15-anos-cnj-aplicou-118-punicoes-a-integrantes-do-judiciario/.

Ministry[187] can file a criminal complaint in the judiciary,[188] which can summarily accept it or not. Such a system operates through a triangulation among the police, Public Ministry and the judiciary, but it operates in an adversarial way,[189] that is, the judiciary can issue warrants when needed but does not participate in the investigation. There is also a controversy over the limits of the Public Ministry's investigation powers and its potential overlap with the police's.[190] At the trial phase, the defendant must be assisted by a private lawyer or a public defender[191] and be guaranteed due process and a fair trial. Criminal cases in Brazil are decided by a single judge in the first instance, except for cases of wilful crimes against life, when there is a jury of seven citizens whose verdict is taken by simple majority. The procedure occurs normally through a set of hearings of witnesses, the Public Ministry and the defendant, but, as is common in the civil law tradition, the procedure is largely written and formal. After sentencing, the case can be appealed to the State Appellate Court or the Regional Federal Court, depending on whether it is a state or federal matter. It can, in some circumstances, even reach both the Superior Court of Justice (STJ) and the Federal Supreme Court (STF).

The practice is, however, far less rosy. The Constitution states that 'no one shall be considered guilty before the issuing of a final and unappealable penal sentence',[192] but, in reality, roughly one third of prisoners are pre-trial detainees who are left in prison as a precautionary measure.[193] Those who are normally well assisted by lawyers can easily postpone the execution of the sentence through numerous appeals, which in the end tend to foster an even more unequal system. It is no wonder that those who are normally better-off financially can see their sentences expire under the statute of limitations. The sense of impunity is fundamentally related to inequality and particularly pronounced in cases of political corruption.[194] Moreover, the Constitution establishes special standing (*foro privilegiado*) in the higher courts for some high-ranking authorities, such as congresspersons, judges, governors, ministers, and, naturally, the president. which normally implies a more condescending treatment.

It is particularly at the bottom of the judicial criminal system and in how law enforcement operates that the crude reality of inequality and violence gains evidence. The high rates of social inequality and violence reflect on a vicious

[187] Exceptionally for some few crimes (eg, honour-related crimes), the victim files the criminal complaint directly in the judiciary. See Brazil's Criminal Code, Articles 138, 139, 140.

[188] Article 129, I, of the 1988 Constitution.

[189] Article 5, LV, of the 1988 Constitution.

[190] See STF, HC 89.837 (2009); 87.610 (2009); 90.099 (2009); 94.173 (2009); RE 593.727 (2015); ADI 1517 MC (1997); ADI 3034 (pending)

[191] Article 5, LXIII, of the 1988 Constitution.

[192] Article 5, LVII, of the 1988 Constitution.

[193] *Reunião Especial de Jurisdição* (CNJ 2017) 3, www.cnj.jus.br/veja-a-integra-do-levantamento-dos-presos-provisorios-no-brasil/.

[194] See Arantes (n 124) 195.

circle in the whole judicial apparatus that feeds further inequality through repression and violence. According to the Monitor of Violence, Brazil, in 2021, was the world's third country in regard to the number of prisoners (746,800),[195] including pre-trial detainees and those on probation, just after the US and China, and features the world's 26th highest incarceration rate (322/100,000 inhabitants).[196] It is an unfair system in which about one third (31.9 per cent) of prisoners are pre-trial detainees, mostly because of drug trafficking (40.5 per cent), all placed inside overcrowded prisons (54.9 per cent of them operating over capacity). There has also been a significant rise in mass incarceration over the years (from 232,755 prisoners in 2000 to 755,274 in 2019), largely due to an increase in drug law enforcement.[197] It is no wonder that, up until May 2021, over 57,000 prisoners tested positive for COVID-19 and more than 200 died of such a disease (237 prison officers also died of COVID-19).[198] These prisons are known as crime schools since organised criminal groups are de facto controllers of the incarcerated population, preparing them to commit crimes once they leave prison.[199]

According to the Brazilian Forum on Public Safety, in 2020, 66.3 per cent of all prisoners identified themselves as Black,[200] a rise from 58.4 per cent in 2005.[201] Police interventions resulting in death targeted mostly Black people: 78.9 per cent.[202] Moreover, the death rate in police interventions is 4.2 for every 100,000 people among Blacks, compared to 1.5 for every 100,000 people among whites. In 2020, 50,033 people were violently killed (a rise of 4 per cent in comparison to 2019), mostly Black (76.2 per cent), young (54.3 per cent) and male (91.3 per cent) and caused by firearms (78 per cent).[203] More importantly, 6,416

[195] CR da Silva et al, 'População Carcerária Diminui, mas Brasil ainda Registra Superlotação nos Presídios em Meio à Pandemia' (*G1, Monitor da Violência*, 17 May 2021) https://g1.globo.com/monitor-da-violencia/noticia/2021/05/17/populacao-carceraria-diminui-mas-brasil-ainda-registra-superlotacao-nos-presidios-em-meio-a-pandemia.ghtml.

[196] CR da Silva et al, 'Com 322 Encarcerados a Cada 100 Mil Habitantes, Brasil Se Mantém na 26ª Posição em Ranking dos Países que Mais Prendem no Mundo' (*G1, Monitor da Violência*, 17 May 2021) https://g1.globo.com/monitor-da-violencia/noticia/2021/05/17/com-322-encarcerados-a-cada-100-mil-habitantes-brasil-se-mantem-na-26a-posicao-em-ranking-dos-paises-que-mais-prendem-no-mundo.ghtml.

[197] See L Boiteux, 'Drugs and Prisons: The Repression of Drugs and the Increase of the Brazilian Penitentiary Population' (2011) *Systems Overload – Drug Laws and Prisons in Latin America.* (Amsterdam, Washington: Translational Institute/Washington Office Latin America) 30.

[198] See CR da Silva et al, 'Sistema Prisional Registra quase 450 Óbitos por Covid-19; Nº de Servidores Mortos É Maior que de Presos' (*G1, Monitor da Violência*, 17 May 2021) https://g1.globo.com/monitor-da-violencia/noticia/2021/05/17/sistema-prisional-registra-quase-450-obitos-por-covid-19-no-de-servidores-mortos-e-maior-que-o-de-presos.ghtml.

[199] See CN Dias and F Salla, 'Organized Crime in Brazilian Prisons: The Example of PCC' (2013) 2 *International Journal of Criminology and Sociology* 397.

[200] *Anuário Brasileiro de Segurança Pública 2021* (Fórum Brasileiro de Segurança Pública, 2021) 213.

[201] *Anuário Brasileiro de Segurança Pública 2020* (Fórum Brasileiro de Segurança Pública, 2020) 13.

[202] *Anuário Brasileiro de Segurança Pública 2021* (n 200) 67 (56.3% of Brazilians are Black).

[203] ibid 14.

deaths resulted from police interventions, but police officers are also victims of violent crimes: 194 died in 2020. In 2020, there were 23.6 intentional homicides/100,000 inhabitants, one of the highest rates in Latin America.[204] These are all symptoms of a country where inequality and violence have been normalised[205] as tolerable in society.[206]

These data point out that the criminal judicial system is itself structured in racism and violence, in a sort of 'democratic simulacrum'[207] that, despite incremental initiatives to combat crime, seems destined to fail in strengthening the rule of law and protecting human rights.[208] Empirical data has shown that Brazil has failed in tackling violence, which has grown significantly over the years.[209] Impunity is a serious issue, and there is a high discrepancy among the federal units. For example, a study revealed that Brazil, from 2006 to 2016, had a clearance rate for homicide that is one of the world's lowest: 92 per cent to 95 per cent of all murders remain unsolved.[210] Some federal units, however, fare much better than others: São Paulo and the Federal District, for example, feature a low impunity index of 1.1,[211] which is even comparable to developed nations, whereas, in Bahia, this index reaches 14.7.[212] Also concerning is the length of the investigation: in São Paulo, a murder investigation takes an average of two years, but in other states, such as Ceará, only 4 per cent of homicides led to a conviction in the same year according to data from 2017.[213]

The constitutional design of public security forces in Brazil helps explain such a dire scenario. The Constitution reinforced the division between investigation and repression among the police forces in Brazil. In the vast majority of cases,[214] the investigation is within the competence of the civilian police,[215] but it is the military police (*polícia militar*) that is responsible for ostensive policing and repression.[216] It is an authoritarian legacy that gained strength during

[204] According to the World Bank, Brazil is only behind El Salvador, Honduras, Venezuela, and Mexico (data from 2018). See https://data.worldbank.org/indicator/VC.IHR.PSRC.P5?most_recent_value_desc=true.

[205] See DS Ng-Mak, et al, 'Normalization of Violence Among Inner-City Youth: A Formulation for Research' (2002) 72 *American Journal of Orthopsychiatry* 92.

[206] See RSD Lima, 'Violence and Public Safety as a Democratic Simulacrum in Brazil' (2018) 7 *International Journal of Criminology and Sociology* 162.

[207] ibid 159.

[208] ibid.

[209] ibid 163 ('since the 1980s, the national homicide rate has grown by an average of 20% a year').

[210] FS Nery and P Nadanovsky, 'Homicide Impunity in Brazil Between 2006 and 2016' (2020) 54 *Revista de Saúde Publica* 153.

[211] ibid 147 ('homicide impunity index was calculated by the ration between the number of homicides committed in five years and the number of individuals *incarcerated for murder* two years after this period').

[212] ibid 148.

[213] ibid 163.

[214] Exceptions are crimes under federal or military jurisdiction.

[215] Article 144, §4, of the 1988 Constitution.

[216] Article 144, §5, of the 1988 Constitution.

the civilian-military dictatorship (1964–85),[217] when the military police became the central force for public security.[218] The existence of a police force that is an 'ancillary [force] and reserve of the Army',[219] reveals how the country, even though having transitioned to democracy, still suffers from a serious difficulty in establishing full civilian control over the military. As with the Army[220] and the military judicial system, the 1988 Constitution kept the clauses that regulate public security virtually untouched, including the military police,[221] whose structure remained practically identical to the dictatorial period.[222] Even though the military police is an 'ancillary [force] and reserve of the Army', the Constitution establishes that both the civilian and military police forces are subject to the governors of the states and the Federal District,[223] but the Union has exclusive power to legislate on 'general organisation rules, troops, matériel, guarantees, drafting and mobilisation of the military police and military fire brigades'.[224] In practical terms, this means that, despite being subject to the governors, who appoint the commanders and pay the officers' salaries,[225] 'the military police has thus two bosses'[226] and the Army has partial control over it, an anomaly for a democratic regime.[227]

What is more, the military police is under the military judicial system or, if subject to civil justice in cases of first-degree murder against a civilian (the only exception), the investigation is carried out by the military.[228] The consequence is one of very deficient oversight and accountability. Overall, the internal corrections units (*corregedorias*), the external oversight by the Military Public Ministry[229] – another authoritarian legacy – and the military judicial system are mostly inoperative. It is no wonder that the rate of impunity among military police officers, even despite the shocking numbers of police violence, is considerably high.

Corruption is also a reality, but the degree varies between the states.[230] The association of violence and corruption gained ground with the rise of militias,

[217] See ML Bretas and A Rosemberg, 'A História da Polícia no Brasil: Balanço e Perspectivas' (2013) 14 *Topoi* 162.
[218] See J Zaverucha (n 35) 56.
[219] Article 144, §6, of the 1988 Constitution.
[220] See ch 3.
[221] Zaverucha (n 35) 45.
[222] ibid 55–56.
[223] Article 144, §6, of the 1988 Constitution.
[224] Article 22, XXI, of the 1988 Constitution.
[225] With the exception of the Federal District, whose budget for the military police comes from the Union.
[226] Zaverucha (n 35) 54.
[227] ibid 46.
[228] See Lei 9.299, de 7 de Agosto de 1996.
[229] Article 129, VII, of the 1988 Constitution.
[230] See AA do Nascimento, 'A Corrupção Policial em Debate: Desvio e Impunidade nas Instituições Policiais do Rio de Janeiro' (2017) 10 *Dilemas-Revista de Estudos de Conflito e Controle Social* 64.

which are paramilitary groups that illegally control parts of the territory, presumably in exchange for providing security and services with the purpose of profit. This phenomenon is seriously pronounced in the city of Rio de Janeiro, where militias already control over 57.5 per cent of the city's territory.[231] The growth of militia groups exacerbated even further the entrenched corruption inside the military and also civilian police, severely undermining the rule of law.[232] All this critical diagnosis is aggravated by the vast evidence that President Bolsonaro and his entourage have close connections with militias in Rio de Janeiro.[233] In fact, *bolsonarismo* is a phenomenon that is intimately connected to the increasing process of politicisation of the police forces, and also the Army, more broadly.[234] Between 2010 and 2020, 25,452 members of the security forces ran for an elective office, mostly men (95.5 per cent) and through centre-right or right parties (87.6 per cent). They were quite successful: 1,860 were elected between 2010–18[235] and at an accelerated pace: in the Chamber of Deputies there were four members originally from the security forces in the 2011–14 legislature, jumping to 19 in the next one (2014–18), and to astonishingly 73 in the 2018–22 legislature (an increase of 1,725 per cent). The intersection between their rise and Bolsonaro's is obvious.[236]

Nonetheless, there are some more positive institutional developments in other areas. The Federal Police, for instance, has gained significant strength over the democratic years. It is subordinate to the executive and is a 'permanent body, organised and maintained by the Union'[237] whose role is to 'investigate criminal offenses against the political and social order', protect the Union's assets, interests and services, and control borders.[238] It is also the institution that investigates drug trafficking, counterfeiting, smuggling, federal tax dodging and money laundering, among other things.[239] It is in the spotlight almost daily as it is normally behind investigations on corruption, which receive catchy names such as 'Operation Car Wash'. The Federal Police works alongside the Federal Public Ministry and the Federal Judiciary in a triangulation where each institution should work independently but in coordination in order to preserve the due process of law.[240] The Federal Police has autonomy to investigate crimes,

[231] 'Apresentação ao Mapa dos Grupos Armados do Rio de Janeiro' (*GENI, NEVI, Fogo Cruzado, Disque Denúncia, Piesta News*, 2020) https://atualprodutora.com/wp-content/uploads/2020/10/apresentacao-16.10.2020.pdf.

[232] See EPN Meyer, *Constitutional Erosion in Brazil: Progresses and Failures of a Constitutional Project* (Hart Publishing, 2021) 141–52.

[233] See BP Manso, *A República das Milícias* (Todavia, 2021).

[234] See ch 3. See also Meyer (n 232) 129–53.

[235] See *Anuário Brasileiro de Segurança Pública 2020* (n 201) 13.

[236] See C Ricardo and F Angeli, 'Policial e Candidato: O Novo Fenômeno Político no Brasil' in *Anuário Brasileiro de Segurança Pública 2020* (n 201) 202–04.

[237] Article 144, §1, of the 1988 Constitution.

[238] Article 144, § 1, I, of the 1988 Constitution.

[239] Articles 109; 144, §1, II, of the 1988 Constitution.

[240] See Arantes (n 124) 192.

but it is overseen by the Public Ministry and, for more intrusive tools such as wiretappings and temporary arrests, it needs prior judicial authorisation.[241] Its autonomy is, however, relative since it is subordinated to the Ministry of Justice and, even though its investigation capacities, personnel, equipment and budget have been improved, there have been attempts to meddle with the federal police by the Bolsonaro government – a fact that led the Supreme Court to approve an investigation.[242] Corruption, though significantly lower than that at the state level (civilian and military police), also occurs, but federal police officers are comparatively more professional, earn better salaries (among the highest in the federal executive), and are more accountable since they are not under observation by the military. It is therefore the police force that is more in tune with democratic principles, but its role is subsidiary: public security is still mostly a state matter, which implies that it is the troublesome binary civilian/military design of police forces that is prevalent nationwide.

Brazil's judicial criminal system continuously struggles with an authoritarian legacy that operates through corruption and violence, whereas, on the other hand, there are some relevant positive achievements in providing new structures and tools to combat crimes, and notably white-collar crimes. The country has adopted strategies to overcome resistance by empowering parallel institutions, such as the Federal Police and the Public Ministry, and providing some degree of liability to sectors that seemed until quite recently virtually untouched. It has not tackled directly the troublesome binary design civilian/military police, but, by creating better structured cross-institutional integration notably at the federal level, it has engendered a sort of institutional bypass[243] that improves law enforcement and weakens potential opposition.

The progress in accountability and transparency through higher coordination and cooperation among the various players in the judicial criminal system is notable. Congress has also passed important legislation to mainly tackle corruption through criminal, administrative and civil liabilities,[244] even if, more recently, it has moved in the other direction.[245] The growth of task forces and anticorruption operations combining efforts by the police, the Public Ministry and the judiciary to combat specific types of crimes has also shown improvement.[246] Despite the setbacks during the Bolsonaro government, there

[241] ibid.

[242] STF, INQ 4831 (pending). See T Philips, 'Jair Bolsonaro Faces Inquiry into Claims of Meddling with Police' *The Guardian* (28 April 2020) www.theguardian.com/world/2020/apr/28/jair-bolsonaro-faces-inquiry-into-claims-of-meddling-with-police.

[243] See MM Prado and MJ Trebilcock, *Institutional Bypasses: A Strategy to Promote Reforms for Development* (Cambridge University Press, 2018).

[244] See the Administrative Improbity Act (Lei n. 8.429, de 2 de Junho de 1992, recently reviewed by Lei n. 14.230, de 25 de Outubro de 2021). See also the Anticorruption Act (Law n. 12.846, de 1 de Agosto de 2913), which establishes penalties for Brazilian and foreign companies for corruption.

[245] See B Mello and E Éboli, 'Congresso Avança na Blindagem a Políticos com Projetos que Limitam Investigação e Punição' (*O Globo*, 15 October 2021) https://oglobo.globo.com/politica/congresso-avanca-na-blindagem-politicos-com-projetos-que-limitam-investigacao-punicao-1-25237172.

[246] See Arantes (n 124) 200.

has also been important coordination with distinct agencies, such as the Central Bank, the Internal Revenue Service, the Financial Activities Control Council (COAF), the Brazilian Institute for Environment and Natural Resources (IBAMA) as well as state agencies, police and the Public Ministry. The rising number of politicians and CEOs and CFOs of Brazilian big companies convicted for crimes are evidence that the criminal system seems to have become slightly less unequal. As Rogério Arantes puts it, 'the police-MP[Public Ministry]-judiciary triangle seems to be moving away from being a Bermuda Triangle – where cases get lost – and has become more effective, thanks to the greater proximity among them and procedural speed'.[247]

There are naturally some caveats to this movement. The balance between improved institutional design, on the one hand, and the risk of abuse of such new powers, on the other, has proven very unstable. The media, by showcasing daily the task forces through this improved cooperation, fosters greater transparency and accountability[248] but can also help frame the public opinion according to its interests. Daily spectacles also challenge the very capacity of such task forces to be diligent and behave according to strict principles of due process of law and fairness.[249] Abuses have led to a growing debate in society over the need to constrain such operations, and it is no wonder that they have provided the perfect argument for those who have long benefitted from impunity to push for measures limiting such powers. On the other hand, abuses by such institutions cannot be tolerated.

This difficult equilibrium reveals that incremental rather than radical change may be a more suitable development to prevent society from spectacles and public agents who present themselves as saviours of criminal justice. It also reveals that incremental change is a better strategy to overcome backlashes from those who have long benefitted from impunity. Yet it is at the bottom of criminal justice, with its alarming numbers of violence and inequality, that the crude perversity of such a system needs to be urgently dealt with. Brazil's criminal justice system significantly contrasts with the institutional improvements the country could achieve in many areas, including in the very judiciary. The paradoxical nature of Brazil's democracy is clearly represented in such contrasting movements: as with the rise of politicisation in the judiciary more broadly, criminal justice is where the country's past, with its longstanding inequality and violence, merges more visibly with its future in the development of the rule of law. In the end, either at the bottom or at the apex of the judicial system, it is still inequality and a certain authoritarian mindset that prevent Brazil from providing a judicial system that is more in accordance with the expectations of inclusiveness, fairness and solidarity that is the basis of Brazil's constitutional project.

[247] ibid 211.
[248] See Arantes (n 124) 201.
[249] ibid 212.

6

The Extra-Legal Influences on the Rule of Law and Mechanisms of Accountability in Brazil

I. INTRODUCTION: THE PARADOXICAL RELATIONSHIP BETWEEN THE PRIVATE AND PUBLIC SECTORS IN BRAZIL

IN HER RECENT book *A Organização: A Odebrecht e o Esquema de Corrupção que Chocou o Mundo* (*The Organisation: Odebrecht and the Corruption Scheme that Shocked the World*),[1] Malu Gaspar, a leading journalist, revealed, with breathtaking details, the rise and the rapid fall of the biggest construction contractor in Brazil, Odebrecht, which had ramifications in several countries all over the world, but particularly in Latin America and Africa. It became a central player in so-called 'Operation Car Wash',[2] a massive criminal investigation involving various politicians, including the presidents of both Houses of Congress, Brazil's largest parties, and CEOs and CFOs of the country's biggest companies, among them Marcelo Odebrecht, Odebrecht's CEO, and many of his entourage. Other countries also filed charges against the company. It was, for example, through a leniency agreement made public by the US Department of Justice and which involved Brazil, the US and Switzerland that the world learned how corruption was a standard practice in many of its operations and how widespread it was. That agreement showed that 'from 2003 to 2014, the company paid 788 million dollars in briberies to Presidents of the Republic and government employees of eleven countries in Latin America and Africa, besides Brazil …'.[3] Such an amount did not include illegal cash transfers to political campaigns, which would increase it to approximately

[1] M Gaspar, *A Organização: A Odebrecht e o Esquema de Corrupção que Chocou o Mundo* (Companhia das Letras, 2020).

[2] See PF Lagunes and J Svejnar, *Corruption and the Lava Jato Scandal in Latin America* (Routledge, 2020); E Valarini and M Pohlmann, 'Organizational Crime and Corruption in Brazil: A Case Study of the "Operation Carwash" Court Records' (2019) 59 *International Journal of Law, Crime and Justice* 100340.

[3] M Gaspar, 'Uma História do Peru: A Ascensão e a Queda da Odebrecht na América Latina' (*Piauí*, July 2017) https://piaui.folha.uol.com.br/materia/uma-historia-do-peru/.

900 million dollars. It was called the biggest leniency agreement ever made and it imposed a penalty on the company of 2.6 billion dollars.[4]

Odebrecht's rise and fall is possibly the most shocking of any private company in Brazilian history. It reveals how this symbiotic relationship between private companies and public officials has been successful in mutually benefitting from corruption: politicians obtain large amounts of money for their political campaigns through slush funds or for their own pockets, and private companies have their access to normally high valued public contracts facilitated through legal benefits, restrained competition via cartel schemes, tax exemptions and other strategies to increase profits such as overbilling. On the other hand, Odebrecht's fall is a sign that some institutional reaction against such practices has gained traction in the country. The fact that not only top executives from Odebrecht and other private companies but also some bigwigs in Congress were convicted and arrested is certainly not an expected outcome for a country where impunity of economic, political and legal elites has long prevailed

The Odebrecht case is especially shocking because of its range and the amount of money involved, but not because of how corruption has operated in the country. It is the corruption playbook seen in various parts of the world whereby big contractors develop a symbiotic relationship with politicians in order to obtain mutual advantages. Yet it is revealing of some contrasting analyses of the quality of the rule of law in Brazil, and this transforms it into a fascinating case in which we can explore some ambiguities raised by prominent comparative indicators of the rule of law, and specifically corruption indicators. Odebrecht is one of only a few cases in which members of the economic and political elites were finally punished and, as part of 'Operation Car Wash', it is at the centre of developments that led to a generalised anti-political sentiment,[5] which, in turn, paved the way for the rise of a populist president in the country. More interestingly, it is also revealing of how punishment of elite groups – which has always been the Achilles heel of Brazil's mechanisms of horizontal accountability[6] – can rapidly and efficiently develop resistance and suffer counterattacks that are detrimental to the rule of law.

This chapter develops as follows. First, it introduces some data on corruption and how interpreting such data may raise more doubts than certainties. The main argument – as the Odebrecht case already suggests – is that there is a structural difficulty in correctly assessing the level of breach of the rule of law when it comes to entrenched corruption in public-private relationships: corruption exists and is highly entrenched, but nonetheless Brazil features one of the most robust oversight and accountability frameworks in Latin America,[7] which

[4] ibid.

[5] See ch 2.

[6] See MA Melo and C Pereira, *Making Brazil Work: Checking the President in a Multiparty System* (Palgrave Macmillan, 2013) 9–10.

[7] ibid.

has provided growing evidence of its capabilities in challenging corrupted practices. Curiously enough, though, Brazil is persistently ranked by some leading corruption indicators as one of the most corrupt countries in the region, exactly when such impactful cases have become general knowledge. Secondly, it will discuss the role of some key accountability institutions in combatting corruption, the major movements that gained momentum in this direction and how they may have paradoxically helped destabilise the political arena, leading to a serious backlash.

Finally, this chapter delves into the involvement of organised civil society in fostering citizenship and democratisation. The main argument is that the private sector has had a paradoxical relationship with the public sector, either through historical clientelism or through demands for more fairness in public institutions, and such a paradox is directly found in the country's longstanding use of law to construct and maintain inequality. While there is a visible longstanding connection between many corporations and sectors of the industry and the public sectors through distinct forms of clientelism, there is also a growing movement of organised civil society in favour of new policies aimed at democratising the institutional framework and designing strategies to tackle the longstanding inequalities in the country. This chapter also examines the role, structure and dynamics of the media, which, though fairly free, are notably concentrated and influential in Brazil. The power of the new media (Facebook, Twitter, WhatsApp, etc) is also addressed by focusing on their impact on Brazil's democracy.

II. THE DATA OF CORRUPTION IN BRAZIL ACCORDING TO INTERNATIONAL INDICATORS

Brazil has scored particularly badly in some perception-based corruption indicators such as Transparency International's Corruption Perception Index (CPI) and World Bank's Control of Corruption (CC). Their low numbers contrast with the country's fairly well-positioned web of accountability and oversight institutions,[8] whose legal frameworks, independence and powers should in principle put Brazil in a better position in comparative perspective,[9] despite some setbacks in the last few years[10] and the still high levels of impunity.[11]

[8] ibid.

[9] ibid 9.

[10] Since President Dilma Rousseff's impeachment, and more emphatically during the Bolsonaro presidency, Brazil has experienced a backlash against anti-corruption movements. See JZ Benvindo, 'The "Rationality of Fear" on the Edge of Brazilian Democracy: Another Shield Against Authoritarianism?' (*International Journal of Constitutional Law Blog*, 31 December 2019) www.iconnectblog.com/2019/12/the-rationality-of-fear-on-the-edge-of-brazilian-democracy-another-shield-against-authoritarianism/.

[11] See LD Carson and MM Prado, 'Mapping Corruption & Its Institutional Determinants in Brazil' (2014) 8 *IRIBA Working Paper*, https://ssrn.com/abstract=2497935; TJ Power and MM Taylor, 'Introduction: Accountability Institutions and Political Corruption in Brazil' in

Brazilian democracy is young but has experienced a gradual self-correcting and self-sustaining process of institutional consolidation and has also achieved a 'broad societal consensus that corruption – and especially political corruption – is a major problem'.[12] A fairly consistent web of accountability and oversight institutions and a general awareness that fighting corruption should be in the national agenda are obviously positive signs for the rule of law. Moreover, if such institutions have increasingly made individuals accountable for their corrupt practices, like the Odebrecht example, and, more broadly, 'Operation Car Wash', there should be some explanation why Brazil is ranked among the most corrupt countries in South America according to those indicators.

Since 2012, when Transparency International CPI started adopting a new methodology, Brazil has scored merely around 40 out of 100 (100 denoting the most non corrupt). In 2017, 2018 and 2019 this figure dropped to 35, rising to 38 in 2020 and 2021. It is currently ranked 96 among 180 countries, and, in South America, it ties with Argentina and only fares better than Peru (36), Ecuador (36), Bolivia (30), Paraguay (30) and Venezuela (14):[13] countries which are either the poorest in the region or authoritarian. World Bank's Worldwide Governance Indicator (100 also denoting the highest rank), in which its Control of Corruption is one marker, has presented more positive results, but the most recent corruption scandals and political crises have driven its Control of Corruption (56.46 in 2009; 43.75 in 2020) and Political Stability and Absence of Violence/Terrorism (51.18 in 2009; 32.08 in 2020), and 'Government Effectiveness' (51.67 in 2009; 36.54 in 2020) indexes into a slump. Its other markers have also declined in a decade, but not as significantly: Brazil's numbers are now mostly below average in Latin America and the Caribbean: 'Voice and Accountability' (62.56 in 2009; 56.52 in 2020), 'Regulatory Quality' (54.55 in 2009; 46.15 in 2020), and 'Rule of Law' (50.71 in 2009; 48.08 in 2020). Its Control of Corruption index is currently way below the indicators of Uruguay (89.42), Chile (84.13), and slightly below Argentina (50.00) and Colombia (47.60).[14]

According to the Transparency International's CPI, such a low score derives from a series of attacks on Brazil's oversight and anti-corruption frameworks during the Bolsonaro administration. In its 2019 report, it highlighted a set of events showing a growing interference with accountability institutions – particularly the Federal Police and the Public Ministry (through the Attorney-General of the Republic's office) – some Supreme Court decisions,[15]

TJ Power and MM Taylor (eds), *Corruption and Democracy in Brazil: The Struggle for Accountability* (University of Notre Dame Press, 2011).

[12] T Power and MM Taylor, 'Conclusion: The Web of Accountability Institutions in Brazil' in Power and Taylor (n 11) 273.

[13] Transparency International, *Corruption Perception Index 2021* (Transparency International, 2021) www.transparency.org/en/cpi/2021.

[14] World Bank, *World Bank's Worldwide Governance Indicators*, https://info.worldbank.org/governance/wgi/.

[15] Transparency International, *Corruption Perception Index 2019* (Transparency International, 2020) 4.

and President Bolsonaro's continuous attacks on civil organisations, the media and institutions more broadly.[16] Interestingly enough, Word Bank's CC pointed out an increase of more than 5 points for Brazil from 2017 to 2020, although, like Transparency International's CPI, its methodology is also largely based upon surveys by experts, non-governmental institutions and private and public sectors.[17]

Even before updating Transparency International's CPI's methodology in 2012, Brazil also scored around 40, if not 30 (as in the 2000s). The World Bank's CC had a slightly more positive assessment of Brazil's control of corruption, grading it around 50–60 until 2013, then dropping the score to around 40 in the following years. Such a fall coincides with the rise of popular protests, the growing dissatisfaction with the political environment, the impeachment of President Dilma Rousseff and the election of Jair Bolsonaro as President. It also coincides with corruption scandals, particularly 'Operation Car Wash', including the Odebrecht case.

Such indicators are mostly based on experts' institutional and organisational responses. When compared with other perceptions-based and experience-based indexes, there are some important contrasts. Transparency International's Global Corruption Barometer 2019, whose data are collected from everyday people's perceptions and experiences, points out that 54 per cent of Brazilians think that corruption increased in the country in the last 12 months (a drop from 2017, when 78 per cent thought so), and 90 per cent answered that corruption is a big problem. Curiously, however, Brazilians have a more positive viewpoint when it comes to the institutional response to corruption: 48 per cent of Brazilians responded that the government has performed well in tackling corruption – an improvement from 2017, when only 35 per cent answered in this way. Moreover, Brazilians feel they are less affected by corruption than most countries in the region: only 11 per cent answered that they had any experience with bribery for basic services[18] – just below Costa Rica (7 per cent).[19] Interestingly, Brazilians feel more optimistic than is average for the region (82 per cent v 77 per cent) as regards their capacity for making a difference in fighting corruption.[20]

Brazil also scores fairly well in some markers of corporate integrity. Transparency International Brazil joined efforts with the Getúlio Vargas Foundation to assess integrity in the corporate sector and its connections with the public sector and civil society.[21] Based on key publications in the field and experts'

[16] ibid 5.

[17] See D Kaufmann, A Kraay and M Mastruzzi, 'The Worldwide Governance Indicators Methodology and Analytical Issues' (2011) 3 *Hague Journal on the Rule of Law* 221.

[18] See Transparency International, *Global Corruption Barometer: Latin America & The Caribbean 2019* (Transparency International, 2020) 17, https://images.transparencycdn.org/images/2019_GCB_LatinAmerica_Caribbean_Full_Report_200409_091428.pdf.

[19] Some countries provided no data, such as Uruguay, Paraguay and Ecuador.

[20] See Transparency International (n 18) 28.

[21] Transparência Internacional, *Integridade e Empresas no Brasil* (Transparência Internacional, 2019) http://portalods.com.br/publicacoes/integridade-e-empresas-no-brasil/.

surveys, it concluded that Brazil features a web of accountability institutions and a legal framework that is quite suitable for carrying out investigations and has improved over the years, such as the vast investigative powers of the Federal Police, the Public Ministry, the Administrative Council for Economic Defence (among others) and the Anti-Corruption (or Clean Company) Act.[22] Among the indicators of efficiency in preventing, detecting and punishing corruption, on a scale from 0 to 100 (100 denoting excellence), Brazil scores well in 'prohibition of bribery by public servants' (75) and 'prohibition of cartels' (83.3); fairly well in 'prohibition of money laundering' (66.6), 'accountability, audit and transparency' (62.5), and 'public procurement' (62.5); fairly badly in 'prohibition of improper influence' (45.8); and badly in protecting whistle-blowers (12.5).[23] Despite the less robust numbers in some markers, Brazilian institutions have been deemed quite efficient when it comes to preventing corruption in foreign relations. According to Transparency International's 'Exporting Corruption Progress Report 2020', among the 47 countries examined comprising 83 per cent of the global exports, Brazil is classified among the 'Moderate Enforcement' countries, along with Germany, France, Italy, Australia, Sweden, Portugal and Spain. It is one of the few countries that have 'moderately [enforced] against companies that pay bribes abroad',[24] and provide 'considerable amount of information in online databases about pending and concluded cases',[25] though some leniency agreements such as those of 'Operation Car Wash' 'are only partially accessible to the public'.[26]

What these last indicators show as being more problematic are data on the corporate world itself and the engagement of civil society against corruption in the private sector. Most markers related to the corporate mechanisms of self-governance and social monitoring of the private sector are less robust than those also involving the public sector. Transparency International's 'Integrity and Companies in Brazil'[27] reveals that Brazilian companies score poorly in some key markers of self-governance (100 denoting excellence), such as compliance (56.2), audit and certification (50), transparency and release of anti-corruption information (37.5), independence of the media from the private sector (25) and social monitoring of the private sector (25), for example.[28] Indeed, the Brazilian corporate sector seems to be a glass half-full or glass half-empty when it comes to preventing corruption, and, with the exception of anti-cartel enforcement, private corruption with no direct

[22] Lei n. 12.846, de 1 de Agosto de 2013.

[23] See Transparência Internacional (n 21).

[24] Transparency International, *Exporting Corruption: Progress Report 2020* (Transparency International, 2020) 14.

[25] ibid 17.

[26] ibid 18.

[27] Transparência Internacional (n 21).

[28] ibid.

participation of the public sector has been left under the radar by Congress. Another interesting study by Transparency International Brazil revealed that, among the Brazilian top 100 companies and top 10 banks, 65 per cent of them publicise anti-corruption programmes, and 48 per cent make public their organisational structure, but only 3 per cent of those with international ramifications (54 companies) publicise their reports by country (below the average of emerging markets of 9 per cent).[29]

These distinct indicators, some from the same organisation through distinct methodologies, reveal that, on the one hand, there is a clear perception that corruption is a serious issue for the rule of law in Brazil. On the other hand, there is a high awareness of the existence of corruption among Brazilians and the potential for civil engagement in fighting it, though targeting more specifically the private-public relationships than the private sector's own practices. Institutional mechanisms to combat corruption exist, are fairly consistent, and have highly improved over the years, but fail to punish crimes, even though some large-scale corruption cases, such as 'Operation Car Wash', have led to punishment of bigwigs in politics and in the business sector.

Overall, however, there are some striking contrasts among such indicators, thereby revealing the difficulties in such types of assessments. There are important variations in relation to trends – for example, the more negative results of Transparency International's CPI versus the more positive results of the World Bank's CC in the last three years – some remarkable gaps between experts' and general perceptions, and some disconnection between perceptions and personal experiences and objective data. They reveal key information about how corruption impacts the reality, but they inevitably suffer from behavioural factors such as biases and limited information and are particularly influenced by how those large-scale corruption scandals and investigations are framed by the media. The correlation between a higher perception of corruption and increasing anti-corruption task forces regularly broadcast on the media is well-documented. In the circumstance of a young democracy, such an effect has proven even greater.[30] On the other hand, it is also known that young democracies need some time before experiencing self-enforcing and self-improving mechanisms to combat corruption. As Timothy Power and Matthew Taylor point out, 'Brazil's democratic accountability institutions have required time to settle into place, to learn how to work on their own and then jointly, and to find ways of cooperating to develop corrective improvements.'[31]

[29] Transparência Internacional, *Transparência em Relatórios Corporativos: As 100 Maiores Empresas e os 10 Maiores Bancos Brasileiros* (Transparência Internacional, 2018), https://transparenciacorporativa.org.br/trac2018/.

[30] See MT Rock, 'Corruption and Democracy' (2009) 45 *The Journal of Development Studies* 55.

[31] Power and Taylor (n 12) 273.

Therefore, even though those indicators – and especially those perception-based indicators – matter and provide some relevant information, they fail particularly in assessing political variables and behavioural biases in their analyses. Brazil has serious problems of corruption, for sure, but it certainly strikes any observer as odd that, for example, for Transparency International's CPI and World Bank's CC, countries that are both non-democratic and whose press is highly constrained, score better than young democracies whose press is much freer, and therefore can regularly report cases of corruption. For example, for Transparency International's CPI and World Bank's CC, Brazil is behind – sometimes way behind – countries such as UAE, Qatar, Cuba, Belarus or China, all non-democracies with limited press freedom. Such a lack of control of behavioural effects and the disregard of political variables lead to the conclusion that surveys should be taken with a pinch of salt and be regarded as just one source whose numbers, especially for young democracies combatting more openly corruption, may fail to provide an accurate depiction of the reality.[32]

III. THE COMBAT OF CORRUPTION IN BRAZIL: THE EFFECTS OF PATH DEPENDENCE, INEQUALITY, AND INSTITUTIONAL DESIGN FLAWS

Since the transition to democracy, Brazil has experienced various corruption scandals[33] but also advanced an anti-corruption agenda, reformed and strengthened oversight and accountability institutions, and passed considerable legislation aimed at curbing corruption.[34] Unlike such perceptions and experienced-based indicators above, empirical data exhibit some relevant achievements in the rule of law over the last few decades: Brazil features, for example, one of the most professionalised bureaucracies in Latin America, whose civil servants are mostly hired after having passed very competitive and merit-based selection processes and integrate a public career with great benefits and incentives.[35] There is also a web of accountability and oversight institutions that is comparatively robust in Latin America, such as the audit courts (*Tribunais de Conta*),[36] the Federal Controller's Office (*Controladoria Geral da União*, (CGU)),[37] the Public Ministry

[32] See L Avritzer, 'Índices de Percepção de Corrupção' in L Avritzer et al (eds), *Corrupção: Ensaios e Críticas* (Editora UFMG, 2008) 423–27.

[33] For a discussion of some such scandals, see Carson and Prado (n 11).

[34] See Melo and Pareira (n 6). See also Power and Taylor (n 12) 273; M Tourinho, 'Brazil in the Global Anticorruption Regime' (2018) 61 *Revista Brasileira de Política Internacional* 14.

[35] See P Cavalcante and P Carvalho, 'The Professionalization of Brazilian Federal Bureaucracy (1995–2014): Advances and Dilemmas' (2017) 51 *Revista de Administração Pública* 2.

[36] See BW Speck, 'Auditing Institutions' in Power and Taylor (n 11) 127–61; Melo and Pereira (n 6) 119–57.

[37] See C Ferraz and F Finan, 'Fighting Political Corruption: Evidence from Brazil' in K Basu and T Cordella (eds), *Institutions, Governance and the Control of Corruption* (Springer, 2018) 253–84.

(*Ministério Público*),[38] the Federal Police[39] and a fairly independent judiciary[40] and media,[41] despite some setbacks in the last years.

These institutions have seen hefty improvements in their capacities over the democratic years, and those that existed before the transition to democracy were greatly empowered by the 1988 Constitution. Moreover, the production of a massive amount of legislation aimed at curbing corruption passed in Congress, largely inspired by the international experience, such as the anti-money laundering,[42] anti-corruption (or clean company)[43] and organised crime acts.[44] These developments have positively reflected on some indicators. For instance, task-forces by the federal police increased from 236, in 2009, to 1,033, in 2018,[45] even though such numbers have decreased under the Bolsonaro government;[46] federal public servants who were punished increased from 110, in 2003, to 619 in 2018 (then decreasing to 491 in 2020);[47] and blacklisted companies included in the National Register of Inapt and Suspended Companies (CEIS) increased from 237, in 2010, to 3,070, in 2017.[48] Transparency has also improved: currently, 75 per cent of all data of the federal government is open to public access, as monitored by the Federal Controllers Office (CGU).[49]

Naturally, professional public servants, greater institutional powers and capacities and a solid body of legislation tell only one side of the story. Underfunding, excessive formalism, burdensome procedural rules[50] and deep-rooted informal practices in private-public relationships[51] have impaired more consistent progress in this area. More specifically, path dependence, inequality

[38] See RB Arantes, 'The Federal Police and the Ministério Público' in Power and Taylor (n 11) 184–217. See ch 5.

[39] ibid. See ch 5.

[40] See Melo and Pereira (n 6) 42; see ch 5.

[41] See Melo and Pereira (n 6) 43.

[42] Lei n. 12.683, de 9 de Julho de 2012; Lei n. 9613, de 3 de Março de 1998.

[43] Lei n. 12.846, de 1º de Agosto de 2013

[44] Lei n. 12.850, de 2 de Agosto de 2013. See Tourinho (n 34) 14.

[45] K Kadanus, 'PF Quintuplica Operações em Dez Anos. Se Depender de Moro, Meta Vai Subir' (*Gazeta do Povo*, 27 February 2019) www.gazetadopovo.com.br/politica/republica/pf-quintuplica-operacoes-em-dez-anos-se-depender-de-moro-meta-vai-subir-4sjs3el4yqkam0rsbo9pwnbvt/.

[46] C Carvalho and G Schmitt, 'Redução de Forças-Tarefa Freia Ritmo de Investigações de Crimes do Colarinho Branho (*O Globo*, 16 July 2021) https://oglobo.globo.com/politica/reducao-de-forcas-tarefa-freia-ritmo-de-investigacoes-de-crimes-de-colarinho-branco-25112236.

[47] Controladoria Geral da União, *Portal da Transparência*, www.portaldatransparencia.gov.br/sancoes.

[48] Transparência Internacional (n 21) 25.

[49] Controladoria Geral da União, *Monitoramento de Dados Abertos*, http://paineis.cgu.gov.br/dadosabertos/index.htm.

[50] See Carson and Prado (n 11) 28–31.

[51] See D Samuels, 'Informal Institutions When Formal Contracting is Prohibited: Campaign Finance in Brazil' in S Levitsky and G Helmke (eds), *Informal Institutions and Democracy: Lessons from Latin America* (The John Hopkins University Press, 2006) 87–206.

and institutional design flaws have hindered efforts to strengthen accountability institutions and their capacity to oversee, investigate and punish corrupt behaviours.

In a country with such a severe level of inequality, any structural reform attacking self-reinforcing practices is costly and tends to backfire,[52] so every step forward to strengthen the rule of law walks on thin ice. In addition to raising switching costs, inequality also thwarts the development of a network of formal and informal ancillary supporting institutions that are needed to produce a more democratic environment for the rule of law, where rights are enforced more equally and institutions and individuals find the incentives to comply with the law.[53] Therefore, despite important developments in Brazil's web of accountability and oversight institutions as well as in its anti-corruption legislation, inequality not only reinforces some negative effects of path dependence but also raises additional barriers to the participation of new members in key sectors of social life, such as public services and public-private partnerships, and weakens civic and political engagement.[54] In the private sector, it means, for instance, that companies that have not participated in corruption networks may find greater barriers to entering the market of public contracts or come across bureaucratic difficulties that are demanding of time or resources. Corruption becomes self-enforcing and increasingly difficult to combat, because the same companies and politicians find mutual benefits in such a partnership of no-competitiveness and impunity. Improvements in institutional capacities and mechanisms of democracy[55] are hence just the tip of the iceberg of a very complex social and institutional fabric.

In addition, institutional design can also weaken efforts to curb corruption, sometimes only noticeable once institutions are examined through their interdependencies. Brazilian constitutionalism demonstrates this phenomenon of half full or half empty institutional capacities quite visibly. The 1988 Constitution and subsequent legislation endowed various institutions with enough powers and tools to curb corruption on several fronts, but, while some innovations may look quite impressive, they come nonetheless with specific design features that help lay the groundwork for backlash, weakening those institutional capacities. Over time, those institutions perform unsatisfactorily and fail to effectively challenge those embedded and self-reinforcing practices. Even if some institutions look powerful by design and have the tools to combat corruption, their capacities can be impaired when a key institution in the web performs poorly. Brazilian institutions suffer from what Timothy J Power and Matthew M Taylor point

[52] See B Weingast, 'The Political Foundations of the Democracy and the Rule of Law' (1997) 91 *American Political Science Review* 59.

[53] See DM Brinks, 'Inequality, Institutions, and the Rule of Law: The Social and Institutional Bases of Rights' (2008) 351 *Kellogg Institute Working Paper* 2.

[54] ibid.

[55] See A Vermeule, *Mechanisms of Democracy* (Oxford University Press, 2007).

out as 'weakness of individual institutions' and 'interdependence of component institutions in the web'.[56]

Brazil's powerful Public Ministry, both at federal and state levels, is a paradigmatic example: the 1988 Constitution significantly enhanced its institutional capacities and it '[represents] one of the most significant institutional innovations undertaken since Brazil's redemocratization'.[57] However, its members can use their vast discretion to advance their own ambitions,[58] which is problematic due to the Public Ministry's lack of vertical and horizontal accountability.[59] Moreover, particularly in criminal investigations, the Public Ministry operates through a 'triangular relationship'[60] with the federal or state policies, which are more vulnerable to politicisation and corruption,[61] and the judiciary, whose punishment rate in corruption cases is rather low.[62] In the end, the Public Ministry itself may be powerful by design, but the same design creates barriers to more successfully fighting corruption.

The same reasoning applies to the judiciary. Brazil features one of the most independent judiciaries in Latin America,[63] but burdensome procedural rules, a bottleneck of cases and a generous statute of limitations strongly affect its capacity to punish white-collar crimes, and specifically corruption. More seriously, the 1988 Constitution provides that 'the law shall not exclude any injury or threat to a right from the consideration of the Judicial Power',[64] which, in other words, means that every case, regardless of its nature, can be the subject of review by the judiciary. Therefore, although Brazil has created a robust web of oversight and investigative institutions, it has nevertheless potentially granted the judiciary the last word for punishment. Even if there is an administrative punishment, for example, by one of the oversight institutions such as the Federal Audit Court (TCU), that decision can be easily brought to review by the judiciary, which is far slower and less equipped with the necessary accounting and anti-corruption expertise. A judiciary that is excessively time-consuming or whose punishment rate is low will also have a deleterious effect on every other institution involved in such cases, even if they are greatly empowered to perform

[56] Power and Taylor (n 12) 252.

[57] RB Arantes, 'The Federal Police and the Ministério Público' in TJ Power and MM Taylor (eds), *Corruption and Democracy in Brazil: The Struggle for Accountability* (University of Notre Dame Press, 2011) 187.

[58] ibid.

[59] See ch 5. See also F Kerche, VED Oliveira and CG Couto, 'The Brazilian Councils of Justice and Public Prosecutor's Office as Instruments of Accountability' (2020) 54 *Revista de Administração Pública* 1334; VE de Oliveira, GS Lotta and NP de Vasconcelos, 'Ministério Público, Autonomia Funcional e Discricionariedade: Ampla Atuação em Políticas Públicas, Baixa Accountability' (2020) 7 *Revista De Estudos Empíricos Em Direito* 181.

[60] Arantes (n 57) 195.

[61] ibid 192.

[62] See Prado and Carson (n 11) 28–30.

[63] See ch 5.

[64] Article 5, XXXV, of the 1988 Constitution.

this task. Lack of independence, politicisation, underfunding and corruption, by the same token, can affect one or another institution in the web, thereby undermining the whole institutional capacity to combat corruption.

IV. ACCOUNTABILITY INSTITUTIONS, INCREMENTAL IMPROVEMENTS IN COMBATTING CORRUPTION AND POLITICAL BACKLASH: TWO STEPS FORWARD, ONE STEP BACK?

A. Accountability Institutions

In such an environment, progress is made with some degree of success through distinct strategies and workarounds that tackle corruption by focusing on incremental and risk-adverse changes instead of structural and radical reforms. For instance, multiple institutions perform overlapping functions (institutional multiplicity)[65] or new institutions create a pathway to change without needing to modify existing institutions (institutional bypass).[66] Both strategies are particularly suitable for realities where the rule of law has deficiently operated, because they may lower the costs of transaction by, in the first case, 'fostering institutional competition, collaboration, complementarity, and compensation',[67] and, in the latter, not directly modifying traditional or dominant institutions nor promoting a whole reform of the institutional framework.[68] In the end, changes are made and institutional dysfunctionalities are attacked, even if at a slower pace and to a lesser extent. Improvements tend to be surgical, risk-adverse and incremental.

For instance, reforms in the Federal Audit Court (TCU)[69] and the creation and later strengthening of the Federal Controller's Office (CGU),[70] with expanded specialisation[71] and monitoring,[72] have improved Brazil's oversight capacities. The Federal Audit Court, which, among other roles,[73] exerts control over federal accounts and expenditures, punishes misconduct and examines – and advises Congress on – the accounts rendered annually by the President, 'saw its institutional design overhauled in the 1988 Constitution'.[74] It is highly professional,

[65] See LD Carson and MM Prado, 'Using Institutional Multiplicity to Address Corruption as a Collective Action Problem: Lessons from the Brazilian Case' (2016) 62 *The Quarterly Review of Economics and Finance* 56; MM Prado and L Carson, 'Brazilian Anti-Corruption Legislation and its Enforcement: Potential Lessons for Institutional Design' (2014) 9 IRIBA Working Paper.

[66] MM Prado and MJ Trebilcock, *Institutional Bypasses: A Strategy to Promote Reforms for Development* (Cambridge University Press, 2018).

[67] Carson and Prado (n 65) 59.

[68] See Prado and Trebilcock (n 66).

[69] See Speck (n 36); Carson and Prado (n 65) 23.

[70] See Carson and Prado (n 65) 25.

[71] ibid 24.

[72] ibid 25.

[73] Article 71, §2, of the 1988 Constitution.

[74] Speck (n 36) 136. See also Melo and Pereira (n 6) 133.

well-funded and, in many respects, outperforms other audit courts in Latin America despite some serious dysfunctionalities.[75] Among them, only two of its nine Ministers (who finally decide matters in the Court) are originally staff members selected among its auditors and prosecutors, whereas the other seven Ministers are normally former politicians with strong ties with Congress and the president.[76] Despite that, it has achieved greater autonomy[77] and can itself directly punish misconducts, which it has done more frequently.[78] As an 'aid'[79] of Congress, however, it usually needs to interact with other institutions to perform its main tasks,[80] whereas its decisions can be appealed to the judiciary.[81] A similar design and function is also found in state and municipal audit courts,[82] even if their performance varies across the states and municipalities depending on the level of political competition and power fragmentation and turnover.[83]

On the other hand, the Federal Controller's Office (CGU), created in 1991 and then empowered in 2006, has added further accountability and transparency to such a web by monitoring federal public expenditures and transfers of federal funds to units of the federation, most notably the municipalities.[84] It has performed as an 'anticorruption agency'[85] and features numerous programmes for auditing public expenditures, such as the 'Random Audits Program in Federative Units'(*Programa de Fiscalização em Entes Federativos*), which, like a lottery, selects some municipalities among the 5,570 in the country that will be audited at a certain given time;[86] the 'Access to Information' *(Acesso à Informação)*[87] and the 'Transparency Portal' (*Portal da Transparência*),[88] which are aimed at providing information and transparency of all activities of the executive; and Time Brazil (*Brazil Team*), whose goal is to help states and municipalities to improve their governance and mechanisms to combat corruption.[89] It works directly with the *Corregedoria-Geral da União*, which has investigative and punishment powers.[90] Particularly notable is that, with the creation and strengthening of CGU, TCU has become more efficient, in what

[75] See Melo and Pereira (n 6) 133, 135, 136, 119.
[76] See Article 73 of the 1988 Constitution. See Speck (n 36) 154–56.
[77] See Speck (n 36) 149.
[78] See Prado and Carson (n 11) 30.
[79] Article 71 of the 1988 Constitution.
[80] See Speck (n 36) 136.
[81] See Prado and Carson (n 11) 30.
[82] See Melo and Pereira (n 6) 119–56.
[83] ibid 132, 155.
[84] See Carson and Prado (n 65) 61–62.
[85] See Melo and Pereira (n 6) 17.
[86] Controladoria-Geral da União, *Programa de Fiscalização em Entes Federativos*, www.gov.br/cgu/pt-br/assuntos/auditoria-e-fiscalizacao/programa-de-fiscalizacao-em-entes-federativos.
[87] Controladoria-Geral da União, *Acesso à Informação*, www.gov.br/acessoainformacao/pt-br.
[88] Controladoria-Geral da União, *Portal da Transparência*, http://transparencia.gov.br/.
[89] Controladoria-Geral da União, *Time Brasil*, www.gov.br/cgu/pt-br/assuntos/transparencia-publica/time-brasil.
[90] See Carson and Prado (n 11) 27.

Carson and Prado see as a major case of 'institutional multiplicity': even if there is some overlap between both institutions, the creation of CGU has led to mutual improvements in accountability and transparency as diverse pathways were opened to monitor expenditures of public funds and punish wrongdoings.[91]

There is also a web of federal and state[92] regulatory agencies with expertise in strategic sectors of the economy,[93] such as telecommunications (ANATEL), oil, natural gas and biofuel (ANP), health (ANVISA), electricity (ANEEL) and water (ANA). They have an important role in oversight, investigation and punishment in the private sector, are bestowed with relative political and financial autonomy through tenured and staggered directorships and have control over their budgets,[94] even though empirical evidence still shows that such an independence is more expected than real.[95] The Administrative Council for Economic Defence (CADE), responsible for antitrust and competition protection, has also seen an impressive learning process at the structural level in particular since the 1990s[96] and should be praised for its technical decisions and expertise. Investigation, especially at the federal level, has also improved, with the Federal Police gaining notoriety with a series of operations with catchy names against corruption largely broadcast by the media.[97] Such empowerment may also have had a positive impact on the Public Ministry's performance.[98]

Legislation such as the Anti-Money Laundering (2012),[99] Anti-Corruption (or Clean Company, 2013),[100] and Organised Crime (2013) Acts[101] have also introduced important mechanisms to curb corruption based on the international experience, such as plea bargains, tracing of assets and financial data, international cooperation[102] and specialised courts. The Anti-Corruption Act (commonly known as the Clean Company Act) is, in many respects, an interesting example of 'institutional multiplicity' since it can reduce the judiciary's bottleneck through the introduction of new players to judge and punish corruption cases, either through administrative proceedings or civil courts, and foster cooperation between parties and authorities in exchange for reduced penalties.[103]

[91] See Carson and Prado (n 65) 62.
[92] See Melo and Pereira (n 6) 97.
[93] See Lei n. 13.848, de 25 de Junho de 2019.
[94] See Melo and Pereira (n 6) 98.
[95] See MM Prado, 'The Challenges and Risks of Creating Independent Regulatory Agencies: A Cautionary Tale from Brazil' (2008) 41 *Vanderbilt Journal of Transnational Law* 436.
[96] See LL de Barros and M Antonio, 'Brazilian Administrative Council for Economic Defense: An Approach from Sociology and History' (2017) 2 *University of Bologna Law Review* 116.
[97] See ch 5. See also Carson and Prado (n 65) 62; Arantes (n 57).
[98] See Carson and Prado (n 65) 62.
[99] Lei n. 12.683, de 9 de Julho de 2012, and Lei n. 9.613, de 3 de Março de 1998.
[100] Lei m. 12.846, de 1° de agosto de 2013.
[101] Lei n. 12.850, de 2 de agosto de 2013.
[102] See Tourinho (n 34) 14.
[103] See Carson and Prado (n 65) 62; MM Prado, L Carson and I Correa, 'The Brazilian Clean Company Act: Using Institutional Multiplicity for Effective Punishment' (2015) 53 *Osgoode Hall Law Journal* 107.

Therefore, some progress in punishment – Brazil's longstanding Achilles Heel in tackling corruption – has been made through strategies aimed at expanding collaboration among distinct institutions.

B. The Expected Political Backlash

However, even if progress is more incremental than structural, backlash tends to be inevitable once punishment reaches prominent figures in the political, economic and legal sectors. More reactive still are those sectors if serious mistakes are made while enforcing this new legislation. A common mistake is the politicisation of corruption scandals and the consequent abuse of the new tools against corruption, such as those brought by the Clean Company Act. 'Operation Car Wash', with its overarching scope, exemplifies this phenomenon quite clearly. Since its inception, it has been challenged as a case of lawfare particularly targeting the Worker's Party (PT), which ruled the country from 2003–16. It was a key factor for President Dilma Rousseff's impeachment in 2016[104] and the imprisonment of former President Lula da Silva for 580 days, who could not then run in the 2018 presidential elections.[105] The federal judge presiding over that operation was Sérgio Moro, who would later become President Jair Bolsonaro's Minister of Justice[106] and even unsuccessfully attempted to run for presidency in the 2022 elections.[107] Judge Moro's objectionable relationship with the prosecutors became a national scandal as conversations between them leaked to the press.[108] 'Operation Car Wash' has since become an interesting case as it showed not only the deep wounds caused by Brazil's dysfunctional relationship between the private and public sectors, but also how the judiciary – and the media that enthusiastically broadcast such developments – looked increasingly partisan.[109]

[104] See T Ginsburg, A Huq and D Landau, 'The Comparative Constitutional Law of Presidential Impeachment' (2021) 88 *The University of Chicago Law Review* 100.

[105] See D Campello, K Belarmino and D Thome, 'Reporting Corruption in Brazil: The Odebrecht Plea Bargain in Jornal Nacional' (2018) Working Paper, https://ssrn.com/abstract=3274967; A Ansell, 'Impeaching Dilma Rousseff: The Double Life of Corruption Allegations on Brazil's Political Right' (2018) 59 *Culture, Theory and Critique* 312; JT Esteves and C Cosentino, 'The Conviction of Former President Lula as the Maximum Expression of the Exercise of Lawfare' in C Proner et al (eds), *Comments on a Notorious Verdict: The Trial of Lula* (CLACSO, 2018) 117–21.

[106] See T Phillips, 'Bolsonaro Appoints Judge Who Helped Jail Lula to Lead Justice Ministry' *The Guardian* (1 November 2018) www.theguardian.com/world/2018/nov/01/bolsonaro-sergio-moro-brazil-justice-ministry-anti-corruption.

[107] 'Former Judge Sergio Moro Back in Brazilian Politics Ahead of 2022 Vote' (*Reuters*, 10 November 2021) www.reuters.com/world/americas/former-judge-sergio-moro-back-brazilian-politics-ahead-2022-vote-2021-11-10/.

[108] See G Greenwald, L Demori and B Reed, 'Secret Brazil Archive' (*The Intercept*, 9 June 2019) https://theintercept.com/2019/06/09/brazil-archive-operation-car-wash/.

[109] See Lagunes and Svejnar (n 2); Campello et al (n 105); TA van Dijk, 'How Globo Media Manipulated the Impeachment of Brazilian Dilma Rousseff' (2017) 11 *Discourse & Communication* 199.

'Operation Car Wash' largely made use of the new tools brought about by the Clean Company Act, such as leniency agreements and whistle blowers. Those tools could, if they were properly implemented, create an important pathway to curb corruption. However, the goal of strengthening the rule of law through such mechanisms was marked by consistent abuses of basic constitutional guarantees, even if the language seemed to express the rule of law ideals.[110] The lack of diligence, impartiality and observance of basic procedural guarantees by authorities when adopting those tools was considerable.

The abuses through the language of the rule of law led to a political backlash, laying the groundwork for reversing some positive features of those instruments aimed at curbing corruption. What could be, in principle, beneficial to the rule of law became then dominated by the conclusion that, in the way those tools had been implemented, they did more harm than good. It is as though the rule of law needed to regain its normative strength against such abuses by sacrificing some potential benefits those tools could have brought. Such an outcome is a two-way street: it brings some justice to the victims of such abuses, but it also provides a strong argument for self-preservationist movements. As long as 'Operation Car Wash' continued to be scrutinised and criticised for non-observance of basic procedural guarantees,[111] the traditional political, economic and legal actors who have benefitted from clientelism and corruption would naturally seize the moment to reposition themselves and attack the operation with reasonable constitutional grounds.

This context is evidence of what rational theorists usually call the 'rationality of fear', according to which 'when citizens or groups are threatened, they take steps to defend themselves'.[112] Even incremental changes are not immune to this phenomenon. In addition to other causes – for instance, corruption in the political realm and loss of political support in society and Congress – self-preservation certainly lay beneath President Dilma Rousseff's impeachment in 2016.[113] Most of those anti-corruption laws were approved during

[110] R Dixon, 'Rule of Law Teleology: Against the Misuse and Abuse of Rule of Law Rhetoric' (2019) 11 *Hague Journal on the Rule of Law* 464 (arguing in favour of Martin Krygier's 'teleogical' account of the rule of law as a 'guard against the danger of misuse in the application of [the rule of law] ideas'). See M Krygier, 'The Rule of Law: Legality, Teleology, Sociology' in G Palombella and N Walker (eds), *Relocating the Rule of Law* (Hart Publishing, 2008); Krygier, M, 'The Rule of Law: Pasts, Presents, and Two Possible Futures' (2016) 12 *Annual Review of Law and Social Science* 199 (sustaining the need to 'support the rule of law ideal'). See also Y Roznai, 'The Rule of Law in 2030' in C Bezemek (ed.), *Constitutionalism 2030* (Hart Publishing, 2022 *forthcoming*) (arguing in favour of recovering some substantive notions of the rule *of* law instead of interpreting it as a rule *by* law).

[111] See T Bustamante and EPN Meyer, 'Operation Car Wash on Trial: What to Expect from Brazilian Federal Supreme Court's Rulings on Lula da Silva' (*Verfassungsblog*, 10 March 2021) https://verfassungsblog.de/operation-car-wash-on-trial/; See EPN Meyer, *Constitutional Erosion in Brazil: Progresses and Failures of a Constitutional Project* (Hart Publishing, 2021) 89–100.

[112] B Weingast, 'Designing Constitutional Stability' in R Congleton and B Swedenborg (eds), *Democratic Constitutional Design and Public Policy Analysis and Evidence* (MIT Press, 2006) 346.

[113] See next Section.

her administration (2011–16),[114] and the reforms in oversight and investigation institutions were largely carried out during the governments of Lula da Silva and Dilma Rousseff, both by the Worker's Party (PT). When such investigations began reaching members of the political class besides the government and PT, the reaction was immediate. Michel Temer, the Vice-President at that time, was an experienced politician who came from such political circles and was in the best position to defend the interests of the traditional political class and 'stop the bleeding'.[115]

The following events revealed how Brazil's embedded and self-reinforcing mechanisms behave in the face of such institutional innovations. President Bolsonaro took advantage of the anti-political sentiment promoted by that agenda against corruption, which was largely broadcast nationwide.[116] However, as a typical would-be autocrat, once in power, he steadily moved to attack that anti-corruption agenda because of graft investigations against his family and allies[117] as well as the desperate need to build a coalition in Congress in order to bar a potential impeachment.[118] There have been a series of attacks on the independence of the Public Ministry, the Federal Police, the Federal Revenue Services and the Financial Intelligence Unit (COAF). A new law aimed at limiting abuses of authority by public officials,[119] though reasonably justified given those violations of constitutional guarantees in cases like 'Operation Car Wash',[120] can nonetheless constrain public officials in carrying out investigations. The Supreme Court, by the same token, has increasingly reversed its political convergence with some anti-corruption task forces and resorted, for this purpose, to a strong emphasis on procedural guarantees.[121] Such a move is justified given the breach of some such guarantees in those large-scale investigations, but the

[114] The Anti-Money Laundering Act (Lei n. 9.613/98) was overhauled by Lei n. 12.683/12. The Clean Company Act was enacted in 2013 (Lei n. 12.846/2013)) and the Organised Crime Act is also from 2013 (Lei n. 12.850/13).

[115] See J Watts, 'Brazil Minister Ousted After Secret Tape Revals Plot to Topple President Rousseff' (*The Guardian*, 23 May 2016) www.theguardian.com/world/2016/may/23/brazil-dilma-rousseff-plot-secret-phone-transcript-impeachment. See also A Ansell, 'Impeaching Dilma Rousseff: The Double Life of Corruption Allegations on Brazil's Political Right' (2018) 59 *Culture, Theory and Critique* 320.

[116] See JZ Benvindo, 'False Consciousness of Time: The Rise of Jair Bolsonaro' (*International Journal of Constitutional Law Blog*, 10 November 2018) www.iconnectblog.com/2018/11/brazils-false-consciousness-of-time-the-rise-of-jair-bolsonaro/.

[117] See E Londoño, M Andreoni and L Casado, '"A Family Business:" Graft Investigation Threatens Brazil's Bolsonaro' *The New York Times* (28 August 2020) www.nytimes.com/2020/08/28/world/americas/brazil-bosonaro-corruption.html.

[118] See JZ Benvindo, 'Tomorrow Knows Better: A New Inflection Point in Brazil's Democracy?' (*International Journal of Constitutional Law Blog*, 1 July 2020) www.iconnectblog.com/2020/07/tomorrow-knows-better-a-new-inflection-point-in-brazils-democracy/.

[119] Lei n. 13.869, de 5 de Setembro de 2019.

[120] See A Fishman et al, 'Breach of Ethics' (*The Intercept*, 9 June 2019) https://theintercept.com/2019/06/09/brazil-lula-operation-car-wash-sergio-moro/.

[121] See E Machado, 'O Supremo, a Lava Jato e o Vale-Tudo Jurídico' (*Piauí*, 10 March 2021) https://piaui.folha.uol.com.br/o-supremo-lava-jato-e-o-vale-tudo-juridico/.

side-effect is the general perception that white-collar crimes will again remain unpunished.[122]

The upshot is that, in order for the rule of law to be strengthened, it demands proper care. Any mistake or abuse is costly and the consequences, as was the case in Brazil, can be dramatic. It may sound paradoxical and can sometimes goes against popular opinion, but at least some such abuses were disclosed and later recognised by Brazilian institutions, such as the Supreme Court[123] – and this is a positive sign for Brazil's rule of law.

V. THE ORGANISED CIVIL SOCIETY AND THE QUEST FOR FAIRNESS AMIDST SELF-PRESERVATION MOVEMENTS: A PERMANENT STRUGGLE

Path-dependence, however, also applies to the premise that key junctures in history can produce a sequence of events that create synergies[124] toward democratic consolidation and strengthen the rule of law. The impacts of democratisation on Brazilian institutions are meaningful: the 1988 Constitution, with its participatory drafting process,[125] has fostered a 'performative meaning'[126] and 'self-correcting learning process'[127] that have contributed to a progressively stable and predictable institutional framework, while encouraging civil society to defend democratic ideals. Naturally, learning processes in politics are not automatic and may even not occur,[128] but an inclusive constitution makes societal consent more visible, thereby stabilising normative expectations,[129] and increases individuals' attachment to the document.[130] In this regard, it promotes

[122] See Transparency International (n 24) 41–43.

[123] See STF, HC 164.493 (the Court ruled that judge Sérgio Moro was biased and abused his powers in a case against former President Lula da Silva, overturning his criminal conviction). See 'Brazil Supreme Court Confirms Ruling that Judge Was Biased Against Lula' (*Reuters*, 23 June 2021) www.reuters.com/world/americas/brazil-supreme-court-confirms-ruling-that-judge-was-biased-against-lula-2021-06-23/.

[124] See P Pierson, *Politics in Time: History, Institutions, and Social Analysis* (Princeton University Press, 2004) 11.

[125] See JZ Benvindo, 'The Forgotten People in Brazilian Constitutionalism: Revisiting Behavior Strategic Analyses of Regime Transitions' (2017) 15 *International Journal of Constitutional Law* 332; C Araújo, 'O Processo Constituinte Brasileiro, a Transição e o Poder Constituinte' (2013) *Lua Nova: Revista de Cultura e Política* 327; L Barbosa, *História Constitucional Brasileira: Mudança Constitucional, Autoritarismo e Democracia no Brasil Pós-1964* (Biblioteca Digital da Câmara dos Deputados, 2012) 143–248; C Paixão, 'Autonomia, Democracia e Poder Constituinte: Disputas Conceituais na Experiência Constitucional Brasileira (1964–2014)' (2014) 43 *Quaderni Fiorentini* 415.

[126] See JZ Benvindo, 'The Seeds of Change: Popular Protests as Constitutional Moments' (2015) 99 *Marquette Law Review* 407.

[127] See J Habermas, 'Constitutional Democracy: A Paradoxical Union of Contradictory Principles?' (2007) 29 *Political Theory* 776.

[128] See Pierson (n 124) 38.

[129] See N Luhmann, *Law as a Social System* (Oxford University Press, 2004) 148.

[130] See Z Elkins, T Ginsburg and J Melton, *The Endurance of National Constitutions* (Cambridge University Press, 2009) 81.

coordination by creating structures and processes[131] that facilitate decision-making and enhance civil engagement toward the enforcement of democratic principles.

Despite the most recent events in the country eroding such principles,[132] Brazilians still show comparatively high levels of awareness of corruption and a willingness to fight it, as those international indicators above have shown. In the new democratic order, the participation of organised civil society reflected on the creation of participatory institutions and councils in numerous areas of social life, notably in health, environment and social welfare – a phenomenon that Leonardo Avritzer called a 'moment of explosion of social participation in Brazil'.[133] There were some successful experiences, such as the participatory budgeting in Brazil's southern city of Porto Alegre,[134] then expanded to over 200 cities, reaching nearly 25 per cent of Brazil's population.[135] This achievement, and the national conferences,[136] were praised as examples of civil activism that had important impacts on defining the social agenda[137] and also combatting corruption and enhancing governance.[138] Even when extinguished, such policies could still foster citizenship and civil mobilisation.[139]

Brazil would experience in the 1990s and 2000s the 'proliferation of participatory governance institutions' as mechanisms to overcome Congress' deficient policy-making.[140] The disconnection of the political system with the demands of society, on the one hand, and the growing civil engagement, on the other, led to the phenomenon of 'funnelling demands emerging from organised communities into the executive branch'.[141] It was the period of organising structures and processes aimed at enhancing the enforcement of individual and social rights that could prevail over embedded self-reinforcing practices[142] such as clientelism.[143] It was the symbiosis of 'the right to have rights', whose goal was to expand

[131] See Weingast (n 112) 345.
[132] See Meyer (n 111).
[133] L Avritzer, 'Um Balanço da Participação Social no Brasil Pós-Constituição de 1988' in L Avritzer (ed), *Experiência Democrática, Sistema Político e Participação Popular* (Fundação Perseu Abramo, 2013) 11.
[134] ibid. See also TR Melgar, 'A Time of Closure? Participatory Budgeting in Porto Alegre, Brazil, After the Workers' Party Era' (2014) 46 *Journal of Latin American Studies* 121.
[135] See B Wampler and L Avritzer, 'The Spread of Participatory Democracy in Brazil: From Radical Democracy to Good Government' (2005) 7 *Journal of Latin American Urban Studies* 37.
[136] See Avritzer (n 133) 12 (explaining that such conferences gathered over six million people and were fundamental for engaging the society in building an agenda on distinct social areas).
[137] See Melgar (n 134) 148; B Wampler, 'Entering the State: Civil Society Activism and Participatory Governance in Brazil' (2012) 60 *Political Studies* 341.
[138] Y Zamboni, 'Participatory Budgeting and Local Governance: An Evidence-Based Evaluation of Participatory Budgeting Experiences in Brazil' (2007) Working Paper, https://citeseerx.ist.psu.edu/viewdoc/download?doi=10.1.1.467.6755&rep=rep1&type=pdf.
[139] See Melgar (n 134) 148.
[140] See Wampler (n 137) 345
[141] ibid.
[142] ibid 344.
[143] ibid 346.

individuals' political voice in public deliberations, and 'participatory publics', which targeted the fair distribution of goods and resources.[144] Though some studies have pointed out that these new practices have not effectively overcome clientelism – and, in some cases, even created new forms for it to operate through involvement of traditional political actors[145] – evidence has also shown that such modalities of participatory governance have indeed enhanced the capacity of coordination of collective actors, the quality of their deliberations and their influence on defining the public agenda inside state institutions.[146]

Yet, this civil engagement toward enhancing the culture of participatory governance has proven far more nuanced. A country marked by high inequality, where the political system is still linked to that authoritarian mindset and behaves according to practices that are incompatible with the new constitutional order, rests upon a very shaky equilibrium. Frances Hagopian, who has long studied clientelism and oligarchs in Brazil,[147] explained such a phenomenon by calling it 'Brazil's accountability paradox'.[148] According to her, 'stronger horizontal accountability institutions and an expanded citizenship have paradoxically eroded the bonds of vertical accountability'.[149] As discussed above, the improvements in horizontal accountability have been consistent, but the legacy of a political system that is incapable of representing the demands of a society increasingly eager for a fairer share of goods and resources may pay a high price. If punishment of members of the political class becomes more tangible, but social demands are not being embraced by political representatives, the crisis is on the radar. Brazilians' high level of disbelief in the political system and the government[150] is a symptom of the wider gap between horizontal and vertical accountability. That equilibrium could be kept relatively undisturbed while some inclusive policies gained strength and the distribution of goods and resources could improve social welfare more broadly,[151] which was particularly possible during the 2000s commodities-boom and the growing economy. That reality started to change in the 2010s and would be more visible from the popular protests of 2013 onwards, when the mood among Brazilians radically changed.[152]

[144] ibid 344.

[145] See AG Lavalle, A Acharya and PP Houtzager, 'Beyond Comparative Anectotalism: Lesson on Civil Society and Participation from São Paulo, Brazil' (2005) 33 *World Development* 951.

[146] See Wampler (n 137) 358.

[147] See F Hagopian, 'The Politics of Oligarchy: The Persistence of Traditional Elites in Contemporary Brazil' (PhD Thesis, Massachusetts Institute of Technology 1986).

[148] F Hagopian, 'Brazil's Accountability Paradox' (2016) 27 *Journal of Democracy* 119, 119–28.

[149] ibid 120.

[150] See ch 2.

[151] See ch 2.

[152] See JZ Benvindo 'Brazilian Elections and Demonstrations of June 2013: The Rise of Conservatism?' (*International Journal of Constitutional Law Blog*, 1 November 2014) www.iconnectblog.com/2014/11/brazilian-elections-and-demonstrations-of-june-2013-the-rise-of-conservatism. See also A Singer, 'Brasil, Junho de 2013, Classes e Ideologias Cruzadas' (2013) *Novos Estudos CEBRAP* 23.

The broken vertical accountability has since clashed with two important variables that would foment social and political backlash. First, the improved checks and balances and accountability institutions made explicit how entrenched and widespread corruption is in the country, a phenomenon well portrayed by those perceptions-based indicators above. Secondly, expanded citizenship and more inclusive institutions progressively foment more inclusiveness, in a self-reinforcing process that is nonetheless quite reactive should it fail or even backslide. Until those 2013 protests, when demonstrators all over the country raised various and conflicting agendas, from calls for social justice and the right to abortion to banning gay marriage and harsher criminal punishments, Brazilians were strongly supportive of the federal government: 65 per cent of Brazilians qualified the Dilma Rousseff presidency as good or great in March 2013. Yet, that support fell sharply to 30 per cent right after those protests in June.[153]

The impeachment of President Dilma Rousseff arose as a direct consequence of such a social catharsis, which was the element needed for the consolidation of a movement of self-preservation by the political class. It was the paradox of a government that enhanced mechanisms of horizontal accountability but saw the rapid crumbling of its party-to-voter linkages.[154] The Worker's Party (PT) and, particularly, its leader, former President Lula da Silva, were the main targets of such corruption scandals. However, it would be naïve to disregard the fact that, beneath this reality, there was a growing oppositional Congress whose members were very much implicated in various corruption scandals and a very experienced Vice-President eager to take office as a more trustworthy defender of the preservationist interests of the political class.

The increasing lack of vertical accountability amidst the strengthening of horizontal accountability and social inclusion is indeed a paradox. However, it explains to a great extent why organised civil society, whose mobilisation was crucial for the transition to democracy, became disillusioned, and therefore was easily co-opted by a populist agenda. The bonds among individuals that make for a vibrant organised civil society were weakened while an anti-systemic rhetoric framed as an anti-corruption campaign gained momentum. Combatting corruption – a serious but diffuse problem usually claimed by populists – became the new mantra, and the association of corruption with the ruling Worker's Party (PT) provided the needed enemy for the populist discourse. Conservative, military, agrarian and religious movements saw in this populist movement the long-sought-after response to their demands.

What is more, Brazil has endured one of the most notable shifts in demographics, with the rise of conservative and right-wing movements anchored in resurrecting and boosting traditionalist and religious values while embracing

[153] See 'Popularidade de Dilma Cai 27 Pontos Após Protestos', (*Folha de S. Paulo*, 29 June 2013) www1.folha.uol.com.br/poder/2013/06/1303541-popularidade-de-dilma-cai-27-pontos-apos-protestos.shtml.

[154] See Hagopian (n 147) 125.

nationalistic feeling and even supporting an illiberal agenda. Particularly strong has been the growth of Evangelicals, especially those from Pentecostal and Neopentecostal churches. In 1991, Evangelicals were only 9 per cent of Brazilians. In the 2000 census, this number grew to 15.4 per cent, and, in the 2010 census, it was already 22.2 per cent, a growth of 61 per cent in 10 years – the biggest expansion of this group worldwide.[155] If the growth rate keeps following such a pattern, it is expected that, by 2022, the number of Catholics, who made up 91 per cent of Brazilians in the 1970s, will amount to less than half of the Brazilian population[156] and, by 2032, be surpassed by Evangelicals.[157] They have to an increasing extent occupied institutional spaces: currently, there are 82 Evangelicals elected among the 513 federal deputies (they numbered 67 in 2014, 65 in 2010, and 35 in 2006),[158] and whoever is running for an elective office increasingly depends on their support. Although there are some important progressive voices in the evangelical community,[159] very few elected Evangelicals have willingly supported progressive values,[160] thus the association with the right-wing caucus is well established. President Bolsonaro, a reported Catholic married to an Evangelical, aggressively defended this agenda, especially through an anti-abortion and anti-gender equality rhetoric. Evangelicals have since been among his most fierce and resilient supporters and were essential for his election in 2018 (69 per cent of valid votes among Evangelicals were for Bolsonaro, whereas the number was just 51 per cent among Catholics).[161]

In this context, an organised civil society willing to defend democratic and progressive principles has clashed more widely with fast-growing movements – religious, right-wing and extremist – that organise themselves around a populist agenda with little or no regard for core democratic values.[162] Polarisation is the immediate consequence while moderate conservatives and liberals have their voice stifled. President Bolsonaro consistently strove to silence progressive voices while constraining checks on his behaviour. He raised barriers to horizontal

[155] See C Queiroz, 'O Crescimento da Fé Evangélica' (*Nexo*, 9 December 2019) www.nexojornal.com.br/externo/2019/12/09/O-crescimento-da-fé-evangélica.

[156] See AV Balloussier, 'Evangélicos Podem Desbancar Católicos no Brasil em Pouco Mais de uma Década' (*Folha de S. Paulo*, 14 January 2020) www1.folha.uol.com.br/poder/2020/01/evangelicos-podem-desbancar-catolicos-no-brasil-em-pouco-mais-de-uma-decada.shtml.

[157] See M Zylberkan, 'Evangélicos Devem Ulltrapassar Católicos no Brasil a partir de 2032' (*Veja*, 4 February 2020) https://veja.abril.com.br/brasil/evangelicos-devem-ultrapassar-catolicos-no-brasil-a-partir-de-2032/.

[158] See Queiros (n 155).

[159] See GD Alencar, 'Grupos Protestantes e Engajamento Social: Uma Análise dos Discursos e Ações de Coletivos Evangélicos Progressistas' (2019) 39 *Religião & Sociedade* 173.

[160] See L Sales and R Mariano, 'Ativismo Político de Grupos Religiosos e Luta por Direitos' (2019) 39 *Religião & Sociedade* 16.

[161] ibid 20. See also JED Alves, 'O Voto Evangélico Garantiu a Eleição de Jair Bolsonaro' (*EcoDebate*, 31 October 2018) www.ecodebate.com.br/2018/10/31/o-voto-evangelico-garantiu-a-eleicao-de-jair-bolsonaro-artigo-de-jose-eustaquio-diniz-alves/.

[162] See MV Bülow, 'The Empowerment of Conservative Civil Society in Brazil' in R Youngs (ed), *The Mobilization of Conservative Civil Society* (Carnegie Endowment for International Peace, 2018) 13.

accountability, extinguished hundreds of forums, such as the national councils aimed at democratising deliberations over national policies,[163] and attacked nongovernmental institutions[164] and the media.[165]

It would be misleading to overlook that Brazilians have already proven in history their capacity to reverse their course.[166] Brazil is no autocracy, but a democracy enduring a serious moment of crisis.[167] Despite the last developments and the worsening in democratic indicators,[168] Brazilians still keep enjoying some freedom and rights, freedom of press remains mostly in place, and there are core institutions working to defend democracy. Political pluralism and participation remain rather strong, and supportive and oppositional forces to the government have had their space for political activities fairly preserved.[169] Besides, nongovernmental organisations, unions and associations of all sorts have been essential players in distinct moments of Brazil's history,[170] and have not only exerted significant pressure on presidents and Congress, but also on the judiciary.[171]

VI. A FREE AND INDEPENDENT MEDIA?

A. The Media as a Key Player in Brazilian Democracy and in its Backsliding

The media in Brazil, by some measures, could be deemed free. Some data related to attacks on journalists and the press more broadly, particularly during the Bolsonaro government, would, however, certainly lead to a less positive conclusion. Like many data on Brazil, media freedom is not a consensus among distinct

[163] See AM Maués, 'Bolsonaro's First Year: Trying to Erode Democracy' (*International Journal of Constitutional Law Blog*, 1 February 2020) www.conjur.com.br/2019-abr-14/presidente-jair-bolsonaro-extingue-centenas-conselhos-federais.

[164] See A Boadle, 'Igniting Global Outrage, Brazil's Bolsonaro Baselessly Blames NGOs for Amazon Fires' (*Reuters*, 21 August 2019) www.reuters.com/article/us-brazil-politics-idUSKCN1VB1BY.

[165] See Repórteres Sem Fronteiras, 'Um Ano Sombrio para a Liberdade de Imprensa no Brasil – 580 Ataques contra a Mídia em 2020' (*Repórteres Sem Fronteira*, 21 January 2021) https://rsf.org/pt/relacoes/um-ano-sombrio-para-liberdade-de-imprensa-no-brasil-580-ataques-contra-midia-em-2020.

[166] See Benvindo (n 125); Benvindo (n 126).

[167] See TG Daly, 'Populism, Public Law, and Democratic Decay in Brazil: Understanding the Rise of Jair Bolsonaro' (2019) 14th International Human Rights Researchers' Workshop: 'Democratic Backsliding and Human Rights, https://ssrn.com/abstract=3350098; Meyer (n 111).

[168] See ch 2.

[169] See, eg, data from Freedom House on political pluralism and participation. Brazil scores 4 out of 4 in two markers and 3 out 4 in the other two. Freedom House, *Freedom in the World 2021*, https://freedomhouse.org/country/brazil/freedom-world/2020.

[170] See Barbosa (n 125) 146–85; D Rollemberg and SV Quadrat (eds), *A Construção Social dos Regimes Autoritários: Legitimidade, Consenso e Consentimento no Século XX – Brasil e América Latina* (Civilização Brasileira, 2010).

[171] See ch 5. For example, the role of the *amici curiae* in hallmark decisions of Brazil's Supreme Court. See MG Godoy, 'As Audiências Públicas e os Amici Curiae Influenciam as Decisões dos Ministros do Supremo Tribunal Federal' (2015) 60 *Revista da Faculdade de Direito UFPR* 137.

international indicators. For instance, for Freedom House, Brazil scores 3 out of 4 on 'free and independent media'. According to its report, 'the media scene is vibrant' – which is quite a strong statement. On the other hand, however, 'journalists who criticised Bolsonaro face online harassment, and outlets that carried out such criticism face economic pressure from the government'. Moreover, 'the legal framework provides inadequate protection for freedom of expression'.[172] The Bolsonaro government has, on several occasions, threatened media outlets with economic pressures and journalists with libel and even criminal prosecution based on the former National Security Act,[173] a vestige of Brazil's civilian-military dictatorship (1964–85),[174] which, also as a reaction by Congress, was replaced by a much more modern and democratic legislation in 2021.[175] Social media has also been largely used as a tool to harass journalists who are critical of the government.[176]

Reporters without Borders (RSF) provides a grimmer picture of the current scenario in Brazil. In a report, they counted 580 attacks against the media under President Bolsonaro in 2020 alone, 85 per cent of which were from Bolsonaro himself and his sons (18.7 per cent from Bolsonaro and 66.5 per cent from his sons Flávio, Eduardo and Carlos). Half of Bolsonaro's cabinet has already attacked the press. Most such attacks were made using social media, especially Twitter (489 of those 580 attacks), and targetting female journalists, in a clear example of misogyny.[177] In 2021, such attacks significantly intensified and were 'cruder and more virulent'.[178] RSF also makes reference to a report by Brazil's Federal Audit Court (TCU), which exposed the 'lack of transparency and absence of technical criteria in the way the President's Special Secretariat for Social Communication (SECOM) was allocating state advertising'.[179] The auditing concluded that the allocation exponentially favoured media outlets that have been in line with the government, such as Record and SBT, while Globo, the one with the widest audience but mostly critical of Bolsonaro, lost substantive shares of advertising.[180]

[172] See 'Freedom in the World 2021: Brazil' (*Freedom House*, 2021) https://freedomhouse.org/country/brazil/freedom-world/2021.

[173] See Lei n. 7.170, de 14 de dezembro de 1983.

[174] See ULS dos Reis and EPN Meyer, 'Undemocratic Legislation to Undermine Freedom of Speech in Brazil' (*International Journal of Constitutional Law Blog*, 3 February 2021) www.iconnectblog.com/2021/02/undemocratic-legislation-to-undermine-freedom-of-speech-in-brazil/.

[175] Lei n. 14.197, de 1° de Setembro de 2021.

[176] See G Amado, 'Bolsonaro e Filhos Proferiram 80% dos Ataques de Autoridades à Imprensa em 2020' (*Época*, 25 January 2021) https://epoca.globo.com/guilherme-amado/bolsonaro-filhos-proferiram-80-dos-ataques-de-autoridades-imprensa-em-2020-24853644.

[177] See 'RSF Tallied 580 Attacks against Media in Brazil in 2020' (*RSF*, 25 January 2021), https://rsf.org/en/reports/rsf-tallied-580-attacks-against-media-brazil-2020.

[178] 'Bolsonaro Family Vents More Anger than ever on Brazil's Media' (*RSF*, 27 July 2021) https://rsf.org/en/reports/bolsonaro-family-vents-more-anger-ever-brazils-media.

[179] See n 177.

[180] See F Fabrini and J Wiziack, 'TCU Vê Falta de Critério do Governo Bolsonaro no Rateio de Verbas para TV' (*Folha de S. Paulo*, 12 August 2020) www1.folha.uol.com.br/poder/2020/08/tcu-ve-falta-de-criterio-do-governo-bolsonaro-no-rateio-de-verbas-para-tvs.shtml?origin=folha.

Specifically due to violence against journalists, RSF has ranked Brazil slightly below 100 among the 180 countries surveyed (103rd in 2017, 102nd in 2018, 105th in 2019, 107th in 2020 and 111th in 2021), which is comparatively behind other Latin American countries (Costa Rica is 5th, Uruguay is 18th, Chile is 54th, Argentina is 69th, Panama is 77th, Peru is 91st, Ecuador is 96th, Bolivia is 110th), but ahead of some countries with a history of narco-guerrillas consistently murdering journalists (Honduras is 151st, Mexico is 143rd, Colombia is 134th). Even though according to its 'Violations of Press Freedom Barometer', Brazil has not counted any further murders of journalists since 2019, there were six in 2015, three in 2016, one in 2017 and four in 2018.[181] For RSF, 'Brazil continues to be an especially violent country for media, and many journalists have been killed in connection with their work', which has become even more serious given that 'any media revelation threatening [Bolsonaro's] or his administration's interests triggers a new round of violent verbal attacks that foster a climate of hatred and mistrust towards journalists'.[182] During the COVID-19 pandemic, such attacks were even more intense.[183]

Based on those reports, it sounds like an overstatement to classify Brazil's media as free or even 'vibrant'. There are naturally nuances here. First, if President Bolsonaro has continuously attacked some specific outlets, such as Globo, the biggest and most influential media conglomerate, and *Folha de S. Paulo*, the biggest newspaper, both (and also many other) media companies have been able to criticise – sometimes very harshly – the government. Secondly, public media outlets, which could become a propaganda tool for the government, have very low audiences and cannot closely compete with private ones. President Bolsonaro took over EBC (*Empresa Brasil de Comunicação*), a public media conglomerate,[184] but its impact seems rather small. On the other hand, some private media organisations, such as SBT, Record, Band and Rede TV, have actually partnered with Bolsonaro and obtained larger shares of governmental advertising as a consequence.[185] However, Globo is still the most influential by far, has a much broader audience, and has usually positioned itself against the government, especially during the COVID-19 crisis. Brazil is not known as a country where journalists are imprisoned, and, currently, no case has been reported of journalists in prison according to the RSF Violations of Press Freedom Barometer 2021,[186] though one such case has indeed happened in the

[181] 'Violations of Press Freedom Barometer' (*RSF*, 2021) https://rsf.org/en/barometer.

[182] 'Brazil: Climate of Hate and Suspicion Fed by Bolsonaro' (*RSF*, 2021) https://rsf.org/en/brazil.

[183] ibid.

[184] EBC employees, for example, have reported 138 cases of curtailment of press freedom from January 2019 to July 2020. See Tallied GT Censura, *2° Dossiê Censura EBC – Inciso VIII* (September 2020) https://fenaj.org.br/wp-content/uploads/2020/09/Dossie_Censura_EBC_2020.pdf.

[185] See J Filho, 'Bolsonaro Se Diz Perseguido pela Imprensa. Mas Band, SBT, Record e Rede TV Estão ao Seu Lado' (*The Intercept*, 23 February 2020) https://theintercept.com/2020/02/23/imprensa-bolsonaro-band-sbt-record-rede-tv/.

[186] 'Violations of Press Freedom Barometer' (*RSF*, 2021) https://rsf.org/en/barometer.

past.[187] In addition, criminal cases against journalists have not achieved much success in the judiciary,[188] even though some cases aiming to remove online content or prohibit the publication of journalistic pieces involving prominent politicians and businesspeople have found moderate acceptance in the courts.[189] On the other hand, President Bolsonaro and his son Eduardo were already ordered to pay damages to some journalists.[190]

Brazil does not suffer from governmental censorship. However, the judiciary has, in some cases, interpreted libel very leniently to the point of curtailing freedom of press. The Constitution has a number of provisions recognising freedom of speech and press, but also sets some limits. It establishes that 'manifestation of thought is free, but anonymity is forbidden'.[191] It also lays down that the 'expression of intellectual, artistic, scientific, and communication activity is free, independent of any censorship or license'[192] and that the 'access to information is assured to everyone, protecting the confidentiality of sources when necessary for professional activity'.[193] It dedicates a whole chapter to social communication, where such provisions are reinforced and detailed.[194] On the other hand, it also defines some protections for potential offences, such as the 'right of reply', which 'is assured, in proportion to the offence …' and the right to 'compensation for pecuniary or moral damages or damages of reputation'.[195] The same principle applies whenever 'personal intimacy, private life, honour and reputation' is violated, 'guaranteeing the right to compensation for pecuniary or moral damages resulting from the violation thereof'.[196]

Lower courts tend to be more favourable to setting libel damages than higher courts. Supreme Court precedents, especially for public authorities, do not leave doubts that the freedom of press should be preserved and guaranteed.[197] The Court has already ruled that the publication of a report or opinion with harsh and even ruthless criticism wards off the intent to offend, mainly when targeting public figures,[198] and that the confidentiality of the journalistic

[187] See 'Brasil: Jornalista Condenado a 6 Meses e 6 Dias de Prisão por Difamação' (*RSF*, 9 November 2016) https://rsf.org/pt/noticia/brasil-jornalista-condenado-6-meses-e-6-dias-de-prisao-por-difamacao.

[188] See 'STF Suspende Inquérito com base na Lei de Segurança Nacional contra Jornalista' (*Congresso em Foco*, 26 August 2020) https://congressoemfoco.uol.com.br/area/justica/stj-suspende-inquerito-com-base-na-lei-de-seguranca-nacional-contra-jornalista/.

[189] See M Bastian, *Media and Accountability in Latin America* (Springer, 2019) 78.

[190] See T Viapiana, 'Presidente Bolsonaro é Condenado a Indenizar Jornalista por Danos Morais' (*CONJUR*, 11 December 2020) www.conjur.com.br/2020-dez-11/bolsonaro-condenado-indenizar-jornalista-danos-morais; 'Eduardo Bolsonaro É Condenado a Indenizar Jornalista Patrícia Campos Mello em R$ 30 Mil' (*O Globo*, 21 January 2021) https://oglobo.globo.com/brasil/eduardo-bolsonaro-condenado-indenizar-jornalista-patricia-campos-mello-em-r30-mil-24849258.

[191] Article 5, IV.

[192] Article 5, IX.

[193] Article 5, XIV.

[194] Articles 220–24.

[195] Article 5, V.

[196] Article 5, X.

[197] STF, ARE 722.744 (2014).

[198] ibid.

source is inviolable.[199] More impactful still, it declared the unconstitutionality of the Press Act (*Lei da Imprensa*),[200] a vestige of the civilian-military dictatorship whose provisions largely limited press freedom.[201] On the other hand, the first appointed justice to that Court by President Bolsonaro, Kassio Nunes Marques and the Attorney General of the Republic, Augusto Aras, filed criminal complaints in the Federal Court against Conrado Hübner Mendes, a professor at the University of São Paulo and a columnist for *Folha de S. Paulo*, for slander, libel and defamation, in a clear sign that even high-ranking officials who act in the Supreme Court have not seriously understood its precedents on freedom of speech.[202]

Hence, there is a reasonable degree of freedom of press and some institutional protection for it, but also some important warnings. The media has been a central player in Brazil's democracy and exerted an important check on the government and public officials. It features some degree of pluralism, but the largest and most influential media outlets are concentrated in the hands of a few. According to Media Ownership Monitor Brasil (MOM-Brasil), which keeps track of the media concentration in the country, the four biggest television organisations – Globo, SBT, Record, and Band – have 71.1 per cent of the national audience combined, and the four biggest news organisations – Globo, Folha, RBS, and SADA – reach 50.42 per cent of the readers of newspapers. There is also a high degree of cross-media ownership concentration: the market share of the eight biggest media companies reaches a staggering 74.7 per cent audience across distinct media sectors.[203] Such characteristics raise some serious risks, such as a lower level of accountability that also contributes to a higher level of politicisation. This is particularly worrying if there is some dependence of such media outlets on state advertising (about 7 per cent of the whole market)[204] and public licences.[205] More seriously, a handful of media outlets, especially communitarian and regional ones, are owned by politicians[206] despite such a practice being constitutionally forbidden for elected officials.[207]

[199] STF, RCL 31.117 MC-AGR (2019).

[200] Lei n. 5250, de 9 de Fevereiro de 1967.

[201] STF, ADPF 130 (2009).

[202] See 'Kassio Nunes Aciona Procuradoria para Apurar Conduta de Colunista da Folha que o Criticou' (*Folha de S. Paulo*, 24 July 2021) www1.folha.uol.com.br/poder/2021/07/kassio-nunes-aciona-procuradoria-para-apurar-conduta-de-colunista-da-folha-que-o-criticou.shtml; K Coura, 'Aras Processa Criminalmente Professor da USP por Críticas a Sua Atuação como PGR' (*Jota*, 20 May 2021) www.jota.info/coberturas-especiais/liberdade-de-expressao/conrado-hubner-mendes-aras-20052021.

[203] 'Indicadores de Riscos à Pluralidade na Mídia' (*Media Ownership Monitor Brasil*, 2022), https://brazil.mom-rsf.org/br/destaques/indicadores/#!184683649287ef5a9e7a369acbbadbd6.

[204] ibid.

[205] See Bastian (n 189) 91.

[206] ibid 87; TC Boas, 'Media Barons and Electoral Politics: Politically-Controlled Broadcasting in Brazil' (2013) Working Paper, www.bu.edu/polisci/files/2010/10/media_boss_politics.pdf.

[207] Article 54 of the 1988 Constitution.

Religious groups have also largely advanced in media ownership, with some significant political impact as they have increasingly been immersed in politics and pushed their doctrines mostly to a very conservative agenda.[208]

Media concentration has also contributed to a more monolithic depiction and interpretation of events, following narratives that reproduce themselves across distinct media companies without much further analysis or self-criticism. The impact on public opinion of a broadly repeated narrative has been meaningful.[209] For instance, most such conglomerates were supportive of the civilian-military dictatorship (1964–85) but reversed course and were very influential during the transition to democracy in 1985 and the constituent process in 1987–88. They were crucial catalysts of President Fernando Collor de Mello's impeachment in 1992 and Dilma Rousseff's impeachment in 2016. 'Operation Car Wash' and other corruption probes would possibly not have the sweeping effects they achieved if they were not reported on daily by those media outlets. In all of these events, the media were fundamental to the outcome, but very few critical and dissenting voices could be found.

This is the paradox of Brazilian media freedom: the media has been a fundamental player in making public officials more accountable, but it can be very selective and biased when reporting on key events in the country.[210] This would not be a serious problem if dissenting views could also find their place more easily in the mainstream media. The high concentration and low self-accountability that is prevalent have nevertheless limited more successful strategies to enhance media pluralism.[211] There is no official censorship, but media organisations may find themselves constrained by indirect means such as state advertising and licensing. Media organisations, in any case, are extremely powerful agents in Brazilian democracy and attempts to interfere more directly in their functioning or merely regulate them have always resulted in fierce backlash.[212] Even movements to democratise the media, which gained ground especially during the presidencies of Lula da Silva and Dilma Rousseff, have receded in recent years.[213] History is evidence that presidents who clash with such powerful organisations – and, in particular, with Globo – tend to pay a high political price. The internet, however, has gradually paved an alternative road of communication that has challenged such dominance, but it has also come with serious side-effects, notably the spread of fake news and misinformation. The traditional media

[208] See AE Smith, *Religion and Brazilian Democracy: Mobilizing the People of God* (Cambridge University Press, 2019) 4; Bastian (n 189) 90.

[209] See Bastian (n 189) 79–85.

[210] See A de Albuquerque, 'Protecting Democracy or Conspiring Against It? Media and Politics in Latin America: A Glimpse from Brazil' (2019) 20 *Journalism* 906.

[211] See Bastian (n 189); TM Rodrigues and M Schneider, 'Five Strategies for Political Participation of the Media Democratization Movement in the New Republic' (2020) 43 *Intercom: Revista Brasileira de Ciências da Comunicação* 189.

[212] See RS Marques, *A Mídia sob o Império da Lei: Políticas de Regulação dos Meios de Comunicação no Brasil e na Argentina no Século XXI* (Appris, 2020).

[213] See Rodrigues and Schneider (n 211) 199.

organisations might have partially lost their influence on people's minds. It does not necessarily follow, though, that through the internet their minds have become freer and better informed.

B. The Power of the New Media: Fake News as the New Normal

For a regular user, the internet in Brazil could be deemed free by some measures: websites are not blocked, there is no governmental censorship, and internet pages are constantly updated with information and opinions from diverse political spectra – all typical signs of a democratic environment. It is also quite widespread, especially for a continental country. According to ICT Households 2019, 74 per cent of Brazilians have access to internet, an impressive expansion compared to the 41 per cent of 10 years ago. Still, there is a high degree of inequality: whereas 97 per cent of Brazilians with higher education have access to the internet, only 16 per cent of those who are illiterate or are still in preschool do so. Income also plays a role: 94 per cent of Brazilians who earn more than 10 times the minimum wage are online, while this proportion falls to 86 per cent among those earning from three to five times the minimum wage, and 61 per cent among those earning less than the minimum wage. The way Brazilians access the internet also reflects such disparities: 99 per cent of Brazilians access it through mobile phones and 58 per cent of them do it exclusively through these devices. In turn, computers, TVs, and videogames are used for internet usage by merely 42 per cent, 37 per cent and 9 per cent of the population, respectively.[214] Although Brazilians frequently access the internet – 90 per cent said they do it daily – WhatsApp and social media platforms, such as Facebook, Instagram, Twitter and Telegram, prevail over any other content. There is a clear divide between rich and poor as regards access to professional journalism.[215]

Whereas the internet looks free because there are no network restrictions and social media and websites are not blocked and nor do they have their content censored, there are some serious issues pointing toward a less positive scenario. Freedom House, for instance, classifies Brazilian internet as 'partly free' (64 out of 100) in its Freedom on the Net 2021 report. It is quite an unexpected result given that, as Freedom House itself reports, 'Brazil's online sphere is vibrant, featuring many frequently updated websites and social media pages that examine the issues of the day from a variety of perspectives.'[216] The same institute also places Brazil as a 'free country' in its annual Freedom in the World Report,

[214] See 'ICT Households 2019' (*Comitê Gestor da Internet no Brasil*, 2020) https://cetic.br/media/docs/publicacoes/2/20201123121817/tic_dom_2019_livro_eletronico.pdf.
[215] ibid.
[216] See 'Freedom on the Net 2021: Brazil' (*Freedom House*, 2021) https://freedomhouse.org/country/brazil/freedom-net/2021.

so it is quite striking that the internet would be in a worse position than Brazil's general freedom status. In fact, Brazil is the only country with such a divergent classification in Latin America in 2021.

The causes for this evaluation are many, but one in particular is critical: Brazilian internet has been overwhelmed by fake news and misinformation, and the federal government has largely used this strategy to strengthen its grip on power and keep its social base engaged. In a country where the largest share of internet users spends most of their time on social media, and where WhatsApp and other messaging services are very widespread across diverse regional and economic social strata, the prerequisites for creating a parallel reality and post-truth politics[217] are all there. Jair Bolsonaro was very successful in occupying these spaces when running for president in 2018 and has since been strongly engaged in keeping the internet as his main platform of communication with his base. More seriously, according to Freedom House, there is an 'apparent coordination of people connected to the government' for this end, notably the so-called *Gabinete do Ódio* (Office of Hate), a group of government advisers whose job is to attack critics of President Bolsonaro, expand pro-Bolsonaro blogs and social media, and spread fake news.[218] This political tactic has proven very deleterious for Brazil's democracy, and its impacts can already be felt in the streets, 'spilling beyond the internet'.[219]

There has been some political reaction to such a strategy. Congress installed a parliamentary committee (CPMI) to investigate the participation of Bolsonaro and his entourage – called 'Fake News CPMI'[220] – which could reveal tactics like mass message firings through WhatsApp – a much used tool for boosting Bolsonaro's election in 2018[221] – as well as interrogate individuals involved in deliberately spreading misinformation.[222] The Supreme Court, by the same token, opened a fake news investigation targeting attacks against its members, which led to police raids on distinct locations for spreading and sponsoring fake

[217] See B Araújo and H Prior, 'Framing Political Populism: The Role of Media in Framing the Election of Jair Bolsonaro' (2021) 15 *Journalism Practice* 1; J Hannan, 'Trolling Ourselves to Death? Social Media and Post-Truth Politics' (2018) 33 *European Journal of Communication* 214.

[218] 'Freedom on the Net 2020: Brazil (*Freedom House*, 2020) https://freedomhouse.org/country/brazil/freedom-net/2020#footnote1_mu82oai; PA Martins, 'Freedom at Stake in Brazil: An Illiberal Project Unfolds under Bolsonaro's Regime' (*International Journal of Constitutional Law Blog*, 17 October 2020) www.iconnectblog.com/2020/10/freedom-at-stake-in-brazil-an-illiberal-project-unfolds-under-bolsonaros-regime/.

[219] See PC Mello, 'Brazil's Troll Army Moves into the Streets' (*The New York Times*, 4 August 2020) www.nytimes.com/2020/08/04/opinion/bolsonaro-office-of-hate-brazil.html.

[220] 'CPMI das Fake News É Instalada no Congresso' (*Senado Notícias*, 4 September 2019) www12.senado.leg.br/noticias/materias/2019/09/04/cpmi-das-fake-news-e-instalada-no-congresso.

[221] R Mota, 'Fake News CPI Lists Top Irregular WhatsApp Accounts' (*Olhar Digital*, 16 January 2020) https://olhardigital.com.br/en/2020/01/16/noticias/cpi-das-fake-news-lista-principais-contas-irregulares-do-whatsapp/amp/.

[222] G Amado, 'Relatório Final da CPI Vai Indicar Extremista Allan dos Santos: Saiba os Crimes (*Metrópoles*, 6 October 2021) www.metropoles.com/colunas/guilherme-amado/relatorio-final-da-cpi-vai-indiciar-extremista-allan-dos-santos-saiba-os-crimes.

news and threats against the Court.[223] Finally, the Superior Electoral Court has already warned the government that such tactics will not be tolerated in the 2022 elections,[224] and the Supreme Court included in the Fake News inquiry[225] President Bolsonaro's continuous attacks on Brazil's electronic voting system. Therefore, spreading fake news and misinformation has become a fundamental catalyst for Bolsonaro's election as well as for keeping his supporters continuously motivated. Attempts to disrupt such a system have been fiercely combatted by Bolsonaro himself and his acolytes through distinct avenues, from calls for freedom of speech to legal battles or even blatant co-optation of political agents.[226]

Some legislation aimed at combatting fake news have been discussed in Congress, and one called 'Brazilian Law on Freedom, Responsibility, and Transparency on the Internet'[227] (or the 'Fake News' bill) has already been passed in the Senate, though it may find further resistance in the Chamber of Deputies. This legislation aims to fight fake news by specifying some criminal offences involving individuals and corporations that either circulate misinformation or finance such activities. It also focuses on electoral campaigns in order to avoid illegal advertisement, as happened in the 2018 presidential elections. Although seemingly justified based on how serious the spread of misinformation has become, legislation as such has the potential to criminalise content, create avenues for personal identification and disrupt privacy by requiring that message apps retain conversations for a period of time.[228] This scenario is more worrying still because the judiciary and mainly the lower courts, similarly to what happens in traditional media, have a record of ordering that some contents be blocked or suspended by reason of a criminal investigation, libel or electoral lawsuits – incidentally a resource largely adopted by politicians.[229] This reality

[223] STF, INQ 4781(pending); E Simões, 'Brazil Police Raid Presidential Allies in Fake News Probe' (*Reuters*, 27 May 2020) www.reuters.com/article/us-brazil-politics-idUSKBN2332KW. This inquiry, however, is controversial because it was opened by the Supreme Court itself based on internal rules aimed at protecting its justices. See 'The Case of the Brazil Fake News Inquiry' (*Global Freedom of Expression, Columbia University*, 2021) https://globalfreedomofexpression.columbia.edu/cases/the-case-of-the-brazil-fake-news-inquiry/. See also M Palau, 'Inside Brazil's Dangerous Battle Over Fake News' (*Americas Quarterly*, 19 October 2021) https://americasquarterly.org/article/inside-brazils-dangerous-battle-over-fake-news/.

[224] PR Netto, 'Moraes: Responsáveis por Disparo de Fake News em 2022 Serão Cassados e Presos (*Poder 360*, 28 October 2021) www.poder360.com.br/justica/moraes-responsaveis-por-disparos-de-fake-news-em-2022-serao-cassados-e-presos/.

[225] STF, INQ 4781(pending); TSE Portaria GP n. 69. See L Paraguassu 'Brazil Court to Probe Bolosonaro for Attacks on Voting System' (2 August 2021) www.reuters.com/world/americas/attacked-by-bolsonaro-brazils-top-judges-say-electronic-voting-is-free-fraud-2021-08-02/; T Phillips, 'Brazil's Election Authority to Investigate Bolsonaro Over Baseless Fraud Claims' (*The Guardian*, 3 August 2021) www.theguardian.com/world/2021/aug/03/brazil-election-authority-bolsonaro-fraud-claims.

[226] See Meyer (n 111) 176–98.

[227] Projeto de Lei n. 2630, de 2020, www.congressonacional.leg.br/materias/materias-bicamerais/-/ver/pl-2630-2020.

[228] See 'Freedom on the Net 2021: Brazil' (n 216).

[229] ibid.

has raised some interesting debates over the limits of freedom of speech[230] and the constitutionalisation of the digital environment.[231]

On the other hand, Brazil provides a reasonable regulatory framework. ANATEL, the Brazilian Agency of Telecommunications, which regulates the internet market (and other communication sectors), is well-known for its technical expertise despite some criticism of it sometimes favouring private interests over public ones.[232] There is also the Brazilian Internet Steering Committee (CGI.br), an independent organisation composed of members of the public and private sectors aimed at promoting studies and setting governance principles for improving the quality of the internet.[233] The 'Brazilian Civil Rights Framework for the Internet' ('*Marco Civil da Internet*'),[234] originated from rich debates with various sectors of organised civil society[235], has since been praised as a world paradigm for the protection of internet freedom, laying down principles such as network neutrality, universality of access, privacy protection and prohibition of censorship, among others.[236] It has nevertheless some worrying provisions on data retention.[237] Brazil also features a modern data protection law called 'Brazilian General Data Protection Law',[238] which is designed for protecting personal data and is basically inspired by the well-regarded European General Data Protection Regulation.[239]

The internet has certainly democratised access to information and competed with traditional media outlets, a phenomenon that is seen in several countries in the world. The same reasoning applies to the paradoxical situation of a more democratised access to information and the expansion of misinformation and fake news through the internet. Brazil has seen this paradox directly affecting the quality of its democracy: the democratisation of information has also meant the democratisation of misinformation with severe consequences for the political environment. Jair Bolsonaro is certainly the most successful politician who has ever ascended from this new environment, proving that the internet has already radically shaken Brazilian politics – a phenomenon that has also been

[230] See FA Medeiros and LA Bygrave, 'Brazil's Marco Civil da Internet: Does it Live Up to the Hype' (2015) 31 *Computer Law & Security Review* 130.

[231] See LFM Moncau and DW Arguelhes, 'The Marco Civil da Internet and Digital Constitutionalism' in G Froslo (ed), *Oxford Handbook of Online Intermediary Liability* (Oxford University Press, 2020) 190–213.

[232] See 'Freedom on the Net 2021: Brazil' (n 216).

[233] See CGI.br, https://cgi.br/about/.

[234] Lei n. 12.965, de 23 de Abril de 2014.

[235] See Medeiros and Bygrave (n 230) 129.

[236] See R Segurado, 'The Brazilian Civil Rights Framework for the Internet: A Pioneering Experience in Internet Governance' in AP Neto and MB Flynn (eds), *The Internet and Health in Brazil: Challenges and Trends* (Springer, 2018) 43.

[237] See Article 10, Lei n. 12.965, de 23 de Abril de 2014.

[238] Lei n. 13.789, de 13 de Agosto de 2018.

[239] See R Koch, 'What is the LGPD? Brazil's Version of the GDPR' (GDPR.EU), https://gdpr.eu/gdpr-vs-lgpd/.

seen elsewhere.[240] It is the challenging reality of a country where citizens have long demanded greater media democratisation amidst such high media concentration, but which has not yet come to grips with the deleterious side-effects of strategic misinformation, let alone strategic misinformation boosted by governmental authorities. This is not an exclusive Brazilian phenomenon, but Brazil is one case that the international community should be looking carefully into in order to diagnose the disease and find solutions for putting the country back on the track of democracy.

[240] See N Persily, 'Can Democracy Survive the Internet' (2017) 28 *Journal of Democracy* 63; J Bartlett, *The People vs Tech: How the Internet is Killing Democracy (and How We Save It)* (Ebury Press, 2018).

7

The Rule of Law in Brazil and the Challenges of International Law

I. INTRODUCTION: BRAZIL AS A SOFT POWER?

THE INTRODUCTION TO this book began with the description of a sequence of covers of *The Economist*, where Brazil's prosperous future and sudden 'entrance onto the world stage'[1] in 2009 would become a monumental 'fall' and a 'disastrous year ahead'[2] in 2016. The events that have since shaken Brazil were nothing short of unsettling, and the election of Jair Bolsonaro as President in 2018 would confirm the diagnosis that things that were already bad can always get worse. From Brazil's emergence as an important internationally praised 'soft power'[3], it would become, under Bolsonaro, increasingly comparable to a pariah state. A country whose diplomacy had long been regarded as highly professionalised, respectful of the international order and aimed at promoting the agenda for human rights would then feature Ernesto Araújo as its Foreign Affairs Minister, a diplomat known for his radical and conspiratorial ideas.[4] In another key area for Brazil's international affairs – the environment – Brazil would be led by Ricardo Salles, correctly dubbed by *Time Magazine* as the '"Terminator" Environment Minister', who was in a position to 'roll back more protections' exactly when the country was going through the worst process of deforestation in a decade.[5] To make things worse, the way Brazil dealt with the COVID-19 crisis, with a president making every single effort to worsen it further and even use it as a political strategy,[6]

[1] 'Brazil Takes Off' (*The Economist*, 14 November 2009) www.economist.com/leaders/2009/11/12/brazil-takes-off.

[2] 'Brazil's Fall' (*The Economist*, 2 January 2016) www.economist.com/leaders/2016/01/02/brazils-fall.

[3] See M Chatin, 'Brazil: Analysis of a Rising Soft Power' (2016) 9 *Journal of Political Power* 369.

[4] See, for instance, Araújo's website *Metapolítica 17*, where such conspiratorial ideas are well exposed: www.metapoliticabrasil.com.

[5] See C Nugent, 'Brazil is Burning – and President Bolsonaro's "Terminator" Environment Minister Is Rolling Back More Protections' (*Time Magazine*, 1 October 2020) https://time.com/5895167/brazil-fires-ricardo-salles-environment/.

[6] See E Brum, 'Study Finds that Brazil's Jair Bolsonaro Carried Out an "Institutional Strategy to Spread the Coronavirus"' (*El País*, 29 January 2021) https://english.elpais.com/americas/2021-01-29/study-finds-that-brazils-jair-bolsonaro-carried-out-an-institutional-strategy-to-spread-the-coronavirus.html;

would lead to the country having the world's second highest death toll – a position clearly exposing how far governance has gone downhill.

The picture of Brazil under Bolsonaro represents, however, a bleak but limited landscape of Brazil's behaviour in the international order over history. Although Brazil's prospects look grim, Brazil is no irrelevant player in the international arena, not only because of its continental size and large population, but also because it is still the largest economy in Latin America and the fourth biggest democracy in the world. It is a giant supplier of commodities, the world's third largest agricultural exporter after the US and the European Union,[7] and the tenth biggest industrial producer in the world.[8] Its presence and influence on the global stage was until recently well regarded, and most analysts depicted it as an increasingly relevant power, a 'soft power broker',[9] a 'global development power',[10] whose two main foreign affairs strategies have been based on persuasion and consensus building through a 'non-interventionist multilateralistic' approach.[11]

Brazil has actively participated in some key peacekeeping missions in countries such as Haiti more recently,[12] advocated for an international human rights agenda as recurrently manifested in distinct international forums, and participated as a mediator in international conflicts.[13] It is not a powerful country in the military sense, but, as Peter Dauvergne puts it, 'it has a longstanding tradition of attracting allies and support with soft power behavior, emphasizing cooperation, multilateral initiatives and diplomacy'.[14] Much of this image Brazil has internationally built of a solidary and multicultural society is not internally corroborated by evidence[15] – the high inequality, violence and political polarisation, as we discussed before, contradict it, after all – but, throughout Brazil's democratic history, Brazil has been more positively than negatively perceived on the global scene, and it is also true that Brazil has long defended multilateralism and liberal values, though 'strongly tempered by its notions of sovereignty'.[16]

R Muggah, 'Opinion: Brazil's President Is a Global Health Threat' (*NPR*, 4 March 2021) www.npr.org/2021/03/04/973662184/opinion-brazils-president-is-a-global-health-threat.

[7] See J Chade, 'Brasil Passa a Ser o 3º Maior Exportador Agrícola, mas Clima Ameaça Futuro' (*Estado de S. Paulo*, 17 September 2018) https://economia.estadao.com.br/noticias/geral,brasil-passa-a-ser-3-maior-exportador-agricola-mas-clima-ameaca-futuro,70002506105.

[8] See 'Perfil da Indústria Brasileira – Indústria Brasileira no Mundo' (*CNI*), https://industriabrasileira.portaldaindustria.com.br/grafico/total/mundo/#/industria-total.

[9] Chatin (n 3) 369.

[10] P Dauvergne and D BL Farias, 'The Rise of Brazil as a Global Development Power' (2012) 33 *Third World Quarterly* 903.

[11] MM Valença and G Carvalho, 'Soft Power, Hard Aspirations: The Shifting Role of Power in Brazilian Foreign Policy' (2014) 8 *Brazilian Political Science Review* 87.

[12] ibid 81.

[13] ibid 78–79; Dauvergne and Farias (n 10).

[14] Dauvergne and Farias (n 10) 913.

[15] See O Stuenkel, 'Do the BRICS Possess Soft Power' (2016) 9 *Journal of Political Power* 355.

[16] ibid 362.

This chapter begins by looking at this unsettling situation of a country that has long been treated as a 'global development power',[17] but which is now enduring a radical twist in its international relations. It will focus on how the international arena and its institutions have impacted the rule of law in Brazil, and vice-versa. More specifically, it will explore how Brazil has advanced proposals for a stronger regional integration through the Common Market of the South (MERCOSUR) and Union of South American Nations (UNASUR), and how it has currently moved towards weakening or even dismantling those associations. The strengthening of the rule of law through such regional dynamics as well as its participation in other international associations – for example, the Organisation for Economic Co-operation and Development (OECD) (of which Brazil is not yet a member, but a key partner currently in accession discussions[18]) and the United Nations – have been a reality, though an imperfect one. This chapter also investigates the relationship of Brazilian institutions with the Inter-American Court of Human Rights, which has issued rulings in contradiction to decisions of the Brazilian Supreme Court. Moreover, though this chapter highlights that Brazil has historically been internationally regarded as an important defender and promoter of the rule of law and human rights despite its internal contradictions, such an international perception has been severely harmed due to recent political developments. Brazil's appeal as a world soft power in promoting democracy and a positive agenda towards the rule of law has thus waned considerably.

II. THE RULE OF LAW IN BRAZIL AND INTERNATIONAL LAW: IMPACTS ON THE DOMESTIC LEVEL

Brazil has been an active player in international forums and has naturally emerged as a regional power in Latin America. It is, along with Argentina, Paraguay and Uruguay, one of the founding members of MERCOSUR, whose function has had its ups and downs since its inception in 1991.[19] It is a member of the Inter-American Human Rights System, which comprises the American Convention on Human Rights (also called Pact of San José), the Inter-American Commission on Human Rights and the Inter-American Court of Human Rights. It is also an active participant of international organisations, such as the United Nations (UN), World Trade Organisation (WTO), World Health Organisation (WHO) and is a key partner (though not yet a member) of the OECD. It has agreed upon a set of international treaties on human rights and governance,

[17] Dauvergne and Farias (n 10) 903.

[18] 'OECD Takes First Step in Accession Discussions with Argentina, Brazil, Bulgaria, Croatia, Peru and Romania' (*OECD*, 22 January 2022) www.oecd.org/newsroom/oecd-takes-first-step-in-accession-discussions-with-argentina-brazil-bulgaria-croatia-peru-and-romania.htm.

[19] See KL Meissner, 'Mercosur: The Ups and Downs of Regional Integration in South America' in S Krapohl (ed), *Regional Integration in the Global South* (Springer, 2017) 147–78.

with natural implications for the rule of law. It has also for many years exerted a strategy of 'soft power' especially through policies aimed at strengthening South-South partnerships and development activities,[20] with the visible consequence of bolstering its presence on the international stage.

Similar to most countries normally participating in such international forums, Brazil has incorporated numerous norms and principles from international agreements into domestic legislation, some with constitutional status. Brazil's 1988 Constitution already features a vast bill of individual and social rights, but the premise that those enumerated rights should be complemented by other norms and principles has existed at least since Brazil's first Republican Constitution of 1891.[21] The 1988 Constitution explicitly extended its application to international law by laying down that 'the rights and guarantees expressed in this Constitution do not exclude others deriving from the regime and from the principles adopted by it, or from the international treaties in which the Federative Republic of Brazil is a party'.[22] It has also established that 'the provisions defining fundamental rights and guarantees are immediately applicable',[23] which can be extended to international law.

These provisions have led to doctrinal disputes over whether international law bears legal, constitutional, supra-legal or even supra-constitutional status when incorporated into domestic law.[24] The Supreme Court had for years upheld the precedent[25] that treaties and conventions have the status of ordinary law. After the Constitutional Amendment n. 45 in 2004, this precedent was partially overturned in a leading case judged in 2008 whereby the Court upheld the thesis that international treaties and conventions on human rights should be interpreted as having supra-legal status[26] (part of the minority even acknowledged they were equivalent to constitutional norms). Their rank, according to the majority opinion, lies thus above ordinary legislation but below the Constitution.[27] Yet they could formally obtain constitutional status if Congress ratifies them according to the same procedure adopted for constitutional amendments. The 1988 Constitution provides that 'international human rights treaties and conventions which are approved in each House of the National Congress, in two rounds of voting, by three fifths of the votes of the respective member shall be equivalent to constitutional status'.[28] Even if not approved according to such a procedure,

[20] See SH Bry, 'Brazil's Soft-Power Strategy: The Political Aspirations of South–South Development Cooperation' (2017) *Foreign Policy Analysis* 297.

[21] Article 78 of the 1891 Constitution. See VA da Silva, *The Constitution of Brazil: A Contextual Analysis* (Kindle edn, Hart Publishing, 2019) pos. 4020.

[22] Article 5, §2, of the 1988 Constitution (emphasis added).

[23] Article 5, §1, of the 1988 Constitution.

[24] See AM Maués, 'Supra-Legality of International Human Rights Treaties and Constitutional Interpretation' (2013) 18 *SUR-International Journal on Human Rights* 205. See also STF, RE 466.343 (1995) 1137.

[25] STF, RE 80.004(1977); STF, HC n. 72.131 (1995).

[26] See Maués (n 24).

[27] STF, HC 87.585 (2008); Maués (n 24); Silva (n 21) pos. 4020–55.

[28] Article 5, § 3, of the 1988 Constitution.

their supra-legal status means, in any case, that they are parameters of constitutional interpretation[29] and sources of the 'control of conventionality', according to which any legal norm should be interpreted not only based on the Constitution but also on international treaties and conventions on human rights.[30] Also interesting is the fact that the Brazilian Constitution expressly recognises the jurisdiction of the International Criminal Court.[31]

The impacts of international law on the domestic level are, therefore, strong and well supported by that protective constitutional framework. As a consequence of Brazil's longstanding history of diplomacy and consensus building, the country is part of various key international treaties and conventions on human rights – a movement that has intensified since the 1988 Constitution. Brazil is a signatory of international treaties or conventions on matters such as combatting torture and other cruel or degrading treatment or punishment;[32] promoting human rights in general[33] and social development;[34] preventing, punishing and eradicating violence and discrimination against women;[35] eliminating racial prejudice;[36] promoting economic, social, cultural,[37] civil, and political rights;[38] protecting children in general[39] and specifically against involvement in armed conflicts,[40] prostitution and pornography,[41] as well as persons with disabilities;[42] preventing and punishing genocide;[43] and protecting the environment,[44] among others. In addition to the International Criminal Court, Brazil has also recognised the jurisdiction of the Inter-American Court of Human Rights[45] since 1998, though such a recognition is far more nuanced in practice.[46]

[29] See Maués (n 24) 217.

[30] F Piovesan, 'Poder Judiciário e os Direitos Humanos' (2014) 101 *Revista USP* 110.

[31] Article 5, § 4, of the 1988 Constitution.

[32] United Nations Convention Against Torture (UNCAT) (UN, 1984); Interamerican Convention to Prevent and Punish Torture (OAS, 1985); Protocol to the American Convention on Human Rights to Abolish the Death Penalty (OAS, 1990).

[33] Declaration on the Right to Development (UN, 1986); American Declaration of the Rights and Duties of Man (IACHR-OAS, 1948).

[34] American Convention on Human Rights (OAS, 1969); Universal Declaration of Human Rights (UDHR-UN, 1948); Vienna Declaration and Programme of Action (UN, 1993).

[35] Inter-American Convention on the Prevention, Punishment, and Eradication of Violence Against Women (OAS, 1994).

[36] International Convention on the Elimination of All Forms of Racial Discrimination (UN, 1969).

[37] American Convention on Human Rights in the Area of Economic, Social, and Cultural Rights ('Protocol of San Salvador') (OAS 1999).

[38] International Covenant on Civil and Political Rights (UN, 1966).

[39] Convention on the Rights of the Child (UN 1989).

[40] Optional Protocol on the Involvement of Children in Armed Conflicts (UN, 2000).

[41] Optional Protocol to the Convention on the Rights of the Child on the Sale of Children, Child Prostitution and Child Pornography (UN, 2000).

[42] Convention on the Rights of Persons with Disabilities (CRPD) (UN, 2006).

[43] Convention on the Prevention and Punishment of the Crime of Genocide (UN, 1948).

[44] Framework Convention on Climate Change (UN, 1992); Kyoto Protocol (UN, 1992); Convention on Biological Diversity (UN, 1992); Paris Agreement (UN, 2015).

[45] See American Convention on Human Rights (OAS, 1969).

[46] See Section IV.

Despite that, the incorporation of international law into domestic law is more intricate and characterised by 'lower interaction and resistance'.[47] The concept of supra-legality and the constitutionalisation of rights and guarantees from international law apply only to international treaties and conventions on human rights. Other cases are interpreted as having the status of ordinary law once they are incorporated into national law.[48] Brazil, similar to most countries,[49] does not adopt the typical monist or dualist system. International treaties and conventions are not automatically incorporated into domestic law once they are ratified by the president nor do they require a law reproducing its content. Instead, the Supreme Court set the precedent that international treaties and conventions, as set out in the Constitution,[50] demand a 'subjectively complex act' involving both the President of the Republic and Congress.[51] Therefore, international treaties are, in principle, only applicable into national territory after an agreement with the other international parties is reached, the congressional endorsement is obtained, the President of the Republic ratifies it, and, finally, an executive decree is published. In the end, there is no law in the strict sense, but a simple presidential decree functioning as an 'executive order'[52] issued after those four steps, a procedure that should thus not be categorised in any of such traditional concepts.[53] Yet, even the congressional endorsement is more mitigated in practice, and many international treaties and conventions are simply incorporated into domestic law through 'executive agreements' which do not require the participation of Congress.[54]

The incorporation of such international norms into the Brazilian legal framework suffers from the natural difficulties of translating international norms and principles into standard practice at the domestic level, a phenomenon that is common worldwide.[55] In any case, though still very limited, Brazilian institutions – and the Brazilian Supreme Court, in particular – have increasingly adopted international treaties and conventions once they are incorporated

[47] M Torelly, 'Transnational Legal Process and Fundamental Rights in Latin America: How Does the Inter-American Human Rights System Reshape Domestic Constitutional Rights?' in P Fortes et al (eds), *Law and Policy in Latin America: Transforming Courts, Institutions, and Rights* (Springer, 2016) 29.

[48] See AW Borges, LC Romeu and AP da Rocha, 'Análise da Jurisprudência do STF Sobre a Forma de Incorporação dos Documentos de Direito Internacional' (2012) 3 *Revista de Direito Brasileira* 55.

[49] See BB Magalhães, 'O Sincretismo Teórico na Apropriação das Teorias Monista e Dualista e sua Questionável Utilidade como Critério para a Classificação do Modelo Brasileiro de Incorporação de Normas Internacionais' (2015) 12 *Revista de Direito Internacional* 88–89; A von Bogdandy, 'Pluralism, Direct Effect, and the Ultimate Say: On the Relationship between International and Domestic Constitutional Law' (2008) 6 *International Journal of Constitutional Law* 397.

[50] Articles 49, I; 84, VIII, of the 1988 Constitution.

[51] STF, ADI/MC 1480 (1997).

[52] Magalhães (n 49) 90.

[53] ibid 93.

[54] See AC Pereira, E Júnior and B Araújo, 'Domestic Law and International Law in Brazil' (2017) 4 *Panorama of Brazilian Law* 204.

[55] See H Krieger and G Nolte, 'The International Rule of Law-Rise or Decline? Points of Departure' (2016) 1 KFG Working Papers, https://papers.ssrn.com/sol3/papers.cfm?abstract_id=2866940.

into domestic law in their procedures and decisions.[56] The enforcement of such rights is, however, less effective than needed, which is mostly a symptom of the whole legal framework, regardless of whether they were originally drafted in Brazil or in international forums. This mismatch between the constitutional promise and the realisation of rights, which is very typical in Latin America, has triggered fascinating discussions of mechanisms that may be able to make such rights more effective in the region. Particularly important are the proposals to integrate Brazil and other Latin American countries into projects aimed at strengthening the realisation of such rights through the development of a network of international institutions, legal frameworks and 'mutually supportive structures'.[57] One such proposal, for example, is the *Ius Constitutionale Commune en América Latina* (ICCAL), whose goal is to promote, through law,[58] what they call 'transformative constitutionalism',[59] which is largely inspired by the belief that a 'rights based, supranationally secured, and regionally rooted constitutionalism'[60] is indispensable in making Latin American constitutionalism achieve its long-sought-after promise of realising human rights and overcoming many of its deficits in the quality of the rule of law and democracy.[61]

The premise that regional integration and international law are key elements for changing the landscape of a region impacted by severe social inequality, institutional weakness and an authoritarian legacy has proven, however, more challenging than expected. Brazil has been a central player in fostering such an integration as a strategy to strengthen its bargain power in Latin America – and also in other South-South partnerships. However, there are still structural self-reinforcing processes[62] that push the country to look inward and even sometimes to act against these integrative developments. This reality has proven even more true during the Bolsonaro administration, which has continuously attacked Brazil's neighbouring countries and regional organisations such as MERCOSUR and UNASUR. Despite that, international law matters greatly and Brazil, the biggest country and economy in the region, obviously needs to be connected to the world, and, more specifically, to its regional partners and institutions.

[56] See A de Carvalho Ramos, 'Supremo Tribunal Federal Brasileiro e o Controle de Convencionalidade: Levando a Sério os Tratados de Direitos Humanos' (2009) 104 *Revista da Faculdade de Direito da Universidade de São Paulo* 241; F Piovesan, 'Tratados Internacionais de Proteção dos Direitos Humanos: Jurisprudência do STF' in LSMD Moura (ed), *O Novo Constitucionalismo Moderno na Era Pós-Positivista. Homenagem a Paula Bonavides* (Saraiva, 2008).

[57] See AV Bogdandy et al, 'Ius Constitutionale Commune en América Latina: A Regional Approach to Transformative Constitutionalism' in AV Bogdandy et al (eds), *Transformative Constitutionalism in Latin America* (Oxford University Press, 2017) 5.

[58] ibid 9.

[59] ibid 4.

[60] ibid 21.

[61] See AV Bogdandy, 'Ius Constitutionale Commune en Anérica Latina: Observations on Transformative Constitutionalism' in Bogdandy (n 57) 28.

[62] See P Pierson, *Politics in Time: History, Institutions, and Social Analysis* (Princeton University Press, 2004) 10.

III. BRAZIL AND REGIONAL INTEGRATION: THE MERCOSUR

Brazil is a founding member of MERCOSUR, the Southern Common Market, which was formed in 1991 through the Treaty of Asunción and was originally established, along with Brazil, by Argentina, Paraguay and Uruguay. The original purpose was to build a common market to promote the free circulation of goods, services and capital by eliminating customs duties and setting a common external tariff. It would also mutually define macroeconomic policies for distinct sectors of the economy and harmonise the legislation among the parties.[63] In 1994, the Treaty of Ouro Preto was signed, which created the institutions of MERCOSUR. Also in 1994, in view of the difficulties in establishing free trade, the MERCOSUR customs union started to operate (though not yet fully) and, over the 1990s, the regional integration was significantly strengthened through gains in international cooperation and investment among its members and also with extra-regional partnerships.[64] In 2013, Venezuela joined MERCOSUR as a full member, though it has since 2017 been suspended because of violations of human rights and democratic principles.[65] Bolivia, which had its protocol of accession to MERCOSUR approved by all the parties in 2015, is currently in the process of gaining full membership.[66]

The MERCOSUR, whose developments have mostly focused on forming a common market, has been, however, far less successful, and the gap between rhetoric and practice is conspicuous.[67] It has not achieved the expected full economic integration through the establishment of a common market. Despite the initial steps toward trade opening, as prompted by the then prevailing neoliberal agenda,[68] structural difficulties mounted.[69] Substantial economic asymmetries – Brazil's GDP is about two thirds of MERCOSUR's GDP, for example – have since hampered the construction of a common market.[70] Yet, there have been some positive gains leading to it being regarded as 'the most successful and ambitions example of regional integration in Latin America'.[71] Though more concentrated in the 1990s, the mutual benefits have been very positive in some areas such as macroeconomic stabilisation and liberalisation, intraregional interdependence, exports and investment.[72] Difficulties escalated particularly from the late 1990s onwards and the regional bloc has since lost

[63] See MERCOSUR official webpage: www.mercosur.int/en/about-mercosur/mercosur-in-brief/.

[64] See Meissner (n 19) 149.

[65] See 'Suspensíon de Venezuela en el MERCOSUR', www.mercosur.int/suspension-de-venezuela-en-el-mercosur/.

[66] See 'MERCOSUR Countries', www.mercosur.int/en/about-mercosur/mercosur-countries/.

[67] GL Gardini, 'MERCOSUR: What You See Is Not (Always) What You Get' (2011) 17 *European Law Journal* 683.

[68] See Meissner (n 19) 149–50; Gardini (n 67) 687.

[69] See Meissner (n 19).

[70] See Gardini (n 67) 683.

[71] ibid 684.

[72] See Meissner (n 19) 155; Gardini (n 67) 684.

much of its momentum,[73] suffering from a series of setbacks such as monetary crises, growing economic asymmetries, trade wars, divergent external trade agenda, fragmentation and overlapping partnerships (UNASUR, for instance).[74] There is also a growing perception that the member states are not seriously engaging in strengthening the bloc and are even attempting to deconstruct some of its achievements.[75]

Furthermore, its evolution has been very reliant on the countries' own agendas, instead of a common one,[76] and decisions have been made by negotiation among member states, not really by supranational institutions.[77] More recently, MERCOSUR was seriously attacked by President Bolsonaro and his Minister of Economy, Paulo Guedes, based on their belief that it is a bloc of 'leftist ideological orientation'.[78] Brazil has become, however, increasingly economically dependent on MERCOSUR's trade surplus, especially now that the country has performed poorly economically.[79] Strategic partnerships are also taking place through MERCOSUR, such as the EU-MERCOSUR Free Trade Agreement, which aims to 'increase bilateral trade and investment', 'create stable rules for trade and investment' and 'promote joint values' in areas such as labour rights, sustainable development, climate change and environmental protection, among others.[80] It has not yet been ratified and it has suffered some obstacles, especially in view of Brazil's disastrous environmental policy under President Bolsonaro, conflicting views among state members and lobby groups.[81]

Moreover, even though originally thought mostly as an economic bloc, MERCOSUR has also invested some energy in fostering democratic principles and the rule of law as well as in designing some mechanisms to protect them. In this regard, MERCOSUR has served as a 'mechanism of constitutional stabilization',[82] which could be observed, for instance, in the suspension of Paraguay's membership in 2012 (after President Fernando Lugo's summary

[73] See Gardini (n 67) 687.

[74] See A Malamud and GL Gardini, 'Has Regionalism Peaked? The Latin American Quagmire and its Lessons' (2012) 47 *The International Spectator* 116; Meissner (n 19) 162. Against this view, see D Nolte and NM Comini, 'UNASUR: Regional Pluralism as a Strategic Outcome' (2016) 38 *Contexto Internacional* 545.

[75] See BE Eleoterio and AL Mesquita, 'The Twenty-First Century Regionalism: Brazil and Mercosur in the New International Scenario' in G Adinolfi et al (eds), *International Economic Law: Contemporary Issues* (Springer, 2017) 106.

[76] See Gardini (n 67) 683; Meissner (n 19) 166.

[77] See Gardini (n 67) 685.

[78] See S Magalhães, 'The Future of MERCOSUR Under the Bolsonaro Administration' (*Wilson Center*, 22 May 2019) www.wilsoncenter.org/blog-post/the-future-mercosur-under-the-bolsonaro-administration.

[79] ibid.

[80] See 'In Focus: EU-MERCOSUR (*European Commission*), https://ec.europa.eu/trade/policy/in-focus/eu-mercosur-association-agreement/.

[81] See F Vieira, 'The Relationship between the MERCOSUR Agreement with the European Union and South American Regionalism' (*Global Americas*, 21 January 2021) https://theglobalamericans.org/2021/01/the-relationship-between-the-mercosur-agreement-with-the-european-union-and-south-american-regionalism/.

[82] See Bogdandy (n 61) 44; Gardini (n 67) 684.

impeachment) and Venezuela in 2017. It had already brought forth the defence of democracy in its Protocol of Ushaia I,[83] whose Article 1 establishes that 'the full effectiveness of democratic institutions is an essential condition for the development of integration processes among the state members' and Article 5 defines the mechanisms to be adopted in the circumstance of violation of democratic principles, such as the 'suspension of participation in distinct organisms of the respective integration process to the suspension of rights and duties resulting from such processes'. Still, the focus on human rights more specifically gained momentum from 2005 onwards through the Protocol of Asunción on the Commitment to Promoting and Protecting Human Rights in MERCOSUR[84] and the creation of organisms and programmes aimed at fostering human rights, also through a more productive dialogue with civil society.[85] This MERCOSUR's emphasis on democratic principles and human rights followed the left-leaning political turn[86] among the member states and, especially, Brazil's South-South strategy during the presidency of Lula da Silva (2003–10).[87]

The Protocol of Asunción on the Commitment to Promoting and Protecting Human Rights in MERCOSUR, adopted in June 2005 and in force since 2010, was a turning point in this policy of fostering human rights in the bloc.[88] Similarly to the Protocol of Ushaia I, but now targeting human rights violations, the Protocol of Asunción defines the measures to adopt when 'serious systematic human rights violations occur in the context of institutional crises or states of emergency in one of the parties'.[89] Its enforcement takes place in circumstances of 'serious and systematic violations of human rights and basic freedoms by one of the parties', though specifically for 'situations of institutional crisis' or 'state of emergency'.[90] If no solution to the crisis is found through consultation with the affected party, some penalties can be imposed, from the 'suspension of participating in the distinct organisms of the integration process to the suspension of the rights and duties originated therefrom'.[91] Various other instruments also address human rights protections and democratic principles,[92] and regional

[83] Protocolo de Ushaia sobre Compromiso Democrático en el Mercosur, la República de Bolívia y la República de Chile (1998).

[84] Protocol of Asunción on the Commitment to Promoting and Protecting Human Rights in MERCOSUR, 20th June 2005, OXIO 89 (*Oxford Public International Law*) https://opil.ouplaw.com/view/10.1093/law-oxio/e89.013.1/law-oxio-e89.

[85] See AR Hoffmann, 'At Last: Protection and Promotion of Human Rights by Mercosur' in TA Börzel and V Van Hüllen (eds), *Governance Transfer by Regional Organizations: Patching Together a Global Script* (Palgrave Macmillan, 2015) 195.

[86] ibid.

[87] ibid 193; Gardini (n 67) 689.

[88] See Hoffmann (n 85) 193.

[89] Article 1 of the Protocol of Asunción.

[90] Article 3 of the Protocol of Asunción.

[91] Article 4 of the Protocol of Asunción.

[92] See the Presidential Declarations of MERCOSUR, www.mercosur.int/documentos-y-normativa/declaraciones-presidenciales/, and Action Plans, such as the *Estatuto de la Ciudadanía del Mercosur – Plan de Acción* (MERCOSUR/CMC/DEC. 64/10) www.raadh.mercosur.int/pt-br/wpdm-package/plan-de-accion-para-el-estatuto-de-la-ciudadania-mercosur/.

bodies and forums[93] were created to disseminate policies and monitor their accomplishment against past[94] and present human rights violations.

They have had, nonetheless, a limited capacity to effectively tackle the long-standing wrongs of the region, such as poverty and inequality.[95] The bloc has not drafted a bill of rights and its Court – the Permanent Review Tribunal – is not really a Court of Justice aimed at deciding cases on human rights or exerting supranational judicial review.[96] Litigations, by the same token, have concentrated basically on matters of economic integration.[97] Its Parliament (PARLASUR), established in 2006 with the purpose of bringing a more political approach to the bloc,[98] has very limited powers and, since its inception, has not effectively functioned as a supranational legislative body.[99] On the other hand, by bringing forward the agenda on human rights and democracy, MERCOSUR has served as a mechanism to promote regional integration and foster governance by 'keeping a hard stance on non-intervention and sovereignty', which is quite a divisive topic at the Organisation of American States (OAS).[100] Despite that, the connection of MERCOSUR with the OAS's Inter-American System of Human Rights is strong and both share similar and complementary ideas on the enforcement of such rights.[101]

The rise of other regional blocs, such as UNASUR in 2004, which Brazil promoted because of conflicts with the MERCOSUR member states and their trade agendas,[102] would reveal the underlying difficulties of South America's regional integration. Instead of strengthening MERCOSUR itself, a new regional bloc would be established from scratch, though potentially targeting other areas such as political cooperation and infrastructure projects.[103] Although UNASUR involved all 12 South American countries (Argentina, Bolivia, Brazil, Chile, Colombia, Ecuador, Guyana, Paraguay, Peru, Suriname, Uruguay and Venezuela) and seemed more politically than economically oriented, the overlap was notorious.

The existence of diverse regional blocs could result in segmentation of policies, difficulties in reaching consensus, loss of focus and greater exposition

[93] See Hoffmann (n 85) 199–201 (for a detailed description of the distinct bodies and forums on human rights of MERCOSUR).

[94] Particularly, human rights violations during the military dictatorships of the state members, such as the 'Condor Operation'. See Hoffmann (n 85) 194.

[95] See Gardini (n 67) 688.

[96] MERCOSUR merely created a Permanent Review Tribunal in 2002, but its powers are very limited and its focus has been on trade. Brazil and Argentina, in particular, have acted against a more robust supranational jurisdiction and instead preferred to maintain the status quo based on consensus-driven initiatives. See C Arnold and AB Rittberger, 'The Legalization of Dispute Resolution in Mercosur' (2013) 5 *Journal of Politics in Latin America* 112–13.

[97] See Hoffmann (n 85) 198.

[98] See Gardini (n 67) 693.

[99] ibid; Meissner (n 19) 168.

[100] Hoffmann (n 85) 207.

[101] ibid 204, 207.

[102] See Meissner (n 19) 166; Nolte and Comini (n 74) 545.

[103] See Meissner (n 19) 165.

to national swings.[104] However, UNASUR could also be seen as a more flexible regional bloc than MERCOSUR in facilitating dialogue and cooperation among the member states because of its design and lower constraints on their foreign policy goals.[105] It could, for example, reconcile countries drawn toward bilateral free trade agreements, such as Chile, with more protectionist ones such as Bolivia, Venezuela, and, to some extent, Brazil and Argentina.[106] Its institutionally flexible architecture aimed at increasing dialogue and cooperation notwithstanding,[107] UNASUR would prove itself not viable enough to facilitate the coordination of interests among its members. In fact, all it took to dismantle UNASUR was the rise of right-wing presidents in some countries in the region. In 2018, a group of countries then led by right-wing presidents in Brazil, Argentina, Chile, Colombia, Paraguay and Peru decided to suspend their participation in the bloc, and created PROSUL (Forum for the Progress of South America). PROSUL was founded by Argentina, Brazil, Chile, Colombia, Ecuador, Paraguay, Guiana and Peru with the clear purpose of antagonising Venezuela. Once again, regional integration would suffer from ideological and political swings.[108] PROSUL, however, looks even more institutionally fragile than UNASUR already was, which may turn out badly in terms of coordinating common interests which have an effective impact.

MERCOSUR, UNASUR, and now PROSUL are examples of the difficulty in establishing regional integration despite the strong cultural, legal, economic and political bonds among the Southern American countries. The movement that led to PROSUL reveals not only incapacity of coordination and 'improvisation',[109] but also that, as Juan Herrera correctly puts it, 'disintegration is a matter of method'.[110] The nonexistence of a strong regional bloc, with effective supranational institutions, not only reduces the capacity of the region to economically compete in the international arena, but also weakens the potential of international law to work as a 'mechanism of constitutional stabilization'[111] and democratic defence. MERCOSUR, the oldest and most institutionally developed of the three, is still far from reaching its potential in terms of economic integration, democratic consolidation and enforcement of the rule of law. It is the bloc that has long survived despite the political and economic swings of its member states and the one whose institutional design, though still very much flawed, comes closer to other more successful models of regional integration.

[104] See Malamud and Gardini (n 74) 123.
[105] See Nolte and Comini (n 74) 546.
[106] See Malamud and Gardini (n 74) 124.
[107] See Nolte and Comini (n 74) 561.
[108] See MV Alvarez, 'A Theory of Hegemonic Stability in South American Regionalism? Evidence from the Case of Brazil in UNASUR and Venezuela in ALBA' (2021) 43 *Contexto Internacional* 71.
[109] See JC Herrera, '"Suramèxit" and Latin American Disintegration' (*International Journal of Constitutional Law Blog*, 6 November 2019) www.iconnectblog.com/2019/11/suramexit-and-Latin-American-disintegration/.
[110] ibid.
[111] See Bogdandy (n 61) 44; Gardini (n 67) 684.

Despite that, a more collaborative and engaged integration in the region demands further coordinated efforts and investment from its member states. Until then, it seems that regional integration will not strengthen the regional economy nor help overcome the longstanding woes of the region, such as poverty, inequality, corruption and institutional deficiencies.

IV. BRAZIL AND INTERNATIONAL TRIBUNALS: THE INTER-AMERICAN COURT OF HUMAN RIGHTS

A more robust system of protection of human rights at the regional level is found in the Inter-American System of Human Rights from the Organisation of American States (OAS). As a member of OAS, Brazil is a signatory of the American Convention on Human Rights ('Pact of San José') of 1969, incorporated into domestic law in 1992,[112] and other international treaties and conventions in matters such as prevention and punishment of torture,[113] economic, social and cultural rights,[114] violence against women,[115] discrimination against persons with disabilities[116] and the prohibition of reestablishment of death penalty,[117] etc. Unlike MERCOSUR, the Inter-American Human Rights System comprises an institutional framework specifically designed to protect human rights, composed of the Inter-American Commission on Human Rights (IACHR) and the Inter-American Court of Human Rights (IACtHR). The American Convention on Human Rights defines the functions of both institutions. The Commission is responsible for '[promoting] respect for and defence of human rights' through a series of activities such as visits, recommendations, studies and reports,[118] and also for examining the suitability of petitions by individuals, organisations and groups in view of alleged violations of human rights by one or more of the member states.[119] If the Commission agrees that there is a case of human rights violation, it can issue a report with recommendations to the member state or submit the case to the Inter-American Court of Human Rights. According to Article 61, 'only the State Parties and the Commission shall have the right to submit a case to the Court'. Therefore, unless it is a member state, the case must be first submitted to the Commission, which, in practice, exerts the discretionary power to bring it (or not) before the Court.

[112] Decreto n. 678, de 6 de Novembro de 1992.
[113] Inter-American Convention to Prevent and Punish Torture (OAS, 1985).
[114] Additional Protocol to the American Convention in the Area of Economic, Social and Cultural Rights ('Protocol of San Salvador') (OAS, 1988).
[115] Inter-American Convention on the Prevention, Punishment and Eradication of Violence against Women ('Convention of Belém do Pará) (OAS, 1994).
[116] Inter-American Convention on the Elimination of All Forms of Discrimination against Persons with Disabilities (OAS, 1999).
[117] Protocol to the American Convention on Human Rights to Abolish the Death Penalty (OAS, 1990).
[118] Article 41 of the American Convention on Human Rights (OAS, 1969).
[119] Article 44 of the American Convention on Human Rights (OAS, 1969).

At first sight, the system looks functional, but the reality is less rosy. It originated in a period when many Latin American countries were not democracies, but dictatorships. It was not therefore a collaborative environment where the 'triad of the rule of law, democracy, and human rights'[120] could be truly adopted as the cornerstone of a model of regional integration. Instead, the dominant mindset was that human rights were 'an agenda against the state'.[121] Latin America has since largely democratised, but that mindset has never really been overcome. MERCOSUR, for example, began focusing on human rights, inspired by the premise that the Inter-American System of Human Rights was still very much influenced by the US and that it could not therefore effectively guarantee the sovereignty of state members[122] in such a degree of economic and political asymmetries. A system that was originally conceived under such a sentiment of mutual hesitation would not foster, in practice, the needed cooperation and engagement to establish supranational institutions that would operate effectively to constrain member states in cases of violations of human rights.

Despite that, the Inter-American System of Human Rights has gained some ground and its legal and institutional framework has had some dialogue with other integration blocs such as MERCOSUR.[123] The Inter-American Commission on Human Rights has issued reports on human rights that have triggered important legal movements toward the protection of human rights,[124] in a growing role whereby domestic demands are examined in an international forum, and then incorporated into domestic law 'with higher pressure for implementation'.[125] Its 2021 report on human rights in Brazil, for instance, mentions that 'the rule of law in Brazil is founded upon solid democratic institutions', but 'has recently been confronting challenges and setbacks'. These challenges are particularly found in inequality, disrespect for minorities, criminal justice, increasing threats to journalists and media workers, hate crimes and violence.[126]

By the same token, the Inter-American Court of Human Rights has issued a series of decisions on human rights that has served as standards of interpretation in the region,[127] creating, as Marcelo Torelly puts it, a 'reflective process [leading] to normative convergence'.[128] It has been a key player in some very

[120] F Piovesan, 'Ius Constitutionale Commune en América Latina: Context, Challenge, and Perspectives' in Bogdandy (n 57) 52.
[121] ibid. See also TG Daly, 'Brazilian "Supremocracy" and the Inter-American Court of Human Rights: Unpicking the Unclear Relationship' in P Fortes et al (ed), *Law and Policy in Latin America: Transforming Courts, Institutions, and Rights* (Springer, 2016) 7–8.
[122] See Hoffmann (n 85) 2017.
[123] ibid 204, 207.
[124] See Torelly (n 47) 21–38.
[125] ibid 26.
[126] 'Situation of Human Rights in Brazil': Approved by the Inter-American Commission on Human Rights on 12 February 2021 (Inter-American Commission on Human Rights, 2021) www.oas.org/en/iachr/reports/pdfs/Brasil2021-en.pdf.
[127] Piovesan (n 120) 53.
[128] Torelly (n 47) 27.

sensitive but crucial topics in Latin America such as human rights violations during dictatorships, transitional justice, realisation of civil and social rights, protection of minorities and vulnerable groups, judicial independence and access to justice, among others.[129]

It should be highlighted that, in Brazil, the IACtHR's decisions have functioned at most as standards of interpretation,[130] and, unlike some other Latin American countries,[131] with little impact especially on topics such as self-amnesty laws and human rights violations during Brazil's civilian-military dictatorship (1964–85).[132] Brazil was not only one of the last countries in the region to accept the IACtHR's jurisdiction but is still one whose Supreme Court has very little dialogue with it.[133] Virgílio Afonso da Silva correctly argues, in this regard, that 'the STF [Brazilian Supreme Court] frequently refers to foreign precedents as an argumentative tool, but almost never to those of the Inter-American Court' and that, although there has been 'an identifiable and increasing trend among the judges of the STF to use decisions of the IACtHR as an argumentative tool', it is not as frequent as 'references to decisions of the Supreme Court of the United States and of the German Constitutional Court …'.[134] Tom Gerald Daly also points out that, 'while the power, centrality and assertiveness of the Supreme Federal Court has increased dramatically, there has been very limited penetration of Inter-American case in the domestic constitutional order … ,'[135] unlike what has happened in other Latin American apex courts.[136]

On the other hand, the IACtHR has also already explicitly criticised the STF. In 2010, in a very controversial decision that challenged the last developments in international law and IACtHR's precedents,[137] the STF, with no dialogue whatsoever with the Inter-American precedents,[138] ruled, by a 7–2 majority, that the Brazilian Amnesty Law,[139] drafted during the civilian-military dictatorship, was constitutional under the new democratic regime.[140] The Supreme Court's decision had come out just six months before the IACtHR in the Gomes

[129] For a detailed description of the main cases in such areas decided by the Inter-American Court of Human Rights, see Piovesan (n 120) 53–62; Torelly (n 47).

[130] See D Lustig and JHH Weiler, 'Judicial Review in the Contemporary World – Retrospective and Prospective' (2018) 16 *International Journal of Constitutional Law* 326.

[131] See Torelly (n 47) 26–29 (for an interesting discussion of the impacts of IACtHR's decisions on amnesty laws in Argentina, Chile, and Brazil).

[132] ibid 30; Daly (n 121) 9.

[133] See Daly (n 121) 11.

[134] Silva (n 21) pos. 4078. See also G Ferreira Santos, 'Treaties x Human Rights Treaties: A Critical Analysis of the Dual Stance on Treaties in the Brazilian Legal System' (2013) 15 *European Journal of Law Reform* 20–28.

[135] Daly (n 121) 4–5.

[136] ibid 5.

[137] ibid 13.

[138] ibid 14.

[139] Lei n. 6.683, de 28 de Agosto de 1979.

[140] STF, ADPF 153 (2010). See EPN Meyer, 'Criminal Responsibility in Brazilian Transitional Justice: A Constitutional Interpretative Process under the Paradigm of International Human Rights Law' (2017) 4 *The Indonesian Journal of International & Comparative Law* 56–60.

Lund case,[141] which unanimously condemned Brazil for crimes committed during the dictatorship. The case involved the disappearance of 62 members of the Communist Party of Brazil (PCdoB) after military troops were sent to the Araguaia region to combat a guerrilla movement in the so-called 'Araguaia Guerrilla'. In a clear criticism of the STF's previous ruling, the IACtHR declared that 'the provisions of the Brazilian Amnesty Law that prevent the investigation and punishment of serious human rights violations are not compatible with the American Convention' and, therefore, 'lack legal effect', and cannot be an impediment for 'the identification and punishment of those responsible' for the 'facts of the present case'. In addition to declaring that Brazil is responsible for various gross human rights violations, it also ordered the country to pursue the investigation of such crimes, give publicity to the case, provide medical and psychological treatment and pay compensation to the victims.[142]

Not only is it a well-founded and strong precedent that is clearly at odds with the STF, but it also shows how divorced from the Inter-American Human Rights System Brazil's domestic law still is. It is true that in the aftermath of the Gomes Lund case Brazil's federal government complied with some of the IACtHR's orders, such as making reparations to the victims and giving publicity to the case, but not much more than that was achieved.[143] There were some positive effects, particularly a shift in the interpretation of the Amnesty Law by the Public Ministry pursuant to the IACtHR's decision,[144] but the cases it brought to justice have seen limited success.[145] NGOs have also been empowered to defend human rights at the domestic level.[146] Other positive effects were the ratification of the International Convention for the Protection of All Persons from Forced Disappearance[147] in 2010[148] and the establishment of the National Truth Commission in 2011[149] to expose rights abuses during the dictatorship.[150] Despite that, it is misleading to ignore that the Inter-American Human Rights System has provided some valuable standards for human rights protection, governance, and the rule of law. If not normatively binding, it has served as a 'reflective interpretative tool' that translates political claims into international law, which then helps shape domestic law.[151] Incrementally, Brazil is opening

[141] *Gomes Lund et al ('Guerrilha do Araguaia') v Brazil* (IACtHR, 24 November 2010).
[142] ibid 113–15. See Meyer (n 140) 61–62.
[143] Meyer (n 140) 63.
[144] See Torelly (n 47) 29.
[145] See Meyer (n 140) 63.
[146] See Torelly (n 47) 34.
[147] International Convention for the Protection of All Persons from Enforced Disappearance (UN, 2006).
[148] Decreto Legislativo n. 661, de 1º de Setembro de 2010; Decreto n. 8.767, de 11 de Maio de 2016.
[149] Lei n. 12.528, de 18 de Novembro de 2011.
[150] See Daly (n 121) 9; M Torelly, 'Assessing a Late Truth Commission: Challenges and Achievements of the Brazilian National Truth Commission' (2018) 12 *International Journal of Transitional Justice* 194; Meyer (n 140).
[151] Torelly (n 47) 34.

itself up to the Inter-American System and to international law, which is encouraging for the enhancement of the rule of law in Brazil, but there are still various open questions as to whether a more fruitful collaboration between Brazil's judiciary and the Inter-American Human Rights System (as is the case in neighbouring countries) will finally take root.

V. THE INTERNATIONAL PERCEPTION OF BRAZIL'S COMPLIANCE WITH THE RULE OF LAW

The prospect of a greater integration with the international order relies on the future of the political landscape in Brazil. Depending on how the chess pieces will move in future elections, Brazil may maintain an isolationist behaviour based on conspiracy theories or it can try to regain some portion of the soft power the country was able to exert up until recently. The results of the 2022 presidential elections will seal the fate of the country and greatly affect the international perception of its compliance with the rule of law, democracy and human rights. The re-election of would-be autocrats like Jair Bolsonaro is normally interpreted as a marker of serious concerns about the prospects of further constitutional[152] and democratic[153] erosion,[154] but Brazilian politics are quite dynamic and may also lead to the election of a president who behaves more rationally and is driven by the purpose of reinstalling Brazil onto the international stage. At the time of writing, the prospects of Jair Bolsonaro's re-election looks increasingly more difficult, and the reappearance as a potential contender of former President Lula da Silva (2003–10), who helped project Brazil as a soft power and invested in South-South relations, may radically change the landscape once again. In the end, Brazil under Bolsonaro may be a transitory, though very disruptive, experience in the country's history, which may be succeeded by the resumption of its soft power, even if an enfeebled one.

The path towards the reconstruction of Brazil's soft power, nevertheless, will be laborious. What Brazil has long built to consolidate itself as a prominent 'soft power' of the underdeveloped world has been rapidly dismantled by a myriad of policies largely inspired by conspiracy theories, lack of strategic vision and confrontational conduct that only reveal how weak Brazil becomes once it throws away its well-known capacity to lead efforts with other middle

[152] See EPN Meyer, *Constitutional Erosion in Brazil: Progresses and Failures of a Constitutional Project* (Hart Publishing, 2021).

[153] See MA Graber, S Levinson and M Tushnet (eds), *Constitutional Democracy in Crisis?* (Oxford University Press, 2018). For a fantastic resource on democratic decay, see the DEM-DEC database at: www.democratic-decay.org/. See also TG Daly, 'Understanding Multi-directional Democratic Decay: Lessons from the Rise of Bolsonaro in Brazil' (2020) 14 *Law & Ethics of Human Rights* 199.

[154] See O Stuenkel, 'Brazilian Democracy is Holding Up – But the Biggest Test Will Come in 2022' (*Americas Quarterly*, 8 March 2021) www.americasquarterly.org/article/brazilian-democracy-is-holding-up-but-the-biggest-test-will-come-in-2022/.

and low-income nations to defend their mutual interests. President Bolsonaro's foreign affairs policy has focused on rolling back key achievements of that past – the weakening of regional integration, for instance – and adopting a subservient and bold alignment with the US at least until President Donald Trump was in office, with no effective gains. Continuous attacks on China by members of Bolsonaro's cabinet and his supporters have shown how reckless and disruptive his government is for Brazil's strategic interests, especially in view of China's position as a major trading partner and a vital supplier of medical equipment and vaccines for combatting COVID-19.

The instruments for fighting corruption and enhancing accountability, which had seen important improvements during the last few decades,[155] have since been progressively undermined.[156] The country's positive image as a defender of the environmental agenda, also backed by previous successes in reducing the deforestation of the Amazon Forest, has been wrecked by the government's incentives to encourage illegal deforestation, mining and agricultural operations. Brazil's well-known cultural heritage, which has long projected Brazil internationally, has been overshadowed by the government's cultural wars and radical views on topics such as abortion, gender equality and religious freedom. To make things worse, the calamitous handling of the COVID-19 crisis, in which Brazil suffered one of the world's highest numbers of deaths/per capita, revealed the country's absence of effective governance.

However, Brazil's longstanding capacity for strengthening diplomatic ties and reaching a consensus in the international arena should not be simply forgotten based on the most recent events. It is also misleading to merely focus on 'executive-led assaults on democratic rule'[157] while there is a multidimensional institutional framework that may help contribute to – but also constrain – such assaults. Brazil's longstanding self-reinforcing processes,[158] many structurally built upon the still pervasive authoritarian mindset[159] and inequality,[160] have indeed been impactful drivers of Brazilian politics – Bolsonaro is, after all, a direct consequence of such a phenomenon.[161] On the other hand, Brazil's history is also impacted by a growing and active civil society and incremental and impactful institutional improvements,[162] which have pushed the country toward democracy[163] and a fruitful dialogue with the international community.

[155] See ch 6.
[156] See ch 6.
[157] See Daly (n 153) 199.
[158] See Pierson (n 62) 35.
[159] See ch 3
[160] See ch 2.
[161] See B Fogel, 'Bolsonaro: Politics as Permanent Crisis' in J Rayner et al (eds), *Back to the'30s?: Recurring Crises of Capitalism, Liberalism and Democracy* (Springer, 2020) 212.
[162] See ch 6.
[163] See JZ Benvindo, 'The Forgotten People in Brazilian Constitutionalism: Revisiting Behavior Strategic Analyses of Regime Transitions' (2017) 15 *International Journal of Constitutional Law* 332.

Although Brazilian institutions – and the judiciary in particular – have been very timid in explicitly incorporating international law and complying with foreign decisions such as those of the Inter-American Court of Human Rights, there is a growing sense of the need to combine constitutional review with conventionality control, thereby adopting international human rights standards such as those of the Inter-American System of Human Rights.[164] The 1988 Constitution had already explicitly recognised this connection in Article 5, §2, by determining the incorporation of unenumerated human rights from international law. There is, therefore, a great deal of potential. Strategic litigation and political pressure from civil society can push Brazilian institutions to incrementally pursue international law standards in human rights and the rule of law.[165] Moreover, unlike what has long been recurrent in southern American integration, the most successful mechanisms for this purpose such as MERCOSUR should be strengthened and not dismantled to build another organisation that features flexibility but lacks basic principles of coordination and institutional capacities.[166] There is still a long way to go before Brazil can seriously integrate into the international order, but the scenario is, as in numerous aspects of Brazil's institutional framework, of a glass half full or half empty.

[164] See Piovesan (n 120) 62.
[165] ibid.
[166] See J Turnpenny et al, 'Why Is Integrating Policy Assessment So Hard? A Comparative Analysis of the Institutional Capacities and Constraints' (2008) 51 *Journal of Environmental Planning and Management* 759.

8

The Future of the Rule of Law in Brazil

I. THE DESTABILISING FACTORS OF THE RULE OF LAW IN BRAZIL

BRAZIL'S CURRENT WORRYING landscape is nothing other than the outbreak of a set of entangled sociological and institutional features that, for a long time, could function with some stability at the expense of 'normalising' their potential conflicts. When such conflicts could no longer be 'normalised', that pressure cooker rapidly and violently burst. This chapter will explore how the structural factors that are beneath Brazil's bumpy road toward democratic consolidation are the major reasons for its current 'democratic decay' and how they should be challenged in order to find a way out of the crisis. The centripetal and longstanding forces that have successfully operated inside Brazilian institutions are the core for understanding why the country fell into such a slump, but they also provide some clues as to whether and how the country can overcome it. The question that will lead the discussion is: what caused this scenario and how can Brazil overcome such a mess and tragedy?

The sociological features – notably the social inequality[1] and the difficulties in challenging the longstanding authoritarian mindset in society[2] – are mutually reinforcing and provide positive feedback that will resist any change to the status quo. Moreover, the 'normalisation' of such social relations anchored in inequality and authoritarianism conceals their disruptive effect in society. As Paul Pierson argues, 'positive feedback over time may simultaneously increase asymmetries of power and, paradoxically, render power relation less visible'.[3] The idea that life goes on despite all the wrongs that have plagued Brazilian democracy is clearly visible in narratives such as the myth of 'racial democracy',[4] the conformism with the high levels of violence[5] and, more recently, the normalisation of the excessive number of deaths due to COVID-19, not to say the brazen disrespect for the victims of such a tragedy. The election of President

[1] See ch 2.
[2] See ch 3.
[3] P Pierson, *Politics in Time: History, Institutions, and Social Analysis* (Princeton University Press, 2004) 37.
[4] See ch 2.
[5] See chs 2 and 5.

Bolsonaro, despite the most blatant evidence of his disregard for democracy and basic moral principles of empathy and solidarity, also speaks volumes about the overarching capacity of this mutual relationship between inequality and authoritarianism to violently react whenever those who have benefitted from it see themselves threatened.

Backlashes can also be found in the resistance to proposals that target a fairer tax system, attack entrenched clientelism in the political realm, promote a more inclusive system of justice, or extend social benefits to underprivileged people. By the same token, any movement whose goal is to tackle the past atrocities committed by the military during the civilian-military dictatorship (1964–85), strengthen the civilian control over the military, or even transform the violent, unaccountable and inefficient police,[6] is met with fierce opposition from leading sectors of society. A 'normalised' society that sees itself threatened can lead to someone like Bolsonaro, whose election is not merely the result of a resentful people but also expresses the 'rationality of fear' by those who will do whatever it takes, even support extra-constitutional actions, to protect themselves.[7]

On the other hand, the institutional and legal frameworks follow a pattern that, in some ways, constructs, reproduces and consolidates this mutual relationship between inequality and authoritarianism. The 'coalition presidentialism' that could offer reasonable governance and stability[8] has seen such a capacity dwindle through increasing party fragmentation and decreasing party institutionalisation in Congress, leading to pork-barrel politics, clientelism and corruption. The judiciary's growing politicisation and lack of accountability have furthered its own non-observance of due process of law as a basic principle of fairness, thus weakening its capacity to combat threats to the rule of law and constitutionalism. It also placed it inside the murky terrain of politics, with all the setbacks of such a move, even of being accused of partisanship, justifiably so in some landmark cases such as those linked to 'Operation Car Wash'.[9]

Mechanisms to combat corruption and foster greater transparency and accountability, which saw some significant progress at least until 2016,[10] have more recently provoked a furious backlash during the Michel Temer and Jair Bolsonaro administrations, in a clear response to an institutional system that was disturbing that 'normalised' sociological pattern. That institutional framework, while advancing in accountability, transparency and punishment, could not 'short-circuit the rationality of fear mechanism'.[11] Instead, particularly with

[6] See ch 5.

[7] See B Weingast, 'Designing Constitutional Stability' in R Congleton and B Swedenborg (eds), *Democratic Constitutional Design and Public Policy Analysis and Evidence* (MIT Press, 2006) 344.

[8] See ch 4. See also AC Figueiredo and F Limongi, 'Political Institutions and Governmental Performance in Brazilian Democracy' in D de la Fontaine and T Stehnken (eds), *The Political System of Brazil* (Springer, 2016).

[9] See chs 5 and 6.

[10] See ch 6.

[11] Weingast (n 7) 344.

the participation of the judiciary in an already troublesome political scenario, the stakes of politics increased, not diminished, thereby leading to greater instability.[12] The other consequence is that the 'institutional equilibrium'[13] that fosters the commitment of political forces to follow the law has become more precarious, and their ability to coordinate interests and constrain the central power turned out to be less efficient. The rule of law has then weakened.

Brazil has thus endured the destabilisation of such an 'institutional equilibrium'. It is a democracy, though a flawed one that is passing through serious junctures challenging its resilience. These junctures are symptoms of longstanding causes that have impaired the consolidation of the rule of law in Brazil, now featuring new shapes and stronger disruptive capacities. They are expressions of sociological and institutional features such as the growing polarisation in society and politics and a dysfunctional institutional framework. While polarisation and the institutional dysfunctionalities could be 'normalised' and their potential conflicts avoided, there was some stability. It is as though, in such a 'normalised' scenario, there is a reasonable level of 'institutional equilibrium' that creates incentives for the political forces to coordinate conflicting interests and equip them with tools to diffuse and control power, even if imperfectly. However, such a balance is susceptible to disruption once that level of 'normalisation' of potential conflicts is affected in one way or another.

A. The Growing Polarisation in Society and Politics

The growing polarisation in society and politics is certainly the Achilles heel of such a balance. It has been increasingly stimulated by new forms of information and disinformation and is, therefore, more open to external inputs. The damage that a divided public can cause to democracy is considerable and is possibly the most impactful variable for a democratic crisis.[14] Brazil's recent developments – similar to various other examples elsewhere[15] – are testimony of the deleterious effect of social and political polarisation. New insights on the effects of the internet and social media on polarisation have popped up across various academic

[12] ibid 344.

[13] See A Przeworski and JM Maravall, 'Introduction' in A Przeworski and JM Maravall (eds), *Democracy and the Rule of Law* (Cambridge University Press, 2003) 3. See also ch 1.

[14] See Z Elkins, 'Is the Sky Falling? Constitutional Crises in Historical Perspective' in MA Graber, S Levinson and M Tushnet (eds), *Constitutional Democracy in Crisis* (Oxford University Press, 2018) 53.

[15] See Graber, Levinson and Tushnet (n 14); T Ginsburg and AZ Huq, *How to Save a Constitutional Democracy* (University of Chicago Press, 2018); A Przeworski, *Crises of Democracy* (Cambridge University Press, 2019); S Levitsky and D Ziblatt, *How Democracies Die* (Crown, 2018); Y Mounk, *The People vs. Democracy: Why Our Freedom is in Danger and How to Save It* (Harvard University Press, 2018); KL Scheppele, 'Autocratic Legalism' (2018) 85 *The University of Chicago Law Review.* 545; R Dixon and D Landau, *Abusive Constitutional Borrowing: Legal Globalization and the Subversion of Liberal Democracy* (Oxford University Press, 2021).

fields, some clearly pointing out that they are catalysers of polarisation[16] and others arguing less emphatically so.[17] However, they can be powerful framers of public opinion especially during electoral moments, as happened during the 2018 elections in Brazil. Emilio Peluso Meyer, for example, '[diagnosed] how Brazilian social-democratic constitutionalism has been affected by the digital age'[18] through a series of events during and after Bolsonaro's election as President, and Wendy Hunter and Timothy J Power examined the 'strategic use of social media' as a key factor for Brazil's democratic backlash under Bolsonaro.[19] The impacts on social and political polarisation in Brazil look undeniable.

However, political and social polarisation in Brazil is naturally marked by its rampant social inequality, first because it creates a divide among distinct social groups (Blacks and whites, poor and rich, women and men, etc) and also because it affects the institutional capacity for coordination, since they fail to deliver incentives for empowering individuals to defend their rights.[20] In such a scenario of lack of coordination, disinformation becomes a much more effective tool of coordination than institutions themselves. *Bolsonarismo* has proven to be an impressive machine of disinformation, but also of engaging diverse interests toward the common goal of defending the government and its leader no matter what. It provides coordination where social relations and institutions have failed to do so. When social relations (religious groups, community associations, unions, etc) or institutions are replaced by a sort of mystifying figure that adopts polarisation as a behavioural strategy of coordination, and such a strategy proves successful, it is not merely polarisation that is the main issue. It is also its capacity of strategically bursting the bubble of 'normalised' social and institutional relations, which have long been marked by inequality, as a psychological weapon of mutual engagement through polarisation. Therefore, social inequality feeds social polarisation, and social polarisation feeds political polarisation as a mechanism of coordination. In this scenario, there is no 'institutional equilibrium' that will lead individuals to understand that abiding by the law is strategically beneficial for them, so there is no rule of law or institutional coordination, but, rather, there is coordination through polarisation.

[16] See CA Bail et al, 'Exposure to Opposing Views on Social Media Can Increase Political Polarization' (2018) 115 *Proceedings of the National Academic of Science* 9216; R Levy, 'Social Media, News Consumption, and Polarization: Evidence from a Field Experiment' (2021) 111 *American Economic Review* 831; A Banks et al, '#PolarizedFeeds: Three Experiments on Polarization, Framing, and Social Media' (2021) 26 *The International Journal of Press/Politics* 609.

[17] See JK Lee et al, 'Social Media, Network Heterogeneity, and Opinion Polarization' (2014) 64 *Journal of Communication* 702; M Yarchi, C Baden and N Kligler-Vilenchik, 'Political Polarization on the Digital Sphere: A Cross-Platform, Over-Time Analysis of Interactional, Positional, and Affective Polarization on Social Media' (2021) 38 *Political Communication* 98.

[18] EPN Meyer, *Constitutional Erosion in Brazil: Progresses and Failures of a Constitutional Project* (Hart Publishing, 2021) 176.

[19] W Hunter and TJ Power, 'Bolsonaro and Brazil's Illiberal Backlash' (2019) 30 *Journal of Democracy* 70.

[20] See ch 1.

B. The Disarrangement of the Political and Judicial Systems

The 'normalisation' was affected by the disarrangement of the political and judicial systems. 'Operation Car Wash' and also some other probes before it[21] yielded a tectonic shift in the 'institutional equilibrium' that had until then prevailed in the relationship between the political and judicial realms. The still entrenched mechanisms of corruption that have long plagued the political system, in a form of clientelism that has shaped the functioning and funding of political parties and politicians for years,[22] felt threatened by new forms of institutional and social oversight and accountability mechanisms.[23] It also needed to readapt itself to a broader, though increasingly uncoordinated, diffusion of political clout as the political system became more fragmented and less institutionalised.[24]

The judiciary, on the other hand, saw itself as empowered by the moral duty of pushing history into a sort of 'illuminist role',[25] which ended up blurring some necessary constraints on the politicisation of judicial discourses. New tools such as the principle of proportionality,[26] the growing methodological syncretism of constitutional concepts[27] and the continuous confusion between moral values and legal principles[28] served well the purpose of transforming the courts into powerful political players, in a mutualism with political parties,[29] with all the risks involved in such a task. Courts have also become more empowered through the expansion of tools to exert judicial review and interbranch oversight.[30] They have done so, however, through the strategic use of their own dysfunctionalities,[31] such as the judges' excessive individual powers,[32] the high inconsistency

[21] For example, the *Mensalão* case before it, in which more than 28 individuals were convicted for a legislative vote-buying scheme. See G Michener and C Pereira, 'A Great Leap Forward for Democracy and the Rule of Law? Brazil's Mensalão Trial' (2016) 48 *Journal of Latin American Studies* 477.

[22] See ch 4.

[23] See ch 6.

[24] See ch 4.

[25] See LR Barroso, 'Countermajoritarian, Representative, and Enlightened: The Roles of Constitutional Tribunals in Contemporary Democracies' (2018) 9 *Revista Direito e Práxis* 2171.

[26] See JZ Benvindo, *On the Limits of Constitutional Adjudication: Deconstructing Balancing and Judicial Activism* (Springer, 2010).

[27] See VAD Silva, 'Interpretação Constitucional e Sincretismo Metodológico' in VAD Silva (ed), *Interpretação Constitucional* (Malheiros, 2005) 115–43.

[28] See K Günther, *The Sense of Appropriateness: Application Discourses in Morality and Law* (SUNY Press, 1993); M Neves, *Constitutionalism and the Paradox of Principles and Rules: Between the Hydra and Hercules* (Oxford University Press, 2021); J Habermas, *Between Facts and Norms* (MIT Press, 1996) 222–37.

[29] See D Bogéa, *Partidos Políticos e STF: Decifrando a Simbiose Institucional* (Appris, 2021).

[30] See ch 5.

[31] See ch 5.

[32] See DW Arguelhes and LM Ribeiro, '"The Court, It is I"? Individual Judicial Powers in the Brazilian Supreme Court and their Implications for Constitutional Theory' (2018) 7 *Global Constitutionalism* 236.

in their decisions and the lack of deliberative performance.[33] The firewall between the murky waters of politics and the sought-after deontological principles of justice became even more fragile, '[destroying] the rational basis for a functional separation of powers justified by the different possibilities of access to certain kinds of reason'.[34]

Such a destruction meant that the 'normalisation' that had prevailed for so long by not encroaching on those clientelist behaviours in the political realm would be disrupted by a judiciary that seemed to be checking those powers at last, but not without also allowing itself to be corrupted by politics in this process. What could in principle seem like a positive development for the rule of law – after all the judiciary would be reaching privileged groups that have historically counted on 'the high probability of their impunity'[35] – turned out to be a breach of the 'institutional equilibrium' that had functioned so far by 'normalising' some of those illegalities, sweeping them under the carpet as a needed 'compromise' to keep the political system stable. In the end, the political system was in tatters – Bolsonaro's election is the most visible example of this[36] – but the judiciary was not far behind. After the judge presiding over 'Operation Car Wash', Sérgio Moro, was declared partial by the Supreme Court in the cases involving former President Lula da Silva because of serious violations of due process of law,[37] the deleterious effects of high politicisation in the judiciary could no longer be denied. Both the political and judicial realms mutually thrived on distrust.

C. A New 'Equilibrium'?

Self-reinforcing processes may suffer from severe disruption, but they tend to find ways to establish a new 'equilibrium'. It did not take long until the political system could, even if erratically, regain control over the disruptive forces that were undermining those longstanding 'compromises' that could keep the political system relatively stable at the expense of weakening its democratic credentials. The growing party fragmentation in Brazil's 'coalition presidentialism' has been pointed out as a dysfunctionality that creates incentives for corruption and clientelism as well as engenders potential gridlocks for

[33] See VA da Silva, 'Deciding without Deliberating' (2013) 11 *International Journal of Constitutional Law* 557.

[34] J Habermas, 'Reply to Symposium Participants, Benjamin N. Cardozo School of Law' in J Habermas, *Habermas on Law and Democracy* (University of California Press 1998) 430.

[35] See M Neves, 'Luhmann, Habermas e o Estado de Direito' (1996) 37 *Lua Nova* 103.

[36] The number of political outsiders was unprecedented both at the federal level (Bolsonaro's Social Liberal Party (PSL) jumped from 8 to 52 seats in the Lower House, and from 0 to 4 in the Senate) but also at the state level (for instance, the elections of the Governor of Rio de Janeiro, Wilson Witzel, and the Governor of Minas Gerais, Romeu Zema).

[37] See ch 5.

governability and instability,[38] even if some controversies arise as to whether 'coalition presidentialism' itself may be more functional and accountable than normally depicted.[39]

In just over three years of his government, Bolsonaro has been nothing other than the most blatant expression of that 'old politics' that he so sharply attacked, to a degree nowhere to be found at least since the transition to democracy in 1985. He has become increasingly dependent on the most clientelist political parties in Congress. Patronage and corruption are his bargaining chips for a government that has proven chaotic and growingly unpopular. Despite Bolsonaro's continuous threats against the democratic regime, whenever he boasts of his strength, he reveals instead a profound level of weakness: his powers have been largely transferred to the fragmented Congress.[40] In a presidential system like in Brazil, a weak president can either be impeached, if he or she does not compromise with Congress (and particularly with some of those most clientelist political parties), or simply be kept in office while Congress takes significant control over the political agenda and the national budget. Whereas former President Dilma Rousseff did not compromise when she rapidly lost popular support and was therefore impeached, Bolsonaro adopted the second strategy. This is a paradox of 'coalition presidentialism': it is dysfunctional by some means, but it also sets high incentives for politics as a condition for governability. A weak president, in such a system, is thus a recipe for instability.

Even Bolsonaro's association with the military, which has engendered analyses of the risk of a *coup d'état*,[41] seems less threatening than is usually depicted. Though the military has been revived in his government as never before since the transition to democracy in 1985, such a close relationship is a consequence of the disruption of the 'normalisation' that has survived over the democratic years by sweeping under the carpet the tensions between civilians and the military. Civilian control over the military seems fragile, just awaiting the opportunity to go off. A would-be autocrat like Bolsonaro would seize the opportunity to explore such a fragility through co-optation and ideological identification in order to raise his bargaining chips through threats and bluffs. Although such

[38] See ch 4.

[39] See ch 4.

[40] See 'Brazil's President Jair Bolsonaro Is Under Siege' (*The Economist*, 29 May 2021) www.economist.com/the-americas/2021/05/29/brazils-president-jair-bolsonaro-is-under-siege.

[41] JV Archegas and L Kreuz, 'The "Constitutional Military Intervention": Brazil on the Verge of Democratic Breakdown' (*Verfassungsblog*, 4 June 2020) https://verfassungsblog.de/the-constitutional-military-intervention-brazil-on-the-verge-of-democratic-breakdown/; S Abranches, 'O Golpe Híbrido de Bolsonaro' (*Sérgio Abranches*, 15 August 2021) https://sergioabranches.com.br/politica/535-o-golpe-hibrido-de-bolsonaro; P Wintour, 'Brazil: Warning Bolsonaro May Be Planning Military Coup Amid Rallies' *The Guardian* (6 September 2021) www.theguardian.com/world/2021/sep/06/brazil-warning-bolsonaro-may-be-planning-military-coup-amid-rallies; T McCoy and GS Pessoa, 'Bolsonaro Once Said He'd Stage a Military Takeover: Now Brazilians Fear He Could Be Laying the Foundation for One' *The Washington Post* (23 July 2021) www.washingtonpost.com/world/2021/07/23/brazil-bolsonaro/.

signs are certainly worrying for Brazil's democracy and rule of law, the power has already shifted to the traditional political realm, where the real disputes defining the functioning of the country's institutions effectively take place. The military owns the tanks and weapons, but it is the political system that has long played the cards of Brazilian democracy, even if at the expense of making it less robust and stable.

The truth is that such an association between the Bolsonaro government and the military has proven not strong enough to challenge those self-reinforcing processes shaping the political system. More seriously, by so strongly aligning with such a weak and chaotic government, the military has also laid bare its own weakness and complicity with that tragic political project: not only has it failed in helping the government to provide good governance, but it also has seen itself engulfed by accusations of mismanagement and corruption. For instance, it was the three-star general Eduardo Pazuello who was in charge of the Ministry of Health during the deadliest period of the COVID-19 crisis. His administration was nothing short of calamitous, some might say criminal. Scandals involving the prescription of ineffective drugs and corruption related to the acquisition of vaccines made international news[42] and implicated not only civilians but several military figures inside the government. Increasingly, the military's association with the Bolsonaro government has become clear as investigations point out the participation of its members in numerous corruption schemes.[43] It has lost some support and trust of general society,[44] so its threats against the democratic system – as happened with Bolsonaro's own threats – have sounded less and less credible, and increasingly frequent and brazen. The military could boast of its strength – after all, it possesses the arms – but, in the end, it needs to compromise with the political system, even as a last hope that its project – and Bolsonaro's – can survive.

In the end, the political system, with all its dysfunctionalities, tends to prevail. Radical and authoritarian movements affect the 'normalisation' that is needed for such a system to work, even more so given the costs of fragmented and concurrent interests. It is no wonder that Brazilian past presidents with successful coalitions have all leaned to the centre of the political spectrum. An authoritarian figure could only succeed if he or she were able to radically disrupt such a system,[45] a move that demands at the very least the massive support of

[42] See T Philips, 'Pressure Mounts on Bolsonaro amid Rising Anger over Vaccine Corruption Scandal' *The Guardian* (1 July 2021) www.theguardian.com/world/2021/jul/01/bolsonaro-brazil-vaccine-covid-scandal.

[43] See S Saxena and F Costa, 'Brazil Senate Inquiry Follows the Money in "Scandalous" Covaxin Deal with India' (*The Wire*, 22 June 2021) https://thewire.in/world/covaxin-brazil-senate-probe-scandal.

[44] See R Bonin, 'Após Pazzuello, Popularidade dos Militares Cai de 62% para 58%' (*Veja*, 11 June 2021) https://veja.abril.com.br/blog/radar/apos-pazuello-popularidade-dos-militares-cai-de-62-para-58/.

[45] See JZ Benvindo, 'The Party Fragmentation in Brazil: A Shield Against Authoritarianism' (*International Journal of Constitutional Law Blog*, 24 October 2019) www.iconnectblog.com/2019/10/the-party-fragmentation-paradox-in-brazil-a-shield-against-authoritarianism/.

key sectors of society, which Bolsonaro has growingly lost. He would need such support for what political scientists call 'gambling for resurrection', that is, to 'maintain power by inducing massive change in the environment that has only a small chance of succeeding'.[46] The vast majority of Brazilians, however, reject the return to an authoritarian regime,[47] so 'gambling for resurrection' increasingly looks like a desperate move. It seems that there is a threshold above which even some of Bolsonaro's supporters may turn against him: they may be on his side now in an environment where democracy still exists, but, if this scenario changes, the 'rationality of fear' may lead to a defensive behaviour against more damaging authoritarian actions. The irony is that, for his authoritarian project, Bolsonaro is a President without enough powers, and a populist without enough people.[48]

On the other hand, the judiciary promotes this new 'equilibrium' by switching from a defiant posture against the 'normalised' political system to a more condescending behaviour toward such a 'normalisation'. The judiciary from 'Operation Car Wash', which revealed corruption schemes but not without also corrupting itself, could not be a reality any longer. The disruptive nature of that defiant posture to the rather stable mutualism[49] between the political and judicial realms, after all, contributed to the perilous rise of a would-be autocrat in the presidency. The upshot is that the judiciary, despite its contribution to such a scenario, found itself in urgent need of resuming its self-restrained behaviour toward the political system. It is no wonder that the Supreme Court has increasingly stressed procedural guarantees in its most recent decisions involving political bigwigs and businessmen,[50] in a movement that contrasts with the more politicised behaviour of the previous years.[51] It is also symptomatic, for example, that Kassio Nunes, the first appointee to the Supreme Court by President Bolsonaro, needed to emphasise that the defence of constitutional guarantees 'should be praised'[52] in his confirmation in the Senate. Yet a defensive

[46] R De Figueiredo and B Weingast, 'The Rationality of Fear: Political Opportunism and Ethnic Conflict' in BF Walter and J Snyder (eds), *Civil Wars, Insecurity, and Intervention* (Columbia University Press, 1999) 263.

[47] See E Gonçalves, 'Quase 80% dos Brasileiros Rejeitam o Retorno de um Regime Autoritário' (*Veja*, 30 July 2020) https://veja.abril.com.br/politica/para-quase-80-dos-brasileiros-democracia-e-a-melhor-forma-de-governo/; 'Apoio à Democracia Atinge 75%' (*Datafolha*, 29 June 2020) https://datafolha.folha.uol.com.br/opiniaopublica/2020/06/1988776-apoio-a-democracia-atinge-75.shtml.

[48] See JZ Benvindo, 'The Rationality of Fear on the Edge of Brazilian Democracy: Another Shield Against Authoritarianism?' (*International Journal of Constitutional Law Blog*, 31 December 2019) www.iconnectblog.com/2019/12/the-rationality-of-fear-on-the-edge-of-brazilian-democracy-another-shield-against-authoritarianism/.

[49] See Bogéa (n 29).

[50] See STF, INQ n. 4781 (2021). See also BM Lorenzetto and RDR Pereira, 'O Supremo Soberano no Estado de Exceção: A (Des)aplicação do Direito pelo STF no Âmbito do Inquérito das "Fake News"' (2020) 41 *Seqüência: Estudos Jurídicos e Políticos* 173.

[51] See ch 5.

[52] See H Freitas, '"O Garantismo Deve Ser Exaltado", Diz Kassio Nunes em Sabatina no Senado' (*Jota*, 21 October 2020) www.jota.info/legislativo/o-garantismo-deve-ser-exaltado-diz-kassio-nunes-em-sabatina-no-senado-21102020.

behaviour against the still destabilising element of this new 'equilibrium' is also needed.

Therefore, if the judiciary has become more condescending toward the traditional political system, it has nevertheless become more reactive to an executive branch that continuously threatens the country's democratic institutions. Inquiries, for example, were opened in the Supreme Court to investigate the spreading of fake news and the promotion of undemocratic acts,[53] the alleged presidential intervention in the federal police[54] and corruption scandals involving the acquisition of COVID-19 vaccines.[55] The judiciary has functioned as a shield against possible attacks on this new 'equilibrium' despite its own fragilities and increasing risks of takeover by the executive, especially in the circumstance of President Bolsonaro's eventual re-election.

The 'institutional equilibrium', even if re-established by some means, has been damaged as never before during the democratic years and is now operating at a lower level. It will take years to recover from the harm inflicted on Brazil's institutions: the political system has become more fragmented, uncoordinated and clientelist; the judiciary has lost credibility after immersing itself so deeply in sheer politics; the oversight institutions in all areas have been weakened; and the military have laid bare their profound incapacity to learn from the years of democratic life, revealing how ingrained in the barracks the authoritarian mindset remains. Overall, Brazil has taken many steps backwards in democratic governance and commitment to the rule of law, which is heart-breaking given the improvements the country could achieve over the democratic years and the immense potentialities of such a resourceful and culturally rich country. However, such a bleak scenario, once overcome, may be the chance for the country to challenge at least some of its longstanding wrongs. The question that remains, however, is whether the country will seize such an opportunity to finally have this encounter with its past.

II. THE FUTURE OF BRAZIL'S RULE OF LAW

This book began by stressing the difficulties of writing it in the middle of the most critical political event in Brazil at least since the transition to democracy in 1985. The risk of history passing us by while the words are put on paper is nothing short of a daily challenge. The rule of law is a concept that spreads over various institutional, sociological and philosophical variables, so a simple change in one of them may bring about a series of developments that demand rewriting entire parts of previous analyses. Despite the high stakes of such an endeavour, there are phenomena that transcend the immediate sequence of

[53] STF, INQ 4781 (pending).
[54] STF, INQ 4831 (pending)
[55] STF, PET 9760 (pending).

events, structures that play an even greater role than junctures and circumstances in shaping the reality. As Paul Pierson argues, 'where historical causation is at work, explanation requires the examination of considerable stretches of time'.[56] In order to understand the rule of law in Brazil, our present history certainly matters, but it may suffer from the natural bias of not only losing the big picture while events and their consequences are still underway, but also highlighting junctures that, even if impactful, may be less so when the whole scenario is examined diachronically rather than merely synchronically.[57]

The main argument of this book has focused on two structural variables that have shaped much of the rule of law in Brazil: the rampant levels of social inequality and the stubborn authoritarian mindset that recurrently appears and gains prominence whenever the opportunity arises. These two structural variables, now understood as features of a long-term history that have been preserved through a series of positive feedbacks,[58] should thus be interpreted as the real determinants of what may happen next in Brazilian reality and in the development of the country's rule of law. In this regard, the phenomenon of Bolsonaro – and *bolsonarismo* more broadly – should be diagnosed as an important symptom, not a cause. The future of the rule of law in Brazil, at least in the short run, certainly hinges on whether Bolsonaro will be re-elected or not, but, in the long run, more important is whether the country's institution can reach a degree of 'normalisation' – and thus a new 'equilibrium' – that can lower the stakes of politics. More important still, the rule of law in Brazil depends largely on whether such a 'normalisation' will mean sweeping those tensions under the carpet and not challenging their structural causes, or whether it may mean gradually challenging them more effectively.

The exercise of behaving as a historian of the future[59] is certainly risky and fallible. It should, therefore, be acknowledged that we are dealing with the imponderable, so the predictions may prove totally or partially wrong. We attempt nevertheless to focus on the long-term history, on such structural variables that we have been discussing in this book by assuming that, as they have lingered for a while, the odds are that they will determine what comes next. Evidently circumstances and critical junctures may change the course of events, but assuming that they tend to follow a certain path relieves a bit of the burden of foreseeing the future.

In the short and medium term, Bolsonaro's eventual re-election certainly means that Brazil will see its democracy backslide even further, but it is more

[56] Pierson (n 3) 46.

[57] ibid 45.

[58] ibid 46.

[59] See JZ Benvindo, 'The Historian of the Future in Brazilian Democracy: The Challenges of Interpreting and Comparing Events of Our Time' (*International Journal of Constitutional Law Blog*, 24 February 2021) www.iconnectblog.com/2021/02/the-historian-of-the-future-in-brazilian-democracy-the-challenges-of-interpreting-and-comparing-events-of-our-own-time/.

likely that such a movement will be bumpier and far more nuanced than normally depicted. The use of strategies leading to forms of abusive constitutionalism[60] or autocratic legalism[61] will be likely to find less institutional resistance, so the constitutional erosion that has already been inflicted prior to and during the Bolsonaro presidency[62] will advance to an even more worrying level. Much of the social-democratic project that Brazil launched with the transition to democracy in 1985 and the drafting of the 1988 Constitution will be at risk. A second term will provide Bolsonaro with the argument and a sort of legitimacy for strengthening his grip on power. It will also be evidence that the institutions were too lenient and failed to protect democracy during his first term, and, when they realised how far he had gone, it was already too late. The premise that usually applies in such cases is that 'unless the incumbent is removed early into the process, he can hardly be removed by democratic means later'.[63]

However, there are relevant caveats for this dire outcome. The first is that, based on current data on popularity,[64] Bolsonaro's electoral victory, if it happens, will be very tight. To promote his election, he has advanced the adoption of polarisation[65] as a strategy. He can no longer behave simply as a populist and count on the popular pressure against the democratic institutions, because his support has significantly dwindled. Corrupting institutions and making them less robust to withstand attacks on democratic principles has thus intensified. The path is well-known for such a strategy: the incumbent gradually '[accumulates] advantage' to the point that, even if citizens do not support him any longer, he has become far more immune to their preferences and can make even bolder movements for such a purpose.[66]

Bolsonaro's first term has been marked by a series of movements against oversight institutions, above all the Public Ministry, through an 'allied' Attorney General of the Republic,[67] the Federal Police[68] and the

[60] See D Landau, 'Abusive Constitutionalism' (2013) 47 *University of California Davis Law Review* 189; R Dixon and D Landau, *Abusive Constitutional Borrowing: Legal Globalization and the Subversion of Liberal Democracy* (Oxford University Press, 2021).

[61] See KL Scheppele, 'Autocratic Legalism' (2018) 85 *The University of Chicago Law Review* 545.

[62] See Meyer (n 18).

[63] See Z Luo and A Przeworski, 'Democracy and Its Vulnerabilities: Dynamics of Democratic Backsliding' (2019) Working Paper 11, https://ssrn.com/abstract=3469373.

[64] According to Datafolha, Bolsonaro's rejection rate reached 59% in September 2021 and would be beaten by most candidates in a run-off. See 'A Um Ano da Eleição, Lula Lidera Disputa Presidencial' (*Datafolha*, 17 September 2021) https://datafolha.folha.uol.com.br/eleicoes/2021/09/1989339-a-um-ano-da-eleicao-disputa-presidencial-tem-lula-na-lideranca-e-bolsonaro-em-segundo.shtml.

[65] See Luo and Przeworski (n 63) 9–10.

[66] ibid 68.

[67] See CH Mendes, 'Aras é a Antessala de Bolsonaro no Tribunal Penal Internacional' (*Folha de S. Paulo*, 26 January 2021) www1.folha.uol.com.br/colunas/conrado-hubner-mendes/2021/01/aras-e-a-antessala-de-bolsonaro-no-tribunal-penal-internacional.shtml.

[68] 'Interferência na PF: Quais Eram os Interesses de Bolsonaro? Confira 12 Perguntas e Respostas' (*Folha de S. Paulo*, 24 February 2021) https://valor.globo.com/politica/noticia/2021/02/24/quais-eram-os-interesses-de-bolsonaro-ao-interferir-na-pf-confira-12-perguntas-e-respostas.ghtml.

Federal Revenue Office.[69] He has also shielded himself against a potential impeachment by expanding his coalition in Congress through pork barrel, patronage and corruption, though such a move is more a sign of weakness than strength.[70] Moreover, in order to regain some electoral support, he has increasingly appealed to public policies aimed at providing some assistance to the most in need – an important initiative especially after the COVID-19 crisis – but without enough planning and merely targeting potential electoral dividends. For example, he replaced the successful *Bolsa Família Program*[71] with the badly designed *Auxílio Brasil*,[72] which, unlike the former, looks like more a paternalist programme than a structural one aiming at lifting people out of poverty. Bolsonaro has historically been very critical of *Bolsa Família* and said that it should be ended,[73] but he naturally saw that increasing the value of the monthly allowance and bringing it to more people, even if through a fiscal manoeuvre,[74] would be his last card to reverse his declining popular support.

Therefore, even if he is successful in gathering support for his re-election, it will not be enough for a 'gambling for resurrection'[75] that could lead to a substantial number of Brazilians to engage themselves in Bolsonaro's agenda of attacking even further the democratic institutions. Stealth will therefore be needed, but the difficulties will possibly lie in the likelihood of a Congress that tends to be composed of a larger number of members of opposition parties. Bolsonaro's re-election will thus not follow the same pattern of his 2018 election, when a social catharsis prompted by 'Operation Car Wash' propelled the election of various newcomers in Congress, many of whom directly associated with Bolsonaro's own unconventional victory. Due to Bolsonaro's closer association with the most clientelist political parties to gain some leverage for re-election, he will already assume office with the rope around his neck. Like his first term,

[69] J Tavares, 'Interferências de Bolsonaro Se Acumulam, de Petrobras e PF a Congresso e Receita' (*Folha de S. Paulo*, 22 February 2021) www1.folha.uol.com.br/poder/2021/02/interferencias-de-bolsonaro-se-acumulam-de-petrobras-e-pf-a-congresso-e-receita.shtml.

[70] 'Brazil's President Jair Bolsonaro is Under Siege' (*The Economist*, 29 May 2021) www.economist.com/the-americas/2021/05/29/brazils-president-jair-bolsonaro-is-under-siege.

[71] See AW Pereira, 'Bolsa Família and Democracy in Brazil' (2015) 36 *Third World Quarterly* 1682; T Campello and MC Neri, *Bolsa Família Program: A Decade of Social Inclusion in Brazil* (IPEA, 2013).

[72] T Campelo and S Brandão, 'Desgoverno de Bolsonaro Destrói o Melhor do Bolsa Família' (*Folha de S. Paulo*, 19 October 2021) www1.folha.uol.com.br/mercado/2021/10/desgoverno-de-bolsonaro-destroi-o-melhor-do-bolsa-familia.shtml; J Camelo, 'Bolsonaro Confirms BRL 400 Stipends for New Cash-Transfer Program' (*The Brazilian Report*, 20 October 2021) https://brazilian.report/liveblog/2021/10/20/cash-transfer-program/.

[73] D Fortuna, 'Bolsonaro e o Programa Bolsa Família: De Crítico Feroz a Defensor' (*Correio Braziliense*, 11 April 2019) www.correiobraziliense.com.br/app/noticia/politica/2019/04/11/interna_politica,748643/bolsonaro-e-o-bolsa-familia-de-critico-feroz-a-defensor.shtml.

[74] R Cunto et al, 'Government, Congress Join Forces in Fiscal Maneuver Over Spending Cap' (*Valor Econômico*, 21 October 2021) https://valorinternational.globo.com/politics/news/2021/10/21/government-congress-join-forces-in-fiscal-maneuver-over-spending-cap.ghtml.

[75] See Figueiredo and Weingst (n 46) 263.

when former General Hamilton Mourão was elected Vice-President, Bolsonaro plans to run with the former General and even closer ally Braga Netto at his side in order to lower risk of an impeachment. Despite that, a second term may only be viable if Bolsonaro behaves like a feeder of pork and patronage, which, in theory, prioritises low-profile behaviour rather than radicalisation. In practice, however, Bolsonaro has already shown that he needs radicalisation as a political platform, so the agreement with the political system will carry on being very unstable and unreliable. The risk is, nevertheless, that radicalism and clientelism may find a common ground for mutual benefits, especially if oversight institutions are increasingly dismantled and lose their capacity of reaction.

Brazil is also a federation of 26 states and the Federal District, so the executive power, even if largely concentrated on the federal government, presents a reasonable level of fragmentation at the state and even municipal levels. In his first term, a number of newcomers were elected governors following Bolsonaro's wave, such as in Rio de Janeiro and Minas Gerais (two leading states in Brazil's Southeast). However, the likelihood is that the next elections will bring professional and experienced politicians back to office as well as increase the share of governors from opposition parties. In his first term, Bolsonaro already had to deal with some serious opposition from distinct governors, especially in relation to the COVID-19 crisis. The Governor of São Paulo, João Doria, was, for example, a fierce opponent of Bolsonaro, even though he had supported him in the 2018 presidential elections. A second term could mean an even stronger opposition, which not only would affect Bolsonaro's influence at both state and local levels, but also how Congress, increasingly operating through pork and patronage, will behave in the face of such potential conflicts.

In a second term, Bolsonaro will have the opportunity to appoint at least two other justices to the Supreme Court. He will not yet reach the majority – and the correlation between appointees and the presidential agenda is far from automatic[76] – but four of the 11 justices will have already been appointed by him.[77] For a Court whose individual powers are highly disproportionate and where collegiate deliberation is low,[78] one single justice can already cause serious damage, let alone four or more. Brazil may then find itself in such a crossroad where not only Congress but also the judiciary may not function as barriers against autocratisation. Along with the increasing co-optation of oversight institutions and the Armed Forces, the scenario could be very bleak at the institutional level.

[76] See DW Arguelhes and LM Ribeiro, 'Indicações Presidenciais para o Supremo Tribunal Federal e seus Fins Políticos: Uma Resposta a Mariana Prado e Cláudia Türner' (2010) 255 *Revista de Direito Administrativo* 115.

[77] See A Spigariol, 'Supreme Court Seat Remains Vacant amid Political Tug-of-War' (*The Brazilian Report*, 20 September 2021) https://brazilian.report/power/2021/09/20/supreme-court-seat-vacant-politics/.

[78] See ch 5.

The path is not, however, that straightforward. Brazil has been a relatively stable democracy for over 30 years and is a very plural country socially, politically and economically. Therefore, a series of positive feedbacks[79] have raised incentives in favour of democracy that cannot be dismantled without suffering fierce opposition. In such a scenario, there will possibly be strong popular resistance and the media will tend to position itself, at least initially, mostly on the side of the opposition, as the main media outlets have already been doing during Bolsonaro's first term. Bolsonaro will move forward in his authoritarian project, but to be successful he will need to count on a conjunction of variables that even a would-be autocrat cannot control. If he wins the 2022 election, autocratisation will be certainly more likely but not assured.

In any case, a Bolsonaro second term is not the most probable scenario according to the current polls.[80] The immediate consequence is that he will probably not concede and will adopt a similar strategy such as the one the US endured right after Donald Trump's defeat in the 2020 presidential elections: Bolsonaro will dispute the results and denounce electoral fraud, even though nonexistent. He has already moved the pieces of the chess board in this direction and has preventively launched an assault on the country's successful system of electronic voting, which, in its over 25 years in operation, has never been faced with cases of fraud and is fast, reliable, and largely accepted among Brazilians.[81] A proposal for constitutional amendment aimed at changing such a system was even presented in Congress, but the reaction, headed by the Superior Electoral Court, was powerful enough to block it in its first steps in the Chamber of Deputies.[82] The message has already been sent, and, if he loses, this may provide him with the argument to either leave office by stating that he had lost only because the election was rigged or, worse, he may lead a counterattack by militias, members of the police forces and even Armed Forces to keep his hold on office. Such a move will very likely fail in the end: a *coup d'état* will probably not work unless he has enough popular and some institutional support, which, especially after losing the elections, he will not, but the damage to democratic institutions and the rule of law will nevertheless be huge.[83] It is no wonder that attacking the electoral system and the members of the Supreme Court

[79] See Pierson (n 3) 37.

[80] According to Datafolha, the former President is leading the dispute with 46% support. Bolsonaro has merely 25%. In a run-off, Lula would beat Bolsonaro by 56% v 31%. See Datafolha (n 64).

[81] See C Avgerou et al, 'Interpreting the Trustworthiness of Government Mediated by Information and Communication Technology: Lessons from Electronic Voting in Brazil' (2009) 15 *Information Technology for Development* 133.

[82] Câmara dos Deputados, PEC 135/2019.

[83] See F Campante, 'Apesar de Arroubos Retóricos, Ameaças Golpistas de Bolsonaro Devem Ser Levadas a Sério' (*Folha de S. Paulo*, 5 August 2021) www1.folha.uol.com.br/poder/2021/08/apesar-de-arroubos-retoricos-ameacas-golpistas-de-bolsonaro-devem-ser-levadas-a-serio.shtml.

and Superior Electoral Court[84] is a win-win strategy once the prospect of his re-election becomes increasingly remote.

In the medium to long term, the future of the rule of law in Brazil hinges, in any case, on whether the country will keep sweeping under the carpet the tensions that helped lead to Bolsonaro's election or whether the country will finally challenge them. For both scenarios, the condition is not only the end of Bolsonaro, even if *bolsonarismo* still remains for a while, but also that the country will be able to recover from the damage inflicted during his years in office and beyond. It will be time for reconciliation, as normally happens during regime transitions. The next presidents will have to reconstruct the bridges between the various political and ideological sectors of society and be able to lead the country to a new democratic moment. There is the risk that instability still remains for a while, but there is also the chance that, after such a cataclysm, the prospects of a stronger national union towards reconstruction gain some traction. Possibly more important is how the country will reconcile with its past. This will speak volumes about which path the country is willing to follow from then onwards. If it repeats the behaviour adopted during the transition from the civilian-military dictatorship (1964–85) to democracy, when reconciliation meant merely amnesty and impunity, 'normalisation' may be achieved, but at the expense of keeping Brazilian institutions under continuous stress, just waiting for a new opportunity to break down.

The stubborn authoritarian mindset gained a new shape and adopted new strategies during the Bolsonaro government. It laid the groundwork for a type of far-right movement that, throughout most of the democratic years, had little power to go much further than in narrow social circles. The most serious consequence for the future of the rule of law in Brazil lies in the higher penetration of a disruptive discourse against democratic institutions in much broader segments of society. Negotiations and compromises between right and left-leaning political players will become far less stable if turmoil is continuously triggered by strategies to antagonise and polarise their stances, in a trend whereby 'democratic publics and elites seem to be considerably less congenial and consensual'.[85] This is the reason why *bolsonarismo*, as the expression of such a movement in Brazil, will certainly linger for a while and will do whatever it takes to make up lost ground after Bolsonaro is no longer in office. The future of the rule of law in Brazil, even if a new democratic momentum takes place, will be negatively affected by the permeability of such a movement, and even more so if it is not seriously challenged or simply swept under the carpet.

[84] M Vargas, 'Bolsonaro Insiste em Ameaça Golpista, Chama Moraes de Ditatorial e Diz que "A Hora Dele Vai Chegar"' (*Folha de S. Paulo*, 5 August 2021) www1.folha.uol.com.br/poder/2021/08/bolsonaro-insiste-em-ameaca-golpista-chama-moraes-de-ditatorial-e-diz-que-a-hora-dele-vai-chegar.shtml.

[85] Elkins (n 14) 65.

On the other hand, it is in such turning points that the opportunity may arise for pushing for change, as they offer the opportunity for reaching a 'new equilibrium' and even a deeper one under which democracy will operate.[86] History has an impressive capacity to reinvent itself for better or for worse, but unless incentives for a self-correcting learning process[87] effectively take place, Brazilian democracy and the functioning of the country's rule of law will always swim in muddy waters. It is time for finally challenging the wrongs of those dictatorial years, the turbulent civilian-military relationship, the violence and unaccountability of the security forces,[88] the legacies of the institutional framework from those dictatorial years[89] and the serious damage to Brazil's rule of law under the Bolsonaro government.

However, if the authoritarian mindset is the Achilles heel of Brazil's democracy and rule of law by raising the stakes of politics and creating incentives for further polarisation, it is the country's outrageous social inequality that feeds it. In such a context, there is an unstable 'equilibrium' whereby those who benefit from such an inequality will do whatever it takes to keep their positions virtually untouched, and, in particular, use the legal framework to construct and maintain inequality for their own benefit. The level of coordination among the distinct segments of society to enforce the rule of law and protect democracy is therefore fragile, demands extra energy to reach consensus, and is less robust in its ability to constrain state powers.[90] It is a fertile ground for resorting to extraconstitutional means and for the rise of would-be autocrats, as happened with Bolsonaro.

On a deeper level, the future of the rule of law in Brazil hinges on how the country will devise public policies aimed at combatting poverty, providing social inclusion and thus transforming de jure equality into de facto distribution of power.[91] Such movements tend to be gradual as pushing for radical changes in such entrenched social relations tends to raise the stakes of politics and destabilise the constitution.[92] In any case, they are necessary, urgent and crucial for laying the groundwork for the country to reach a new level of commitment to the rule of law and to establish an 'equilibrium culture' where democracy is

[86] See Pierson (n 3) 157.

[87] See J Habermas, 'Constitutional Democracy: A Paradoxical Union of Contradictory Principles' (2001) 29 *Political Theory* 776.

[88] See J Zaverucha, 'Relações Civil-Militares: O Legado Autoritário da Constituição Brasileira de 1988' in E Teles and V Safatle (eds), *O Que Resta da Ditadura: A Exceção Brasileira* (Boitempo, 2010) 41–76.

[89] See G Bercovici, '"O Direito Constitucional Passa, o Direito Administrativo Permanece": A Persistência da Estrutura Administrativa de 1967' in Teles and Safatle (n 88) 77–90.

[90] See B Weingast, 'The Political Foundations of Democracy and the Rule of Law' (1997) 91 *American Political Science Review* 246.

[91] See D Acemoglu et al, 'Democracy, Public Policy, and Inequality' (2013) 11 *Comparative Democratization* 17.

[92] See Weingast (n 7) 345.

'the only game in town'.[93] Brazil has, throughout its democratic years, achieved significant institutional progress, created relevant mechanisms of social inclusion and enhanced its culture of democracy. Yet, it is still a country of deep social exclusion, extractive institutions[94] and where the legal construction of inequality prevails. In such a context, 'normalisation' through oblivion becomes Brazil's historical hallmark. The future of the rule of law in Brazil is certainly a vast unknown, but unless its wrongs are finally combatted, it may reach a new democratic equilibrium, but, once again, one that is fragile and unstable, just awaiting a new crisis. May Brazil learn from its past. May Brazil's rule of law finally mean the legal construction of *equality*.

[93] See A Przeworski, 'Democracy as an Equilibrium' (2005) 123 *Public Choice* 253.

[94] See D Acemoglu and JA Robinson, *Why Nations Fail: The Origins of Power, Prosperity and Poverty* (Crown Business, 2012) 124.

Bibliography

Abranches, S, 'Presidencialismo de Coalizão: O Dilema Institucional Brasileiro' (1988) 31 *Dados – Revista de Ciências Sociais* 5.

Abranches, S, *Presidencialismo de Coalizão* (Companhia das Letras, 2018).

Abranches, S, 'Polarização Radicalizada e Ruptura Eleitoral' in Abranches, S, et al (eds), *Democracia em Risco? 22 Ensaios sobre o Brasil Hoje* (Companhia das Letras, 2019) 7–28.

Abranches, S, et al, *Democracia em Risco? 22 Ensaios sobre o Brasil Hoje* (Companhia das Letras, 2019).

Acemoglu, D and Robinson, JA, 'De Facto Political Power and Institutional Persistence' (2006) 96 *American Economic Review* 325.

Acemoglu, D and Robinson, JA, *Economic Origins of Dictatorship and Democracy* (Cambridge University Press, 2006).

Acemoglu, D and Robinson, JA, *The Narrow Corridor: States, Societies, and the Fate of Liberty* (Penguin, 2019).

Acemoglu, D and Robinson, JA, *Why Nations Fail: The Origins of Power, Prosperity and Poverty* (Crown Business, 2012).

Acemoglu, D, et al, 'Democracy, Public Policy, and Inequality' (2013) 11 *Comparative Democratization* 2.

Acemoglu, D, et al, 'Democracy, Redistribution, and Inequality' in Atkinson, AB and Bourguignon, F, (ed), *Handbook of Income Distribution* (Elsevier, 2015) 1885–966.

Adams, M, Meuwese, A and Ballin, EH, *Constitutionalism and the Rule of Law* (Cambridge University Press, 2017).

Albert, R, *Constitutional Amendments: Making, Breaking, and Changing Constitutions* (Oxford University Press, 2019).

Albert, R, et al, 'Constitutional Reform in Brazil: Lessons from Albania' (2017) 4 *Revista de Investigações Constitucionais* 12.

Albertus, M and Menaldo, V, *Authoritarianism and the Elite Origins of Democracy* (Cambridge University Press, 2018).

Albuquerque, AD, 'Protecting Democracy or Conspiring Against It? Media and Politics in Latin America: A Glimpse from Brazil' (2019) 20 *Journalism* 906.

Alencar, GD, 'Grupos Protestanttes e Engajamento Social: Uma Análise dos Discursos e Ações de Coletivos Evangélicos Progressistas' (2019) 39 *Religião & Sociedade* 173.

Almeida, MHTD and Guarnieri, FH, 'The Unlikely President' (2020) 1 *Revista Euro Latinoamericana de Análisis Social y Político* 139.

Alvarez, MV, 'A Theory of Hegemonic Stability in South American Regionalism? Evidence from the Case of Brazil in UNASUR and Venezuela in ALBA' (2021) 43 *Contexto Internacional* 55.

Alves, JA, 'On Mules and Bodies: Black Captivities in the Brazilian Racial Democracy' (2016) 42 *Critical Sociology* 229.

Alves, JA, *The Anti-Black City: Police Terror and Black Urban Life in Brazil* (University of Minnesota Press, 2018).

Ames, B, *The Deadlock of Democracy in Brazil* (University of Michigan Press, 2001).

Amorim Neto, O, 'Presidential Cabinets, Electoral Cycles, and Coalition Discipline in Brazil' in Morgenstern, S and Nacif, B (eds), *Legislative Politics in Latin America* (Cambridge University Press, 2002).

Anderson, N, 'REDDy or Not? The Effects on Indigenous Peoples in Brazil of a Global Mechanism for Reducing Emissions from Deforestation and Degradation' (2009) 2 *Journal of Sustainable Development* 18.

Anis – Insstituto de Bioética, *Aborto: Por Que Precisamos Descriminalizar? Argumentos Apresentados ao Supremo Tribunal Federal na Audiência Pública da ADPF 442* (Letras Livres, 2019).
Ansell, A, 'Impeaching Dilma Rousseff: The Double Life of Corruption Allegations on Brazil's Political Right' (2018) 59 *Culture, Theory and Critique* 312.
Arantes, RB, 'Judiciário: Entre a Justiça e a Política' in Avelar, L and Cintra, AO (eds), *Sistema Político Brasileiro: Uma Introdução* (Konrad-Adenauer-Stiftung, 2007) 79–108.
Arantes, RB, 'The Federal Police and the Ministério Público' in Power, TJ and Taylor, MM (eds), *Corruption and Democracy in Brazil: The Struggle for Accountability* (University of Notre Dame Press, 2011) 184–217.
Arantes, RB and Couto, CG, 'Construção Democrática e Modelos de Constituição' (2010) 53 *Dados – Revista de Ciências Sociais* 545.
Arantes, RB and Moreira, TMQ, 'Democracia, Instituições de Controle e Justiça sob a Ótica do Pluralismo Estatal' (2019) 25 *Opinião Pública* 97.
Arantes, RB and Sadek, MT, *Ministério Público e Política no Brasil* (Sumaré, 2002).
Araújo, B and Prior, H, 'Framing Political Populism: The Role of Media in Framing the Election of Jair Bolsonaro' (2021) 15 *Journalism Practice* 226.
Araújo, C, 'O Processo Constituinte Brasileiro, a Transição e o Poder Constituinte' (2013) 88 *Lua Nova: Revista de Cultura e Política* 327.
Araújo, C and Alves, JED, 'Impactos de Indicadores Sociais e do Sistema Eleitoral sobre as Chances das Mulheres nas Eleições e suas Interações com as Cotas' (2007) 50 *Dados – Revista de Ciências Sociais* 535.
Arguelhes, DW, 'Poder Não É Querer: Preferências Restritivas e Redesenho Institucional no Supremo Tribunal Federal Pós-Democratização' (2014) 25 *Universitas Jus* 25.
Arguelhes, DW, 'La Moderación Judicial como Legado Constitucional Autoritario: El Supremo Tribunal Federal Brasilero y las Facultades Legislativas Presidenciales' (2020) 24 *Discusiones* 143.
Arguelhes, DW and Hartmann, IA, 'Timing Control without Docket Control' (2017) 5 *Journal of Law and Courts* 105.
Arguelhes, DW and Prado, MM, '"Resistance by Interpretation": Supreme Court Justices as Counter-Reformers to Constitutional Changes in Brazil in the 90s' in Albert, R, Bernal, C, and Benvindo, JZ (eds), *Constitutional Change and Transformation in Latin America* (Hart Publishing, 2019) 167–88.
Arguelhes, DW and Ribeiro, LM, 'Indicações Presidenciais para o Supremo Tribunal Federal e seus Fins Políticos: Uma Resposta a Mariana Prado e Cláudia Türner' (2010) 255 *Revista de Direito Administrativo* 115.
Arguelhes, DW and Ribeiro, LM, 'O Supremo Individual: Mecanismos de Atuação Direta dos Ministros sobre o Processo Político' (2015) 46 *Revista Direito, Estado e Sociedade* 121.
Arguelhes, DW and Ribeiro, LM, 'Courts as the First and the Only Legislative Chambers? The Brazilian Supreme Court and the Legalization of Same-Sex Marriage' (2017) 50 *Verfassung in Recht und Übersee* 281.
Arguelhes, DW and Ribeiro, LM, '"The Court, It is I"? Individual Judicial Powers in the Brazilian Supreme Court and their Implications for Constitutional Theory' (2018) 7 *Global Constitutionalism* 236.
Arias, O, Yamada, G, and Tejerina, L, 'Education, Family Background and Racial Earnings Inequality in Brazil' (2004) 25 *International Journal of Manpower* 355.
Arnold, C and Rittberger, AB, 'The Legalization of Dispute Resolution in Mercosur' (2013) 5 *Journal of Politics in Latin America* 97.
Arretche, M, 'Federalism, Bicameralism, and Institutional Change: General Trends and One Case-Study' (2010) 4 *Brazilian Political Science Review* 10.
Arretche, M, 'Conclusion: A Half-Century of Change' in Arretche, M (ed), *Paths of Inequality in Brazil: A Half-Century of Changes* (Springer, 2019) 331–54.
Arretche, M, 'The Geography of Access to Basic Services in Brazil' in Arretche, M (ed), *Paths of Inequality in Brazil: A Half-Century of Changes* (Springer, 2019) 137–62.

Avgerou, C, et al, 'Interpreting the Trustworthiness of Government Mediated by Information and Communication Technology: Lessons from Electronic Voting in Brazil' (2009) 15 *Information Technology for Development* 133.

Avritzer, L, 'Reforma Política e Participação no Brasil' in Avritzer, L and Anastasia, F. (eds) *Reforma Política no Brasil* (Belo Horizonte, Editora UFMG, 2006) 35–45.

Avritzer, L, 'Índices de Percepção de Corrupção' in Avritzer, L, et al (eds), *Corrupção: Ensaios e Críticas* (Editora UFMG, 2008) 423–27.

Avritzer, L, 'Um Balanço da Participação Social no Brasil Pós-Constituição de 1988' in Avritzer, L (ed), *Experiência Democrática, Sistema Político e Participação Popular* (Fundação Perseu Abramo, 2013) 11–20.

Avritzer, L, 'The Impeachment of Dilma Rousseff: Introduction' (2017) 11 *Critical Policy Studies* 349.

Avritzer, L and Marona, M, 'A Tensão entre Soberania e Instituições de Controle na Democracia Brasileira' (2017) 60 *Dados – Revista de Ciências Sociais* 359.

Azevedo Amaral, AJD, *O Estado Autoritário e a Realidade Nacional* (eBooksBrasil (CPDOC/FGV), 2002).

Azevedo, DDL, *Espectros da Ditadura: Da Comissão da Verdade ao Bolsonarismo* (Autonomia Literária, 2020).

Bähre, E and Diniz, D, 'Women's Rights and Misogyny in Brazil: An Interview with Debora Diniz' (2020) 36 *Anthropology Today* 17.

Bail, CA, et al, 'Exposure to Opposing Views on Social Media Can Increase Political Polarization' (2018) 115 *Proceedings of the National Academic of Sciences of the United States of America* 9216.

Bailey, SR, Loveman, M, and Muniz, JO, 'Measures of "Race" and the Analysis of Racial Inequality in Brazil' (2013) 42 *Social Science Research* 106.

Banks, A, et al, '#PolarizedFeeds: Three Experiements on Polarization, Framing, and Social Media' (2021) 26 *The International Journal of Press/Politics* 609.

Barros, LLD and Antonio, M, 'Brazilian Administrative Council for Economic Defense: An Approach from Sociology and History' (2017) 2 *University of Bologna Law Review* 116.

Barbosa, L, *História Constitucional Brasileira: Mudança Constitucional, Autoritarismo e Democracia no Brasil Pós-1964* (Biblioteca Digital da Câmara dos Deputados, 2012).

Barroso, LR, 'Countermajoritarian, Representative, and Enlightened: The Roles of Constitutional Tribunals in Contemporary Democracies' (2018) 9 *Revista Direito e Práxis* 2171.

Bastian, M, *Media and Accountability in Latin America* (Springer, 2019).

Ben Yahmed, S, 'Formal but Less Equal. Gender Wage Gaps in Formal and Informal Jobs in Urban Brazil' (2018) 101 *World Development* 73.

Bennett, DL and Nikolaev, B, 'Factor Endowments, the Rule of Law and Structural Inequality' (2016) 12 *Journal of Institutional Economics* 773.

Benvindo, JZ, *On the Limits of Constitutional Adjudication: Deconstructing Balancing and Judicial Activism* (Springer, 2010).

Benvindo, JZ, 'The Seeds of Change: Popular Protests as Constitutional Moments' (2015) 99 *Marquette Law Review* 364.

Benvindo, JZ, 'The Forgotten People in Brazilian Constitutionalism: Revisiting Behavior Strategic Analyses of Regime Transitions' (2017) 15 *International Journal of Constitutional Law* 332.

Benvindo, JZ, 'Brazil in the Context of the Debate over Unamendability in Latin America' in Albert, R and Oder, B (eds), *An Unamendable Constitution?* (Springer, 2018) 345–64.

Benvindo, JZ and Acunha, F, 'Tempos na Atuação da Jurisdição Constitucional: A Interpretação Inicial do STF a respeito do Mandado de Injunção e as Oportunidades que Não Voltam' in Martins, A, Roesler, CR and Paixão, C (eds), *Os Tempos do Direito: Diacronias, Crise e Historicidade* (Max Limonad, 2020) 93–108.

Benvindo, JZ, Bernal, C, and Albert, R, 'Introduction: Facts and Fictions in Latin America Constitutionalism' in Albert, R, Bernal, C and Benvindo, JZ (eds), *Constitutional Change and Transformation in Latin America* (Hart Publishing, 2019) 1–18.

Beramendi, P and Rueda, D, 'Inequality and Institutions: The Case of Economic Coordination' (2014) 17 *Annual Review of Political Science* 251.

Bercovici, G, '"O Direito Constitucional Passa, o Direito Administrativo Permanece": A Persistência da Estrutura Administrativa de 1967' in Teles, E and Safatle, V (eds), *O Que Resta da Ditadura: A Exceção Brasileira* (Boitempo, 2010) 77–90.

Bernardino-Costa, J and De Carli Blackman, AE, 'Affirmative Action in Brazil and Building an Anti-Racist University' (2017) 20 *Race Ethnicity and Education* 372.

Bianchi, B, et al, 'De-Democratization in Contemporary Brazil: From 2015 to 2020' in Bianchi, B, et al (eds), *Democracy and Brazil: Collapse and Regression* (Routledge, 2020) 1–15.

Biroli, F and Miguel, LF, *Feminismo e Política* (Boitempo Editorial, 2015).

Boas, TC, 'Media Barons and Electoral Politics: Politically-Controlled Broadcasting in Brazil' (2013) Working Paper, www.bu.edu/polisci/fi les/2010/10/media_boss_politics.pdf.

Bogdandy, AV, 'Pluralism, Direct Effect, and the Ultimate Say: On the Relationship between International and Domestic Constitutional Law (2008) 6 *International Journal of Constitutional Law* 397.

Bogdandy, AV, 'Ius Constitutionale Commune en América Latina: Observations on Transformative Constitutionalism' in Bogdandy, AV, et al (eds), *Transformative Constitutionalism in Latin America* (Oxford University Press, 2017) 27–48.

Bogdandy, AV, et al, 'Ius Constitutionale Commune en América Latina: A Regional Approach to Transformative Constitutionalism' in Bogdandy, AV, et al (eds), *Transformative Constitutionalism in Latin America* (Oxford University Press, 2017) 3–23.

Bogéa, D, *Partidos Políticos e STF: Decifrando a Simbiose Institucional* (Appris, 2021).

Boiteux, L, 'Drugs and Prisons: The Repression of Drugs and the Increase of the Brazilian Peintentiary Population' (2011) *Systems Overload – Drug Laws and Prisons in Latin America. Amsterdam/Washington: Transnational Institute/Washington Office Latin America* 30.

Boix, C, *Democracy and Redistribution* (Cambridge University Press, 2003).

Borges, A, 'Razões da Fragmentação: Coligações e Estratégias Partidárias na Presença de Eleições Majoritárias e Proporcionais Simultâneas' (2019) 62 *Dados – Revista de Ciências Sociais* 1.

Borges, AW, Romeu, LC and da Rocha, AP, 'Análise da Jurisprudência do STF Sobre a Forma de Incorporação dos Documentos de Direito Internacional' (2012) 3 *Revista de Direito Brasileira* 55.

Bresser Pereira, LC, 'Ideologias Econômicas e Democracia no Brasil' (1989) 3 *Estudos Avançados* 46.

Bretas, ML and Rosemberg, A, 'A História da Polícia no Brasil: Balanço e Perspectivas' (2013) 14 *Topoi* 162.

Brinks, DM, 'Inequality, Institutions, and the Rule of Law: The Social and Institutional Bases of Rights' (2008) 351 *Kellogg Institute Working Paper*.

Bry, SH, 'Brazil's Soft-Power Strategy: The Political Aspirations of South–South Development Cooperation' (2017) 13 *Foreign Policy Analysis* 297.

Bülow, MV, 'The Empowerment of Conservative Civil Society in Brazil' in Youngs, R (ed), *The Mobilization of Conservative Civil Society* (Carnegie Endowment for International Peace, 2018) 13–18.

Bustamante, T and Decat, TL, *Philosophy of Law as an Integral Part of Philosophy: Essays on the Jurisprudence of Gerald J. Postema* (Hart Publishing, 2020).

Câmara, HF, 'STF na Ditadura Militar Brasileira: Um Tribunal Adaptável?' (PhD Thesis, Federal University of Paraná 2017).

Cameron, MA, 'The Return of Oligarchy? Threats to Representative Democracy in Latin America' (2021) 42 *Third World Quarterly* 775.

Camou, MM and Maubrigades, S, 'The Lingering Face of Gender Inequality in Latin America' in Bértola, L and Williamson, J (eds), *Has Latin American Inequality Changed Direction?: Looking Over the Long Run* (Springer, 2017).

Campello, D, Belarmino, K and Thome, D, 'Reporting Corruption in Brazil: The Odebrecht Plea Bargain in Jornal Nacional' (2018) Working Paper, https://ssrn.com/abstract=3274967.

Campello, T and Neri, MC, *Bolsa Família Program: A Decade of Social Inclusion in Brazil* (IPEA, 2013).

Campos, F, *O Estado Nacional: Sua Estrutura, Seu Conteúdo Ideológico* (José Olímpio, 1940).

Canotilho, JJG, *Estado de Direito* (Gradiva Publicações, 1999).

Canotilho, JJG, *Direito Constitucional e Teoria da Constituição* (Almedina, 2003).

Cardoso, BB, Vieira, FMDSB and Saraceni, V, 'Aborto no Brasil: O Que Dizem os Dados Oficiais' (2020) 36 *Cadernos de Saúde Pública*.

Carson, LD and Prado, MM, 'Mapping Corruption & Its Institutional Determinants in Brazil' (2014) 8 *IRIBA Working Paper*, https://ssrn.com/abstract=2497935.

Carson, LD and Prado, MM, 'Using Institutional Multiplicity to Adress Corruption as a Colective Action Problem: Lessons from the Brazilian Case' (2016) 62 *The Quarterly Review of Economics and Finance* 56.

Carvalho, ADZD, 'Entre o Dever da Toga e o Apoio à Farda: Independêncica Judicial e Imparcialdiade no STF durante o Regime Militar' (2017) 32 *Revista Brasileira de Ciências Sociais* e329415.

Carvalho, JAD, Wood, CH and Andrade, FC, 'Estimating the Stability of Census-Based Racial/Ethnic Classifications: The Case of Brazil (2004) 58 *Population Studies* 331.

Castro, MFD, 'The Courts, Law, and Democracy in Brazil' (2009) 49 *International Social Science Journal* 241.

Cattoni de Oliveira, MA, 'Democracia Sem Espera e Processo de Constitucionalização: Uma Crítica aos Discursos Oficiais sobre a Chamada "Transição Política Brasileira"' (2010) 3 *Revista Anistia Política e Justiça de Transição* 200.

Cattoni de Oliveira, MA and Patrus, RD, 'Constituição e Poder Constituinte no Brasil Pós-1964: O Processo de Constitucionalização Brasileiro entre "Transição e Ruptura"' (2016) 45 *Quaderni Fiorentini* 171.

Cavalcante, P and Carvalho, P, 'The Professionalization of Brazilian Federal Bureaucracy (1995–2014): Avances and Dilemmas' (2017) 51 *Revista de Administração Pública* 1.

Cave, AA, 'Genocide in the Americas' in Stone, D (ed), *The Historiography of Genocide* (Palgrave Macmillan, 2008) 273–95.

Cerqueira Neto, JN, 'O Supremo Contra a Constituição' (PhD Thesis, University of Brasília 2020).

Chang, H-J, *Kicking Away the Ladder: Development Strategy in Historical Perspective* (Anthem Press, 2002).

Chatin, M, 'Brazil: Analysis of a Rising Soft Power' (2016) 9 *Journal of Political Power* 369.

Cheibub, JA, Elkins, Z and Ginsburg, T, 'Latin American Presidentialism in Comparative and Historical Perspective' (2011) 89 *Texas Law Review* 1707.

Chitolina, L, Foguel, MN, and Menezes-Filho, NA, 'The Impact of the Expansion of the Bolsa Família Program on the Time Allocation of Youths and their Parents' (2016) 70 *Revista Brasileira de Economia* 183.

Ciaschi, M, et al, 'A Reversal in Shared Prosperity in Brazil' (2020) 344111 *The World Bank*.

Codato, AN, 'Political Transition and Democratic Consolidation in Brazil: A Historical Perspective' in Codato, AN (ed), *Political Transition and Democratic Consolidation: Studies on Contemporary Brazil* (Nova Publishers, 2006) 1–26.

Coelho, VSP and Dias, M, 'Health and Inequalities' in Arretche, M (ed), *Paths of Inequality in Brazil: A Half-Century of Changes* (Springer, 2019) 183–205.

Cord, L, et al., 'Inequality Stagnation in Latin America in the Aftermath of the Global Financial Crisis' (2017) 21 *Review of Development Economics* 157.

Costa, AA and Benvindo, JZ, 'A Quem Interessa o Controle Concentrado de Constitucionalidade? O Descompasso entre Teoria e Prática na Defesa dos Direitos Fundamenetais' (2014) University of Brasília Working Paper, https://ssrn.com/abstract=2509541.

Costa, P, 'The Rule of Law: A Historical Introduction' in Costa, P and Zolo, D (eds), *The Rule of Law: History, Theory and Criticism* (Springer, 2007) 73–151.

Costa, P and Zolo, D (eds), *The Rule of Law: History, Theory and Criticism* (Springer, 2007).

Cott, DLV, 'Latin America's Indigenous Peoples' (2007) 18 *Journal of Democracy* 127.

Couso, J, 'Trying Democracy in the Shadow of an Authoritarian Legality: Chile's Transition to Democracy and Pinochet's Constitution of 1980' (2013) 29 *Wisconsin International Law Journal* 393.

Cunha, MCD, 'Índios na Constituição' (2018) 37 *Novos Estudos CEBRAP* 429.
Cypher, JM, 'Pinochet Meets Polanyi? The Curious Case of the Chilean Embrace of "Free" Market Economics' (2004) 38 *Journal of Economic Issues* 527.
Da Ros, L and Taylor, M, 'Opening the Black Box: Three Decades of Reforms to Brazil's Judicial System' (2017) School of International Service Research Paper 2017-3, https://ssrn.com/abstract=3028731.
Daflon, VT, *Tão Longe, Tão Perto: Identidades, Discriminação e Estereótipos de Pretos e Pardos no Brasil* (Mauad Editora Ltda, 2018).
Daly, TG, 'Brazilian "Supremocracy" and the Inter-American Court of Human Rights: Unpicking the Unclear Relationship' in Fortes, P, et al (eds), *Law and Policy in Latin America: Transforming Courts, Institutions, and Rights* (Springer, 2016).
Daly, TG, 'Public Law and the Puzzle of Democratic Decay in Brazil' (2017) Working Paperr presented at the Law and Society Association Annual Meeting 2017.
Daly, TG, 'Populism, Public Law, and Democratic Decay in Brazil: Understanding the Rise of Jair Bolsonaro' (2019) Working Paper presented at the 14th International Human Rights Researchers' Workshop: 'Democratic Backsliding and Human Rights', https://ssrn.com/abstract=3350098.
Daly, TG, 'Understanding Multi-directional Democratic Decay: Lessons from the Rise of Bolsonaro in Brazil' (2020) 14 *Law & Ethics of Human Rights* 199.
Daly, TG and Jones, BC, 'Parties versus Democracy: Addressing Today's Political Party Threats to Democratic Rule' (2020) 18 *International Journal of Constitutional Law* 509.
Dauvergne, P and BL Farias, D, 'The Rise of Brazil as a Global Development Power' (2012) 33 *Third World Quarterly* 903.
Derrida, J, *Rogues: Two Essays on Reason* (Stanford University Press, 2005).
Diamond, L, Linz, JJ and Lipset, SM, *Democracy in Developing Countries: Latin America* (Adamantine Press, 1999).
Dias, CN and Salla, F, 'Organized Crime in Brazilian Prisons: The Example of PCC' (2013) 2 *International Journal of Criminology and Sociology* 397.
Dias Lopes, A, 'Affirmative Action in Brazil: How Students' Field of Study Choice Reproduces Social Inequalities' (2017) 42 *Studies in Higher Education* 2343.
Dijk, TAV, 'How Globo Media Manipulated the Impeachment of Brazilian Dilma Rousseff' (2017) 11 *Discourse & Communication* 199.
Diniz, D, et al, 'National Abortion Survey 2016' (2017) 22 *Ciência & Saúde Coletiva* 653.
Dixon, R, 'Rule of Law Teleology: Against the Misuse and Abuse of Rule Rhethoric' (2019) 11 *Hague Journal on the Rule of Law* 464.
Dixon, R and Landau, D, *Abusive Constitutional Borrowing: Legal Globalization and the Subversion of Liberal Democracy* (Oxford University Press, 2021).
Drybread, K, 'When Corruption Is Not a Crime: 'Innocent' White Politicians and the Rationalization of Criminality in Brazil' (2018) 59 *Culture, Theory and Critique* 332.
Dworkin, R, *Sovereign Virtue: The Theory and Practice of Equality* (Harvard University Press, 2002).
Eisenstadt, TA, LeVan, AC, and Maboudi, T, *Constituents Before Assembly: Participation, Deliberation, and Representation in the Crafting of New Constitutions* (Cambridge University Press, 2017).
Eleoterio, BE and Mesquita, AL, 'The Twenty-First Century Regionalism: Brazil and Mercosur in the New International Scenario' in Adinolfi, G, et al (eds), *International Economic Law: Contemporary Issues* (Springer, 2017) 99–110.
Elkins, Z, 'Is the Sky Falling? Constitutional Crises in Historical Perspective' in Graber, MA, Levinson, S and Tushnet, M (eds), *Constitutional Democracy in Crisis* (Oxford University Press, 2018) 49–66.
Elkins, Z, Ginsburg, T and Melton, J, *The Endurance of National Constitutions* (Cambridge University Press, 2009).
Encarnación, OG, 'A Latin American Puzzle: Gay Rights Landscapes in Argentina and Brazil' (2018) 40 *Human Rights Quarterly* 194.

Esteves, JT and Cosentino, C, 'The Conviction of Former President Lula as the Maximum Expression of the Exercise of Lawfare' in Proner, C, et al (eds), *Comments on a Notorious Verdict: The Trial of Lula* (CLACSO, 2018) 117–21.

Fajnzylber, P, Lederman, D and Loayza, N, 'Inequality and Violent Crime' (2002) 45 *The Journal of Law and Economics* 1.

Faoro, R, *Democratização e as Forças Armadas* (Ordem dos Advogados do Brasil, 1984).

Faoro, R, *Os Donos do Poder: A Formação do Patronato Político Brasileiro* (Globo Livros, 2001).

Faria, JE, 'O Sistema Brasileiro de Justiça: Experiência Recente e Futuros Desafios' (2004) 18 *Estudos Avançados* 103.

Fausto, B, *O Pensamento Nacionalista Autoritário (1920–1940)* (Zahar, 2001).

Feinrider, M, 'Judicial Review and the Protection of Human Rights under Military Governments in Brazil and Argentina' (1980) 5 *Suffolk Transnational Law Journal* 171.

Fenwhick, TB, 'Avoiding Governors: The Success of Bolsa Família' (2009) 44 *Latin American Research Review* 102.

Ferrajoli, L, 'The Past and the Future of the Rule of Law' in Costa, P and Zolo, D (eds), *The Rule of Law: History, Theory and Criticism* (Springer, 2007) 323–52.

Ferraz, C and Finan, F, 'Fighting Political Corruption: Evidence from Brazil' in Basu, K, Cordella, T (eds), *Institutions, Governance and the Control of Corruption* (Springer, 2018) 253–84.

Ferreira de Souza, PHG and Medeiros, M, 'Diferencial Salarial Público-Privado e Desigualdade de Renda per Capita no Brasil' (2013) 43 *Estudos Econômicos* 5.

Ferreira de Souza, PHG, 'A History of Inequality: Top Incomes in Brazil, 1926–2015' (2017) 167 Working Paper – International Policy Centre for Inclusive Growth (IPC-IG), https://www.econstor.eu/handle/10419/200608.

Ferreira de Souza, PHG, 'A Desigualdade Vista do Topo: A Concentração de Renda entre os Ricos no Brasil, 1926–2013' (PhD Thesis, University of Brasília 2016).

Ferreira de Souza, PHG, *Uma História da Desigualdade: A Concentração de Renda entre os Ricos no Brasil (1926–2013)* (Hucitec, 2018).

Ferreira Filho, MG, 'Nova Perspectiva do Processo Constitucional' (1985) 60/61 *Revista Brasileira de Estudos Políticos* 129.

Ferreira Filho, MG, 'Significação e Alcance das "Cláusulas Pétreas"' (1995) 202 *Revista de Direito Administrativo* 11.

Ferreira Santos, G, 'Treaties x Human Rights Treaties: A Critical Analysis of the Dual Stance on Treaties in the Brazilian Legal System' (2013) 15 *European Journal of Law Reform* 20.

Figueiredo, AC and Limongi, F, 'Constitutional Change, Legislative Performance and Institutional Consolidation' (2000) Special Issue No. 1 *Brazilian Review of Social Sciences* 1.

Figueiredo, AC and Limongi, F, 'Presidential Power, Legislative Organization, and Party Behavior in Brazil' (2000) 32 *Comparative Politics* 151.

Figueiredo, AC and Limongi, F, *Executivo e Legislativo na Nova Ordem Constitucional* (Editora FGV, 2001).

Figueiredo, AC and Limongi, F, 'Instituições Políticas e Governabilidade: Desempenho do Governo e Apoio Legislativo na Democracia Brasileira' in Ranulfo, C (ed), *A Democracia Brasileira: Balanços e Perspectivas para o Século 21* (Editora UFMG, 2007).

Figueiredo, AC and Limongi, F, 'Political Institutions and Governamental Performance in Brazilian Democracy' in Fontaine, DDL and Stehnken, T (eds), *The Political System of Brazil* (Springer, 2016).

Fleming, JE, *Getting to the Rule of Law* (NYU Press, 2011).

Fogel, B, 'Bolsonaro: Politics as Permanent Crisis' in Rayner, J, et al (ed), *Back to the'30s?: Recurring Crises of Capitalism, Liberalism and Democracy* (Springer, 2020).

Freitas, A and Silva, GPD, 'Das Manifestações de 2013 à Eleição de 2018 no Brasil' (2019) 38 *Novos Estudos CEBRAP* 137.

Freire, SDM, 'Pensamento Autoritário e Modernidade no Brasil' (2009) 6 *Revista da Faculdade de Serviço Social da Universidade do Estado do Rio de Janeiro* 203.

Freyre, G, *The Masters and the Slaves: A Study in the Development of Brazilian Civilization* (University of California Press, 1986).
Fuller, LL, *The Morality of Law* (Yale University Press, 1969).
Gardini, GL, 'MERCOSUR: What You See Is Not (Always) What You Get' (2011) 17 *European Law Journal* 683.
Gargarella, R, *Latin American Constitutionalism,1810–2010: The Engine Room of the Constitution* (Oxford University Press, 2013).
Gargarella, R, 'Latin America's Contribution to Constitutionalism' in Sieder, R, Ansolabeher, K and Alfonso, T (eds), *Routledge Handbook of Law and Society in Latin America* (Routledge, 2019) 25–50.
Gaspar, M, *A Organização: A Odebrecht e o Esquema de Corrupção que Chocou o Mundo* (Companhia das Letras, 2020).
Gaspari, E, *A Ditadura Envergonhada* (Companhia das Letras, 2002).
Gay, R, 'The Even More Difficult Transition from Clientelism to Citizenship: Lessons from Brazil' in Fernández-Kelly, P and Shefner, J (eds), *Out of the Shadows: Political Action and the Informal Economy in Latin America* (The Pennsylvania State University Press, 2006) 195–21.
Ginsburg, T, '¿ Fruto de la Parra Envenenada? Algunas Observaciones Comparadas sobre la Constitución Chilena' (2014) 133 *Estudios Públicos* 1.
Ginsburg, T, Huq, A and Landau, D, 'The Comparative Constitutional Law of Presidential Impeachment' (2021) 88 *The University of Chicago Law Review* 81.
Ginsburg, T and Versteeg, M, 'Constitutional Correlates of the Rule of Law' in Adams, M, Meuwese, A and Ballin, EH (ed), *Constitutionalism and the Rule of Law* (Cambridge University Press, 2017) 506–25.
Godoy, MG, 'As Audiências Públicas e os Amici Curiae Influenciam as Decisões dos Ministros do Supremo Tribunal Federal' (2015) 60 *Revista da Faculdade de Direito UFPR* 137.
Goes, EF, et al, 'Racial Vulnerability and Individual Barriers for Brazilian Women Seeking First Care Following Abortion' (2020) 36 Suppl 1 *Cadernos de Saúde Pública* e00189618.
Gomes, FDBC, 'Cooperação, Liderança e Impasse entre o Legislativo e o Executivo na Produção Legislativa do Congresso Nacional do Brasil' (2012) 55 *Dados – Revista de Ciências Sociais* 911.
Gomes, KO, 'Em Defesa da Sociedade? Atuação da Procuradoria Geral da República em Controle Concentrado de Constitucionalidade (1988–2012)' (MsC Dissertation, University of Brasília, 2015).
Gomes, S, 'O Impacto das Regras de Organização do Processo Legislativo no Comportamento dos Parlamentares: Um Estudo de Caso da Assembléia Nacional Constituinte (1987–1988)' (2006) 49 *Dados-Revista de Ciências Sociais* 193.
Gonçalves, LAO, Silva, NND and Brooke, N, 'Brazil' in Stevens, PAJ and Dworkin, AG (eds), *The Palgrave Handbook of Race and Ethnic Inequalities in Education* (Palgrave Macmillan, 2019).
Gozzi, G, 'Rechtsstaat and Individual Rights in German Constitutional History' in Costa, P and Zolo, D (eds), *The Rule of Law: History, Theory and Criticism* (Springer, 2007) 237–59.
Graber, MA, Levinson, S and Tushnet, M, *Constitutional Democracy in Crisis?* (Oxford University Press, 2018).
Graber, MA, Levinson, S and Tushnet, M, 'Constitutional Democracy in Crisis? Introduction' in Graber, MA, Levinson, S and Tushnet, M (eds), *Constitutional Democracy in Crisis?* (Oxford University Press, 2018) 1–12.
Grimm, D, 'The Role of Fundamental Rights after Sixty-Five Years of Constitutional Jurisprudence in Germany' (2015) 13 *International Journal of Constitutional Law* 9.
Grugel, J, 'Transitions from Authoritarian Rule: Lessons from Latin America' (1991) 39 *Political Studies* 363.
Guerchon, CW, 'Institutional Acts of the Brazilian Government' (1971) 1 *International Journal of Politics* 258.
Guimarães, ASA, *Preconceito e Discriminação: Queixas e Ofensas e Tratamento Desigual dos Negros no Brasil* (Editora 34, 2004).

Günther, K, *The Sense of Appropriateness: Application Discourses in Morality and Law* (SUNY Press, 1993).
Habermas, J, 'Reply to Symposium Participants, Benjamin N. Cardozo School of Law' in Habermas, J, *Habermas on Law and Democracy* (University of California Press, 1998).
Habermas, J, *Between Facts and Norms* (MIT Press, 1996).
Habermas, J, 'Constitutional Democracy: A Paradoxical Union of Contradictory Principles?' (2007) 29 *Political Theory* 766.
Haggard, S and Kaufman, RR, *Dictators and Democrats: Masses, Elites, and Regime Change* (Princeton University Press, 2016).
Haggard, S, MacIntyre, A and Tiede, L, 'The Rule of Law and Economic Development' (2008) 11 *Annual Review of Political Science* 205.
Hagopian, F, 'The Politics of Oligarchy: The Persistence of Traditional Elites in Contemporary Brazil' (PhD Thesis, Massachusetts Institute of Technology, 1986).
Hagopian, F, '"Democracy by Undemocratic Means"?: Elites, Political Pacts, and Regime Transition in Brazil' (1990) 23 *Comparative Political Studies* 147.
Hagopian, F, 'Brazil's Accountability Paradox' (2016) 27 *Journal of Democracy* 119.
Hannan, J, 'Trolling Ourselves to Death? Social Media and Post-Truth Politics' (2018) 33 *European Journal of Communication* 214.
Helmke, G and Ríos-Figueroa, J, 'Introduction: Courts in Latin America' in Helmke, G and Ríos-Figueroa, J (eds), *Courts in Latin America* (Cambridge University Press, 2011) 1–26.
Higley, J and Gunther, R, *Elites and Democratic Consolidation in Latin America and Southern Europe* (Cambridge University Press, 1992).
Hirata, G and Soares, RR, 'Competition and the Racial Wage Gap: Evidence from Brazil' (2020) 146 *Journal of Development Economics* 102519, 102519.
Hiroi, T, 'Paradox of Redistribution: Legislative Overrepresentation and Regional Development in Brazil' (2018) 49 *The Journal of Federalism* 642.
Hirschl, R, *Towards Juristocracy: The Origins and Consequences of the New Constitutionalism* (Harvard University Press, 2004).
Hirschl, R, *Comparative Matters: The Renaissance of Comparative Constitutional Law* (Oxford University Press, 2014).
Hobsbawm, E, *The Age of Extremes: A History of the World* (Pantheon, 1994).
Hobsbawm, E, 'The Present as History: Writing the History of One's Time' in Bates, D, Wallis, J and Winters, J (eds), *The Creighton Century, 1907–2007* (University of London Press, 2002) 273–85.
Hoffmann, AR, 'At Last: Protection and Promotion of Human Rights by Mercosur' in Börzel, TA and Van Hüllen, V (eds), *Governance Transfer by Regional Organizations: Patching Together a Global Script* (Palgrave Macmillan, 2015) 192–208.
Holmes, S, 'Lineages of the Rule of Law' in Przeworski, A and Maravall, JM (eds), *Democracy and the Rule of Law* (Cambridge University Press, 2003) 19–61.
Houle, C, 'Inequality and Democracy: Why Inequality Harms Consolidation but Does Not Affect Democratization' (2009) 61 *World Politics* 589.
Hunter, W, 'Negotiating Civil-Military Relations in Post-Authoritarian Argentina and Chile' (1998) 42 *International Studies Quarterly* 295.
Hunter, W and Power, TJ, 'Bolsonaro and Brazil's Illiberal Backlash' (2019) 30 *Journal of Democracy* 68.
Huntington, SP, 'Will More Countries Become Democratic?' (2016) 131 *Political Science Quarterly* 237.
Huq, A and Ginsburg, T, 'How to Lose a Constitutional Democracy' (2018) 65 *UCLA Law Review* 1.
Janusz, A, 'Candidate Race and Electoral Outcomes: Evidence from Brazil' (2018) 6 *Politics, Groups, and Identities* 702.

Kapiszewski, D, 'Power Broker, Policy Maker, or Rights Protector? The Brazilian Supremo Tribunal Federal in Transition' in Helmke, G and Rios-Figueroa, J (eds), *Courts in Latin America* (Cambridge University Press, 2011) 154–86.
Karl, TL, 'Dilemmas of Democratization in Latin America' (1990) 23 *Comparative Politics* 1.
Katz, AS, 'Making Brazil Work? Brazilian Coalitional Presidentialism at 30 and Its Post-Lava Jato Prospects' (2018) 5 *Revista de Investigações Constitucionais* 77.
Kay, K, Mitchell-Walthour, G and White, IK, 'Framing Race and Class in Brazil: Afro-Brazilian Support for Racial versus Class Policy' (2015) 3 *Politics, Groups, and Identities* 222.
Kaufmann, D, Kraay, A and Mastruzzi, M, 'The Worldwide Governance Indicators Methodology and Analytical Issues (2011) 3 *Hague Journal on the Rule of Law* 220.
Kinzo, MDG, 'A Democratização Brasileira: Um Balanço do Processo Político desde a Transição' (2001) 15 *São Paulo em Perspectiva* 3.
Koerner, A, 'Ativismo Judicial? Jurisprudência Constitucional e Política no STF Pós-88' (2013) 96 *Novos Estudos CEBRAP* 69.
Koerner, A and Freitas, LBD, 'O Supremo na Constituinte e a Constituinte no Supremo' (2013) 88 *Lua Nova* 141.
Kopkin, N and Mitchell-Walthour, G, 'Color Discrimination, Occupational Prestige, and Skin Color in Brazil' (2020) 15 *Latin American and Caribbean Ethnic Studies* 44.
Krieger, H and Nolte, G, 'The International Rule of Law-Rise or Decline? Points of Departure' (2016) KFG Working Papers, n. 1, https://ssrn.com/abstract=2866940.
Krygier, M, 'Four Puzzles about the Rule of Law: Why, What, Where? and Who Cares?' in Fleming, JE (ed), *Getting to the Rule of Law* (NYU Press, 2011) 64–104.
Krygier, M, 'The Rule of Law: Legality, Teleology, Sociology' in Palombella, G and Walker, N (eds), *Relocating the Rule of Law* (Hart Publishing, 2008).
Krygier, M, 'The Rule of Law: Pasts, Presents, and Two Possible Futures' (2016) 12 *Annual Review of Law and Social Science* 199.
Kucinski, B, *O Fim da Ditadura Militar* (Contexto, 2001).
Lagunes, PF and Svejnar, J, *Corruption and the Lava Jato Scandal in Latin America* (Routledge, 2020).
Landau, D, 'Abusive Constitutionalism' (2013) 47 *University of California, Davis* 189.
Landau, D, 'Populist Constitutions' (2018) 85 *The University of Chicago Law Review* 521.
Laquièze, A, 'État de Droit and National Sovereignty in France' in Costa, P and Zolo, D (eds), *The Rule of Law: History, Theory and Criticism* (Springer, 2007) 261–92.
Lavalle, AG, Acharya, A and Houtzager, PP, 'Beyond Comparative Anectotalism: Lesson on Civil Society and Participation from São Paulo, Brazil' (2005) 33 *World Development* 951.
Lavalle, AG and Barone, LS, 'Councils, Associations, and Inequality' in Arretche, M (ed), *Paths of Inequality in Brazil: A Half-Century of Changes* (Springer, 2019) 25–46.
Layton, ML and Smith, AE, 'Is It Race, Class, or Gender? The Sources of Perceived Discrimination in Brazil' (2017) 59 *Latin American Politics and Society* 52.
Lee, JK, et al, 'Social Media, Network Heterogeneity, and Opinion Polarization' (2014) 64 *Journal of Communication* 702.
Leirner, PC, 'Hybrid Warfare in Brazil' (2020) 10 *HAU: Journal of Ethnographic Theory* 41.
Levitsky, S and Ziblatt, D, *How Democracies Die* (Crown, 2018).
Levitt, BS, 'Discrimination and Distrust of Democratic Institutions in Latin America' (2015) 3 *Politics, Groups, and Identities* 417.
Levy, R, 'Social Media, News Consumption, and Polarization: Evidence from a Field Experiment' (2021) 111 *American Economic Review* 831.
Lewin, L, *Politics and Parentela in Paraíba: A Case Study of Family-Based Oligarchy in Brazil* (Princeton University Press, 2014).
Lewis, N, *A View of the World* (Eland Publishing, 2011).
Lima, RSD, 'Violence and Public Safty as a Democratic Simulacrum in Brazil' (2018) 7 *International Journal of Criminology and Sociology* 159.

Limongi, F, 'A Democracia no Brasil: Presidencialismo, Coalizão Partidária e Processo Decisório' (2006) 76 *Novos Estudos CEBRAP* 17.

Limongi, F and Figueiredo, AC, 'Partidos Políticos na Câmara dos Deputados: 1989–1994' (1995) 38 *Dados – Revista de Ciências Sociais* 497.

Limongi, F and Figueiredo, AC, 'A Crise Atual e o Debate Institucional' (2017) 36 *Novos Estudos CEBRAP* 79.

Limongi, F, Cheibub, JA and Figueiredo, A, 'Political Participation in Brazil' in Arretche, M (ed), *Paths of Inequality in Brazil: A Half-Century of Changes* (Springer, 2019) 3–24.

Linz, JJ, 'The Perils of Presidentialism' (1990) 1 *Journal of Democracy* 51.

Linz, JJ and Valenzuela, A, *The Failure of Presidential Democracy* (John Hopkins University Press, 1994).

Lopes, FDM, 'Television and Judicial Behavior: Lessons from the Brazilian Supreme Court' (2018) 9 *Economic Analysis of Law Review* 47.

Loveman, B, '"Protected Democracies" and Military Guardianship: Political Transitions in Latin America, 1978-1993' (1994) 36 *Journal of Interamerican Studies and World Affairs* 105.

Luhmann, N, *Law as a Social System* (Oxford University Press, 2004).

Luo, Z and Przeworski, A, 'Democracy and Its Vulnerabilities: Dynamics of Democratic Backsliding' (2019) Working Paper, https://ssrn.com/abstract=3469373.

Lustig, D and Weiler, JHH, 'Judicial Review in the Contemporary World – Retrospective and Prospective' (2018) 16 *International Journal of Constitutional Law* 315.

Macaulay, F, 'Dilma Rousseff (2011–2016): A Crisis of Governance and Consensus in Brazil' in Montecinos, V (ed), *Women Presidents and Prime Ministers in Post-Transition Democracies* (Palgrave Macmillan, 2017) 123–40.

MacCormick, N, 'Der Rechtsstaat und die Rule of Law' (1984) 39 *JuristenZeitung* 65.

MacCormick, N, *Rhetoric and the Rule of Law: A Theory of Legal Reasoning* (Oxford University Press, 2005).

Magalhães, BB, 'O Sincretismo Teórico na Apropriação das Teorias Monista e Dualista e sua Questionável Utilidade como Critério para a Classificação do Modelo Brasileiro de Incorporação de Normas Internacionais' (2015) 12 *Revista de Direito Internacional* 77.

Magaloni, B, 'Authoritarianism, Democracy and the Supreme Court: Horizontal Exchange and the Rule of Law in Mexico' in Mainwaring, S and Welna, C (eds), *Democratic Accountability in Latin America* (Oxford University Press, 2003) 266–305.

Mainwaring, S, 'Dilemmas of Multiparty Presidential Democracy: The Case of Brazil' (1992) 174 Kellog Institute Working Paper, http://davidefendi.staff.umy.ac.id/files/2013/04/dilemmas-of-multyparty-presidential-Scott.pdf.

Mainwaring, S, 'Introduction' in Mainwaring, S (ed), *Party Systems in Latin America: Institutionalization, Decay, and Collapse* (Cambridge University Press, 2018) 1–13.

Mainwaring, S, *Rethinking Party Systems in the Third Wave of Democratization: The Case of Brazil* (Stanford University Press, 1999).

Mainwaring, S, Bizzarro, F and Power, TJ, 'The Uneven Institutionalization of a Party System: Brazil' in Mainwaring, S (ed), *Party Systems in Latin America: Institutionalization, Decay, and Collapse* (Cambridge University Press, 2018) 164–200.

Mainwaring, S and Pérez-Liñán, A, 'Cross-Currents in Latin America' (2015) 26 *Journal of Democracy* 114.

Mainwaring, S and Shugart, MS, *Presidentialism and Democracy in Latin America* (Cambridge University Press, 1997).

Malamud, A and Gardini, GL, 'Has Regionalism Peaked? The Latin American Quagmire and its Lessons' (2012) 47 *The International Spectator* 116.

Mallinder, L, 'The End of Amnesty or Regional Overreach? Interpreting the Erosion of South America's Amnesty Laws' (2016) 65 *International and Comparative Law Quarterly* 645.

Malloy, JM and Seligson, MA, *Authoritarians and Democrats: Regime Transition in Latin America* (University of Pittsburgh Press, 1987).

Manso, BP, *A República das Milícias* (Todavia, 2021).
Marques, AA, 'A Conexão Porto Príncipe-Brasília: A Participação em Missões de Paz e o Envolvimento na Política Doméstica' in Filho, JRM (ed), *Os Militares e a Crise Brasileira* (Alameda, 2021).
Marques, ECL, 'Housing and Urban Conditions in Brazil' in Arretche, M (ed), *Paths of Inequality in Brazil: A Half-Century of Changes* (Springer, 2019) 163–82.
Marteleto, LJ and Dondero, M, 'Racial Inequality in Education in Brazil: A Twins Fixed-Effects Approach.' (2016) 53 *Demography* 1185.
Martins, JDS, 'Clientelism and Corruption in Contemporary Brazil' in Little, W and Posada-Carbó, E (eds), *Political Corruption in Europe and Latin America* (Palgrave Macmillan, 1996) 195–218.
Martins Filho, JR (ed), *Os Militares e a Crise Brasileira* (Alameda, 2021).
Maués, AM, 'Supra-Legality of International Human Rights Treaties and Constitutional Interpretation' (2013) 18 *Sur – International Journal on Human Rights* 205.
McCallum, C, 'Racionalized Bodies, Naturalized Classes: Moving Through the City of Salvador da Bahia' (2005) 32 *American Ethnologist* 100.
McCoy, J and Somer, M, 'Toward a Theory of Pernicious Polarization and How It Harms Democracies: Comparative Evidence and Possible Remedies' (2019) 681 *The Annals of the American Academy of Political and Social Science* 234.
Medeiros, FA and Bygrave, LA, 'Brazil's Marco Civil da Internet: Does it Live Up to the Hype' (2015) 31 *Computer Law & Security Review* 120.
Medeiros, M, *O Que Faz os Ricos Ricos: O Outro Lado da Desigualdade Brasileira* (Hucitec, 2005).
Medeiros, M and Souza, PHGF, 'Estado e Desigualdade de Renda no Brasil: Fluxos de Rendimentos e Estratificação Social' (2013) 28 *Revista Brasileira de Ciências Sociais* 141.
Medeiros, M, Souza, PHGF and Castro, FÁD, 'O Topo da Distribuição de Renda no Brasil: Primeiras Estimativas com Dados Tributários e Comparação com Pesquisas Domiciliares, 2006–2012' (2015) 58 *Dados – Revista de Ciências Sociais* 7.
Medeiros, M and Souza, PHGF, 'A Estabilidade da Desigualdade no Brasil entre 2006 e 2012: Resultados Adicionais' (2016) 46 *Pesquisa e Planejamento Econômico* 7.
Meirelles, HL, 'Natureza, Conteúdo e Implicações do Ato Institucional N.º 5: Notas e Comentários' (1969) 20 *Revista de Direito da Procuradoria Geral* 1.
Meissner, KL, 'Mercosur: The Ups and Downs of Regional Integration in South America' in Krapohl, S (ed), *Regional Integration in the Global South* (Springer, 2017) 147–78.
Melgar, TR, 'A Time of Closure? Participatory Budgeting in Porto Alegre, Brazil, After the Workers' Party Era' (2014) 46 *Journal of Latin American Studies* 121.
Melo, MA, 'Latin America's New Turbulence: Crisis and Integrity in Brazil' (2016) 27 *Journal of Democracy* 50.
Melo, MA and Pereira, C, *Making Brazil Work: Checking the President in a Multiparty System* (Palgrave Macmillan, 2013).
Mendes, CH, *Constitutional Courts and Deliberative Democracy*, (Oxford University Press 2013).
Mendes, G, 'New Challenges of Constitutional Adjudication in Brazil' (2008) Brazil Institute Special Report.
Menezes Filho, N and Kirschbaum, C, 'Education and Inequality in Brazil' in Arretche, M (ed), *Paths of Inequality in Brazil: A Half-Century of Changes* (Springer, 2019) 69–88.
Meyer, EPN, *Constitutional Erosion in Brazil: Progresses and Failures of a Constitutional Project* (Hart Publishing, 2021).
Meyer, EPN, 'Criminal Responsibility in Brazilian Transitional Justice: A Constitutional Interpretative Process under the Paradigm of International Human Rights Law' (2017) 4 *The Indonesian Journal of International & Comparative Law* 41.
Meyerhenrich, J and Loughlin, M (ed), *The Cambridge Companion to the Rule of Law* (Cambridge University Press, 2021).
Michener, G and Pereira, C, 'A Great Leap Forward for Democracy and the Rule of Law? Brazil's Mensalão Trial' (2016) 48 *Journal of Latin American Studies* 477.
Michiles, C, *Cidadão Constituinte: A Saga das Emendas Populares* (Paz e Terra, 1989).

Miguel, LF, 'Political Representation and Gender in Brazil Quotas for Women and their Impact' (2008) 27 *Bulletin of Latin American Research* 197.

Miguel, LF and Biroli, F, 'Mídia e Representação Política Feminina: Hipóteses de Pesquisa' (2009) 15 *Opinião Pública* 55.

Milanez, F, et al, 'Existência e Diferença: O Racismo Contra os Povos Indígenas' (2019) 10 *Revista Direito e Práxis* 2161.

Mitchell, MJ and Wood, CH, 'Ironies of Citizenship: Skin Color, Police Brutality, and the Challenge to Democracy in Brazil' (1999) 77 *Social Forces* 1001.

Møller, J and Skaaning, S, *The Rule of Law: Definitions, Measures, Patterns and Causes* (Springer, 2014).

Moncau, LFM and Arguelhes, DW, 'The Marco Civil da Internet and Digital Constitutionalism' in Froslo, G (ed), *Oxford Handbook of Online Intermediary Liability* (Oxford University Press, 2020) 190–213.

Monk, EP, 'The Consequences of "Race and Color" in Brazil' (2016) 63 *Social Problems* 413.

Moreira, AJ, 'We Are a Family! Legal Recognition of Same-Sex Unions in Brazil' (2012) 60 *American Journal of Comparative Law* 1003.

Morgenstern, S, 'Towards a Model of Latin American Legislatures' in Morgenstern, S and Nacif, B (eds), *Legislative Politics in Latin America* (Cambridge University Press, 2002) 1–22.

Motta, RPS, 'João Goulart e a Mobilização Anticomunista de 1961–64' in Ferreira, MDM (ed), *João Goulart: Entre a Memória e a História* (FGV Editora, 2006) 129–48.

Mounk, Y, *The People vs. Democracy: Why Our Freedom is in Danger and How to Save It* (Harvard University Press, 2018).

Moura, LSMD (ed), 'Poder Judiciário e os Direitos Humanos' (2014) 101 *Revista USP* 99.

Mucinhato, RMD, 'Quem São os Deputados Brasileiros? Um Balanço do Perfil Biográfico de 1986 a 2012' in Moisés, JÁ (ed), *O Congresso Nacional, os Partidos Políticos e o Sistema de Integridade: Representação, Participação e Controle Institucional no Brasil Contemporâneo* (Konrad Adenauer Stiftung, 2014) 61–89.

Müller, J-W, *What Is Populism?* (University of Pennsylvania Press, 2016).

Nascimento, AAD, 'A Corrupção Policial em Debate: Desvio e Impunidade nas Instituições Policiais do Rio de Janeiro' (2017) 10 *Dilemas – Revista de Estudos de Conflito e Controle Social* 64.

Neri, MC, *Qual Foi o Impacto da Crise sobre a Pobreza e a Distribuição de Renda* (FGV Social, 2018).

Nery, FS and Nadanovsky, P, 'Homicide Impunity in Brazil Between 2006 and 2016' (2020) 54 *Revista de Saúde Pública* 144.

Neves, IBS, 'Fragmentação Partidária e a Cláusula de Desempenho da Emenda Constitucional n. 97/2017: Uma Análise dos Aspectos Ideológicos dos Estatutos Partidários' (2021) 23 *Confluências* 153.

Neves, M, 'Luhmann, Habermas e o Estado de Direito' (1996) 37 *Lua Nova* 93.

Neves, M, *Constitutionalism and the Paradox of Principles and Rules: Between the Hydra and Hercules* (Oxford University Press, 2021).

Ng-Mak, DS, et al, 'Normalization of Violence Among Inner-City Youth: A Formulation for Research' (2002) 72 *American Journal of Orthopsychiatry* 92.

Nichter, S, 'Political Clientelism and Social Policy in Brazil' in Brun, DA and Diamond, L (eds), *Clientelism, Social Policy, and the Quality of Democracy* (JHU Press, 2014) 131–151.

Nicolau, J and Stadler, J, 'The Brazilian Electoral System' in Fontaine, DDL and Stehnken, T (eds), *The Political System of Brazil* (Springer, 2016) 103–20.

Nino, CS, 'The Debate over Constitutional Reform in Latin America' (1992) 16 *Fordham International Law Journal* 635.

Nino, CS, 'Transition to Democracy, Corporatism, and Presidentialism with Reference to Latin America' in Greenberg, D, et al (ed), *Constitutionalism and Democracy: Transitions in the Contemporary World* (Oxford University Press, 1993) 46–64.

Nolte, D and Comini, NM, 'UNASUR: Regional Pluralism as a Strategic Outcome' (2016) 38 *Contexto Internacional* 545.

O'Donnell, G, Schmitter, PC and Whitehead, L, *Transitions from Authoritarian Rule* (Johns Hopkins University Press. 1986).
Oliveira, RCD, *Na Teia do Nepotismo: Sociologia Política das Relações de Parentesco e Poder Político no Paraná e no Brasil* (Insight, 2012).
Oliveira, VED, Lotta, GS and Vasconcelos, NPD, 'Ministério Público, Autonomia Funcional e Discricionariedade: Ampla Atuação em Políticas Públicas, Baixa Accountability' (2020) 7 *Revista de Estudos Empíricos em Direito* 181.
Oliveira Vianna, FJ, *Problemas de Política Objetiva* (Record Cultural, 1974).
Osiel, MJ, 'Dialogue with Dictators: Judicial Resistance in Argentina and Brazil' (1995) 20 *Law & Social Inquiry* 481.
Paixão, C, 'Direito, Política, Autoritarismo e Democracia no Brasil: da Revolução de 30 à Promulgação da Constituição da República de 1988' (2011) 26 *Araucária* 146.
Paixão, C, 'Autonomia, Democracia e Poder Constituinte: Disputas Conceituais na Experiência Constitucional Brasileira (1964–2014)' (2014) 43 *Quaderni Fiorentini* 415.
Paixão, C, 'The Protection of Rights in the Brazilian Transition: Amnesty Law, Violations of Human Rights and Constitutional Form' (2014) *forum historiae iuris*, http://www.forhistiur.de/2014-08-paixao.
Paixão, C, 'Past and Future of Authoritarian Regimes: Constittuion, Transition to Democracy and Amnesty in Brazil and Chile' (2015) 30 *Journal of Constitutional History* 89.
Pasinato, W, 'The Maria da Penha Law: 10 Years On' (2016) 24 *SUR – International Journal on Human Rights* 155.
Pereira, AC, Júnior, E, and Araújo, B, 'Domestic Law and International Law in Brazil' (2017) 4 *Panorama of Brazilian Law* 197.
Pereira, AW, 'Bolsa Família and Democracy in Brazil' (2015) 36 *Third World Quarterly* 1682.
Pereira, AW, *Political (in)Justice: Authoritarianism and the Rule of Law in Brazil, Chile, and Argentina* (University of Pittsburgh Press, 2005).
Pérez-Liñan, A and Castagnola, A, 'Presidential Control of High Courts in Latin America: A Long-Term View (1904–2006)' (2009) 1 *Journal of Politis in Latin America* 87.
Persily, N, 'Can Democracy Survive the Internet' (2017) 28 *Journal of Democracy* 63.
Pierson, P, *Politics in Time: History, Institutions, and Social Analysis* (Princeton University Press, 2004).
Piketty, T, *Capital in the Twenty-First Century* (Harvard University Press, 2017).
Pinho, HDBD and Paumgarten, MP, 'The Challenges of Court Mediation from the Brazilian Perspective' (2015) *International Journal of Procedural Law* 301.
Pinheiro, L and Medeiros, M, 'Desigualdades de Gênero em Tempo de Trabalho Pago e Não-Pago no Brasil' (2015) 33 *Revista Sociedade e Estado* 161.
Pinheiro, PS, 'Eric Hobsbawm: Um Espelho do Mundo em Mutação' (1989) 3 *Estudos Avançados* 86.
Piovesan, F, 'Tratados Internacionais de Proteção dos Direitos Humanos: Jurisprudência do STF' in Moura, LSMD (ed), *O Novo Constitucionalismo Moderno na Era Pós-Positivista. Homenagem a Paula Bonavides* (Saraiva, 2008).
Piovesan, F, 'Ius Constitutionale Commune en América Latina: Context, Challenge, and Perspectives' in Bogdandy, AV, et al (eds), *Transformative Constitutionalism in Latin America* (Oxford University Press, 2017) 49–65.
Postema, GJ, 'Law's Rule: Reflexivity, Mutual Accountability and the Rule of Law' in Zhai, X and Quinn, M (eds), *Bentham's Theory of Law and Public Opinion* (Cambridge University Press, 2013) 7–39.
Power, T and Taylor, MM, 'Conclusion: The Web of Accountability Institutions in Brazil' in Power, TJ and Taylor, MM (eds), *Corruption and Democracy in Brazil: The Struggle for Accountability* (University of Notre Dame Press, 2011) 250–275.
Power, TJ, *Political Right in Postauthoritarian Brazil: Elites, Institutions, and Democratization* (Penn State Press, 2010).

Power, TJ and Taylor, MM, *Corruption and Democracy in Brazil: The Struggle for Accountability* (University of Notre Dame Press, 2011).
Power, TJ and Taylor, MM, 'Introduction: Accountability Institutions and Political Corruption in Brazil' in Power, TJ and Taylor, MM (eds), *Corruption and Democracy in Brazil: The Struggle for Accountability* (University of Notre Dame Press, 2011) 1–28.
Prado, MM, 'The Challenges and Risks of Creating Independent Regulatory Agencies: A Cautionary Tale from Brazil' (2008) 41 *Vanderbilt Journal of Transnational Law* 435.
Prado, MM, 'Institutional Bypass: An Alternative for Development Reform' (2011) Working Paper, https://ssrn.com/abstract=1815442.
Prado, MM and Carson, L, 'Brazilian Anti-Corruption Legislation and its Enforcement: Potential Lessons for Institutional Design' (2014) 9 IRIBA Working Paper, http://www.brazil4africa.org/wp-content/uploads/2014/07/IRIBA-working-paper-09-Brazilian-Anti-Corruption-Legislation-and-its-Enforcement.pdf.
Prado, MM, Carson, L and Correa, I, 'The Brazilian Clean Company Act: Using Institutional Multiplicity for Effective Punishment' (2015) 53 *Osgoode Hall Law Journal* 107.
Prado, MM and Trebilcock, MJ, *Institutional Bypasses: A Strategy to Promote Reforms for Development* (Cambridge University Press, 2018).
Proner, C, et al, *Comments on a Notorious Verdict: The Trial of Lula* (CLACSO, 2018).
Proni, TTDRW and Proni, MW, 'Discriminação de Gênero em Grandes Empresas no Brasil' (2018) 26 *Revista Estudos Feministas* 1.
Przeworski, A, *Democracy and the Market: Political and Economic Reforms in Eastern Europe and Latin America* (Cambridge University Press, 1991).
Przeworski, A, et al, *Democracy and Development: Political Institutions and Well-Being in the World: 1950-1990* (Cambridge University Press, 2000).
Przeworski, A, 'Democracy as an Equilibrium' (2005) 123 *Public Choice* 253.
Przeworski, A, 'Self-Enforcing Democracy' in Wittman, DA and Weingast, BR (eds), *The Oxford Handbook of Political Economy* (Oxford University Press, 2006) 312–28.
Przeworski, A and Maravall, JM (eds), *Democracy and the Rule of Law* (Cambridge University Press, 2003).
Przeworski, A and Maravall, JM, 'Introduction' in Przeworski, A and Maravall, JM (eds), *Democracy and the Rule of Law* (Cambridge University Press, 2003) 1–18.
Queiroz, RMR, 'Abuse of Rhetorical Power and Presidential Impeachment in Brazil: Reflections from Legal History' (2020) 40 *Journal of Constitutional History* 215.
Queiroz, RMR, *Como Remover um Presidente: Teoria, História e Prática do Impeachment* (Zahar, 2021).
Ramos, AC, 'Supremo Tribunal Federal Brasileiro e o Controle de Convencionalidade: Levando a Sério os Tratados de Direitos Humanos' (2009) 104 *Revista da Faculdade de Direito, Universidade de São Paulo* 241.
Reale, M, 'Como Deverá Ser a Nova Constituição' (1985) 60/61 *Revista Brasileira Estudos Politicos* 9.
Recondo, F, *Tanques e Togas: O STF e a Ditadura Militar* (Companhia das Letras, 2018).
Rezende, MJD, 'Raymundo Faoro e os Enigmas da Transição Política no Início da Década de 1980 no Brasil' (2008) 42 *Revista de Ciências Humanas* 165.
Rezende, MJD, 'As Forças Armadas e a Reflexão de Raymundo Faoro sobre a Abertura Política, 1984' (2009) 43 *Revista de Ciências Humanas* 97.
Ribeiro, CAC and Schlegel, R, 'Horizontal Stratification in Brazil's Higher Education (1960–2010)' in Arretche, M (ed), *Paths of Inequality in Brazil: A Half-Century of Changes* (Springer, 2019) 89–112.
Ríos-Figueroa, J, 'Institutions for Constitutional Justice in Latin America' in Helmke, G and Rios-Figueroa, J (eds), *Courts in Latin America* (Cambridge University Press, 2011) 27–54.
Rock, MT, 'Corruption and Democracy' (2009) 45 *The Journal of Development Studies* 55.
Rodrigues, LM, *Mudanças na Classe Política Brasileira* (Centro Edelstein de Pesquisas Sociais, 2009).

Rodrigues, TM and Schneider, M, 'Five Strategies for Political Participation of the Media Democratization Movement in the New Republic' (2020) 43 *Intercom: Revista Brasileira de Ciências da Comunicação* 189.
Rollemberg, D and Quadrat, SV, 'Apresentação' in Rollemberg, D and Quadrat, SV (eds), *A Construção Social dos Regimes Autoritários: Legitimidade, Consenso e Consentimento no Século XX – Brasil e América Latina* (Civilização Brasileira, 2010) 12–32.
Rosenfeld, M, 'The Rule of Law and the Legitimacy of Constitutional Democracy' (2001) 74 *Southern California Law Review* 1307.
Rosenfeld, M, *The Identity of the Constitutional Subject: Selfhood, Citizenship, Culture, and Community* (Routledge, 2009).
Rosenn, KS, 'Recent Important Decisions by the Brazilian Supreme Court' (2013) 45 *University of Miami Inter-American Law Review* 297.
Rousseau, D, 'The Conseil Constitutionnel Confronted with Comparative Law and the Theory of Constitutional Justice (or Louis Favoreu's Untenable Paradoxes)' (2007) 5 *International Journal of Constitutional Law* 28.
Roznai, Y, 'The Rule of Law in 2030' in Bezemek, C (ed), *Constitutionalism 2030* (Hart Publishing, 2002 *forthcoming*).
Roznai, Y, *Unconstitutional Constitutional Amendments: The Limits of Amendment Powers* (Oxford University Press, 2017).
Sá e Silva, FD, 'SIPS Justiça: Opinião Pública, Pesquisa Aplicada e Reforma da Justiça: Contribuições e Desafios, Polítiticos e Analíticos' in Schiavinatto, F (ed), *Sistema de Indicadores de Percepção Social (SIPS)* (IPEA, 2011) 17–42.
Saad-Filho, A, 'Mass Protests under "Left Neoliberalism": Brazil, June–July 2013' (2013) 39 *Critical Sociology* 657.
Saad-Filho, A and Boffo, M, 'The Corruption of Democracy: Corruption Scandals, Class Alliances, and Political Authoritarianism in Brazil' (2020) 124 *Geoforum* 300.
Sales, L and Mariano, R, 'Ativismo Político de Grupos Religiosos e Luta por Direitos' (2019) 39 *Religião & Sociedade* 9.
Samuels, D, 'Informal Institutions When Formal Contracting is Prohibited: Campaign Finance in Brazil' in Levitsky, S and Helmke, G (eds), *Informal Institutions and Democracy: Lessons from Latin America* (The John Hopkins University Press, 2006) 87–206.
Samuels, DJ, 'Incentives to Cultivate a Party Vote in Candidate-Centric Electoral Systems: Evidence from Brazil' (1999) 32 *Comparative Political Studies* 487.
Santos, JAF, 'Desigualdade Racial de Saúde e Contexto de Classe no Brasil' (2011) 54 *Dados – Revista de Ciências Sociais* 5.
Santos, NCB and Gasparini, CE, 'Orçamento Impositivo e Relação entre Poderes no Brasil' (2020) 31 *Revista Brasileira de Ciência Política* 339.
Santos, PAGD and Wylie, K, 'The Representation of Women' in Ames, B (ed), *Routledge Handbook of Brazilian Politics* (Routledge, 2019) 57–71.
Scheppele, KL, 'Autocratic Legalism' (2018) 85 *The University of Chicago Law Review* 545.
Schinke, VD and Castro, RS, 'O Relatório da Comissão Nacional da Verdade: O Capítulo sobre a Atuação do Poder Judiciário durante a Ditadura' (2017) 18 *Espaço Jurídico Journal of Law* 143.
Schleiter, P and Voznaya, A, 'Party System Institutionalization, Accountability and Governmental Corruption' (2018) 48 *British Journal of Political Science* 315.
Schlink, B and Jacobson, AJ, 'Introduction – Constitutional Crisis: The German and the American Experience' in Schlink, B and Jacobson, AJ (eds), *Weimar: A Jurisprudence of Crisis* (University of California Press, 2000) 1–40.
Schneider, N, 'Impunity in Post-authoritarian Brazil: The Supreme Court's Recent Verdict on the Amnesty Law' (2011) 90 *Review of Latin American and Caribbean Studies* 39.
Schwartzman, LF, 'Does Money Whiten? Intergenerational Changes in Racial Classification in Brazil' (2007) 72 *American Sociological Review* 940.
Schwartzman, S and Zimmerman, B, 'Conservation Alliances with Indigenous Peoples of the Amazon' (2005) 19 *Conservation Biology* 721.

Scully, TR and Mainwaring, S, *Building Democratic Institutions: Party Systems in Latin America* (Stanford University Press, 1995).
Segurado, R, 'The Brazilian Civil Rights Framework for the Internet: A Pioneering Experience in Internet Governance' in Neto, AP and Flynn, MB (eds), *The Internet and Health in Brazil: Challenges and Trends* (Springer, 2018) 27–46.
Sheriff, RE, *Dreaming Equality: Color, Race, and Racism in Brazil* (Rutgers University Press, 2001).
Shugart, MS and Carey, JM, *Presidents and Assemblies: Constitutional Design and Electoral Dynamics* (Cambridge University Press, 1992).
Silkenat, JR, Hickey, JE and Barenboïm, P, *The Legal Doctrines of the Rule of Law and the Legal State (Rechtsstaat)* (Springer, 2014).
Silva, GMD and Reis, EP, 'Perceptions of Racial Discrimination among Black Professionals in Rio de Janeiro' (2011) 46 *Latin American Reseearch Review* 55.
Silva, GM and Saldivar, E, 'Comparing Ideologies of Racial Mixing in Latin America: Brazil and Mexico' (2018) 8 *Sociologia & Antropologia* 427.
Silva, GHGD and Skovsmose, O, 'Affirmative Actions in Terms of Special Rights: Confronting Structural Violence in Brazilian Higher Education' (2019) 11 *Power and Education* 204.
Silva, JAD, 'O Estado Democrático de Direito' (1988) 173 *Revista de Direito Administrativo* 15.
Silva, JAD, *Aplicabilidade das Normas Constitucionais* (Malheiros, 2008).
Silva, JM, 'Mapeando o Supremo: As Posições dos Ministros do STF na Jurisdição Constitucional (2012-2017)' (2018) 37 *Novos Estudos CEBRAP* 35.
Silva, TD and Silva, JMD, 'Reserva de Vagas para Negros em Concursos Públicos: Una Análise a partir do Projeto de Lei 6.738/2013' (2014) 17 *IPEA (Nota Técnica)*.
Silva, VAD, 'Interpretação Constitucional e Sincretismo Metodológico' in Silva, VAD (ed), *Interpretação Constitucional* (Malheiros, 2005) 115–43.
Silva, VAD, 'Deciding without Deliberating' (2013) 11 *International Journal of Constitutional Law* 557.
Silva, VAD, 'Review: Making Brazil Work: Checking the President in a Multiparty System' (2017) 15 *International Journal of Constitutional Law* 519.
Silva, VAD, *The Constitution of Brazil: A Contextual Analysis* (Hart Publishing, 2019).
Silva, VAD, *Direito Constitucional Brasileiro* (Editora da Universidade de São Paulo, 2021).
Singer, A, 'Brasil, Junho de 2013, Classes e Ideologias Cruzadas' (2013) 97 *Novos Estudos CEBRAP* 23.
Smith, AE, *Religion and Brazilian Democracy: Mobilizing the People of God* (Cambridge University Press, 2019).
Speck, BW, 'Auditing Institutions' in Power, TJ and Taylor, MM (eds), *Corruption and Democracy in Brazil: The Struggle for Accountability* (University of Notre Dame Press, 2011) 127–61.
Stepan, AC, *Rethinking Military Politics: Brazil and the Southern Cone* (Princeton University Press, 1988).
Stuenkel, O, 'Do the BRICS Possess Soft Power' (2016) 9 *Journal of Political Power* 353.
Sunde, U, Cervellati, M, and Fortunato, P, 'Are All Democracies Equally Good? The Role of Interactions between Political Environment and Inequality for the Rule of Law' (2008) 99 *Economics Letters* 552.
Sunstein, CR and Vermeule, A, 'Interpretation and Institutions' (2010) 101 *Michigan Law Review* 885.
Suteu, S, *Eternity Clauses in Democratic Constitutionalism* (Oxford University Press, 2021).
Taylor, MM, 'The Troubling Strength of Brazilian Institutions in the Face of Scandal' (2019) 15 *Taiwan Journal of Democracy* 91.
Telles, EE, 'Residential Segregation by Skin Color in Braizl' (1992) 57 *American Sociological Review* 186.
Teorell, J, *Determinants of Democratization: Explaining Regime Change in the World, 1972–2006* (Cambridge University Press, 2010).
Thomassen, L, 'A Bizarre, Even Opaque Practice: Habermas on Constitutionalism and Democracy' in Thomassen, L (ed), *The Derrida-Habermas Reader* (The University of Chicago Press, 2006) 176–94.

Torelly, M, 'Transnational Legal Process and Fundamental Rights in Latin America: How Does the Inter-American Human Rights System Reshape Domestic Constitutional Rights?' in Fortes, P, et al (ed), *Law and Policy in Latin America: Transforming Courts, Institutions, and Rights* (Springer, 2016) 21–38.

Torelly, M, 'Assessing a Late Truth Commission: Challenges and Achievements of the Brazilian National Truth Commission' (2018) 12 *International Journal of Transitional Justice* 194.

Torre, CDL, 'Populism and the Politics of the Extraordinary in Latin America' (2016) 21 *Journal of Political Ideologies* 121.

Torre, CDL, 'Populism in Latin America' in Kaltwasser, CR, et al (eds), *The Oxford Handbook of Populism* (Oxford University Press, 2017) 195–213.

Tourinho, M, 'Brazil in the Global Anticorruption Regime' (2018) 61(1) *Revista Brasileira de Política Internacional* e004.

Turnpenny, J, et al, 'Why Is Integrating Policy Assessment So Hard? A Comparative Analysis of the Institutional Capacities and Constraints' (2008) 51 *Journal of Environmental Planning and Management* 759.

Uslaner, EM, *Corruption, Inequality, and the Rule of Law* (Cambridge University Press, 2008).

Valarini, E and Pohlmann, M, 'Organizational Crime and Corruption in Brazil: A Case Study of the "Operation Carwash" Court Records' (2019) 59 *International Journal of Law, Crime and Justice* 100340.

Valença, MM and Carvalho, G, 'Soft Power, Hard Aspirations: The Shifting Role of Power in Brazilian Foreign Policy' (2014) 8 *Brazilian Political Science Review* 66.

Vermeule, A, *Mechanisms of Democracy* (Oxford University Press, 2007).

Vermeule, A, *The System of the Constitution* (Oxford University Press, 2011).

Viana, N, *Dano Colateral: A Intervenção dos Militares na Segurança Pública* (Companhia das Letras, 2021).

Vianna, ARB and Carrara, S, 'Sexual Politics and Sexual Rights in Brazil: A Case Study' in Corrales, J and Pecheny, M (eds), *The Politics of Sexuality in Latin America* (University of Pittsburgh Press, 2010) 122–134.

Vieira, OV, *Supremo Tribunal Federal: Jurisprudência Política* (Revista dos Tribunais, 2002).

Vieira, OV, 'Inequality and the Subversion of the Rule of Law' (2007) 4 *Sur – International Journal on Human Rights* 26.

Vilaça, A and Wright, R, *Native Christians: Modes and Effects of Christianity among Indigenous Peoples of the Americas* (Ashgate, 2009).

Voigt, S, Gutmann, J and Feld, LP, 'Economic Growth and Judicial Independence, A Dozen Years On: Cross-Country Evidence Using an Updated Set of Indicators' (2015) 38 *European Journal of Political Economy* 197.

Wacquant, L, 'Toward a Dictatorship over the Poor? Notes on the Penalization of Poverty in Brazil' (2003) 5 *Punishment & Society* 197.

Waldron, J, *Law and Disagreement* (Oxford University Press, 1999).

Waldron, J, 'The Rule of Law as a Theatre of Debate' in Burley, J (ed), *Dworkin and His Critics: With Replies by Ronald Dworkin* (Blackwell, 2004) 319–36.

Waldron, J, 'The Concept and the Rule of Law' (2008) 43 *Georgia Law Review* 1.

Waldron, J, 'The Rule of Law and the Importance of Procedure' in Fleming, JE (ed), *Getting to the Rule of Law* (NYU Press, 2011) 3–31.

Wampler, B, 'Entering the State: Civil Society Activism and Participatory Governance in Brazil' (2012) 60 *Political Studies* 341.

Weffort, F, 'Novas Democracias. Que Democracias?' (1992) 27 *Lua Nova* 5.

Weingast, B, 'The Political Foundations of Democracy and the Rule of Law' (1997) 91 *American Political Science Review* 245.

Weingast, B, 'Designing Constitutional Stability' in Congleton, R and Swedenborg, B (eds), *Democratic Constitutional Design and Public Policy Analysis and Evidence* (MIT Press, 2006) 343–66.

Weingast, BR, 'A Postscript to "Political Foundations of Democracy and the Rule of Law"' in Przeworski, A and Maravall, JM (eds), *Democracy and the Rule of Law* (Cambridge University Press, 2003) 109–13.

Williamson, JG, 'Latin American Inequality: Colonial Origins, Commodity Booms or a Missed Twentieth-Century Leveling' (2015) 16 *Journal of Human Development and Capabilities* 324.

Wright, R, *Transformando os Deuses: Igrejas Evangélicas, Pentecostais e Neopentecostais entre os Povos Indígenas no Brasil* (Editora da Unicamp, 2004).

Wylie, K and dos Santos, P, 'A Law on Paper Only: Electoral Rules, Parties, and the Persistent Underrepresentation of Women in Brazilian Legislatures' (2016) 12 *Politics & Gender* 415.

Yarchi, M, Baden, C and Kligler-Vilenchik, N, 'Political Polarization on the Digital Sphere: A Cross-platform, Over-time Analysis of Interactional, Positional, and Affective Polarization on Social Media' (2021) 38 *Political Communication* 98.

Yashar, DJ, *Contesting Citizenship in Latin America: The Rise of Indigenous Movements and the Postliberal Challenge* (Cambridge University Press, 2005).

Zamboni, Y, 'Participatory Budgeting and Local Governance: An Evidence-Based Evaluation of Participatory Budgeting Experiencies in Brazil' (2007) Working Paper, https://citeseerx.ist.psu.edu/viewdoc/download?doi=10.1.1.467.6755&rep=rep1&type=pdf.

Zaverucha, J, 'Relações Civil-Militares: O Legado Autoritário da Constituição Brasileira de 1988' in Teles, E and Safatle, V (eds), *O Que Resta da Ditadura: A Exceção Brasileira* (Boitempo, 2010) 41–76.

Zhouri, A, '"Adverse Forces" in the Brazilian Amazon: Developmentalism Versus Environmentalism and Indigenous Rights' (2010) 19 *The Journal of Environment & Development* 252.

Zolo, D, 'The Rule of Law: A Critical Reappraisal' in Costa, P and Zolo, D (eds), *The Rule of Law: History, Theory and Criticism* (Springer, 2007) 3–72.

Index

A

abortion
- deaths and hospitalisations caused by 48–49
- legislation 48–49, 126
- populist anti-abortion rhetoric 167
- protests demanding right to 166

Abranches, Sérgio 82, 98, 103, 108
academic freedom 126
ação civil pública 129, 132
ação declaratória de constitucionalidade **(ADC)** 124
ação direta de inconstitucionalidade **(ADI)** 124, 130
accountability
- 1988 Constitution 72
- 'accountability paradox' 165–166
- anti-corruption measures 148, 149, 151, 153–155, 157–160
- Bolsonaro administration 196
- constitutional provisions 25, 34
- criminal justice system 144, 145, 156–157
- institutional bypass strategy 157
- institutional multiplicity strategy 157, 159–160
- judiciary 114, 128, 137–138, 199
- political system 1, 106, 111, 112, 147–148
- regional differences 58
- rule of law 147

Administrative Council for Economic Defence 159
administrative merits doctrine 127
Advocacy-General of the Union 129, 132
alternative dispute resolution 134
Amaral, AJD Azevedo 68
Amazon rainforest
- deforestation 52–53
- illegal mining 53
- Indigenous people 52–53

American Convention on Human Rights 189, 191, 194
Ames, Barry 104–105, 108
Amnesty Law 65, 79–80, 193–194, 213
antipetismo 96–97, 108
antitrust regulation 159
Arantes, Rogério 131, 145
Aras, Augusto 130
Araújo, Ernesto 179
Argentina
- corruption in 149
- democracy in 61
- Indigenous people 51
- transition from dictatorship 65, 79

arguição de descumprimento de preceito fundamental **(ADPF)** 124
Arretche, Marta 37–38, 46, 57
Attorney-General of the Republic 130, 149, 209
authoritarian mindset *see also* **dictatorships**
- Bolsonaro administration 64–66, 67, 78–84, 85, 196, 198–199, 206, 208, 213–214
- Brazil, generally 3, 66–71, 84–86, 90
- civil society institutions 165
- clientelism 10, 67, 68, 71, 72
- Cold War 68
- Constituent Assembly of 1987–88 71–78, 84
- Constitution 1967 23–24
- Constitution 1988 9–10, 24–25, 29, 72–78
- continuity despite regime changes 66–67
- corruption and 10
- criminal justice system 144, 145
- democracy 6, 7–8, 9, 23–24, 62, 63–66, 71–78, 84, 90, 208, 214
- depoliticisation of society 67, 68, 71, 72
- *Estado de Direito* 8, 18, 21–25
- inequality and 26, 31, 67, 185, 198–199
- Institutional Acts 23, 69–71, 120
- Inter-American System of Human Rights 192
- judiciary 11, 206
- Latin America, generally 87–88
- military, revival under Bolsonaro 78–84, 85, 97, 143, 204–205, 207, 211, 212
- oligarchical elites 101
- popular support for 66, 108
- preservationism 21–25, 26, 29
- resistance to redistributive policies 32
- rule of law and 6, 7–8, 9–10, 18, 26, 29, 82, 84, 198–199
- social inequality and 65–66
- support for authoritarian governments 61, 68–69

technocracy, institutionalisation 67, 68–69, 71, 72
theoretical justification for 66–67
Auxílio Brasil 210
Avritzer, Leonardo 77, 164

B

Barbosa, Leonardo 22, 23, 69
***Bolsa Família* programme**
decentralisation 58
generally 34, 44, 57
replacement 210
Bolsonaro, Jair
anti-abortion rhetoric 167
anti-gender equality rhetoric 167
attacks on civil organisations 150, 162, 167–168
attacks on electronic electoral system 176, 212
attacks on the media 150, 168–172, 175–176
attacks on oversight institutions 209–210, 211
authoritarian mindset in Brazil 64–66, 67, 78–84, 85, 206, 208, 213–214
Auxílio Brasil 210
bolsonarismo 3–6, 32, 143, 201, 208–209, 213
coalition presidentialism and 111–112, 204
corruption under 97, 110, 149–150, 154, 196, 204–205, 207, 210–211
COVID-19 pandemic 170, 179–180, 196, 205, 207, 210, 211
democracy, deterioration under 61–62, 103, 110, 167–168, 199, 201, 204–213
dwindling support for 209, 212
election 2, 3–6, 32, 60, 62, 64–66, 85–86, 96–97, 103, 107, 108–109, 111, 113–114, 147, 150, 162–163, 179, 199–206, 210
environmental policy 52–53, 179, 187, 196
Evangelical churches' support for 167
fake news and misinformation 175–176, 201
foreign policy 195–196
'gambling for resurrection' 206, 210
gender rights under 46
impact on future developments 5–6
Indigenous people, policy on 52–53
investigations against 130
judiciary and 82, 160, 206–207, 211, 212–213
MERCOSUR 187
militias, connections to 143, 212
Office of Hate 175
police forces and 128, 143, 144–145, 149, 207, 209, 212
populism 59–60
pork-barrel politics 109–110, 199, 210–211
re-election, prospect of 195, 207–215
revival of the military 78–84, 85, 97, 204–205, 207, 211, 212
rule of law and Bolsonaro administration 2, 4, 208–209, 214
social media, use of 175–176, 177–178, 201
social and political polarisation under 201, 209
Supreme Court and 128, 149, 211, 212–213
Brazilian Democratic Movement Party (PMDB) 69, 76
Brazilian Social Democracy Party (PSDB) 1, 94

C

Campos, Francisco 68–69
Canotilho, JJ Gomes 21
Cardozo, Fernando Henrique 94
Carson, LD and Prado, MM 159
Castro, Fábio Ávila de 35
Castro, Marcos Faro de 121
census classification 42
Cheibub, JA et al 88–89
Chile
corruption in 149
democracy in 61
Indigenous people 51
multiparty presidential system 91
transition from dictatorship 65, 77, 133
citizenship
civil society fostering 148
civil law tradition
emphasis on the state 19–22
legality principle 19
rule of law, concept of 16–17, 19–22
Civil Procedural Code 134
civil society
'accountability paradox' 165–166
Bolsonaro administration attacks on 150, 167–168
Brazil's authoritarian mindset 165
combatting corruption 151–152
democracy, impact of 163–164, 166
generally 34, 148
inequality and 165
participatory governance institutions 75–76, 164–165

rise of populism and 167–168
self-correcting learning process 163–164
clientelism
antipetismo 96–97, 108
authoritarian mindset and 10, 67, 68, 71, 72
Bolsonaro administration 204, 210–211
coalition presidentialism and 10, 103–110, 111
combatting 164–165
corruption and 58
generally 11, 21, 104, 109, 112, 148
National Congress 111
oligarchical elites and 101–102
participatory governance institutions and 164–165
political institutions, generally 10
political parties and 202, 203
poverty levels and 58
Codato, Adriano Nervo 74
Cold War
authoritarian mindset 68
Collor de Mello, Fernando 90, 173
Colombia
corruption in 149
democracy in 61
common law tradition
rule of law concept 14, 16, 17, 19, 27
Communist Party of Brazil (PCdoB)
Gomes Lund et al v Brazil 193–194
competition, regulation 159
Congress
clientelism 111
executive and 105
fragmented and oligarchical nature 98–103
grip on national budget 109
Constituent Assembly of 1987–88
authoritarian mindset and 71–78
compromise with the military 79–81
judiciary and courts 115, 121–122
Constitution 1891 182
Constitution 1934
gender equality 45
Constitution 1937
authoritarianism 32
Constitution 1946 93
Constitution 1967
civilian-military dictatorship 22–24, 32, 73, 93
Constitution 1976 21
Constitution 1988
accountability strengthened by 72
authoritarian mindset and 72–78
basic rights under 29, 34, 132–135
bolsonarismo, threat of 209
civilian-military relationship 79–81, 142
constitutional transition 65
democratic core 21, 25, 26, 28–29, 32–33, 34, 72, 75–77, 163
Estado Democrático de Direito 8, 21, 24–25
evolutionary Constitution, as 73
executive powers expanded by 93–94, 105
Federal Audit Court 157–158
formal equality under 29
gender equality 45–46
generally 106, 154
Indigenous people 52
military, provisions as to 80, 142
military judicial system 118–119, 142
preservationist use 9–10, 23–25, 26, 29
Public Ministry 129
public security 142
rights, individual and social 29, 34, 132–135, 182–183
social and economic exclusion 29
social welfare provisions 133–134
strategy against 32–33
unamendable clauses 46
constitutionalism
attacks on 32–33
defence of 11, 206–207
democracy and, generally 7, 20–21, 28–29
Estado de Direito 20–21
future of, generally 197
interpretation of Constitution 125–126
Ius Constitutionale Commune en América Latina 185
judiciary, role of 116, 125–126, 206–207
Latin American 92, 185
stabilization 187–188
state's centrality in Brazil 28–29
coordination dilemmas
societal 18, 30
unequal societies, in 26–30, 34–35
corruption
accountability and 148, 149, 151, 153–155, 157–160
anti-corruption crusade under Rousseff 81
anti-corruption legislation 143, 151, 154–155, 159, 160, 161
anti-corruption societal consensus 149, 150, 151–152, 164

audit courts, oversight by 153, 156, 157–158
authoritarian mindset and 10
blacklisted companies 154
Bolsonaro/*bolsonarismo* 5, 32, 96–97, 110, 149–150, 154, 196, 204–205, 207, 210–211
Brazil's international ranking 148–153
clientelism *see* clientelism
combatting 147–148, 150–178
corporate integrity 150–151
COVID-19 pandemic 205, 207
data, generally 148–153
Federal Controller's Office, role 153, 154, 157, 158–159
foreign relations, in 151
generally 5, 11, 91, 104, 147–148, 202
inequality reinforcing 59, 154–155
international cooperation in combatting 159
investigations into 131, 143–144, 151
justice system 114, 137–138, 206
leniency agreements 146–147, 151, 161
Lula da Silva linked to 166
militias and 142–143
money laundering 143, 151, 154, 159
oligarchical elites and 102
Operation Car Wash 5, 96, 97, 103, 113–114, 116, 131, 143, 146–147, 149, 150, 151, 160–163, 199, 202, 206, 210
oversight institutions 157–160
police 142–143, 144
political system 5, 103, 104–105, 108–109, 127, 146–148, 149, 202, 203
politicisation of corruption scandals 160
populists claiming to combat 166
pork-barrel politics 97–98, 102–103, 104–105, 106, 108–110, 111, 199, 210–211
poverty levels and 58
private and public sectors, relationship 146–148, 152
punishment rate 152, 156
punishment regime 147, 154, 157, 158–160
regional differences 58
transparency of anti-corruption provisions 151, 158–160
whistle-blowers 151, 161
Worker's Party 108, 166

Costa Rica
corruption in 150
democracy in 61

courts *see* **justice system and judiciary**

Covas, Mario 76

COVID-19 pandemic
Indigenous population 54
prison population 140
response to 2, 5, 126, 170, 179–180, 196, 198, 205, 207, 210, 211

criminal justice system *see also* **prison system**
accountability 144, 145
appeals 139
authoritarian legacy 144, 145
Bolsonaro administration and 128, 143, 144–145, 149, 207, 209
civilian police 141, 143
conviction rates 141
corruption and 142–143, 144, 156
dysfunctionality 138–139
federal police 128, 143–145, 149, 151, 153, 156, 207, 209
foro privilegiado 139
generally 61
harsher punishments, calls for 166
inefficiency 11
inequality 139, 140–141, 145, 147
inter-agency coordination 145
judiciary and 139
jury trials 139
military police 141–143
police 11, 138–143, 156, 212
pre-trial detention 139
Public Ministry 138–139, 144, 156
transparency 144, 145
trials 139
violence and 139–143, 144, 145, 214
warrants, issue 139

criminal law
Military Criminal Code 119

D

Da Ros, Luciano and Taylor, Matthew 136

Daly, Tom Gerald 62, 193

data protection 177

Dauvergne, Peter 180

deforestation
Bolsonaro administration 179, 196

democracy
1988 Constitution 21, 25, 26, 28–29, 32–33, 34, 72, 75–77, 163
authoritarian mindset impacting 6, 7–8, 9, 23–24, 62, 63–66, 71–78, 84, 90, 214
bolsonarismo 2, 3–6, 61–62, 64–66, 103, 168–169, 175, 196, 201, 204–207, 208–213
civil society and 11, 148, 163–164, 166

civilian-military dictatorship and 69–71
constitutionalism and 7, 20–21, 28–29
distrust in democratic institutions 62, 64
erosion 4–5, 7, 59–62, 164, 168–169, 173, 195, 204–210
Estado de Direito 20, 23–24
Estado Democrático de Direito 8, 21, 24–25
fake news and misinformation 175–176, 201
inclusion of outsiders 39
indexers of 60–61
inequality and 33–34, 38, 44, 59–60, 214–215
institutional capacities and 3, 4, 5–6
international perception of Brazil 195–197
internet and 177, 201
judiciary, politicisation 5, 10–11, 113–116
judiciary and democratisation process 114–116
Latin American 88–89
Latinobarómetro Informe 2021 60–62
media, importance of 168–174
MERCOSUR and 187–188, 189
military and 142
multiparty presidential system 90–91
party fragmentation 5, 10, 90, 91, 94–95, 111–112, 127, 203–204
polarisation of political system 200–201, 209
presidential elections 94–97
'racial democracy' myth 40–41
Rechtsstaat 20
rule of law and 7–8, 16, 24
self-correcting learning process 163–164
self-reinforcing processes 3
social inequality and 26, 55
stability 33–34, 90–91, 212
support for 61
Supreme Court and 114–116, 120–121, 125, 128
transition to 2–5, 7–10, 12–13, 23–25, 26, 28, 33, 63–64, 65, 71–78, 79, 103, 104, 115, 166, 173, 213

determinacy
rule of law and 15

dictatorships *see also* **authoritarian mindset**
1967 Constitution 22–24
abuses of legal concepts 8
Amnesty Law 65, 79–80, 193–194, 213
Brazil's history of 3–4, 6, 7
civilian-military 22–24, 31, 32, 51, 66, 67, 68–71, 81, 93, 114, 119, 120, 142, 169, 214
Estado de Direito 8, 21–25
Estado Novo 8, 31, 32, 66, 67, 68, 69
human rights violations 66, 71, 114, 119
inequality and 31
Institutional Acts 23, 69–71, 120
judiciary and 114, 120
legacy 214
media during 173
rule of law and 18
support for 67, 68–69
transition from 3–4, 7, 23–24, 26, 65, 115, 213

Diniz, Debora 46–47

discrimination
class 41
racial 39–43
residential segregation 42

Doria, João 211

E

economic exclusion
inclusion, democracy and 39
invisibility of the extreme poor 29

economic inequality
Auxílio Brasil 210
Bolsa Família 34, 44, 57, 210
economic rights enforcement 134–135
generally 61
GINI Index 37, 56
pervasiveness in Brazil 26–27, 29, 31, 33–34, 35–39
racial inequality 40, 42, 43
regional differences 54–58
resistance to redistributive policies 32
rule of law and 26, 214–215
wealth distribution 61
'whitening' phenomenon 41
women 47

Economist Intelligence Unit (EUI) Democracy Index 60–61

economy
generally 1–2, 179–180
social welfare state 133
stagnation and decline 1–4, 179, 187

education
Bolsa Família programme 57, 210
gender and sex education 126
illiteracy levels 43, 55, 57
provision, generally 33–34, 38, 133
quota system for university access 126
racial inequality 41, 42, 43, 44–45, 126
regional inequality 55, 57
'whitening' phenomenon 41
women 38, 46, 47

electoral system *see* **political system**

Elkins, Zachary 4
Elkins, Zachary et al 73
employment
racial inequality 42, 43, 44–45
unemployment levels 43, 58
women 46–47
Encarnación, Omar 49
environmental policy
Bolsonaro administration 52–53, 179, 187, 196
environmental protection
EU-MERCOSUR and 187
Indigenous people and 51
equality *see also* **economic inequality; inequality; social inequality**
constitutional 29
Estado de Derecho
generally 14
Estado de Direito *see also* ***Estado Democrático de Direito*; rule of law**
1967 Constitution 22–23
civilian-military dictatorship and 18, 22
constitutionalist approach to 20–21
democracy and 20–22, 23–25
generally 14
legality principle 20
meaning 15–16
modernisation 25
preservationist use 8, 18, 21–25
Revolution and 23, 24
social, risks of 21
social inequality and 18–19, 22, 26–28
social justice and 18, 21, 27–30
solidarity and inclusion 20
substantive values and 19–22
transition from formalist to substantive conception 20, 28–30
use of term 8, 14, 15–16, 26–27
Estado de Direito Democrático
1976 Constitution 21
modernisation 25
Estado Democrático de Direito *see also* ***Estado de Direito*; rule of law**
1988 Constitution 8, 21, 23–25
evolution of concept 8, 16–17, 18, 19–22, 24–25, 27–28
institutional equilibrium, reliance on 17–18, 19, 29
rule of law and 16–17
Estado Novo 8, 31, 32, 66, 67, 68, 69
estamentos 101
État de Droit 14, 19, 20
État Légal 20
Evangelical churches 45, 167
executive *see also* **political system; presidential system**
1988 Constitution 93–94, 105–106
Access to Information 158
capacity to check 111
Transparency Portal 158

F
fairness, rule of law and 15
Faoro, Raymundo 67, 101
Fausto, Boris 67
Federal Controller's Office 153, 154, 157, 158–159
Federal Judiciary 143
Federal Public Ministry 143
Federal Revenue 94, 210
Federal Supreme Court *see* **Supreme Court**
federalism
generally 94, 99–100, 104–105, 116, 211
presidential system and 94
fertility, decline in 44
***Figueiredo Commission* report** 50
freedom of speech
constitutional provisions 171
generally 126, 171, 176–177
internet 174
press freedom 169–174, 176–177
Freire, Silene de Moraes 67
Freyre, Gilberto 40
fundamental rights *see* **human rights**

G
'gambling for resurrection'
Bolsonaro 206, 210
Gargarella, Roberto 93
Gaspar, Malu 146
gender issues *see also* **LGBTQIA+ community; Women**
generally 33, 38, 45–46
populist rhetoric 167
same-sex marriage 46, 49, 126, 166
trans rights 126
generality principle
constitutional provisions 34
rule of law and 29
global south
stereotypes associated with 88
Gomes Lund et al v Brazil 193–194
Goulart, João 68–69
Great Depression 32, 36–37
Guedes, Paulo 187
Guimarães, Ulysses 76

H
habeas corpus
civilian-military dictatorship 69
generally 117–118
political crimes 120
Haddad, Fernando 96
Hagopian, Frances 74, 165
health care provision
Bolsa Família programme 57, 210
generally 33–34, 38, 133
response to COVID-19 pandemic 2, 5, 54, 126
unequal distribution 42, 126
Herrera, Juan 190
Hobsbawm, Eric J
'The Present as History' 63–64, 65, 85, 86
housing
inequality 43
residential segregation 42
human rights *see also* **rights**
1988 Constitution 182–183
American Convention on Human Rights 189, 191, 194
Amnesty Law decision 65, 79–80, 193–194
authoritarian mindset and 192
Bolsonaro administration 179
Brazil's ranking 61
dictatorship, violations by 66, 71, 114, 119, 193
enforcement 185
freedom of speech *see* freedom of speech
Gomes Lund et al v Brazil 194–195
increasing rights culture 132–134
Inter-American Commission on Human Rights 191
Inter-American Court of Human Rights 12, 181, 183, 191–195, 197
Inter-American System of Human Rights 189, 191, 195, 197
International Convention for the Protection of All Persons from Forced Disappearance 195
international perception of Brazil's compliance 195–197
international treaties and conventions 34, 182–183, 188–189, 191–195
Supreme Court decisions 49–50, 125–126
Hunter, Wendy and Power, Timothy J 201

I
illiteracy levels 43, 55, 57
inclusiveness *see* **inequality**
Indigenous people *see also* **racial inequality**
1988 Constitution 52
abortion and 48–49
acculturation 53
COVID-19 deaths 54
environmental protection and 51
Figueiredo Commission report 50
genocide 53
inequality 9, 26–27, 33, 50–54
land rights 52–54
inequality *see also* **economic inequality; social inequality**
1988 Constitution 45–46
authoritarian mindset and 65–66, 67, 185, 198–199
bolsonarismo 32, 46, 201, 208
civil society initiatives to tackle 148
coordination dilemmas 26–30, 34–35
corruption reinforced by 59, 154–155
declining rule of law and 59–62
democracy and, generally 38, 39, 44, 59–62, 214–215
democratic stability and 33–34
dictatorial periods 31
difficulty in assessing 33, 37
gender 33, 38, 45–50
generally 61, 180
health care provision 42, 126
historical 33–34, 38, 39–62
housing 43
income 33–34, 35–39
increasing 89
Indigenous people 33, 50–54
institutional framework impacted by 33
internet access 174
justice system 11, 135–138, 139, 145, 147
LGBTQIA+ community 45–46, 49–50, 126
oligarchical elites 101
pervasiveness in Brazil 26–27, 29–39, 165
racial *see* racial inequality
regional 33, 39, 47, 54–58, 99, 141
religious legacy 45, 46
resistance to redistributive policies 32
rights enforcement 135
rule of law impacted by 6, 8, 9, 13, 18–19, 29, 59–62, 198–199, 208, 214–215
social and political backlash 165–166
social and political polarisation 201, 209, 214–215
technocracy, institutionalisation 67, 68–69, 71, 72
violence and inequality 34, 41, 42, 43–44, 58, 139–141

wealth distribution 61
welfare provision *see* welfare provision
women 9, 26–27, 33, 38, 45–49
innocence, presumption of 126
Institutional Acts 23, 69–71, 120
institutional capacity
Brazil, generally 27
democracy and 3, 4, 5, 6
dysfunctionalities 3, 4, 5–6
erosion 5
evolution 3, 4, 6, 27–28
increasing social participation 26
inequality impacting 33
Inter-American Commission on Human Rights (IACHR) 191, 192
Inter-American Court of Human Rights (IACtHR) 12, 181, 183, 191–195, 197
Gomes Lund et al v Brazil 193–194
Inter-American System of Human Rights 189, 191–195, 197
interna corporis doctrine 127
International Convention for the Protection of All Persons from Forced Disappearance 195
International Criminal Court (ICC)
genocide of Indigenous Brazilians 53
recognition by Brazil 183
international law
Brazil and, generally 11–12
human rights 182–183, 185, 188–189
incorporated into domestic legislation 182–185, 191, 197
international perception of Brazil's compliance 195–197
rights under, enforcement 185
rule of law concept, generally 16–17, 19
international relations
Bolsonaro administration 195–196
Brazil's soft power 179–182, 195–196
EU-MERCOSUR Free Trade Agreement 187
generally 179–182
Ius Constitutionale Commune en América Latina 185
MERCOSUR 12, 181, 185, 186–191, 192, 197
multilateralism and non-interventionism 180, 189
OAS 12, 189
OECD, accession discussions 181
peacekeeping missions 180
PROSUL 190
regional integration 185
UNASUR 12, 181, 185, 187, 189–190
weak regional institutions 190–191
internet
access to 174
Civil Rights Framework for 177
data protection 177
democracy and 177, 201
fake news and misinformation 173, 174–178, 201
freedom of speech 174
power of the new media 174–178
regulatory framework 177
***Ius Constitutionale Commune en América Latina* (ICCAL)** 185

J

judicial review system
Constitution, interpretation 125
generally 120–121, 123–125, 130
juizados especiais 134
justice system and judiciary
accountability 114, 128, 137–138, 197, 199
administrative cases 117
alternative dispute resolution 134
Amnesty Law ruling 65, 79–80, 193–194
appeal courts and system 117–118, 119–120, 121, 123, 139
appointment and tenure 117–119, 122–123, 137
audit courts 94, 130, 153, 156, 157–158
authoritarian mindset 11
Bolsonaro administration 82, 160, 206–207, 211, 212–213
caseload 120, 124–125, 156
civilian-military dictatorship 69, 70, 114, 120
conception of rule of law 28
Constituent Assembly and 115, 121–122
constitutionalism, protection 116, 206–207
corruption 114, 137–138, 206
courts system 115–129
criminal justice system *see* criminal justice system
democratisation process and 114–116
disarrangement 202–203
during Constituent Assembly 115
elections, oversight 118
fair trials and procedures 15
fake news investigations 175–176
federal courts 116–117
Federal Judiciary 143

Federal Supreme Court *see* Supreme Court
financial expenditure on 136–138
general repercussion requirement 123, 134
independence 1, 11, 94, 106, 115, 120, 134, 136, 138, 154, 156
individual rights, interpretation 126, 133–135
inequality and 135–138, 139
innocence, presumption of 126
international law and 182, 184, 195, 197
interpretative role 125–126
Judicial Reform 2004 123, 125, 131, 134, 137
jury trials 139
Latin America, generally 87–88
legal impartiality 29
libel law, interpretation 171–172
military judicial system 118–119, 142
Operation Car Wash 5, 113–114, 116, 160–163, 199, 202, 206–96
oversight 125
politicisation 5, 10–11, 90, 113–116, 123, 126–129, 138, 145, 199–200, 202–203, 206–207
prison system *see* prison system
privilege 135–138, 139
Public Defender's Office 129, 131–132
rule of law, fostering 116
salaries 135–136
small claims courts 134
social inequality embodied by 11
specialised courts 117, 118
state courts 116–117
Superior Courts 117–118
Supreme Court *see* Supreme Court
transparency 114, 125, 138
Tribunais de Justiça 117, 119
Tribunais Regionais Federais 117
TV Justiça 122–123, 125
warrants, issue 139

K
Krygier, Martin 17, 19

L
labour law
generally 34
labour rights
EU-MERCOSUR 187
land ownership
Indigenous people 52–53
Latin America
stereotypes associated with 87–88, 92
***Latinobarómetro Informe* 2021** 60–62
Layton, ML and Smith, AE 40
legal system *see also* **justice system and judiciary; legislation**
constitutional provisions 34
legality principle
civil law tradition 19
emphasis on the state 19
Estado de Direito 20
rule of law, generally 20, 29
legislation
anti-corruption 143, 151, 154–155, 159, 160, 161
international law, incorporation 182–185
Medidas Provisórias 93–94, 110
non-retroactivity 29
pace of deliberations, Supreme Court ruling 127
presidential power to issue 93–94, 110, 111
publicity of 29
Leirner, Piero 78
Lewis, Norman 51
LGBTQIA+ community
criminalisation of homophobia 126
criminalisation of transphobia 126
inequality 45–46, 49–50
same-sex marriage 46, 49, 126, 166
Limongi, Fernando 111
Limongi, Fernando and Figueiredo, Angelina Cheibub 85, 91, 93, 105, 111
Locke, John 15
Lugo, Fernando 187–188
Lula da Silva, Luiz Inácio 94
corruption scandals 166
imprisonment 113, 160
media and 173
MERCOSUR 188
Operation Car Wash 113–114, 116, 131, 146–147, 160–163, 203
reappearance as potential contender 195
reforms of judiciary 125

M
Mainwaring, Scott 104–105
Mainwaring, Scott et al 95, 107–108
Mainwaring, Scott and Pérez-Liñán, Aníbal 107
Medeiros, Marcelo et al 35
media
access to 174
bias 173
Bolsonaro administration, opposition to 212
Bolsonaro administration attacks on 150, 168–172, 175–176
Bolsonaro's use of social media 175–176, 177–178, 201

civilian-military dictatorship and 173
confidentiality of sources 171–172
COVID-19 pandemic 170
fake news and misinformation 173, 174–178, 201
freedom of speech 169–174, 176–177
harassment of journalists 168–170
importance to democracy 168–174
independence 1, 62, 106, 151, 154, 168–174
influence 11, 145, 168–178
internet, power of 174–178
libel law, judicial interpretation 171–172
murdered journalists 170
ownership 170, 172–173
public media outlets 170
social media 169, 175–176
state advertising and licensing constraining 172, 173
Medidas Provisórias 93–94, 110
Melo, Marcus André and Pereira, Carlos 91, 106, 111
MERCOSUR
Bolsonaro administration 187
Brazilian membership 12, 181, 185
democracy and the rule of law 187–188, 189
development 186–187
economic asymmetries within 186
establishment and membership 186
EU-MERCOSUR Free Trade Agreement 187
human rights, promotion and protection 188–189
PARLASUR 189
Permanent Review Tribunal 189
Protocol of Asunción 188
Protocol of Ushaia I 188
purpose 186, 197
UNASUR and 187, 189
Meyer, Emílio Peluso 201
Meyer, Emílio and Reis, Ulisses dos 78
military
1988 Constitution and 79–81
Amnesty Law 80, 193–194
civilian control over 10, 79
civilian-military dictatorship 22–24, 31, 32, 51, 66, 67, 68–71, 81, 119
command of *Minustah* 80–81
Constituent Assembly compromise with 79–80
Military Criminal Code 119
military judicial system 118–119, 142
military police 141–143
National Truth Commission 80–81, 195
politicisation 80–84, 143
revival under Bolsonaro 78–84, 85, 97, 143, 204–205, 207, 211, 212
militias
Bolsonaro administration and 143, 212
corruption and 142–143
rise of 142–143
Milovic, Miroslav 4
minority groups
inclusion, generally 9, 10
political representation 112
money laundering
legislation against 143, 151, 154, 159
Montgomery, Paul L 51
Morgenstern, Scott 88
Moro, Sergio 114, 160, 203
Mourão, Hamilton 210–211
murder rates
racial inequality 43–44

N
National Congress *see* **Congress**
National Council of Justice 46, 125, 134, 136, 137
National Council of the Public Ministry 134, 137
National Renewal Alliance (ARENA) 69, 72
nationalism, populism and 167
Neves, Aécio 95
Neves, Marcelo 26
Nunes, Kassio 206

O
Odebrecht corruption scandal 146–147, 149, 150
OECD, accession discussions 181
Office of Hate 175
oligarchical elites
'accountability paradox' 165
clientelism and 101–102
corruption and 102
National Congress 98–103
political system, in 98–103
Operation Car Wash 5, 96, 97, 103, 113–114, 116, 131, 146–147, 149, 150, 151, 160–163, 202, 206, 210
Organisation of the American States (OAS) *see also* **Inter-American System of Human Rights**
Brazilian membership 12, 189

P
Pact of San José 189
Paixão, Cristiano 66, 71, 73
Panama 61
Passarinho, Jarbas 71
Pazuello, Eduardo 205
Pereira, Anthony 7
Pierson, Paul 198, 208
Pimentel, Marcelo 78
Pinheiro, Paulo Sérgio 63
Pinochet, Augusto 133
police *see* **criminal justice system**
political system *see also* **democracy; presidential system**
1988 Constitution 105–106
accountability 1, 106, 111, 112, 147, 197
authoritarian mindset *see* authoritarian mindset
banned candidates 127
bicameralism 99
campaign financing 127, 146, 147
candidate selection 102
Chamber of Deputies 99–100, 105
clientelism *see* clientelism
coalition presidentialism 10, 90–98, 101, 103–112, 199, 204, 205–206
corruption *see* corruption
courts *see* justice system and judiciary
depoliticisation of society 67, 68, 71, 72
disarrangement 202–203
elections, oversight 118
electoral quota 100
electoral system 99–100, 104–105, 127, 176, 212
electoral threshold 100
electronic voting, Bolsonaro's attacks on 176, 212
estamentos 101
executive powers 93–94, 105–106, 111
federalism 94, 99–100, 104–105, 116, 211
female representation in parliament 102
generally 87–92
improvement in political liberty 33
inequality and 34, 42–43, 88–89, 214–215
instability 204, 211, 214
judiciary, politicisation 5, 10–11, 90, 113–116, 123, 126–129, 138, 145, 202–203
Latin America, generally 88–89, 92–93
level of participation in 168
locally-oriented 109
malapportionment 99–100
media influence 11, 145, 168–178
media ownership 170, 172–173
military, politicisation 80–84, 143
military judicial system 118–119, 142
minority groups, representation 112
National Congress 98–103, 105, 111
oligarchical elites 58, 98–103
open-list proportional representation 100–101, 102, 104–105
participatory governance institutions 164–165
party fragmentation 5, 10, 90, 91, 94–95, 98–103, 105, 108, 110, 111–112, 127, 203–204
perception of, generally 87–90
pluralism 168
polarisation 4, 46, 59, 69, 89, 94–97, 108, 110, 112, 167–168, 180, 200–201, 209, 214–215
political advertising 176
pork-barrel politics 97–98, 102–103, 104–105, 106, 108–110, 111, 199, 210–211
racial inequality 42, 43
rule of law, impact on 103–104
'secret budget' 109–110
stability 33–34, 90–91, 212
structural dysfunctionalities 95–96, 103–105, 107–108, 109, 112
Supreme Court politicisation 10–11, 90, 123, 126–129
transition to democracy 103, 104
transparency 106, 111, 112
under civilian-military dictatorship 69
weak party institutionalisation 101–102, 103, 105, 107, 108–109
political voluntarism 131
populism
anti-abortion rhetoric 167
anti-gender equality rhetoric 167
authoritarian mindset and 66
bolsonarismo 2, 3–6, 32, 59–62, 64–66, 103, 143, 168–169, 175, 179, 196, 201–214
civil society institutions and 167–168
claiming to combat corruption 166
nationalism and 167
rise of, causes 4–5, 59–60, 89, 166–167
pork-barrel politics 97–98, 102–103, 104–105, 106, 108–110, 111
Bolsonaro administration 109–110, 199, 210–211

poverty *see also* **economic exclusion; economic inequality**
rule of law impacted by 58
Power, Timothy and Taylor, Matthew 152
predictability
constitutional provisions 34
rule of law and 15
presidential system *see also* **democracy; political system**
Brazil, generally 92–110
clientelism and 10, 103–110, 111
coalition presidentialism 10, 90–98, 101, 103–112, 199, 204, 205–206
electoral system 94–97
executive powers, generally 105–106
federalism constraining 94, 211
impeachment 90, 92, 94, 95–96, 103, 113, 150, 160, 173, 204
Latin American tradition 88–89, 90, 92
legislative powers 93–94, 110, 111
Medidas Provisórias 93–94, 110
pork-barrel politics 104–106, 111
powers 93–94
public spending, power over 93
press freedom *see* **media**
prison system *see also* **criminal justice system**
COVID-19 deaths within 140
incarceration rate 140
organised criminal groups 140
pre-trial detainees 139, 140
prison conditions 140
prisoners' rights 46
probation 140
racial inequality 42, 140
private and public sectors *see also* **clientelism**
corporate integrity 150–151
corruption and 146–148, 152
dysfunctional relationship 146–148, 152, 160
public sphere 'privatisation' 101
regulatory agencies 159
Progress of South America (PROSUL) 190
proportionality principle
generally 203
Supreme Court 125
protests of 2013
right-wing populism 4, 166–167
social and political backlash 165–166
Przeworski, Adam 4, 82, 88
Przeworski, Adam et al 33
Przeworski, Adam and Maravall, JM 18, 24, 28
Public Class Actions 129, 132
Public Defender's Office 129, 131–132, 134
Public Ministry
Bolsonaro administration 149, 209–210
Operation Car Wash 131
police and 138–139, 144
politicisation 131
role 129–131, 132, 134, 138–139, 153–154, 156
public sector *see* **private and public sectors**

R
racial inequality *see also* **Indigenous people**
abortion and 48–49
census classification 42
death rate in police interventions 140–141
economic inequality 41, 42, 43
education levels and 41, 42, 43, 44–45, 126
generally 9, 26–27, 33, 38, 39–45
murder rates 43–44
political families 58
political representation 42, 43
prison demographics 42, 140
quota system for university access 126
'racial democracy' myth 40–41, 45
racial discrimination 39–43
residential segregation 42
state-orchestrated violence and 41, 42, 140–141
rationality of fear 161
Rechtsstaat
constitutional 20
democratic 20
emphasis on the state 19–20
influence 14, 19–20, 28
recurso especial 117
recurso extraordinário 121, 123
religion
growth of Evangelical churches 45, 167
Indigenous acculturation 53
influence in Brazil 45, 46, 49, 72, 173
media ownership 173
Roman Catholic church 45, 72, 75, 167
repercussão geral 123, 134
Revolution
Estado de Direito and 23, 24
rights *see also* **freedom of speech; human rights**
1988 Constitution, under 29, 34, 132–135, 182–183
Civil Rights Framework for the Internet 177
enforcement 185
increasing rights culture 132–134
judiciary's interpretative powers 133–135
'right to have rights' 164–165

unamendability 34
unequal enforcement 135
Roman Catholic church 45, 72, 75, 167
Rousseff, Dilma
generally 1–2, 32, 94–95
impeachment 60, 81, 90, 92, 95–96, 97, 103, 113, 150, 160–162, 166, 173, 204
media and 173
National Truth Commission 80–81, 195
public support for 166
rule of law *see also* ***Estado de Direito; Estado Democrático de Direito***
accountability and 147
Anglo-American legal tradition 14, 16, 17, 19, 27, 28
authoritarian mindset and *see* authoritarian mindset
authoritarian use of concept 8
Bolsonaro administration 2, 4, 208–209, 214
civil law counterparts 16–17, 19–22
concept of, generally 14–16
coordination dilemmas, societal 18, 30
decline 59–62
democracy and 7–8, 16, 24
destabilising factors 198–207
economic inequality and 26
economic and social development, impact of 58
evolution of concept in Brazil 8, 16–17, 18, 19–30
evolution of institutional capacities 3, 4, 6, 27–28
fairness of trials and procedures 15
future developments 12, 207–215
generality principle 29
inequality and *see* economic inequality; inequality; social inequality
institutional equilibrium, reliance on 17–18, 19, 29
international adoption of concept 16–17, 19
international perception of Brazil's compliance 195–197
judiciary, role of 116
legality principle 20, 29
meaning 15–16
political system, impact of 103–104
procedural safeguards, based on 15
raison d'être 17–18
regional inequalities 33
social justice and 18, 21, 27–30
state, individual's capacity to police 27
state's duty of protection 27
structural fragilities 34
threats to 7
translation into Brazilian system 8, 14, 15–16, 26–27
universalist and contextual values 16–17
World Justice Project Rule of Law Index 60

S
Salles, Ricardo 179
Sarney, José 72, 76
Schwarcz, Lilia 82
separation of powers
1988 Constitution 29
importance 15
politicisation of judiciary 10–11
Silva, José Afonso da 21
Silva, Virgílio Afonso da 193
social development 55–58
social exclusion 29, 39
social inequality
authoritarian mindset and 65–66, 185
Bolsonaro administration 185, 208
coordination in unequal societies 26–30
democracy and 26, 55
Estado de Direito and 18, 22, 26–28
generally 61, 87–88, 133, 200–201
justice system and 11, 135–138, 139–140, 145, 147
mechanisms maintaining 6
pervasiveness in Brazil 26–27, 29–39
preconceptions of Latin American 88
regional integration and international law 185
rising level of 2, 4
rule of law impacted by 6, 8, 9, 13, 18–19, 29, 31–62, 214–215
social rights enforcement 134–135
state, individual's capacity to police 27
structural 9, 26–27
social justice
Estado de Direito and 18, 21, 27–30
rule of law and 27–30
Social Liberal Party (PSL) 5, 96
social media *see also* **internet; media**
fake news and misinformation 174–178, 201
social mobility, democracy and 4
social polarisation 4, 46, 59, 69, 89, 94–97, 108, 110, 112, 200–201, 209, 214–215
social security system *see also* **welfare provision**
access to 38
generally 34, 133

social welfare *see* **welfare provision**
Souza, Pedro Ferreira de 35–37
state
centrality in Brazilian constitutionalism 28–29
citizens, relationship with 25
civil law tradition emphasis on 19–22
duty of protection 27
individual's capacity to police 27
Stato di Diritto 14
Supreme Court
ação direta de inconstitucionalidade 124, 130
accountability 128
Amnesty Law decision 65, 79–80, 193–194
appointment and tenure of justices 122
Bolsonaro administration and 128, 149, 206–207, 211, 212–213
Chamber of Deputies President suspended by 127
civilian-military dictatorship and 69–70, 114, 120, 122
Constituent Assembly and 121–122
creation 120
criminal case appeals 139
democratisation process and 114–116, 120–121, 125, 128
electoral system, decisions as to 127
excessive individual judicial powers 128
fake news investigation 175–176
Federal Senate President suspended by 127
foreign precedents, referral to 193–194
generally 117
guardian of the Constitution, as 117, 120–121, 125
human rights decisions 49–50, 125–126
inconsistency 127, 202
independence 120
influence 116
international treaties and conventions 182, 184–185
Judicial Reform 2004 123, 125, 131, 134, 137
judicial review system 120–121
LGBTQIA+ rights 46, 49–50, 126
libel law, interpretation 171–172
mediation and conciliation centre 134
number of justices 120
Operation Car Wash 114, 162–163, 199
pace of legislative deliberations, ruling on 127
politicisation 10–11, 90, 123, 126–129
proportionality principle 125, 202
recurso extraordinário 121, 123
repercussão geral 123, 134
role 117, 118, 120, 125
seriatim deliberative model 122–123
stability 120–121, 122
strategic collaboration with press 128
TV Justiça 122–123

T
Taylor, M 92
Temer, Michel 81, 82, 130, 162, 166, 199
Time Brazil 158
Torelly, Marcelo 192
totalitarianism *see* **dictatorships**
trans rights 126
transparency
Access to Information 158
anti-corruption provisions 151, 158–160
constitutional provisions 25, 34, 106
criminal justice system 144, 145
justice system 114, 125, 138
political system 106, 111, 112
Transparency Portal 158
Transparency International Corruption Perception Index 148–153
Treaty of Asunción 186
Treaty of Ouro Preto 186
Tribunais de Conta 153
Tribunais de Justiça 117, 119
Tribunais Regionais Federais 117
Trump, Donald 196, 212

U
UNASUR
Brazilian membership 12, 181, 185, 187, 189
establishment and membership 189–190
MERCOSUR and 187, 189–190
role 189–190
United Nations 181
urbanisation 68, 102
Uruguay
corruption in 149
democracy in 61
Indigenous people 51
transition from dictatorship 65, 79

V
Vargas, Getúlio
Estado Novo 8, 31, 32, 66, 67, 68, 69
Varieties of Democracy (V-Dem) 60
Venezuela 81

Vianna, FJ Oliveira 67–68
Vieira, Oscar Vilhena 26, 29
violence
against Indigenous people 50–51
against LGBTQIA+ community 49–50
against women 43–44, 48
Amnesty Law 65, 79–80, 193–194
civilian-military dictatorship, under 71, 80–81, 214
conviction rates 141
criminal justice system and 139–143, 144, 145
deaths resulting from police interventions 140–141
increase in 141
inequality and 34, 41, 42, 43–44, 58, 139–140, 180
National Truth Commission 80–81, 195
rise of militias 142–143
security forces, generally 214
state, racial inequality and 41, 42

W
Weffort, Francisco 74
welfare provision *see also* **education; health care provision**
1988 Constitution 133–134
Bolsa Família programme 34, 44, 57, 210
improvements in 33, 35, 39, 44, 55–58
inclusion, democracy and 39
racial inequality 42
regional inequalities 55–58
rule of law impacted by 27–28, 38, 58
worsening 60
women
abortion rights 48–49, 126, 166, 167
education 38, 46, 47
employment 46–47
female journalists 169
female representation in parliament 102
inequality 9, 26–27, 33, 38, 45–49
labour market 38
reproductive rights 48–49
violence against 43–44, 48
Worker's Party (PT)
backlash against 32, 166
corruption scandals 108, 166
decline 5
elector identification with 101
generally 1, 94, 96
Operation Car Wash 5, 96, 97, 113–114, 116, 131, 160–163
World Bank Control of Corruption indicators 148–153
World Health Organisation (WHO) 181
World Justice Project (WJP) Rule of Law Index 60
World Trade Organisation (WTO) 181
World War II 32, 36–37
Wylie, Kristin N 102

www.ingramcontent.com/pod-product-compliance
Ingram Content Group UK Ltd.
Pitfield, Milton Keynes, MK11 3LW, UK
UKHW021908150926
475560UK00003B/256

9 781509 934959